The BILLBOARD ILLUSTRATED ENCYCLOPEDIA of
COUNTRY MUSIC

Publisher and Creative Director: Nick Wells
Commissioning Editor: Julia Rolf
Picture Researchers: Melinda Revesz and Elena Verrecchia
Designer: Mike Spender
Production: Chris Herbert and Claire Walker

Special thanks to: Meryl Greenblatt, Bob Nirkind, Sara Robson and Polly Willis

First Published in 2007 by Billboard Books
An imprint of Watson Guptill Publications
A Division of VNU Business Media, Inc.
770 Broadway, New York, New York 10003
www.watsonguptill.com

Created and produced by
FLAME TREE PUBLISHING
Crabtree Hall, Crabtree Lane
Fulham, London SW6 6TY
www.flametreepublishing.com

07 09 11 10 08 06
1 3 5 7 9 10 8 6 4 2

Flame Tree is part of The Foundry Creative Media Company Limited
© 2006 Flame Tree Publishing

Library of Congress Control Number 2006930549
ISBN-10: 0-8230-7781-0
ISBN-13: 978-0-8230-7781-6
Library of Congress cataloguing-in-publication data for this title
can be obtained from the Library of Congress

Printed and bound in China

The BILLBOARD ILLUSTRATED ENCYCLOPEDIA of
COUNTRY MUSIC

GENERAL EDITOR: TONY BYWORTH

FOREWORD BY JACK CLEMENT

Billboard Books
An imprint of Watson Guptill Publications/New York

How To Use This Book

Each chapter covers a particular era or movement within country music.

Cross-references pinpoint the interplay of influences between the artists and music styles of the genre, enabling the reader to follow specific areas of interest into other parts of the book.

Classic Recordings chronologically highlight important albums, tracks and session line-ups from the artist's career.

Quotes from fellow musicians, contemporary figures and the artist themself provide insight into their playing style and accomplishments.

Key Track boxes examine a well-known tune or song that gives a good example of a player's overall sound, delving into the melody, lyrics and instrumentation used.

Influences & Development

Sam Bush & Bela Fleck

Contents

Foreword

Scene: Office at Cowboy Jack Clement's Cowboy Arms Hotel & Recording Spa. Cowboy is behind his desk, talking with John Lomax III. Numerous stringed instruments festoon the walls.

JL3: Hey Cowboy, what do you think of this new *Encyclopedia of Country Music*?

Cowboy: Well, there's country music and there's hillbilly music. If this book does its job the readers will be able to tell the difference.

JL3: The difference is?

Cowboy: Country music is basic, even primal, music that has its inception in a rural situation, out on the farm, in the woods, at the old swimming hole.

JL3: But that's not so true today.

Cowboy: Yeah, they took it to the city, tried to make it into music for city folk.

JL3: You mean they slicked it up?

Cowboy: Yeah, where's that twangy lilt that captured my young ears some 70 years ago? You can take Billy out of the hills but you can't take the hills out of Billy. So call me a hillbilly, I like that, I consider it a badge of honor. Call me a shit-kicker, I like that even better.

JL3: What do you think about where music is today?

Cowboy: The good news is you can find a CD of just about anything that's ever been recorded, all that great stuff from the past, like 'Blue Eyes Crying In The Rain' before Willie sang it.

JL3: The bad news?

Cowboy: Music's categorized too much, the labels and distribution system is too much like a dictatorship.

JL3: The *Encyclopedia* looks like it really covers the ground...

Cowboy: Yes, it seems really comprehensive – looks to me like a book I'd use myself – hope it makes a case that there might be a future for country music.

JL3: Kinda looks like it does.

Cowboy: It's got plenty of the artists I like in it: Bradley Kincaid, Carson Robison, Lulu Belle & Scotty, The Sons Of The Pioneers, Bill Monroe – all hillbillies – and a bunch of people I worked with who are hillbillies but don't know it: Charley Pride, Waylon Jennings, George Jones, Townes Van Zandt, Don Williams, John Prine...

JL3: So you'd recommend this book?

Cowboy: Yep – far as I can tell if you want to learn about country music and hillbilly music this is a great place to start (breaks into song):

> *I like mountain music*
> *Good ol' mountain music*
> *Played by a real hillbilly band**

(fade to the stage of the Grand Ole Opry. The curtains begin to part...)

*1933 pop music hit song

Cowboy Jack Clement, 2006

Introduction

It's a question that has been asked many, many times and one that always remains difficult, perhaps impossible, to answer. *What is country music?* Everybody will venture their own explanation and, frequently, there's never a particularly satisfactory answer. More likely, it will evoke a lively debate where everyone will purport the validity of their own argument.

Certainly, like jazz and blues, country music is an art form native to America, though its roots were planted in the British Isles and Europe, then transported to the New World with the early settlers. Like other musical genres it has seen constant change, and those early recordings by Fiddlin' John Carson and Uncle Dave Macon are 80 years – and a universe – away from the million-selling sounds of latter-day superstars Garth Brooks and Shania Twain. Transcending a shorter time-span, the raw lyricism of Hank Williams' plaintive ballads or Ray Price's honky-tonk stylings might be just as foreign to the smooth strings and choruses that created the Nashville Sound just a few years later. Time does, as that old country song proclaims, change everything.

It might be simpler to say that, in many people's minds, country music began when they first jumped on the train. Those who first experienced country in the 1950s, listening to the likes of Kitty Wells and Webb Pierce, might believe the big-band sounds of Western-swing king Bob Wills to be alien and claim that brass instruments have no place in country music, yet a few years earlier, Jimmie Rodgers – a founding father – recorded with Louis Armstrong. Similarly, today's young audiences might favour the recordings of such stars as Gillian Welch, Ryan Adams and Lambchop, and dismiss the work of Jim Reeves or Patsy Cline, George Jones or Tammy Wynette. All qualify as country music, though.

In addition to the changes experienced over the years, country music is equally diverse in its regional presentations. There is the early acoustic 'hillbilly' sound that flourished in rural Eastern surroundings and established Roy Acuff as the king of country music; Cajun music is a French variant predominant in Louisiana; Western swing developed from a mish-mash of musical styles found in Texas, Oklahoma and the Southwest; bluegrass was a wholly new sound attributed to Kentucky's Bill Monroe; and, in the 1950s, several strands joined forces to create rockabilly.

Further differences came with the presentation of the music – and country music, like a chameleon, fitted its surroundings. While it had one face in the South – a quieter, more revered presence that befitted family life and the church – out West it took on rowdier, louder aspects, perfect for the bars and the dancehalls, where it competed with the roar of the crowds for whom country was the main attraction for a wild Saturday night out.

Today, country music – once representing a 'cottage-industry' slice of the music scene and possessing a loyal, dedicated audience – sells in its millions as it grows increasingly linked to pop and rock music. Such 'progression' has rubbed away much of country's original characteristics, though, and with few exceptions, it has been the small independent labels that continue to support the more traditional country-music artists. There you can still hear singers with the distinctive, nasal intonations, prominent fiddles and steel guitars, and the occasional honky-tonk piano that were the music's major selling-points to an earlier generation. At the same time, though, it has also been those independent labels that have been at the forefront of developing a new generation of creative singers and songwriters, collectively reigning under the title '.alt country'.

So, back to the original question, *What is country music?* Perhaps, these days, it's more a state of mind and, as Kris Kristofferson once remarked, 'if it feels country, it is'. Hopefully this book, which covers the music's diverse history and the many colourful characters that created its popularity, will provide a greater insight into a music that, although always changing, shows no signs of fading away.

Tony Byworth, 2006

For The Wonder State We'll Sing A Song:
The Roots Of Country Music

The roots of country music are entwined with the roots of America itself. What we call 'country music' today was planted some 300 years ago by the earliest European explorers of the New World. Adventurers and exiles, religious dissenters and slave traders, farmers, merchants, freemen and women, indentured workers, slaves, criminals and members of native tribes that had lived there for eons, but were to suffer decimation – all sowed songs there like seeds in a fertile field.

Those seeds nestled deep, and their shoots gained a permanent hold on the soil. American music was spread by tenacious people who rooted themselves in the land itself. Music was a bounty of that land, and of American rural life. Country music expresses the values of rural Americans – even those who left it, or only dreamed they were once there. The roots of country music represent those values in raw form, before self-conscious cultivation and commercialism changed the shape of the music.

The dominant seeds of early American music were Anglo-Celtic story-songs that arrived from the British Isles with the Pilgrims and with the colonizing immigrants who followed them. Their music evolved as their settlements and frontiers developed, influenced by contact with other cultures, idiosyncratic choices, regional differences, historical events and socio-economic trends. The first Americans' descendants bent this or that musical shoot to tap diverse resources or to achieve particular goals. Country music is an adaptive art form, but has always been a conservative one. It still honours and feeds off its original roots.

Despite abundant variety, country music retains indelible DNA. Its eternal themes are faith and its lapses, the high lonesome ache of isolation and the satisfactions of a close-knit clan, the power of self-reliance and the pre-eminence of freedom. Country music has come to fruition over its history in the most remote hamlets of America, independently and simultaneously, as if by spontaneous generations. It also arose in the cities – indeed, country music is often about tradition confronting change. The roots of country music have drawn from – and nourished – virtually all aspects of American culture since the seventeenth century.

Influences & Development

'Anyone who wants to be a
songwriter should listen to as
much folk music as they can.'
Bob Dylan

Country music is identified with the American South
and West, but its roots were established on the Atlantic
seaboard, from Cape Breton to New
England, then filtered into the lower-central
USA through the 2,400-km (1,500-mile)
Appalachian mountain range. Eventually it
proliferated everywhere. And if such a reach
seems so vast as to defy a single culture, look at it this
way: wherever country music comes from or gets to, it
hearkens back to a rustic American past – real or mythic.

musical practice – not its ritual chanting or insistent
drumming or instrumental evocation of nature – looms
large in country music.

Nor does Spanish liturgical music register obvious
impact on country music, although the first book printed
in America was an *Ordinary of the Mass*, produced in
1556. Spanish culture contributed hugely to American
country, which enthusiastically embraced the Spanish
guitar. However, guitars weren't generally available until
the late 1800s, when mass production made them
affordable. And although French Huguenots settled on
America's East Coast – from Acadia to Florida's southern
tip – during the 1560s, French musical culture survives
mostly in Nova Scotia and Louisiana's Cajun communities
as a grace-note to Great Britain's cultural dominion over
North America.

Psalms From Europe

Jamestown, Virginia, established in 1607, was the first
enduring English settlement in the New World. There,
Captain John Smith's 104 men and boys entertained
themselves by singing around campfires whatever bits
of ballads and broadsides they recalled from their lives
in Elizabethan England, and worshipped by singing the
Psalms of David. Even the Pilgrims, who arrived in
North America in 1620, sang psalms, and brought with
them on the *Mayflower* Henry Ainsworth's 342-page
Book Of Psalmes, which featured 39 British, French
and Dutch melodies.

The Puritans, who followed the Pilgrims in 1630,
brought a psalter of their own – the *Sternhold And
Hopkins* collection. This was the source for several
hymns that remain in use in America today, notably
'Old Hundredth' (named for the hundredth psalm),
known now as the 'Doxology'.

Just as the first book printed by the Spanish in
America was a Mass, the first printed in New England was
the *Bay Psalm Book*, which originally had no music for the

Above

*Spanish musical
traditions, particularly
the Spanish guitar,
were among the earliest
influences on American
country music.*

Indigenous Roots

The music of indigenous people of North America
certainly had some bearing on the roots of country music
from the start. Aboriginal Californians are documented as
having encouraged Sir Francis Drake's sailors to sing in
1579 by saying, 'Gnaáh, gnaáh'– perhaps referring to the
nasal quality of their vocalizations. But little of native

Left

Captain John Smith and his fellow settlers brought to America the traditional songs of their native Britain.

psalms, only suggestions of 48 appropriate tunes in four-part settings by English composers.

With or without music, early American congregations would have found it difficult to sing anything like harmoniously. Hymns were typically 'lined out' by a church elder, who 'sang' a line then paused for the assembly to repeat his rendition. This custom was highly problematic, yet when challenged it was fiercely defended, and succumbed only after serious debate to a newly emergent class of itinerant New England singing teachers. The most famous of these was William Billings, a misshapen Bostonian tanner whose original compositions, including anthems supporting the Revolution, stand as the first truly American musical works.

The Rise Of Musical Life

As Americans secured a modicum of leisure time, musical life soon emerged. The fiddle, brought by the first colonists, proved irresistible to every ethnic group or community of kinsmen, despite being condemned by some Christians as a tool of the Devil. Fiddles attracted crowds; as early as 1736 amateur fiddlers competed for prizes at county fairs and similar gatherings.

Other instruments were also surprisingly plentiful in the young colonies. Wealthy men imported 'chests of viols' – sets of basses, violas and violins. There were woodwinds, trombones, kettledrums, virginals, harps, lutes, hammered dulcimers, and – in 1711 – an organ. Music was played in taverns and private salon-like recitals, as well as sung in church. In 1731, a Boston newspaper advertised a public concert taking place in the 'great room' of a local engraver's home.

Below

Massachusetts Bay was one of the first areas settled by the British Pilgrims in the seventeenth century.

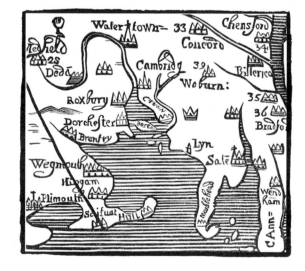

Ballads – Stories In Song

Secular music was popular in Philadelphia, Pennsylvania and Charleston, South Carolina, while musically oriented German sects such as the Moravians and Piests founded towns in other parts of Pennsylvania. This was the American field in which one particular strain of transplanted European music gained an especially firm hold.

Story-songs, sub-classified as ballads, broadsides and lyrics, enjoyed far more immediate popularity and dissemination than instrumental music. Many of these early songs – including 'Barbara Allen', 'Billy Boy' and 'Froggy Went A-Courtin'' – are still remembered. Closely related jigs, reels, frolics and hoe-downs ('Old Joe Clark', 'Cumberland Gap' and 'Cripple Creek', for example) started to shift attention from the stories told in the songs and place more emphasis on the music. This resulted in early ensembles of semi-professional players – primordial string bands.

These ballads had originated in Scottish and Irish border regions, where conflict with English rulers – one of the main topics of the songs – was rife. Some ballads found their way to London, where they were written down in simplified forms or published as one-sheet broadsides. Most, however, were simply passed around by word of mouth. Conveyed across the ocean, they became Anglo-American folk songs, encapsulating feelings about love, death and other inescapable struggles that must have seemed as apt in the New World as they were in the old.

Francis James Child detailed more than 100 such songs in his multivolume collection *The English And Scottish*

Below

Dr Humphrey Bates (second from left with harmonica) formed one of the first professional string bands in the late 1890s. His fellow players hold a fiddle, a guitar, a banjo and a cello.

American folk songs as preserved by people from the Appalachian highlands, though country-music stars may play the pieces and others derived from them without thought of their origins. The style of The Carter Family, who stand with Singing Brakeman Jimmie Rodgers (1897–1933) at the headwaters of contemporary country music, folded Anglo-American folk songs in with religious songs of the rural white American Protestant church. This repertoire received its own boost of popularity at evangelical camp meetings of the Great Revival, launched in Kentucky in 1799.

This meeting of Anglo-Celtic ballads and Protestant hymnody was undoubtedly a turning-point in the development of country music as we know it today. However, of the many subsets comprising country music in the twenty-first century, few of them bear direct resemblance to Scots-Irish balladry, psalms, hymns – or even one another. The plain-spoken nature of old-timey music contrasts sharply with the florid sentiment or slick jocularity of highly polished Nashville studio productions, the up-tempo ensemble virtuosity of bluegrass, the high-times and wages-of-sin hangovers of honky-tonk, the jazzy underpinnings of western swing or the outlaw ethos of rockabilly. Yet these styles, too, were filtered through white Southern Christian sensibility to become country music. They have ancestry, artists and audiences in common, and some essence that marks them as country.

Left
A young Jimmie Rodgers was the jaunty star of country music in the late 1920s.

Below
The first family of country music – the Carters (Maybelle, A. P. and Sara), recorded traditional songs that became country-music standards.

Popular Ballads (1882–98). Beginning around 1840, researchers had discovered these ballads among communities throughout the Appalachian mountains, a low, rolling, frequently interrupted system of ranges. Some 200,000 Scottish and Irish Protestants are estimated to have arrived in America prior to the Revolution of 1776, and many pushed into sparsely populated Appalachia to avoid the unfriendly British governance that had prompted their emigration in the first place. Besides their favourite songs, they brought with them beliefs tying education to religion, skills at distilling corn whiskey, a reputation for stubborn severity, and words like the Irish *seisiun* ('session') to denote a musical gathering.

Due to the isolation the Scots-Irish both sought and found, their age-old ballads were accurately preserved for an unusually long time. Typically, the songs relate dramatic incidents in verse form from the perspective of a distant or understated third person. Their stories, subtexts and structures remain touchstones for mainstream country music to this day.

Old-Timey And New Country

When aficionados speak of 'old-timey' music, they are referring to more-or–less traditional versions of Anglo-

The Black Influence

How does so much variety evolve from a single source? One answer is that the geographic placement, the energy of the people involved and the inexorable processes of time have all influenced the country-music mix. On the other hand, the people who preserved Anglo-American folk song were never as reclusive as claimed.

Of an estimated 900,000 immigrants new to the USA in 1790, more than a third were Africans brought to America as slaves. Of the nation's total population of almost 3.9 million (according to the first US census), 20 per cent were of African extraction. White Americans had regular contact with black Americans, and reports from

Below
Slaves brought from Africa to work on the American plantations provided a key influence on the development of early musical styles.

rescued from work in the fields to perform less onerous services in the master's residence.

Songs Of The Workers

So ballads, broadsides and up-beat dance tunes had penetrated rural America by 1800, along with Protestant church music (sung by both black and white congregations). There were occupational songs and work hollers of lumberjacks, field hands, canal-men and river-boaters, seafarers' chanties and shepherds' airs. But the nineteenth century was an age of enormous expansion and industrial transformation in the USA. The dynamics of change were mirrored in popular entertainments and the performing arts. Restlessness and inquiry were the spirit of the era; exploration and settlement of the frontier national imperatives. Traders, ministers, medicine-show purveyors, teachers and ne'er-do-wells took to the roads, carrying news to hills and vales, farms and free ranges where residents might be interested or might resent intimations that their ways had become outmoded.

If any medium allowed the new to be absorbed and applied without harm to the tried and true, it was music. Novelty could pique the tastes of listeners, while tradition supplied secure foundation for otherwise uncertain life.

Right
Minstrel troupes such as the Ethiopian Serenaders were popular touring entertainers.

New York in the Federal era (1785–1811) as well as New Orleans' Congo Square before the Louisiana Purchase (1803) demonstrate a fascination with the expressive power of the music of the slaves and free blacks. Conventional racial prejudices may have denied that blacks – slave or free – were whites' social equals, but white observers were universally awed by how people out of Africa sang and played.

Residents of America's cities and rural regions alike were aware of the non-European music of the African-American population. In the cities, blacks might be street-corner musicians, playing brass horns, drums, fiddles and banjos, the long-necked lutes with skin-headed resonators assumed to be of African origin. On plantations, musically talented slaves were well-treated, and sometimes

Far Right
Christy's Minstrels were formed in Buffalo, New York, in 1843 and were one of the most commercially successful of all the blackface groups of the period.

Minstrel Music

In 1843, America produced its first original theatrical style – the blackfaced minstrel show. This was a staged presentation of songs, dances and jokes performed by white men who wore black make-up to caricature Negroes. Blackface dates to 1769, when an actor blacked-up as a character named Mungo for a comic opera in New York City. By the late 1820s black-faced singers, appearing as openers in variety shows, were all the rage.

George Washington Dixon's urban black dandy (the 'zip coon') and Thomas Dartmouth 'Daddy' Rice's 'Jim Crow' song-and-dance impersonation were blackface favourites of the 1830s. But when Daniel Decatur Emmett rehearsed a musical act in his New York City rooming house that featured Emmett himself on fiddle, Billy Whitlock playing

banjo and rhythmic accompaniment from tambourine and rattling bones players, the fully fledged minstrel show was born. Emmett, an Irish-American from frontier Ohio, called his troupe the Virginia Minstrels to give his pseudo-Negroes a Southern tag.

The Virginia Minstrels lasted less than a year, disbanding after successful, if stressful, appearances in England. But their formula for a show persisted – music (Emmett is credited with writing 'Dixie', 'Polly-Wolly-Doodle' and 'Old Dan Tucker'), speciality dances and jokes that were old and corny even then. Their model was adopted and polished by such troupes as Edwin P. Christy's Minstrels, and minstrelsy served as coin-of-the-entertainment-realm into the early twentieth century, when it was supplanted by vaudeville.

For more than 60 years, blackface minstrel shows traipsed through every corner of America. Sheet-music arrangements of minstrel tunes were published from the 1840s, and much of the minstrel repertoire entered the canon of old-timey music.

Country Songs

Fiddlin' John Carson (1875–1949) played Emmett's 'Old Dan Tucker' in 1924 for one of the first hillbilly recordings, and the format of the Grand Ole Opry radio broadcasts (see page 98) echoed the minstrel shows, too. By the late 1800s, after the Civil War and the end of slavery, genuinely black entertainers toured in minstrel troupes such as the Mississippi-based Rabbit Foot Company, in which blues singers Ma Rainey, Bessie Smith and Ida Cox got their starts. Legendary Emmett Miller, a genre-bending pre-pop singer cited as a key influence by country-music heroes from Rodgers to Bob Wills (1905–75) to Hank Williams (1923–53), was a white blackface minstrel of the early twentieth century.

Below

Swedish singer Jenny Lind set off 'Lind fever' with the arias, polkas and waltzes of her repertoire.

A more respectable version of blackface emerged in direct response to one of Dan Emmett's first hits. Stephen Foster is acknowledged as America's first professional songwriter. His resumé contains around 175 compositions, about 30 of which treated Negro themes in pseudo-Negro dialect. In 1845, Foster wrote 'Uncle Ned' as an answer to Emmett's 'Old Dan Tucker', infusing genteel sentimentality into the rowdiness that music-lovers then attributed to the 'Ethiopian delineation'.

Foster wrote at a considerable distance from his presumed inspiration – what he knew of black life came from minstrel music rather than his own experience. Yet he wrote memorably spirited songs ('Oh! Susanna' and 'Camptown Races') as well as melodramatic tearjerkers ('The Old Folks At Home', 'Massa's In De Cold, Cold Ground' and 'Old Black Joe'). His songs were promoted by the Christy Minstrels in a mutually beneficial arrangement, but Foster died – young, drunk and penniless – in a flophouse on New York's Bowery. Country-music history abounds with such stories of self-destruction, and also with the parlour romanticism that Foster employed in classics such as 'Jeanie With The Light Brown Hair' and 'Beautiful Dreamer'.

Rural musicians and listeners did not shy away from such excess, which perhaps balanced the straight-faced, straitlaced suppression of emotion characteristic of Anglo-American folk songs. Certainly America was ripe for gentility, as demonstrated by the huge success of Jenny Lind, the 'Swedish Nightingale' who, contracted by P. T. Barnum, made 93 stops on her 1850 US tour.

Hillbilly Breaks Through

By the time the American Civil War ended in 1865, the roots of country music were almost fully formed. In the next decades, the processes of musical assimilation by rural people slowed – perhaps in reaction to the increasing momentum of every other kind of change.

Rurally rooted musicians contributed Anglo folk-song variants to both armies of the Civil War and to cowboys who sought solace in song during the long cattle-drives of the Old West era (1865–90), and offered up their tropes to select Tin Pan Alley professionals who penned commercial music aimed at rustic tastes. The Industrial Workers Of The World, trying to unite labourers in work camps across the United States, popularized songs about unions with implicit or explicit political critiques. Only the African-

American folk music known as the blues (a wellspring itself fed by Scots-Irish ballads, African retentions, minstrel and medicine-show music, plantation songs and bits and pieces gleaned from cosmopolitan transients), its formal brethren ragtime and infant jazz, had further major impact on the white southern styles that, after Al Hopkins' casual remark about his fellow string-band players, came to be called 'hillybilly music' in 1925.

This is not to say that momentous transformations affecting all the world – advances in mining, photography, communications, electricity, sound recording, telephones and transcontinental transportation, as well as the

Industrial Revolution, capitalism, a world war and a stock-market crash, circumvented the communities that produced country music. Of course rural people were touched by all that change – and Jimmie Rodgers, for one, demonstrated how a country feller could interact with modernity, giving a jaunty tip to his hat, wearing fine clothes in the city with ease, relying on a country yodel to remind himself – and everyone else – where he was from. The yodel was a pre-language call, from one hill to another. It was Rodgers' expression of his roots in the country, akin to the cry of the first British voyagers to see the New World – as in, 'Land, ho!'

Below
Cowboys would sing tunes based on old folk songs during the long cattle drives.

There Is Sunshine In The Shadows:
The Early Years Of Hillbilly Music

in the nineteenth century, country music belonged to fireside and family, to the frontier town and the backwoods hamlet. Four decades into the twentieth, it was utterly transformed, driven headlong into the new world of the new century. First, fiddlers' conventions and other public events provided a context of competition and offered the musician the chance of going professional. Then radio and records carried the notes of old-time songs and fiddle tunes far beyond schoolroom and courthouse square. Musicians who seldom left their home town, and whose audiences were numbered in dozens or a few hundreds, could now be heard by tens of thousands in places they would never visit, might never even have been heard of. Rural singers and pickers gazed upon a vista of commercial possibility, a broad highway to fame and fortune.

That road would eventually lead to a pan-American country music, in which the rough edges of regional difference would be planed and smoothed to form a standardized product. But in the crucial decades of the 1920s and 1930s, there was still room for the variety of local styles and the idiosyncrasy of individual performers: for the blind street singer and the cowboy, the hoedown fiddler from Georgia and the waltz fiddler from Mississippi, the mountain banjo picker and the guitar-playing blue yodeller; for musicians as saltily distinct – both from each other and from the rest of the musical world – as Fiddlin' John Carson and Roy Acuff, or Jimmie Rodgers and The Carter Family. Guided by style-setters like these and the innumerable artists who followed them, country music arrived at the end of the 1930s as a major player on radio, on record, on film and on the road. The poor relation of American music had come into its inheritance.

Key Artists

Roy Acuff

The Carter Family

Uncle Dave Macon

Jimmie Rodgers

Influences & Development

'Country music is three chords and the truth.' **Harlan Howard**

'The fiddle and guitar craze is sweeping northward!' ran Columbia Records' ad in *Talking Machine World* on 15 June 1924. 'Columbia leads with records of old-fashioned southern songs and dances. [Our] novel fiddle and guitar records, by Tanner and Puckett, won instant and widespread popularity with their tuneful harmony and sprightliness... The records of these quaint musicians which are listed here need only to be heard to convince you that they will "go over big" with your trade.'

The Song Is The Thing

This was not mere adspeak. In December 1925 the Nashville *Tennesseean* spotted a 'recent revival in the popularity of the old familiar tunes' and observed: 'America may not be swinging its partners at a neighbor's barn dance but it seems to have the habit of clamping on its ear phones and patting its feet as gaily as it ever did when old-time fiddlers got to swing.' In the same month *Talking Machine World* returned to the subject with an article headed 'What The Popularity Of Hill-Billy Songs Means In Retail Profit Possibilities', suggesting that the vogue for such material 'shows the earmarks of a new phase of the popular music and record business' and 'may mark the initial move in the passing of jazz'. 'The great American public,' it concluded, 'is returning to songs and after all "the song is the thing".'

Talking Machine World was the trade paper of the American record industry, and its claim that there was, in the famous phrase of another magazine article, 'gold in them thar hillbillies' echoed a buzz running through the business. There had been a few random recordings in 1922–24, but over the next three years the leading labels of the day – Columbia, Victor, Brunswick and OKeh, followed by smaller rivals like Gennett and Paramount – got seriously into the business of marketing southern country music. (It would be many years, though, before they gave it that name. At this point it was called 'Old Familiar Tunes', or 'Native American Melodies', or 'Songs From Dixie'.) In carefully organized 'field trips' – usually in spring and autumn – teams of producers and engineers travelled through the South, stopping off for a week or two in Atlanta, Memphis, Dallas, New Orleans and other cities,

Victor Records
OF OLD FAMILIAR TUNES
and NOVELTIES

"HIS MASTER'S VOICE"
REG. U.S. PAT. OFF.

installing their equipment in hotel rooms or warehouses, and recording local talent by the bushel.

Old Familiar Tunes

What was that talent? What kind of music did they make? Historian and reader alike must take a deep breath here. A song might be an Old World ballad of knights and fair ladies, a cowboy's tale of life on the trail, a yodel song, a Victorian narrative of lost love or an old home left behind, a comic piece from the blackface minstrel show, or a newly written story of a murder, shipwreck or train crash. A tune might be a reel, a waltz, a rag, blues or a medley. And the song might be accompanied – or the tune played – on fiddle, banjo, harmonica or guitar, or by combinations of two of them, or by a string band embracing all of them and mandolins, pianos and ukuleles besides.

Who were the men and women making this music? Over the years a mythology would develop, fostered by television shows like *The Beverly Hillbillies* and *Hee Haw*, and later by movies like *O Brother, Where Art Thou?* and *Cold Mountain*, that country music was made by and for muddy-booted, tobacco-chewing crackers from the backwoods. Some of the early stars were folk like that, but many were not; often they were professional men, doctors, schoolteachers and small-town lawyers, or prosperous local tradesmen. Some had formal musical training, thanks to itinerant music teachers who held classes in violin-playing or choral singing in rural schools. Others had learned their

music in stringed-instrument societies sponsored by leading manufacturers like Gibson and Martin, or had their grounding in the brass bands that most towns boasted in the late nineteenth and early twentieth centuries. Many singers had learned their craft in church.

Their audiences were equally mixed. The periodical *Musical America*, describing the 1914 Atlanta Old Fiddlers' Convention, listed several prominent Atlantans who attended the opening night, among them the mayor and 'one of the South's leading bankers'. The reporter marvelled that 'From front row to back sat richly gowned society leaders, side by side with working folk in rough attire,' and before long 'Atlanta society folk shuffled their feet to the lilting strains of "Wild Hog In The Cane Brake".'

Early Stars

The boiling variety of the music recorded in the guise of 'Old Familiar Tunes', or any of its other names, in the 1920s and 1930s makes simple definitions impossible. All we can do is observe certain trends that many artists followed. Some of them would fade away, but others would persist, to mould the country music of the 1940s and 1950s.

Though several of the early stars were solo acts – like Fiddlin' John Carson (1875–1949), Uncle Dave Macon (1870–1952), Riley Puckett (1894–1946) and Bradley Kincaid (1895–1991) – country music in the 1920s and 1930s was essentially collaborative, typically made by family string bands and singing groups: The Carter Family, The Crocketts and Pickards, fiddle-and-guitar teams like the Kessinger and Stripling brothers, and scores of brother (or sister) vocal duets and trios. Even the soloists often led parallel working and recording lives as bandleaders – Carson with his Virginia Reelers, Macon with his Fruit Jar Drinkers, Puckett as featured singer with the Skillet Lickers, first of the hillbilly show-bands. Family and community solidarity is intrinsic to this music, as it so signally is not in the African-American music that was made alongside it, but when a performer emerged to offer country music a different direction, it was one who drew

Below
The Powers Family, led by Fiddlin' Cowan Powers, was the first family string band to make a commercial recording, in 1924.

his inspiration from that black tradition: Jimmie Rodgers (1897–1933), the first country artist to devote himself to the essentially solo idiom – one man and his guitar – of the blues.

Rodgers and The Carter Family serve as signposts to the two main directions country music would take in the 1930s and 1940s. The Carters, with their repertoire of sentimental and religious songs, stand at the head of a line that includes Roy Acuff (1903–92), The Blue Sky Boys and, in due course, bluegrass – music that affirms the timeless values of family, home and the little country church. Rodgers, by contrast, is a wholly twentieth-century figure: mobile, self-sufficient, forward-looking, hedonistic, a bit of a lad. In his wake comes the procession of hillbilly bluesmen like Cliff Carlisle (1904–83) and his brother Bill (1908–2003), or Gene Autry (1907–98) and Jimmie Davis (1899–2000), both of whom began their recording careers as arrant Rodgers imitators before remaking themselves as all-purpose country singers.

A Musical Medley

The mingling of white and black strains gives us some of the most potent music of the period: the roistering Charlie Poole (1892–1931) singing the 'Beale Street Blues', Dock Boggs (1898–1971) with 'Down South Blues', The Delmore Brothers' jolly 'Brown's Ferry Blues' – tiny sparks in the powder-trail that would burn through the blues-loving western-swing bands of Bob Wills (1905–75) and Milton Brown (1903–36), and eventually explode in the rockabilly and hillbilly boogie of the 1950s, revealing, when the smoke cleared, Elvis Presley. But even blues-aware artists like Wills or the Delmores were never just that. Playing

the Rodgers card was only one of their tricks, and they maintained throughout their careers the flexibility that would ensure that they had careers, shuffling blues and 'heart' songs, train and hobo songs, gospel and comedy, refreshing their repertoires for the radio programmes and personal appearances that, far more than records, gave them an income and a future.

Because records are there, permanent documents, we may assign them too much importance. It is in the evanescent idiom of radio that country music made its national, pan-American impact, reaching millions on shows like Nashville's Grand Ole Opry, Chicago's *National Barn Dance* and countless others on stations from Cincinnati to Dallas, from Charlotte, North Carolina, to Shenandoah, Iowa. America no longer needed to 'clamp on its ear phones', as that Nashville journalist wrote in 1925. Radio – aided by rural electrification – brought country music loud and clear into factory and farm home alike. In doing so, it groomed a new generation of media-conscious artists such as Lulu Belle And Scotty, Patsy Montana And The Prairie Ramblers, Mainer's Mountaineers and The Sons Of The Pioneers. As the old-timers blinked and hung up their fiddles, country music poised itself for a leap into a bright post-war future.

Left
Bradley Kincaid – one of the first solo stars of country music.

Below
Fiddle and guitar duo Clark (centre) and Luches (right) Kessinger teamed up with dance-caller Ernest Legg (left) to record a series of tunes for Brunswick in 1928.

The Bristol Sessions

If you look for country music's Big Bang, there is nothing more momentous than Bristol, 1927. Within four summer days, two stars appeared that would change the cosmology of country – remap the sky. And it all happened in a disused office building in a quiet mountain town perched on the state line between Virginia and Tennessee.

Why Bristol?

What brought Jimmie Rodgers and The Carter Family to Bristol? Atlanta would have made sense, or even Memphis or Dallas – these were cities with large populations and thriving musical cultures. To answer the question it is necessary to go back four years, to when OKeh Records' Ralph Peer, acting on a local tip-off, went to Atlanta to record Fiddlin' John Carson. That June 1923 trip was the first time a New York record company sent a producer and engineers into the South to uncover local talent.

Such location recording soon became routine. Several times a year, OKeh, Columbia and Victor sent teams to Atlanta, Memphis, New Orleans and St Louis, set up their equipment in a warehouse or hotel room and solicited the musical offerings of the region's blues singers, jazz bands, banjo-pickers, cowboy songsters – whatever was going.

Peer, now with Victor, had quickly realized that location recording had several advantages over the previous practice of doing it in New York. Some southerners were made nervous by big cities and formal studios. Recording on the artists' own ground meant drawing more of them, even if they only came out of curiosity. This opened up a wider range of possibilities – you never knew what you might get. So when Peer and his assistants rolled up in Bristol in the last week of July 1927, they were doing nothing they hadn't done before. All the same, this would be a trip like no other.

Twelve Days That Shook The World

The Bristol sessions began with a safe bet. Ernest Stoneman (1893–1968) and his family had worked with

Peer before and know how to make records. By the end of Monday 25 July, they had given him 10 good discs of mountain love-songs and hymns. Over the next few days the Taylor-Christian building on State Street saw a procession of talent from the surrounding area – men like the banjoist and ballad-singer B. F. Shelton and the gospel-singing guitarist Alfred G. Karnes from Corbin, Kentucky, or the fiddling songwriter Blind Alfred Reed from Princeton, West Virginia.

It was wonderful stuff, but Peer would have had no thoughts of a bestseller like Vernon Dalhart's (1883–1948) 'The Wreck of the Old 97', which was still moving very nicely for Victor after three years. Then, on the Monday of the second week in Bristol, prompted by a couple of articles about the session that had appeared in Bristol's papers, a homely looking trio from Virginia stopped by to sing 'Bury Me Under The Weeping Willow' – and Peer knew he had a hit on his hands.

The six songs the Carters recorded for him would have justified the entire Bristol excursion, financially and aesthetically, but fate had another surprise gift for Ralph Peer. It is not clear whether he knew Jimmie Rodgers before their encounter on Thursday 4 August – there may have been correspondence, and possibly a brief meeting – but when he heard the consumptive ex-brakeman sing 'The Soldier's Sweetheart' and 'Sleep, Baby, Sleep', he felt again that frisson of possibility. 'I was elated,' he wrote later. 'He had his own personal and peculiar style, and I thought that his yodel alone might spell success. I arranged to have his record issued quickly. The dealers ordered heavily and then reordered. It was obvious that Jimmie Rodgers was the best artist uncovered by the Bristol expedition.'

Peer wrapped up the trip with a few more string-band recordings and an unaccompanied choir of 20 local singers

chanting the hymns 'Standing On The Promises' and 'Shall We Gather At The River?' It was a curious conclusion to 12 days that shook the world of country music.

Roy Acuff

Key Artist

There were people coming in here from New York, California, Chicago, all different places that had publishing companies, trying to buy my songs.'
Roy Acuff

If Jimmie Rodgers is the father of country music, Uncle Dave Macon its first radio star and the Carters its first family group, Roy Acuff (1903–92) has a claim to be called the father of the country-music business. Not only was he a key figure in the Grand Ole Opry – indeed, for many, its figurehead – but he was also a prime mover in making Nashville the home of country-music publishing.

'To Hell With Roy Acuff!'

As a boy in east Tennessee he wanted to play pro baseball, but illness ruled that out. His second choice was music. His father was a fiddler, and he had inherited some of this talent. Acuff made a regional name on WNOX in Knoxville, Tennessee, on the station's famous *Midday Merry-Go-Round*, and in 1936 began making records. His first session produced two of his biggest hits, 'Wabash Cannonball' (actually sung, that first time, by one of his band-members) and the sacred song 'Great Speckled Bird', which shares the tune of that country standby 'I'm Thinking Tonight Of My Blue Eyes'. He would be condemned to sing both of them for the rest of his career.

A couple of years later he joined the Grand Ole Opry and by the early 1940s he was its most potent artist, drawing fans from hundreds of miles away. On records he was as famous as Gene Autry and Bob Wills, thanks to wartime hits like 'Wreck On The Highway' and 'Fire Ball Mail'. Indeed, an oft-told story has it that Japanese soldiers, when attacking American outposts in the South Pacific, would scream 'To hell with Roosevelt! To hell with Babe Ruth! To hell with Roy Acuff!'.

His voice quivered with emotion and it hardly mattered that he wasn't much of a player, because he had such a fine band, stocked with men like fiddler Howdy Forrester (1922–87) and Dobro player Pete Kirby (1911–2002), professionally known as Bashful Brother Oswald, both of whom would stay with him for decades. In the tradition of earlier aggregations like J. E. Mainer's Mountaineers, The Smoky Mountain Boys were less a band than a revue act. In between the songs, Howdy would be featured on a fiddle breakdown, Oswald on a Hawaiian tune or Jimmy Riddle on a harmonica solo, while Roy himself took time out from singing to show what he could do with a yo-yo. In later line-ups, harmonica player Onie Wheeler would demonstrate the curious art of 'eephing' – a kind of rhythmic grunting.

Grand Old Man Of The Opry

After the Second World War, though he remained a charismatic figure on the Opry, and had enough clout in Tennessee to run for Governor (unsuccessfully), Acuff's

Right
Country music's Grand Old Man – Roy Acuff, who continued to work in the music business well into his seventies.

Top Far Right
Roy Acuff entertains the other members of his band with a balancing trick.

Bottom Far Right
Acuff and The Crazy Tennesseans – an earlier incarnation of Acuff's band The Smoky Mountain Boys.

heart-on-sleeve sincerity was increasingly out of touch with prevailing tastes in country music, which leaned towards honky-tonkers like Ernest Tubb or country crooners like Eddy Arnold. But he had other catfish to fry: his partnership with the songwriter Fred Rose in Acuff-

Rose Publications was highly successful (they would acquire the entire Hank Williams catalogue), and in the 1950s the two men and Fred's son Wesley invested in a label, Hickory Records. In 1962 Acuff was the first musician to be elected to the Country Music Hall Of Fame while still alive, and a decade later he surprised some by agreeing to work with a longhaired rock group on the – as it proved – milestone album *Will The Circle Be Unbroken?* by the Nitty Gritty Dirt Band. When the Opry relocated to Opryland, he had a house in the centre of the theme park, and he spent his last years as the show's Grand Old Man, his dressing-room a place of pilgrimage for musicians and fans.

Classic Recordings

1936
*'Great Speckled Bird',
'Freight Train Blues'*

1940
'The Precious Jewel'

1942
'Fire Ball Mail', 'Wreck On The Highway', 'Low And Lonely'

Key Track

'Wabash Cannonball' (1936)
There are few sounds more evocative of the South than a train-whistle in the night, few sights more thrilling than a speeding train with its smokestack gleaming in the sun. Country music is full of train songs, but few are better known and loved than the story of the *Wabash Cannonball*.

The Carter Family

Key Artist

'It's good for young people to know this kind of music. There was a time when music told a story; it wasn't just some beat.'
Janette Carter

Above
The extended Carter Family pose during one of their shows on border radio in the 1930s.

The Carters (A. P. 1891–1960, Sara 1899–1979 and Maybelle 1909–78) are the most extensive clan in country music, encompassing three generations of performers and connections by marriage to other artists. This is fitting, for their musical influence is pervasive, too. Near the dawn of country music as a commercial entity, they were its first successful family group, expressing domestic and Christian values in the face of the seamy, bluesy music purveyed by Jimmie Rodgers. Yet, in the guise of a group dedicated to the ethos of the Victorian parlour song and the mountain ballad,

they initiated the process of creative recomposition – rewriting songs in the public domain in order to turn them into profitable copyrights.

A Family Business

The Carter Family took shape in the early 1920s, when Alvin Pleasant Carter and his wife Sara Dougherty Carter began singing at local gatherings around their home in Maces Springs, in south-west Virginia. In 1926, A. P.'s brother Ezra's wife, Maybelle Addington Carter, joined them, adding her guitar to Sara's autoharp as the trio's musical accompaniment. The following year they made their first records, for Victor. Ralph Peer, who supervised the session, said that when he first heard Sara's deep, sober voice, 'That was it. I knew that was going to be wonderful.' But while it was the singing that initially sold The Carter Family's records, the music behind it would in the long term be no less important. Maybelle's melody-picking on the lower strings, featured in songs like 'Wildwood Flower', would inspire a generation of country guitarists.

Under Peer's careful direction The Carter Family made scores of records, their settings varying from solo vocal to duet to trio, and from autoharp and guitar to two guitars. A. P. was the rogue element: sometimes he chimed in with a low harmony line, sometimes not, as he felt moved. To fill their recording schedule he sought material from amateur singers, content even with fragments if he could build and shape them into a three-minute work. In effect he was a collector, though his goal was not folkloric documentation but practical use.

Break For The Border

A. P. and Sara's marriage broke up in 1932, but they continued to work together. In 1938 the clan moved to Texas to be close to the border radio stations, which, by transmitting from Mexico, evaded US broadcasting regulations and beamed a powerful signal across the entire nation. Sponsored by the manufacturers of hair products

Left
*Johnny Cash heads up
The Carter Family, into
which he married in 1968.*

and tonic medicines, their programmes attracted enormous audiences and fan mail. By then, a second generation of Carters had joined the original trio: Sara's daughter Janette (1923–2006) and Maybelle's daughters Helen (1927–98), June (1929–2003) and Anita (1933–99).

The Texas adventure ended in 1941, as did the recording log of the original Carter Family. A. P. and Sara reunited in the 1950s to record for the small Acme label, but Sara was disinclined to stay in music and moved to California. Meanwhile Maybelle and her daughters worked on various south-eastern stations before joining the Grand Ole Opry in 1950. Anita, Helen and June all had independent careers; in 1952 June married the singer Carl Smith, and in 1968 Johnny Cash. Maybelle and Sara had their own reunion at the 1967 Newport Folk Festival. Maybelle, having done all

she could for country guitar, took up the autoharp and became equally influential on that instrument.

The Carter legacy is clear in the groups that followed them devotedly, including The Phipps Family in Kentucky, but it also permeated bluegrass, through admirers like Mac Wiseman and Flatt & Scruggs. The third generation of Carters includes June's daughters Carlene Carter (by Carl Smith) and Rosanne Cash (by Johnny Cash).

Key Track

'Keep On The Sunny Side' (1928)
'It will help you every day, it will brighten all your way, if you keep on the sunny side of life.' It was a timely message during the Depression – a musical pick-me-up for the downhearted, and The Carter Family made it their theme song, opening and closing their every broadcast.

Uncle Dave Macon

Key Artist

'My name is Dave Macon and I'm from Rutherford County. I suppose most of you don't know anything about Rutherford County. Well let me tell you about Rutherford County...' **Uncle Dave Macon**

Right

'Bile Them Cabbage Down' was the first recording of what was known as a 'shout tune' – one that the entire cast would sing together at the end of a show.

Below

Uncle Dave Macon – the first major star of the Grand Ole Opry (with his son Dorris Macon on guitar).

Uncle Dave Macon (1870–1952) was the first star of country music. Other artists got on disc first: men like Eck Robertson, Henry Whitter, Fiddlin' John Carson, Gid Tanner and Riley Puckett. Uncle Dave didn't enter a recording studio until July 1924 – whereupon he proved to be quite productive – but he had another route to the affections of the country music audience: radio.

An Old-Timer On The Opry

Georgia boys like Carson and Puckett might show up at the studios of WSB in Atlanta from time to time, but Macon had a weekly spot on the Grand Ole Opry, which was heard practically all the way across the USA. Sitting on

a chair on the Opry stage, he didn't just sing a few songs. He had the time to create a character – that of a rambunctious old fellow, brimming with songs and jokes. It was a veritable one-man show.

He probably got a lot of the songs and jokes from older entertainers, since his parents ran a Nashville hotel that catered to show people. He played banjo as a young man, but if he entertained any hopes of entering the music profession he subdued them, making his living as a farmer. As he approached 50, however, he began to venture on to the stages of the southern vaudeville circuit. In 1926, he joined the Opry roster, even then one of its older members. They called him 'The Dixie Dewdrop'. He was sometimes accompanied by the fiddler Sid Harkreader (1898–1988), and often by the guitarist and banjoist Sam McGee, with whom he would make some particularly exuberant records. On other records he would have a whole string band behind him, consisting of Sam and Kirk McGee and fiddler Mazy Todd. Some 50 years later, their vibrant playing of 'Sail Away Ladies' would be one of the ingredients of skiffle, the homemade, folksy roots music that came just before rock'n'roll.

Not So Much A Record, More A Revue

A notable feature of Macon's records is that they are often not simply a song or a tune but a whole routine: first a comic introduction, a flourish on the banjo, a joke, a short banjo tune, then some verses of a song, or even two or three songs. Remarkably for a man in his fifties,

Left
Uncle Dave continued to play the Grand Ole Opry until just three weeks before his death at the age of 81.

conservative in many of his views, Macon looked at this new technology, the recording medium, and not only embraced it, but actually found a new way to use it. Take the sequence of songs and comic storytelling that were issued on discs such as 'Uncle Dave's Travels, Parts I–IV'. Macon sings about Nashville, stops off in Louisville, tells a story about Arkansas and concludes with a vignette called 'Visit At The Old Maid's', where he impersonates a plummy-voiced spinster taking a leaf out of some faded Victorian folio – 'Come, deeearest, the daylight is faaalling...'. As the final note of his cruel parody dies away, Macon cackles 'Hot dog!'

Uncle Dave is a splendid example of someone growing old disgracefully. He might have described himself in the title of one of his songs, 'The Gayest Old Dude That's Out'. In truth, he wasn't always a merry old devil; as artists who worked with him have revealed, he was subject to occasional fits of depression. You would never guess it from his music, nor from the priceless two minutes of screen time he occupies in the 1940 movie *Grand Ole Opry* – breaking off in mid-song, old pro that he was, to fan his banjo with his hat.

Key Track

'Keep My Skillet Good and Greasy' (1924 and 1935)
Country music began in the home, being sung and played by family and friends around hearth or wood-burning stove, and many early country songs evoke that domestic setting. Uncle Dave conjures up a rural kitchen, where a skillet is always ready for frying a hoecake or a slice of country ham.

Jimmie Rodgers

Key Artist

'Jimmie ... is the voice in the wilderness of your head.'
Bob Dylan

Below

Jimmie Rodgers (second from left in glasses) with his Entertainers.

Although routinely – and fairly – described as the father of country music, Jimmie Rodgers (1897–1933) was actually something more. Having established himself in that genre, he gradually moved towards mainstream popular music and, but for his early death, would probably have found a niche there.

So far as country music is concerned, though, his unique achievement was to create a wholly original concept out of apparently disparate elements, fusing cowboy and hobo songs with the blues – and adding a yodel. That single invention inspired dozens of copyists, from artists still finding their feet for the journey to fame, such as Gene Autry, Jimmie Davis, Cliff Carlisle, Hank Snow and Ernest Tubb, to many lesser figures who were content to make slight adaptations to Rodgers' model.

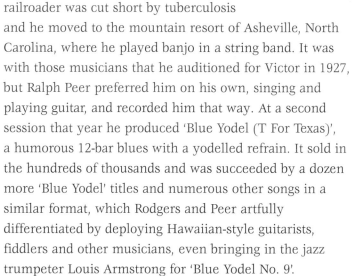

'T For Texas, T For Tennessee'

Rodgers grew up in Meridian, Mississippi. His career as a railroader was cut short by tuberculosis and he moved to the mountain resort of Asheville, North Carolina, where he played banjo in a string band. It was with those musicians that he auditioned for Victor in 1927, but Ralph Peer preferred him on his own, singing and playing guitar, and recorded him that way. At a second session that year he produced 'Blue Yodel (T For Texas)', a humorous 12-bar blues with a yodelled refrain. It sold in the hundreds of thousands and was succeeded by a dozen more 'Blue Yodel' titles and numerous other songs in a similar format, which Rodgers and Peer artfully differentiated by deploying Hawaiian-style guitarists, fiddlers and other musicians, even bringing in the jazz trumpeter Louis Armstrong for 'Blue Yodel No. 9'.

Interspersed among these blues compositions were sentimental songs, western themes, songs rooted in the experiences of railroaders, gamblers and prisoners, and a group of topographical songs, such as 'Peach Pickin' Time In Georgia' and 'Roll Along Kentucky Moon', which were calculated to appeal to regional audiences. Many were written or co-written by Rodgers himself, some with his sister-in-law Elsie McWilliams, while others were supplied by professional songwriters. Whatever the material, Rodgers unfailingly personalized it with his warm,

Classic Recordings

1927
'Away Out On The Mountain'

1928
'In The Jailhouse Now',
'Waiting For A Train'

1929
'Any Old Time'

1930
'Blue Yodel No. 8
(Mule Skinner Blues)',
'Blue Yodel No. 9'

1933
'Mississippi Delta Blues'

Left

Rodgers invested his considerable earnings in building a large house in Kerrville, Texas, where he also ordered this new roadster.

ingratiating delivery, plainly drawn guitar lines and, of course, the yodel.

Like everyone else in country music, Rodgers could not sustain the huge sales of his early records through the lean years of the Depression. Unlike almost everyone else, he had another market, overseas. Most of his releases came out in the UK and Australia (where he exercised enormous influence on the nascent record industry, practically blueprinting the style of artists like Tex Morton), and many also in India, Ireland and other territories.

'Got The T. B. Blues'

Throughout what an album title would later call his 'short but brilliant life' Rodgers made personal appearances on major theatre circuits and, in a publicist's neat move, toured with the humorist Will Rogers. He even made a short film, *The Singing Brakeman* (1929). But he had never shaken off tuberculosis – a fact that inspired a couple of blackly humorous songs – and by May 1933, when he cut his last records, he had to take a break between each song and rest on a cot in the studio. He died in his New York hotel a few days later.

Death only enhanced his fame. All his records were reissued on cheap labels and multiplied their sales many times over. Twenty years after his death, his daughter Anita and admirers like Tubb and Snow instituted a Jimmie Rodgers Day in his home town, which has continued ever since. Albums brought his songs to a new audience and made fans out of musicians as diverse as Duane Allman and Bob Dylan. The legacy of Jimmie Rodgers remains a thick, bright, unfrayed thread in the fabric of country music.

Left Middle

'Blue Yodel' was recorded at the second session Rodgers undertook with Ralph Peer, the Victor talent scout.

Key Track

'Blue Yodel' (1927)
'T for Texas, T for Tennessee – T for Thelma, that gal that made a wreck out of me.' It's not only one of the most famous opening verses in country music, but also a road sign pointing in a new direction: down the blues highway walked by countless black singers whose music would shape that of Rodgers and his followers.

A-Z of Artists

Clarence 'Tom' Ashley
(Vocals, banjo, 1895–1967)

Tom Ashley (as everyone but record companies called him) learned his trade as an entertainer by working on travelling shows. In the 1920s he played in The Carolina Tar Heels and recorded exceptional banjo-accompanied versions of 'The Coo Coo Bird' and the traditional ballad 'The House Carpenter'. As late as the 1950s he was working with Ralph Stanley, performing in blackface. His Folkways LP *Old-Time Music At Clarence Ashley's* introduced the world to Doc Watson.

The Blue Sky Boys
(Vocal duo, 1936–76)

This prettiest and most poignant of country harmony duos was first heard on southern radio in 1935. The North Carolina-born Bolick brothers – Bill (b. 1917) and Earl (1919–98) – also recorded prolifically, accompanying themselves on mandolin and guitar, from 1936 to 1951, making definitive discs of traditional Americana like 'Down On The Banks Of The Ohio' and 'Story Of The Knoxville Girl'. In later years, though they had ceased working together, they were persuaded to reunite for occasional festival appearances and albums.

Dock Boggs
(Vocals, banjo, 1898–1971)

Boggs grew up in south-western Virginia at a time when mountain people were reluctantly quitting the backwoods for the hell of the coalmines. His music, too, reflects adaptation – 'Country Blues', 'Pretty Polly' and 'Down South Blues' making an eerie connection between the dispassionate narrative of the hillbilly ballad and the personal testimony of the blues. His 1920s recordings having achieved almost legendary status, he was tracked down in the 1960s and persuaded to perform and record again.

Dick Burnett
(Vocals, banjo, guitar, 1883–1977)

A singer, banjoist and guitarist from southern Kentucky, blinded in a shooting accident in his early twenties, Burnett wrote (but did not record) 'Man Of Constant Sorrow', made famous again through its use in the film *O Brother, Where Art Thou?* He and his playing partner, the fiddler Leonard Rutherford, were one of the most gifted duet acts on early country records, and even today there are musicians faithful to their fluid, close-knit style.

The Callahan Brothers
(Vocal duo, 1930s–40s)

Contemporaries of the Delmores, Dixons and other brother acts, Homer (1912–2002) and Walter (1910–71) Callahan (professionally, Bill and Joe respectively) stood out with their duet yodelling and their fondness for bluesy themes.

Below

The Callahan Brothers (middle row, centre) at the Big D. Jamboree in 1949.

Starting out on radio in Asheville, North Carolina, in 1933, they recorded copiously through the 1930s, enjoying moderate success with 'She's My Curly Headed Baby'. In the 1940s they were on radio in Texas, where Homer remained active in music to an advanced age.

Bill & Cliff Carlisle

(Vocal/instrumental duo, 1930s–50s)

Raised near Louisville, Kentucky, Cliff Carlisle (1904–83) was attracted as a boy to blues and Hawaiian music. His fusion of the two would make him one of the most distinctive musicians of his time. Playing the dobro resonator guitar with a slide, he transmuted the blue yodels of Jimmie Rodgers, becoming a popular performer on radio and records. In the 1930s he worked on WBT in Charlotte, North Carolina, with his brother Bill (1908–2003) an equally talented singer and a fast flatpicking guitarist, who also recorded prolifically in his own name. Both men adapted to the changes in country music after the Second World War, scoring in their family group The Carlisles with records like 'Too Old To Cut The Mustard' (1951) and 'No Help Wanted' (1953). Cliff retired in the 1950s, but Bill maintained his career for another 50 years, making his last appearance on the Grand Ole Opry 10 days before his death.

Left

Country bluesman Cliff Carlisle, one of the most talented steel guitarists in country music's early years.

Left Below

After separating from brother Cliff in the early 1950s, Bill Carlisle worked with family group The Carlisles, which became a regular on the Grand Ole Opry.

Fiddlin' John Carson

(Fiddle, vocals, 1875–1949)

Carson's June 1923 disc of 'The Old Hen Cackled And The Rooster's Going To Crow' and 'Little Old Log Cabin In The Lane' was the first country record made in the South, in a temporary studio in Atlanta. A farmer by trade, Carson had been famous for years in Northern Georgia as an entertainer and a contestant at fiddling contests, but his many records in the 1920s and 1930s made him more widely known. He came across chiefly as a gnarly old comedian, playing antique fiddle tunes, singing crazy old songs like 'It's A Shame To Whip Your Wife On Sunday' and swapping repartee with his daughter Rosa Lee, known as 'Moonshine Kate'. But his band sides with his Virginia Reelers, like 'Hell Bound For Alabama', are some of the wildest string music ever recorded. After a long career he took a job in local government, operating the lift in Atlanta's State Capitol.

Below

Fiddlin' John Carson and his daughter, 'Moonshine Kate', who recorded as a comedy duo despite Carson's considerable fiddling talents.

In all, he recorded more than 1,000 tracks, issued on innumerable labels and under dozens of pseudonyms. These embraced every kind of country song, from topical ('The Death Of Floyd Collins') to weepie ('The Letter Edged In Black') to mock-gospel ('Golden Slippers'). He was typically accompanied by his own harmonica, a studio fiddler and Carson Robison, playing guitar and singing harmony. It was not genuine southern music, but as an impression of it for a non-southern audience it was evidently very effective – at least until the Depression. By 1932 his popularity was fading, and he ended his life as a penurious voice coach.

Tom Darby & Jimmie Tarlton
(Vocal/instrumental duo, 1927–33)

The sound of the steel guitar has been part of country music almost from the beginning. An influential early exponent was Jimmie Tarlton (1892–1979), who partnered singer-guitarist Tom Darby (1980–*c.* 1971) in a series of duet recordings between 1927 and 1933, including two of the biggest hits of the period, 'Birmingham Jail' and 'Columbus Stockade Blues'. With their plaintive harmonies and Tarlton's swooping slide guitar – particularly effective on blues – they were one of the most distinctive acts of their day.

Above

The Cumberland Ridge Runners – (l–r) Hartford Taylor, Red Foley, Karl Davis and Slim Miller – from the WLS Family Album of 1934.

The Cumberland Ridge Runners
(Vocal/instrumental group, 1930–35)

This group, created by the Berea, Kentucky, entrepreneur John Lair in 1930 for the WLS *National Barn Dance*, genially exploited popular perceptions of mountain folk through music and costume, and was an ancestor of shows like *The Beverly Hillbillies* and *Hee Haw*. The group lasted only five years, but its members went on to enjoy long careers in country music, among them Karl & Harty and singer-guitarists Doc Hopkins (1899–1988) and Red Foley (1910–68).

Vernon Dalhart
(Vocals, harmonica, 1883–1948)

Right

Singer and politician Jimmie Davis, who was elected to the Country Music Hall Of Fame in 1972.

Although a trained singer with experience in opera – and from 1917 a full-time recording artist in the popular field – the Texas-born Dalhart is best known for his vast catalogue of recordings in the hillbilly idiom, beginning with 'The Wreck Of The Old '97' and 'The Prisoner's Song' in 1924.

Jimmie Davis

(Vocals, 1899–2000)

Born in rural Louisiana, Davis first made his name singing on radio station KWKH in Shreveport. From 1928 onwards, he was a popular recording artist, initially with sentimental and cowboy songs, then with raunchy blue yodels in the manner of Jimmie Rodgers. These included 'She's A Hum Dum Dinger From Dingersville' and 'Bear Cat Mama From Horner's Corners', and were sometimes accompanied by black guitarists. Switching labels in 1934 to the new Decca company, he had a crossover hit with the love song 'Nobody's Darlin' But Mine', and thereafter left the blues behind. His career-best hit, 'You Are My Sunshine' – one of many songs that he bought from the writers and claimed as his own – made him a country star of comparable magnitude to Gene Autry, and he used that fame to boost his political career, serving two terms as Governor of Louisiana (1944–48 and 1960–64). His later recordings are heavily weighted towards gospel music.

The Delmore Brothers

(Vocal duo, 1926–52)

The sound of The Delmore Brothers – a humorous blues or a wistful train song, told to the rhythm of two mellow guitars – echoed through country music across three decades. Alton (1908–64) and Rabon (1916–52) were among the first stars of the microphone era, their voices linked in soft, confidential harmony fit for the intimacy of radio. Between 1932 and 1938, as stalwarts of the Grand Ole Opry, they travelled with fellow cast-member Uncle Dave Macon and recorded behind fiddler Arthur Smith (1898–1971). Their comic piece 'Brown's Ferry Blues' was a major hillbilly hit of the period. Later they were on WLW in Cincinnati and in at the birth of King Records, for whom they had hits like the sombre 'Blues Stay Away From Me' (1949), with the lonesome harmonica of Wayne Raney, and up-tempo numbers like 'Hillbilly Boogie', in which they transformed the easygoing swing of their earlier music into something close to rock'n'roll.

Curly Fox & Texas Ruby

(Vocal/instrumental duo, 1940s–50s)

The hard-driving, bluesy fiddling of Tennessee-born Curly Fox (1910–95) had been heard on radio, and on records by The Shelton Brothers, but his career took an upswing around 1936 when he teamed with Texan singer-guitarist

Ruby Owens (1909–63), whom he subsequently married. Over 25 years they had spells on the Grand Ole Opry and WLW's *Boone County Jamboree*, as well as on television in Houston. Fox's recordings of tunes like 'Black Mountain Rag' were influential among other fiddlers.

BELOW

The style of The Delmore Brothers laid the foundations for rockabilly and early rock'n'roll.

Above
Frank Hutchison is believed to have learnt to play the blues by watching a disabled black man, Bill Hurt.

Right
Banjo-playing Baptist minister Buell Kazee continued in the music industry until his death in 1976.

Kelly Harrell
(Vocals, 1889–1942)

A mill-hand from Fieldale, Virginia, Harrell was a contemporary and acquaintance of Charlie Poole, but had little of his raunchy zest; instead he sang old parlour pieces like 'In The Shadow Of The Pine' with bleak sobriety. He made his finest recordings with Poole's fiddler Posey Rorer – among them the ballad 'Charles Guiteau' about the assassination of US President James Garfield. He also wrote 'Away Out On The Mountain', an early hit for Jimmie Rodgers.

George D. Hay
(Radio showman, 1895–1968)

Best known as the emcee of the Grand Ole Opry from its start until the late 1940s, Hay had an earlier career as a newspaper columnist and radio announcer in Memphis, followed by a spell on WLS in Chicago, where he presented the ancestor of the *National Barn Dance*. Joining WSM in Nashville in 1925, he created similar programming that

became the Opry. He is seen in a characteristic role in the 1940 movie *Grand Ole Opry*.

The Hill Billies
(Vocal/instrumental group, 1920s)

The Hill Billies, led by pianist Al Hopkins (1889–1932), was the first band to employ the slighting term 'hillbilly', initiating a terminological debate that went on for decades. Originally based in Galax, Virginia, the band included fiddlers Tony Alderman (1900–83) and Charlie Bowman (1889–1962) and banjoist John Rector (d. 1985). The Hill Billies' records on Vocalion and Brunswick – a mixture of songs and dance tunes, ingeniously arranged with solo passages – were steady sellers in the 1920s.

Frank Hutchison
(Guitar, vocals, harmonica, 1897–1945)

Hutchison, a singer, slide-guitarist and harmonica player from West Virginia, was one of the more striking exponents of 'hillbilly blues' – music learned from, or influenced by, African-American sources, which in his case was acquired from railroad workers and miners. His ragtime picking piece 'Coney Isle', retitled 'Alabam'', was a hit years later for Cowboy Copas, while his slide guitar-accompanied 'Worried Blues' and 'Train That Carried My Girl From Town' continue to attract musicians.

Blind Andy Jenkins
(Vocalist, songwriter, 1885–1957)

The Rev. Andrew Jenkins, a blind Georgia minister, made numerous records in the 1920s, both solo and with family members, but his importance lies chiefly in his huge folio of songs, particularly topical pieces like 'The Death Of Floyd Collins' and 'Ben Dewberry's Final Run' (recorded by Jimmie Rodgers), and gospel songs such as 'God Put A Rainbow In The Clouds'. He and two stepdaughters formed The Jenkins Family, which sang sacred music on Atlanta's WSB throughout the 1920s.

Karl & Harty
(Vocal/instrumental group, 1935–40s)

After the dissolution of The Cumberland Ridge Runners around 1935, Karl Davis (vocal, mandolin, 1905–79) and Hartford Taylor (vocal, guitar, 1905–63) maintained their popularity on the WLS *National Barn Dance* and other Chicago radio shows until the late 1940s. Echoing an earlier

WLS mandolin-guitar duet, Mac & Bob (Lester McFarland and Robert Gardner), they recorded sentimental and humorous songs such as 'I'm Here To Get My Baby Out Of Jail' and 'Kentucky' (later recorded by the Everly Brothers).

Buell Kazee

(Banjo, vocals, 1900–76)

A trained musician who thought he had left old-time music behind him in rural Kentucky, Kazee nevertheless became an important early country recording artist. His banjo-accompanied versions of traditional American ballads like 'East Virginia' and 'The Wagoner's Lad' influenced generations of singers, incuding Joan Baez. His career didn't outlast the Depression, but by then he was a Baptist minister, and his later years were devoted to writing operas and cantatas based on folk themes.

Bradley Kincaid

(Vocals, guitar, 1895–1991)

The Kentuckian singer-guitarist was a superstar of early country radio, appealing to the vast mid-western audience of the WLS *National Barn Dance* with gentle renditions of old songs like 'Barbara Allen' and 'The Fatal Wedding'. In the 1920s and 1930s he sold hundreds of thousands of songbooks and records. After retiring to run a music store in Springfield, Ohio, he returned to a studio in 1963 and over four days rerecorded his entire repertoire of 162 songs.

Lulu Belle & Scotty

(Vocal duo, 1933–58)

In Chicago in the early 1930s, Myrtle Cooper (Lulu Belle, 1913–99) and Scott Wiseman (1909–81) were young North Carolinians performing on WLS's *National Barn Dance*.

When they fell in love, the station exploited them as sweethearts of the radio, increasing their fan mail and attracting record and movie companies. Their rapport and old-fashioned music endeared them to a generation. Despite retiring in 1958, they continued to record, and Lulu Belle served as a Democrat in the North Carolina State Legislature.

Below

Even after he retired, Bradley Kincaid continued to play in folk festivals, and always considered himself a folk singer rather than a country musician.

J. E. Mainer & His Mountaineers
(Vocal/instrumental group, 1930s)

Right

Sam McGee on guitar, Arthur Smith with his fiddle, and Kirk McGee on banjo. The McGee brothers were active for nearly 60 years.

In 1934 Joseph E. Mainer (1898–1971) and his brother Wade (b. 1907), playing fiddle and banjo respectively, secured a slot on WBT in Charlotte, North Carolina. The group they assembled – adding singer-guitarists Daddy John Love and Zeke Morris – was an immediate hit, not only on radio but also on Bluebird Records with numbers like 'Maple On The Hill'. They were essentially a country variety act in the tradition of the minstrel- or medicine-show, a character maintained by successive line-ups as they dispensed old-time comic numbers, gospel selections and heart songs in the 'brother duet' manner. Wade and Zeke Morris left in 1936 to form their own band, eventually called The Sons Of

Below

Mainer's Mountaineers – one of the most popular string bands of the 1930s.

The Mountaineers. The Mainers' music was an important precursor of bluegrass, several of J. E.'s numbers turning up in the repertoire of The Stanley Brothers. J. E. continued to record into the 1960s; Wade was still making occasional appearances 30 years later.

Sam & Kirk McGee
(Vocal/instrumental duo, 1920s–70s)

The McGee brothers, Sam (1894–1975) and Kirk (1899–1983) from Franklin, Tennessee, were the first guitar stars of the Grand Ole Opry, and remained affiliated to the show for half a century. Sam's adroit picking is exemplified by his own discs, including 'Buck Dancer's Choice' and others with Uncle Dave Macon, whom he and his brother (Kirk doubling on bluesy fiddle) accompanied on records and personal appearances. They later worked with fiddler Arthur Smith, and continued to perform and record into their seventies.

Bob Miller
(Piano, vocals, songwriter, publisher, 1895–1955)

A Memphis riverboat pianist and bandleader, Miller got into the publishing and songwriting business in his twenties. Moving to New York, he worked for several labels as a record producer, supplying acts like Gene Autry and Cliff Carlisle with material of his own, such as 'Twenty-One Years', 'Seven Years With The Wrong Woman' and 'Rockin' Alone (In An Old Rockin' Chair)' and often playing keyboards on their records. One of his biggest successes was Elton Britt's Second World War hit 'There's A Star-Spangled Banner Waving Somewhere' (1942). He is reputed

to have written 4,000 songs; the true number may be about 10 per cent of that, but it included many interesting topical pieces like 'Eleven Cent Cotton, Forty Cent Meat' (1928), 'Dry Voters And Wet Drinkers' (1929) and a sheaf of true-crime compositions, all of which he recorded himself under several pseudonyms.

Ralph S. Peer
(Producer, 1892–1960)
Peer entered the record business at the age of 19 in his home town of Kansas City, Missouri. By 1920, he was in New York running the OKeh label, where he supervised the first vocal blues recording by a black artist – Mamie Smith – and created a 'race series' of exclusively African-American recordings. He matched this in 1925 with an 'old-time' list, following the success of his recordings of Fiddlin' John Carson. From 1926, he worked as a talent-scout and record-producer for Victor, discovering and overseeing sessions by Jimmie Rodgers, The Carter Family and innumerable other country, blues and jazz artists. He also published their compositions through his companies Southern Music (which in the 1930s had huge success with mainstream pop repertoire like 'Rockin' Chair' and 'Lazy River' and South American music) and (from 1940) Peer International, which is still a significant player in the country-music publishing business.

Charlie Poole
(Vocals, banjo, 1892–1931)
A textile-mill worker and banjo player, Poole led one of the finest of old-time bands, The North Carolina Ramblers, with guitarist Roy Harvey (1892–1958) and a succession of fiddlers headed by Posey Rorer. Their first release, 'Don't Let Your Deal Go Down Blues' and 'Can I Sleep In Your Barn Tonight,

Mister?' in 1925, sold in six figures. With his rowdy lifestyle and endearingly creaky singing, Poole was much loved in Appalachia and his music is still remembered there.

Riley Puckett
(Vocals, guitar, 1894–1946)
Much of the success of The Skillet Lickers, the north Georgia string band led by Gid Tanner, was due to the warm, friendly singing of the blind Riley Puckett, who also anchored them with eccentric single-note guitar runs dictated by his own sense of time and melody. In 1924, he and Tanner had made some of the earliest recordings of fiddle-and-guitar music, and after The Skillet Lickers broke up he had a long career on radio and records.

Above
Riley Puckett (right), one of Columbia's most successful acts, jamming with the fiddler A. A. Gray.

Blind Alfred Reed

(Vocals, fiddle, 1880–1956)

Reed, a singer and fiddler from Princeton, West Virginia, made his living playing at dances and church meetings and giving music lessons. Recording in the late 1920s, he observed contemporary life in songs like 'How Can A Poor Man Stand Such Times And Live?'– a catalogue of the ills that afflicted Depression-hit rural southerners. His favourite theme was the tragicomedy of marriage, epitomized in his line 'God made woman after man – and she's been after man ever since'.

Eck Robertson

(Fiddle, 1887–1975)

To fiddler Eck Robertson, and his often overlooked partner Henry Gilliland, goes the credit for recording, in June 1922, the first unequivocal country record: 'Arkansaw Traveler', an intricate fiddle duet, and 'Sallie Gooden', a virtuoso version of the traditional tune played by Robertson alone. He recorded again in the late 1920s with his family band, and reappeared at folk festivals in the 1960s, wearing a goatee like the cartoon Uncle Sam – and still playing brilliantly.

Right
Ernest 'Pop' Stoneman demonstrates his skill with the harmonica and autoharp.

Below
The prolific Carson Robison inherited his musical talent from his father, a championship fiddler.

Carson Robison

(Vocals, guitar, 1890–1957)

Initially a New York session guitarist (with a talent on the side for whistling), Kansas-born Robison became the regular accompanist and vocal duet partner of Vernon Dalhart on hundreds of recordings in the 1920s. He also learned the skill of songwriting for the hillbilly market, specializing in topical subjects like bank raids and train crashes, but extending to local-colour compositions such as 'When It's Springtime In The Rockies' and 'Sleepy Rio Grande', many of which he recorded in duet with the singer Frank Luther (1899–1980). During the 1930s Robison And His Pioneers were popular in Europe, recording for many English labels and broadcasting on Radio Luxembourg. In later years this supremely versatile man recorded square-dance albums and rockabilly before finding a last hit with the slow-talking, rocking-on-the-porch narration 'Life Gets Tee-Jus, Don't It?'.

Ernest Stoneman

(Vocals, harmonica, guitar, autoharp, 1893–1968)

Stoneman might be considered the first fully professional country artist. He saw the music's potential and was involved in it from the 1920s to the 1960s, spanning music technology from the cylinder recording to the stereo LP. In the 1920s and 1930s, singing and playing harmonica, guitar and autoharp, he made almost 200 recordings – some solo, some in groups with his wife Hattie on fiddle. He embraced dance tunes, Victorian parlour songs, native American ballads, sacred music and novelties like 'Possum Trot School Exhibition', which combined old-time music and a spelling competition. After the Second World War, some of his sons and daughters, notably the brilliant fiddler Scotty (1932–73) and mandolin player Donna (b. 1934), played in The Bluegrass Champs, which developed into The Stonemans, featuring further siblings and 'Pop' Ernest himself. They made several albums and had their own television show before fading from view in the 1970s.

Gid Tanner
(Fiddle, banjo, vocals, 1885–1960)
An old-time fiddler and comic singer from Dacula, Georgia, Tanner gave his name to the most famous of old-time string bands, The Skillet Lickers, though his medicine-show routines were regarded as an embarrassment by younger members of the band, which included fiddler Clayton McMichen (1900–70), who was determined to turn the old-time fiddle band into a modern swing unit. Yet, thanks to the singing of Rilcy Puckett and the brilliant harmonized fiddling of McMichen, Lowe Stokes (1898–1983) and Bert Layne, The Skillet Lickers were the bestselling string band of the 1920s, both with musical records like 'Pass Around The Bottle And We'll All Take A Drink' and 'Watermelon On The Vine' and with the comedy sketch series 'A Corn Licker Still In Georgia' – about making moonshine and dodging the law during Prohibition. The band broke up in 1931 but Tanner led another line-up at an exhilarating swansong session in 1934.

Uncle Jimmy Thompson
(Fiddle, 1848–1931)
The first man to play on the Nashville radio station that would house the Grand Ole Opry, Thompson was a Tennessee-born, Texas-raised fiddler with many contest rosettes to his name when he sat down at a WSM microphone in November 1925. Accompanied by his daughter Eva, who played piano or danced, he toured small-town Tennessee in a homemade mobile home, playing, on 'Old Betsy', fiddle tunes that dated back to the Civil War.

Henry Whitter
(Harmonica, guitar, vocals, 1892–1941)
Competent harmonica player, average singer and guitarist, Whitter holds a place in history as one of country music's pioneering disc artists, recording in 1923 strong sellers like 'Fox Chase' and 'The Wreck Of The Old '97', which

enabled him to quit his job at a Fries, Virginia, textile mill and become a professional musician. Later he accompanied the fiddler and singer G. B. Grayson (1888–1930) on some classic ballad recordings, but his career withered after the 1920s.

Below
Uncle Jimmy Thompson, with his daughter and accompanist, Eva Thompson Jones.

Sons of the Pioneers

I've Sold My Saddle For An Old Guitar:
Cowboys & Playboys

It is ironic that western music – be it cowboy vocal balladry or ranch-house dance fiddling – began seriously to engage the imagination of the American public as the real West slipped further and further into the past and the country became increasingly urbanized and sophisticated.

This capturing of the public imagination was perhaps inevitable, too, not only because of the nostalgia for what was lost – and sometimes never was – but also because of the huge impact of new technologies such as the phonograph and, in particular, radio. These made the wide dissemination of music possible, while on a more practical level the introduction of microphones and electrical public-address systems allowed for – and even demanded – stylistic growth and facilitated the explosion of the music's popularity in the 1930s. At the same time, improved road systems and cheaper and more reliable transportation further aided the music's spread and evolution.

It is also ironic that while western music and offshoots such as western swing long ago ceased to be dominant musical styles in mainstream country music, the trappings of these styles – western dress and a certain mystique – have remained at the forefront. There are few modern male country stars, from Hank Williams to the cowboy hat-wearing young singers of recent generations far removed stylistically from anything remotely 'western', who don't present themselves as cowboys – Stetson hat, boots and all. This lingering affectation is a testimony to the huge impact of western music and western swing from the 1930s to the early 1950s, and to the continuing attraction of a mythic West that had gripped the nation so strongly in these years.

Key Artists

Gene Autry

Milton Brown

Roy Rogers & The Sons Of The Pioneers

Hank Thompson

Bob Wills

Influences & Development

The western music – be it jazzy, danceable western swing or spare cowboy songs – that thrived for more than two decades from the 1920s grew out of several strains of American folk tradition, chiefly balladry and fiddle-band music, each of which had over time developed its own regional flavours and stylistic quirks.

'I didn't play much early on. What I really liked was cowboy movies. I was a big cowboy fan and liked western music.... I hung out at a little theater that played Gene Autry and Tex Ritter movies. Tex Ritter is still my favourite singer.'

Otis Blackwell

Below

Louise Massey And The Westerners in the mid-1930s. A seminal and slickly professional group, they combined a western image and musical base with pop and jazz sensibilities.

The Development Of Cowboy Music

The eclectic instrumental style that flourished west of the Mississippi evolved naturally in the cultural melting-pot of the south-west and beyond. Its ultimate origins may have been Old World – Scottish and Irish fiddle tunes, for example, carried west by pioneers – but by the twentieth century this frontier music had been impacted, whether overtly or subtly by myriad influences, including popular music of the day, the music of slaves and their descendents, and that of other ethnic groups like Czechs, Germans, Poles and Mexicans.

The historical development of the cowboy song and singing cowboys, however, was less straightforward, even controversial. N. Howard Thorpe and others had collected cowboy songs since the late-nineteenth century, but it remains unclear how much of this music actually sprang from authentic cowboys or authentic ranch life. What is certain is that the growing popularity of such songs reflected a national fascination with all things cowboy that grew apace into the early decades of the twentieth century.

The 1920s was a pivotal decade. Radio and the growth of the phonograph industry greatly enhanced the exposure and expanded the commercial possibilities of the music, while large population shifts from the countryside into urban areas brought rural music into towns and cities. There it found not only a built-in audience among transplanted country folk, but also potentially huge new audiences among city dwellers. As *Time* magazine put it in 1946, trying to put its finger on Bob Wills' enormous popularity, 'His trick was to bring ranch-house music nearer to the city.'

Influential Inventions

Wills himself felt that the introduction of PA (public address) systems was the key factor that facilitated the development of his western swing in the early 1930s. This technology allowed fiddle bands, previously restricted to small venues like house dances because of the lack of amplification, to move into dancehalls. Almost overnight, a band could play for hundreds of dancers instead of a few dozen. The new environment demanded the addition of further instruments and with this growth came a mandate of sorts to expand the horizons of the music – to please an audience that had been newly exposed to a variety of styles and was no longer content with just the old fiddle tunes.

Following closely behind the introduction of the PA system was that of electrically amplified instruments. Originally a necessity to enable the instruments to be heard over the din, electrification of instruments such as guitar and steel guitar opened up huge possibilities for the artistic development of these instruments and country music was at the forefront of this progress.

While cowboy music and the nascent western string-band style often evolved within the same group – for example, Otto Gray's Oklahoma Cowboys band featured both cowboy singer Owen Gray and a string band playing traditional and modern fiddle music – more often they developed separately. Early cowboy singers like Carl T. Sprague (1895–1979), Jules Verne Allen (1883–1945) or Marc Williams (1903–73) were, if they performed regularly

at all, chiefly show and radio singers, solo artists, with spare accompaniment, if any, beyond their own guitar. The western string bands, however, were dance bands. Gray's pioneering Oklahoma Cowboys was a show band, and those it inspired in the Midwest and East were generally the same. But west of the Mississippi, string bands generally played for dancers.

Into the 1930s, both these styles became increasingly influenced by popular music. A cowboy singer was as likely to feature a faux cowboy song written by a Tin Pan Alley pro like Billy Hill as a traditional number like 'Whoopi-Ti-Yi-Yo'. Performers began writing their own material, too, and the songs of, for example, Bob Nolan of The Sons Of The Pioneers were western pop songs, not variations of earlier and earthier folk fare.

Left

Gene Autry was the most famous and influential 'singing cowboy' of the 1930s. He made over 90 movies throughout his career.

Below

Another singing cowboy – Tex Ritter (left), with guitarist Eldon Shamblin (centre) and the 'king of western swing', Bob Wills (right).

Pop Influences & Western Swing

Below

*Clayton McMichen,
whose early string-band
work drew heavily from
jazz, pop and blues.*

The influence of pop music and other musical styles, particularly jazz and blues, was even more pronounced in the evolving fiddle bands, and the music that eventually came to be known as western swing was heavily

Below

*Clayton McMichen,
whose early string-band
work drew heavily from
jazz, pop and blues.*

influenced by these modern styles and drew extensively from black music. It must be stressed, though, that the influence of pop, jazz and blues in country music did not originate with the western-swing bands of the 1930s. Jimmie Rodgers (1897–1933) had of course drawn deeply from them. Less widely acknowledged are others, like fiddler Clayton McMichen (1900–70), best known for his work with 1920s' old-time stalwarts The Skillet Lickers, but whose heart lay firmly in the modern era and whose own music profoundly anticipated styles that came into vogue a decade later.

Western swing became the dominant country-music style in the south-west from the mid-1930s, with artists like Milton Brown (1903–36) and Bob Wills (1905–75) at the forefront. It would enjoy a national vogue during the 1940s, when its epicentre shifted to the West Coast, with stars like Wills, Spade Cooley (1910–69) and Tex Williams (1917–85) leading the way.

Cowboy styles and more straightforward western music enjoyed its greatest popularity at the same time western swing thrived. Its classic era was ushered in via the movies, heralded by the arrival of Gene Autry (1907–98) in 1935 and by the emergence of The Sons Of The Pioneers, from whose ranks sprang another star, Roy Rogers (1911–98), around the same time. Autry's popularity and impact were nationwide and immeasurable.

The Cowboy Style

Autry's style and that of other cowboys like The Pioneers or Ray Whitley increasingly shared characteristics with western swing and was certainly influenced by it from the late 1930s. The influence was two-way, however, with western dance bands increasingly donning cowboy garb and singing western-themed material in response to the rise of the singing cowboys. Indeed, the early spread of jazzy western string music probably owed more on a national level to The Sons Of The Pioneers, through the fiddle and guitar work of group members Hugh and Karl Farr, than it did to the western-swing bands operating in the south-west, who had chiefly regional impact until the 1940s.

The influence of south-westerners like Bob Wills slowly but tellingly increased beyond the region. Even Milton Brown, whose 1936 death cut short an important career, had residual influence far beyond his lifetime, partly through recordings but no significantly via the work of later singers and musicians who had been heavily influenced by Brown, and brought the music to new listeners far beyond Texas.

Indeed, the 1940s West Coast scene was heavily populated by musicians who had honed their skills in the Southwest. Which is not to say that this scene didn't have its innovators and its native practitioners. Spade Cooley's highly sophisticated string orchestra, all the rage in the mid-1940s, drew from myriad earlier sources, but the flashy, influential mix that resulted was distinctly southern Californian.

gaining popularity. Both strains survive into the twenty-first century, as do – sometimes in much-altered form – such long-lived bands as The Sons Of The Pioneers and The Light Crust Doughboys, not to mention the Cajun swing band The Hackberry Ramblers, who as of 2006 still included two musicians whose tenures began in the early 1930s.

Cowboy Revival

The polish and sophistication of Cooley and the earthier but still relatively uptown Texas Playboys of Bob Wills eventually found itself out of style – the victim of a backlash that saw country-music audiences easing towards the more rural and straightforward, emotionally raw music of artists like Hank Williams. The popularity of cowboy singers like Autry and Rogers and vocal groups like The Sons Of The Pioneers faded around the same time. The last of the singing film cowboys, Rex Allen, flourished for a short time in the early 1950s – and that was it. The bigger names, like Bob Wills, survived in the decades that followed; a few, like Hank Thompson, sustained admirably successful recording and touring careers during the lean years dominated by television, rock'n'roll and other changes in taste and lifestyle.

There was a revival of sorts in the 1970s and beyond, with young western-swing bands like Asleep At The Wheel and cowboy vocal groups like Riders In The Sky

Left
West Coast cowboy Spade Cooley with The Sons Of The Pioneers.

Below
The Sons Of The Pioneers, the ultimate cowboy band, whose influence can still be felt today.

Country Music In The Dancehalls & On The Airwaves

Right

The Light Crust Doughboys were named for the sponsor of their radio show, which made Light Crust Flour.

Country music today retains little of the regional identity that characterized it in its early days. There are pockets of resistance to this homogeneity and to the hegemony of Nashville – a honky-tonk dance circuit and a fiercely independent singer-songwriter tradition in Texas, for example – but overall the scene is one of major stars playing huge venues.

The middle ground of regional stardom has largely disappeared, but it was once the norm. The popularity of an artist like western swing pioneer Milton Brown was limited to the area in which he or she operated – limited by the reach of local radio and by hard travel in the days before superhighways.

Below

Curley Williams' Georgia Peach Pickers were one of the chief exponents of the hot-swing style in the south-east.

Dance Music

It is almost a cliché of country-music scholarship to underscore the differences in regional styles in black and

white: east of the Mississippi the music was for 'show', west of the Mississippi its primary purpose was for dancing. This is largely true, though certainly there were plenty of exceptions on both sides of the river to disprove the rule. The south-eastern band of Curley Williams (1914–70), for example, flourished on a dance circuit in southern Georgia and northern Florida prior to its arrival on the Grand Ole Opry in 1943. At the same time, non-dance shows that featured more straightforward country music were popular all over the south-west and beyond, including such major Saturday-night radio barn dances as the *Louisiana Hayride* in Shreveport and the *Big D Jamboree* in Dallas.

Even among the western-swing groups in the south-west, dance bands in a region in which dancing – whether in large dancehalls or small honky-tonks – was dominant, there were bands that were exclusively radio and show bands. These included some of the most important and influential bands in the style: Fort Worth's Light Crust Doughboys and Dallas' Bill Boyd's Cowboy Ramblers and Roy Newman And His Boys. The Doughboys and Boyd toured widely as purely show bands behind their regionally

popular radio shows, while Newman's band, though it played locally on a limited basis, was chiefly a radio band.

The Rise And Decline Of The Dancehall

Far more common, however, were dance bands like Bob Wills And His Texas Playboys, who in their pre-war heyday operated with stunning success within a region defined by the coverage of their radio broadcasts. In the case of the Playboys, who played over powerful 50,000-watt KVOO, this was a fairly large range of several hundred miles beyond their Tulsa home base. In the days before prerecording was common and radio shows were performed live, such performers were also limited by how far they could realistically travel to perform and still make it back for the radio show the following morning.

What Wills' dance band and the Doughboys' show group had in common was radio sponsorship – in both cases flour companies. This was a new development in the 1930s and it proved lucrative for both band and sponsor. At the same time, many bands had no such sponsorship and often traded their music simply for airtime, a practice that was also mutually beneficial. The radio station got cost-free entertainment and the band was able to plug its dance schedule.

As with so much else, this all began to change after the Second World War. Radio became more network- and record-dominated, and the entertainment industry grew more centralized. Stars tended to be national ones, touring – and broadcasting – from coast-to-coast. Regional circuits like that in which Wills or Brown operated became smaller, more localized, or died out altogether. Television and other changes in entertainment habits altered the scene even more, limited the impact of radio and effectively killed off the dancehall scene in which so many bands had flourished.

Below
The Renfro Valley Barn Dance – one of the earliest and most popular of the radio dance shows.

Gene Autry

Key Artist

Above

Singing cowboy legend Gene Autry in performance at a Dallas rodeo, c. 1948.

'When I went to the movies and heard cowboys like Roy Rogers and Gene Autry yodelling, when I came out of the movie, I was that guy.'

Aaron Neville

It's hard to fathom now – 70 years on – the enormous impact that the laid-back, unassuming Gene Autry (1907–98) had when he rose to national stardom in 1935. Cowboys and western music had enjoyed a certain currency and mystique before he came along, but the first singing movie cowboy's phenomenal rise inspired an entire generation and changed the course of country music.

The First Singing Cowboy

Autry was born Orvon Gene Autry in Tioga, Texas, in 1907 and moved to Oklahoma in his teens. Little is known about his early musical influences. He learned guitar from his mother, briefly worked in a medicine show, and in the late 1920s began pursuing music while working for the railroad. On a trip to New York, he met the Marvin Brothers, Frankie and Johnnie – pop stars from Oklahoma who would remain important figures in his career. Frankie gave him the advice that changed his life: forget the pop music and try hillbilly. Autry chose Jimmie Rodgers as his role model and, beginning in 1929, recorded dozens of songs in the Rodgers style. He developed confidence as both a performer and songwriter, but blue yodelling was just the means to an end. As he came into his own, he abandoned the Rodgers style and later never cited Rodgers as a formative influence.

Autry's first hit, a duet with his uncle-in-law Jimmy Long, was the sentimental 'That Silver Haired Daddy Of Mine'. The song took him to Chicago radio station WLS where, guided by his recording producer Art Satherley, he began to style himself as 'Oklahoma's Singing Cowboy'. Hollywood soon beckoned. After a successful appearance in a Ken Maynard film (*In Old Santa Fe*, 1934), he was signed by Republic Pictures as essentially the first of a new breed: the singing cowboy. Within a year, Gene Autry was a major star and singing cowboys were all over the place.

King Of The Hill

Autry's film career skyrocketed, though his recording career developed at a slower pace. Despite a few classics like 'Riding Down The Canyon', written with sidekick

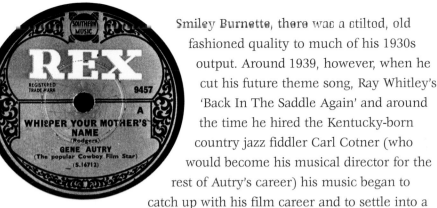

Smiley Burnette, there was a stilted, old fashioned quality to much of his 1930s output. Around 1939, however, when he cut his future theme song, Ray Whitley's 'Back In The Saddle Again' and around the time he hired the Kentucky-born country jazz fiddler Carl Cotner (who would become his musical director for the rest of Autry's career) his music began to catch up with his film career and to settle into a distinctive style that boasted twin fiddles, Frankie Marvin's unobtrusive steel guitar backing and muted trumpet. His singing remained straightforward, as did most of his songwriting with partners like Johnnie Marvin or Fred Rose, which yielded classics like 'Dust' and 'Be Honest With Me'.

Despite increasing competition, Autry remained king of the hill until the Second World War; he served with distinction in the Army Air Corps for four years, then resumed his career. He scored major hits with songs like the Christmas classic 'Rudolph The Red Nosed Reindeer', but his major focus became making money, which he did with a consistency that rivalled his success on film and record.

By the early 1950s, the singing-cowboy phenomenon had played itself out, and Autry slowly eased out of the public eye, gaining some new notoriety as the owner of the California Angels baseball team. A living legend, he remained something of an enigma. From what depths he'd drawn to become the idol of American youth and one of the most influential of all country or western performers was a mystery that died with him at age 91 in 1999.

Classic Recordings

1931
'That Silver Haired Daddy Of Mine'

1935
'Ridin' Down The Canyon'

1940
'Be Honest With Me'

1945
'At Mail Call Today'

1949
'Rudolph The Red Nosed Reindeer'

Left Above
Autry recorded this, and a number of other Jimmie Rodgers songs early in his career, but later eschewed the 'blue-yodel' style.

Left
Autry's horse, Champion, became as famous as his rider.

Key Track

'Back In The Saddle Again' (1939)
This jaunty anthem was written and first recorded by Ray Whitley, but Autry made it his own and it became the song most identified with him. It also heralded the arrival of a smoother, more sophisticated sound that would characterize Autry's recordings, previously rather spare, from this point onwards.

Milton Brown

Key Artist

'At the time, there was no one to compare him to.... The figure I'm repeatedly reminded of is Elvis Presley.' **Robert Palmer**

Below

Milton Brown And His Musical Brownies were among the first to meld country, jazz and pop influences to create the sound of western swing.

There was a time during the western-swing revival of the 1970s when it looked as if the pioneering legacy of Milton Brown (1903–36) And His Musical Brownies would be entirely subsumed amid the accolades given to the music's most popular, enduring figure, Bob Wills. Fortunately, that didn't happen, though Wills continues to reign supreme in the popular imagination. But it was under the guidance of Milton Brown that the music first gelled into a recognizable, influential and popular regional style. Brown didn't pull western swing, fully formed, like a rabbit out of a hat, in his home base of Fort Worth, Texas, in the 1930s – others were easing towards it, too – but it was in the orientation, instrumentation and repertoire of The Musical Brownies that the music fully coalesced into a distinctive style.

Jazz Child

Milton Brown was born at Stephenville, Texas, in 1903. His father was a fiddler and younger brother Derwood

Brown's Brownies

From this point – but even more so after the hiring of the exciting and pioneering electric steel guitarist Bob Dunn at the end of 1934 – the Brownies defined the basic style and instrumentation of what would eventually become known as western swing. Brown mostly eschewed things overtly 'western', however, dressed his band like a pop band and played a similar repertoire, though fiddle and old-time tunes remained in the mix.

The band began recording for Bluebird in 1934 and switched to the upstart Decca the following year. The recordings spread their influence beyond the territory they carved out via their radio show and dances. The Brownies were the most important and popular string band in the south-west, and their sound transformed the approach of almost every string musician in that region. Brown's singing was admired and copied, steel guitarist Dunn was perhaps the most influential instrumentalist of the period, and Brownie fiddlers Cecil Brower and Cliff Bruner also made their mark on aspiring musicians of the era. The Brownies' rhythm and use of piano and twin fiddles all became hallmarks of western swing.

Brown enjoyed several hits, including 'St. Louis Blues', 'My Mary' and 'El Rancho Grande', but he tragically died following a car accident in April 1936. Derwood held the band together for a while, but the magic was gone. The Brownies faded and Bob Wills, who, like Brown, had charisma to burn and a searching musical mind, quickly became the music's major figure – a position he never relinquished.

Classic Recordings

1934
'Precious Little Sonny Boy'
'Garbage Man Blues'

1935
'St. Louis Blues'
'My Mary'
'Taking Off'

Left

Milton Brown, flanked by his radio announcers, sits proudly in front of an early line-up of The Musical Brownies, c. 1933.

(1915–78) learned to second his father on guitar. The personable Milton sang, but it was not until early in the Depression that he began seriously to pursue a musical career. Like so many who came of age in the increasingly urbanized America of the 1920s, Milton's musical loyalties were split between rural and city sensibilities. He was, like his friend Bob Wills, a child of the Jazz Age, who loved hot jazz, blues and pop music.

Brown teamed with Wills in 1930 in a band that soon evolved into The Light Crust Doughboys. The group quickly gained a loyal regional following. The presence of pop-tinged vocalist Brown marked the band as different, as did an eclectic repertoire, but it was when Brown departed in 1932 to form his own group that the scene was set for Texas string dance bands to develop into something quite different from the traditional fiddle bands. The Musical Brownies embraced a new ethos. Brown began to hire musicians who could do more than play basic rhythm and melody. He added to Derwood's rhythm guitar the Dixieland-tinged tenor banjo of Ocie Stockard, the energetic bass of Wanna Coffman and the jazzy fiddle of Jesse Ashlock. Soon after, he added the trained swing violinist Cecil Brower and the jazz pianist Fred Calhoun.

Left

The cover of the first LP reissue of Milton Brown's recordings, released almost two decades after his untimely death.

Key Track

'Yes Suh!' (1936)
Other songs are more readily associated with Brown, but his importance lies in his style rather than any hits. All his records sold well, but this hopped-up, jivey novelty is among those that most closely captures Brown's charisma and the spirit, innovation and excitement of his Musical Brownies.

Roy Rogers & The Sons Of The Pioneers

Key Artist

'When my time comes, just skin me and put me up there on Trigger, just as though nothing ever changed.' **Roy Rogers**

Above
The Sons Of The Pioneers support their former member Roy Rogers in 1945's Don't Fence Me In.

The Sons Of The Pioneers are one of the most influential vocal groups in American history – an impeccable hallmark of fluid precision and musical integrity since 1933, universally admired for their tight sound and gorgeous harmonies. The group also boasted two great American songwriters in Tim Spencer and Bob Nolan, and two of the most influential country instrumentalists of the 1930s–40s in Hugh and Karl Farr. The third member of the group's original vocal trio, Leonard Slye, was perhaps the least conspicuously talented of the lot, but he ultimately rose to a level of

individual stardom – under the name of Roy Rogers (1911–98) – that eclipsed that of the group he had been instrumental in forming.

Sons Of The West

The Sons Of The Pioneers were formed when the western music scene in southern California was still in its infancy, though there had been other western groups in the area, most notably the influential Beverly Hill Billies, an early role model for the Pioneers. After a few false starts, the original Pioneer Trio of Len Slye, Bob Nolan and Tim Spencer first came together in 1933. In 1934, they added the Texas-born country-jazz fiddler Hugh Farr and began recording for the fledgling Standard Transcription company, which spread their name and style nationally even before they had made a commercial recording or appeared on film. In early 1935, Hugh Farr's talented guitarist younger brother Karl joined the group.

Tight harmonies, a beautiful vocal blend and the instrumental virtuosity of the Farrs set the Pioneers apart from the beginning, as did the songwriting abilities of Spencer and particularly Nolan, whose early efforts include all-time American classics such as 'Tumbling Tumbleweeds' and 'Cool Water'.

Recording, together with film appearances with Gene Autry and Charles Starrett, spread the Pioneers' fame and influence, but with success came upheaval. Spencer left for a while, replaced by Lloyd Perryman, who possessed one of the most loved voices in western-music history and who would become the band's sturdy lynchpin for much of its later existence. Rogers left in 1937 to pursue a solo career, replaced by bassist-comedian Pat Brady. Despite the

Classic Recordings

1934
'Tumbling Tumbleweeds',
'Way Out There'

1941
'Cool Water'

1949
'My Best To You',
'Roomful Of Roses'

Left
Roy Rogers with his on- and off-screen partner Dale Evans, and his horse Trigger.

changes, the band went from strength to strength into the war years, when the departure of Perryman and Brady for war service necessitated further personnel changes, including the adding of veteran western vocalist Ken Carson and bassist-comedian Shug Fisher.

Pioneering Film Stars

In 1941, the band appeared in the first of some 40 films in support of old colleague Rogers, by then a star in his own right for Republic Pictures. Rogers had been signed by the studio in 1937 when its disgruntled star Autry had walked out on his contract. By the 1940s, Rogers was billed the 'king of the cowboys', and had become one of the biggest stars in the country.

After the war, both Rogers and the Pioneers began long associations with RCA Victor, recording numerous classics, including, together, the lovely hit 'Blue Shadows On The Trail'. A widowed Rogers married co-star Dale Evans, a former pop singer and a talented songwriter herself; the pair remained a professional

team as well as a real-life one for the remainder of their performing careers.

The Pioneers ended their film series with Rogers in 1948 and the end of the 1940s also saw the retirement of Tim Spencer and Bob Nolan. Their initial replacements were Ken Curtis, a former big-band crooner turned western film star, and Nolan sound-alike Spike Doss. Roy Rogers became a television star in the 1950s, and though his career faded in the ensuing decades, he remained a well-loved American institution until his death. The Pioneers endure, led first by Lloyd Perryman until his death in 1977 and by Dale Warren after that. They retain a loyal following and an admirably high standard into the twenty-first century.

Key Track

'Blue Shadows On The Trail' (1947)
The Pioneers' body of work contains numerous classics better known than this, but this lovely collaboration between Roy Rogers and his former band mates was Rogers' biggest hit. Rogers knew instinctively that his voice was best suited to a vocal-group sound and this track finds both him and the Pioneers in peak form.

Hank Thompson

Key Artist

'Hank Thompson was ... my idol, and I had seen him in the big western swing band when I was younger. He called me one day ... and invited me to sing with his band the following week.... I told him I would love to, but would have to ask my mother.'
Wanda Jackson

Hank Thompson (b. 1925) is one of the most difficult country stars to classify. His Brazos Valley Boys were for a number of years one of the most talented and revered of western-swing bands, yet Thompson was never really a western-swing performer. He recorded a number of songs that

remain honky-tonk classics, but he was never just a honky-tonk singer. Nor is he associated with a particular era, sustaining an admirable level of popularity over decades.

Nashville And Back
What is beyond question is that Thompson is a living legend. Deservedly – almost inevitably – elected to the Country Music Hall Of Fame in 1989, he was still recording in his eightieth year, releasing two albums in

2005, 59 years after his recording debut. A highly distinctive stylist, he never had a great voice, but it was unmistakable and widely copied. A consistently impressive songwriter, he was uncommonly astute, too, in his choice of non-original material, turning moderate hits like 'The Wild Side Of Life' into all-time classics.

Born in Waco, Texas, in the heart of western-swing country, Thompson grew up instead with his ear cocked towards the sounds coming out of the Grand Ole Opry in Nashville. He admired Roy Acuff, fellow Texan Ernest Tubb, and pioneers Jimmie Rodgers, and The Carter Family. He landed his own radio show on WACO at 16, but his career was interrupted by military service in the Second World War. After the war, he returned to Texas and recorded his classics 'Whoa Sailor' and 'Swing Wide Your Gate Of Love' for the Globe label. In 1947, he recorded for another small company, Blue Bonnet, before signing with the up-and-coming Capitol label. His first release was a hit, 'Humpty-Dumpty Heart'. One of the musicians on Thompson's early recording sessions was steel guitarist Lefty Nason, who created several distinctive licks that became Thompson trademarks.

Thompson briefly flirted with Nashville in 1949 and Ernest Tubb helped secure him a spot on the Grand Ole Opry. But he quickly resigned and headed back to Texas. Significantly, prior to this Thompson had been a show performer, not a dancehall singer, but, as historian Rich Kienzle puts it, Thompson had 'done the math and realized real money was in playing clubs and dance halls'.

Living Legend

Rather than appear as a single artist with local bands – as was increasingly the case with stars, who were expected to travel greater distances than in earlier years, when scenes were more regional and nationally known country stars were few – Thompson hired a young but seasoned veteran, Billy Gray, to build a road band, a versatile dance group that could satisfy club and ballroom patrons. Within months, The Brazos Valley Boys had evolved into one of the biggest and best western bands in the country, featuring at various times the cream of western-swing players of the era, including fiddlers Keith Coleman, Bob White and Curly Lewis, and steel guitarists Curley Chalker and Bobby White.

Thompson's easing toward a western-swing identity was deftly managed without the singer changing his essentially mainstream country style. Ironically, it also came when the popularity of western swing in general was in decline. Thompson and The Brazos Valley Boys thrived, however, and hit after hit followed, from 'The Wild Side Of Life' early in the 1950s to 'Six Pack To Go' in 1959. The momentum continued well into the 1960s.

As times and tastes changed, Thompson persevered, faring far better than most of his contemporaries, enjoying Top 10 hits as late as 1974. With no illusions about regaining the level of fame and success he'd once enjoyed, Thompson has continued to do it his own way, with verve – and a following that many performers half his age would envy.

Far Left
Hank Thompson stands out in white in the WKY-TV studio in Oklahoma.

Left
A signed publicity photograph, from Hank Thompson to fellow western-swinger Cliff Bruner.

Key Track
'The Wild Side Of Life' (1952)
Most of Thompson's hits were self-penned, but his biggest was this honky-tonk classic – originally a regional hit for fellow Texan Jimmie Heap – that he initially didn't want to record. It underscores the fact that at heart, despite the western-swing trappings, Thompson was a great country singer.

Bob Wills

Key Artist

Above
Bob Wills (left, with vocalist Tommy Duncan) – the most influential and dynamic artist of the western-swing era.

'I'm from the Bob Wills and the Little Richard school of music. Bob Wills did what the hell he thought … and those were my big influences.' **Buck Owens**

Right
Bob Wills licensed a mill so that he could use the name of Playboys (after Playboy Flour) for his band.

Texas Playboy

James Robert Wills was born in east-central Texas in 1905 and was reared in West Texas. His father 'Uncle' John was a highly revered fiddler and Bob, the oldest of 10, was one of four brothers who became professional musicians and bandleaders. Johnnie Lee, Luther Jay and Billy Jack all began their careers as Texas Playboys.

In addition to the fiddle music of his father, Wills was from childhood affected by the music of black field workers. His deliberate mixing of white and black musical styles would give his music much of its vibrancy, and lend his fiddle playing a haunting, vocal quality. Fiddling from age 10, Wills reached maturity at the height of the Jazz Age. The music of that era – from the hopped-up hillbilly of The Skillet Lickers, to the classic blues of Bessie Smith and the southern minstrel jazz of Emmett Miller – shaped his musical vision.

After gaining experience in medicine shows, Wills formed the Wills Fiddle Band, which would eventually become The Light Crust Doughboys. He left the band in 1933 and after a stop in Waco took his Texas Playboys to Oklahoma in early 1934. The band caught on at Tulsa's 50,000-watt KVOO and soon virtually owned Oklahoma. Wills expanded upon Milton Brown's model, adding horns and drums to his string band – his early 1940s band boasted a full horn section. Among many early important

Observers who saw him in his prime have likened the charisma of the 'king of western swing' Bob Wills to that of latter-day superstars such as Elvis and The Beatles. The Texas fiddler, with his trademark high-pitched folk hollers and jivey, medicine-show asides, was an irresistible force of nature. Although he was, in the earliest days of his band-leading career, in the shadow of Milton Brown – who left Fort Worth's Light Crust Doughboys a year ahead of him – Wills soon came into his own. He was musically open-minded, daring and innovative, and his Texas Playboys evolved from a rag-tag crew that was more spirited than skilled into perhaps the most talented, influential group in country-music history, while Wills became a living legend.

Left
The style of The Texas Playboys blurred the boundaries between genres and created a type of music that was instantly popular and enduringly influential.

band members were vocalist Tommy Duncan, steel guitarist Leon McAuliffe and guitarist Eldon Shamblin.

Western-Swing Legend

The Playboys began recording for ARC-Brunswick in 1935 and immediately scored hits like 'Spanish Two-Step', 'Steel Guitar Rag' and 'San Antonio Rose'. Wills' development as a songwriter culminated in 1940 with the all-time classic 'New San Antonio Rose', when he added lyrics to his 1938 hit fiddle instrumental.

In 1943, Wills turned the Tulsa territory over to brother Johnnie Lee and left for California, where western swing was riding the crest of a wartime boom. Before long he had become one of the most popular bandleaders in the country in any genre. Further hits followed and Wills led excellent, innovative bands. The Playboys' dynamic use of electric guitars and mandolins was particularly influential in this era. Wills and The Playboys also appeared in a number of movies.

Wills enjoyed a final hit with the classic 'Faded Love' in 1950, but after a few successful years in California, he spent a difficult decade looking for a new home base to compare with Tulsa, with short spells in Oklahoma City and Dallas, among other places. Despite a number of personal setbacks, he survived, achieving legendary status. His health failed during the 1960s, but he persevered until a massive stroke in 1969.

A year earlier he'd been elected to the Country Music Hall Of Fame. He died in 1975, having lived just long enough to see a major revival of his music that began with superstar Merle Haggard's Wills tribute album in 1970.

Key Track

'New San Antonio Rose' (1940)
An American classic, this song epitomizes the exciting eclecticism of Bob Wills' music. A fiddle instrumental transformed into a pop song, wrapped in a big-band arrangement and crooned by Tommy Duncan, it was a massive hit – a song, Wills later joked, that 'took us off the hamburgers and put us on the steaks'.

A-Z of Artists

Jules Verne Allen
(Guitar, vocals, 1883–1945)

Jules Verne Allen was significant among early singing cowboys in that he had actually been a working cowboy. After years of trail driving he became a professional cowboy singer in an era when such a thing scarcely existed. In addition to radio, he recorded 24 sides for Victor during 1928–29. In 1933–34, he led a cowboy band in San Antonio that included several future western-swing stalwarts, but he soon faded from the scene.

Rosalie Allen
(Vocals, 1924–2003)

Rosalie Allen was one of a number of western stars who called New York home, for despite being seemingly removed from anything remotely western, the city boasted a thriving scene. Born Julie Bedra in Pennsylvania, Allen idolized Patsy Montana and became an adept yodeller. From 1943, she was a star on New York radio. In addition to recording successfully for RCA, including popular duets with Elton Britt, she became a popular dj before fading from the scene after the mid-1950s.

Below
Bill Boyd And The Cowboy Ramblers were a radio mainstay in the 1930s and 1940s.

Shelly Lee Alley
(Songwriter, bandleader, fiddle, vocals, 1894–1964)

Shelly Lee Alley is best remembered for writing the classic 'Traveling Blues' for Jimmie Rodgers in 1931. Texan Alley led his own pop and jazz orchestras in the 1920s, but also enjoyed success as a western-swing bandleader a decade later. At various times, his Alley Cats included such stars as Cliff Bruner, Ted Daffan, Floyd Tillman and Clyde Brewer, and he continued to write after giving up bandleading in 1946, scoring a hit via Moon Mullican's version of 'Broken Dreams' in 1948.

The Blue Ridge Playboys
(Vocal/instrumental group, 1934–42)

The Blue Ridge Playboys were a key early western-swing band. Based in Houston, they were formed in 1934 and were fronted by fiddler Leon 'Pappy' Selph (1914–99). Although Selph remained musically active to his death, the original band broke up soon after the US entry into the Second World War. The Playboys were not particularly influential as a working entity, but importantly served as a training ground for such future stars as Ted Daffan, Floyd Tillman and Moon Mullican.

Bill Boyd
(Vocals, guitar, bandleader, 1910–77)

Bill Boyd led one of the most prolific and important western-swing groups, The Cowboy Ramblers. A guitarist, Boyd and brother Jim (1914–93), a bassist and guitarist who also became an important figure, were reared in Greenville, Texas and began their careers in nearby Dallas in the early 1930s. Boyd signed to Victor's Bluebird label in 1934. He recorded more than 200 sides for the label through 1951 and such hits as 'Under The Double Eagle', 'New Steel Guitar Rag' and 'Spanish Fandango' earned him the nickname 'the king of the instrumentals'. More musically conservative than most of his contemporaries – a fact that might have contributed to his longevity – Boyd's career waned from the mid-1950s. Jim remained active

into the 1990s, working with The Light Crust Doughboys, with whom he had first worked in 1938–39; he recorded for RCA Victor during 1949–51.

Cliff Bruner
(Fiddle, bandleader, 1915–2000)

Cliff Bruner was one of the most influential western-swing fiddlers and bandleaders of the late 1930s–40s era. Born in Texas City, Texas, the self-taught Bruner was playing professionally by his mid-teens and joined the music's pioneering ensemble, Milton Brown's Musical Brownies, in 1935. His stint with Brown made him a name, and following Brown's death, Bruner formed his own Texas Wanderers, which included such important figures as steel guitarist Bob Dunn, pianist Moon Mullican and vocalist Dickie McBride. He recorded for Decca and was instrumental in introducing the songs of both Floyd Tillman ('It Makes No Difference Now') and Ted Daffan ('Truck Driver's Blues') to a wider public. Based along Texas's Gulf Coast, Bruner continued to lead popular regional bands through the 1940s before giving up full-time music in 1950. He continued to play on a part-time basis until his death.

Harry Choates
(Fiddle, guitar, vocals, 1922–51)

Harry Choates is one of the tragic figures of country music. A charismatic fiddler reared along the Louisiana-Texas Coast, he combined Cajun styles with western swing and hit with 'Jole Blon' in 1946. The hard-living, alcoholic Choates (who was even more skilled on guitar than fiddle) soon spiralled out of control. When he died in an Austin, Texas jail, locked up for non-support, he was not yet 30.

The Girls Of The Golden West
(Vocal group, 1930s)

The Girls of the Golden West were Millie (1913–93) and Dolly (1915–67) Good (real name Goad). They starred during the 1930s on Chicago's WLS and recorded for Bluebird and ARC. Regionally popular and influential – they inspired Pee Wee King, among others – they were particularly renowned for their close harmony and harmonized yodelling. Marrying, they retired by the end of the 1940s, though they would record again in the 1960s.

Left
Influential fiddler Cliff Bruner And His Texas Wanderers ruled the Texas-Louisiana Gulf Coast in the 1940s.

Below
Although publicity claimed they hailed from Texas, The Girls Of The Golden West were actually Illinois farm girls.

Otto Gray

(Bandleader, 1884–1967)

Otto Gray, leader of the first truly professional western band The Oklahoma Cowboys, is often given only perfunctory attention in country-music histories. But his group was both popular and significant – and introduced hundreds of future musicians, particularly in the Midwest and Northeast, to country music. Gray, an astute businessman from Stillwater, Oklahoma, didn't play an instrument (though he was a trick roper). He formed The Oklahoma Cowboys in 1926 from a band created shortly before by Spanish-American War hero Billy McGinty. The group featured Gray's son Owen on vocals and guitar and wife Florence ('Mommie') on vocals. The Cowboys' often-lacklustre recordings fail to adequately convey their musical abilities or reflect their popularity, and have contributed to a diminished reputation among both fans and historians. The group was extremely important in its day, however, though it fell victim to changing tastes and the Depression, breaking up around 1936.

The Hi-Flyers

(Vocal/instrumental group, 1930s–42)

The Hi-Flyers were among the earliest and most important of Texas western-swing bands. The Fort Worth band predated even the seminal Light Crust Doughboys, though it didn't ease towards a string swing style until inspired by Brown's Musical Brownies. Led by guitarist Elmer

Below

Fort Worth's Hi-Flyers, shown c. 1935, were one of the earliest and best of the Texas swing bands.

Scarbrough, the band also included such key musicians as fiddler Darrell Kirkpatrick and steel guitarist Billy Briggs.

Adolph Hofner

(Vocals, guitar, bandleader, 1916–2000)

Adolph Hofner successfully combined the musical heritage of his Texas-Czech youth with hillbilly, pop and swing influences in a career that stretched from the mid-1930s to the late 1990s, with his steel guitar-playing brother Emil (nicknamed 'Bash') at his side throughout. Equally influenced by Milton Brown and Bing Crosby, Hofner was the first western-swing crooner, and his San Antonio-based bands featured such top-flight musicians as fiddler J. R. Chatwell and pianist Walter Kleypas.

Pee Wee King

(Accordion, bandleader, 1914–2000)

Pee Wee King And His Golden West Cowboys were the chief exponents of western music and western swing east of the Mississippi, best known for high-profile years on the Grand Ole Opry. An accordionist from Wisconsin of German-Polish heritage (born Kuczynski), King eased towards country music during the 1930s and towards stardom under the auspices of manager J. L. Frank (his father-in-law). King and his right hand, fiddler-vocalist Redd Stewart, were among the most successful country-music songwriters, penning such classics as 'Tennessee Waltz', 'Slow Poke' and 'You Belong To Me'. King left the Opry in 1947, originally for Louisville, Kentucky. Extensive tours and television work followed. He was elected to the Country Music Hall Of Fame in 1974.

Texas Jim Lewis

(Guitar, bass, bandleader, 1909–90)

Texas Jim Lewis is a largely unheralded figure in western swing, but his varied activities deserve far more attention. His career encompassed 1930s stints on New York radio and in vaudeville, and a 1940s run in Hollywood making movies and recording. His Lone Star Cowboys were one of the best bands of the era and served as the training ground for a number of key musicians. A Georgia native, Lewis was in Texas by the early 1930s, working with the Swift-Jewel Cowboys before heading north at mid-decade. Lewis veered between western swing and novelty (in addition to guitar and bass, he played a homemade contraption called the hootenannie and he eventually became a Seattle children's television-show host), but his bands were musically impeccable and included such notable players as guitarist-vocalist (and Lewis's half-brother) Jack Rivers, accordionist-arranger Pedro DePaul and guitarist-banjoist Smokey Rogers.

The Light Crust Doughboys
(Vocal/instrumental group, 1930–present)

Formed in Fort Worth in 1930, The Light Crust Doughboys were one of the seminal bands of western swing. The original group, essentially a traditional Texas string band, included the music's future architects Milton Brown and Bob Wills. The band name came from the group's flour-company sponsor and from soon after their formation The Doughboys were led by the company's president W. Lee O'Daniel. O'Daniel was fired in 1935, by which time Wills and Brown had gone their own ways, too. The reconstituted Doughboys thrived, featuring such stalwarts as tenor banjoist Marvin Montgomery (who remained with the band to his death in 2001), jazz pianist Knocky Parker and electric-guitar pioneer Zeke Campbell. Recording for ARC (later Columbia), they were musically impeccable and widely influential. They disbanded during the Second World War but reformed afterwards and remained a popular attraction into the 1950s. The band was still going strong in 2006.

Below

Texas Jim Lewis And The Lone Star Cowboys was one of the best bands of the era and served as a training ground for a number of key musicians.

Louise Massey & The Westerners
(Vocal/instrumental group, 1930s–40s)

Below

*Patsy Montana And
The Prairie Ramblers –
Jack Taylor, Chick Hurt,
Ken Houchins and
Tex Atchison.*

Louise Massey And The Westerners are largely forgotten today, but in their heyday, this was one of the most successful western acts in the USA. Polished, versatile and influential, they boasted a smooth sound that obscured their origins as rural musicians under their fiddling father Henry's tutelage in New Mexico. The band included three Masseys – Louise (vocals; 1902–83), Allen (guitar, vocals, 1907–83), Curt (fiddle, trumpet, vocals, 1910–91), as well as Louise's husband, bassist Milt Mabie, and accordionist Larry Wellington. They hit stride upon arrival at Chicago's WLS in 1933. Louise was the group's nominal focal point, her fame peaking with her classic 1941 hit 'My Adobe Hacienda'. However, Curt was arguably the band's true star. An excellent jazz fiddler and trumpeter, as well as a fine pop-tinged vocalist, he enjoyed a major hit with 'The Honey Song' in 1942, and when the band broke up soon after, he went on to mainstream media stardom in California.

Patsy Montana & The Prairie Ramblers
(Vocal/instrumental group, 1933–50s)

Patsy Montana And The Prairie Ramblers were stars of the WLS *National Barn Dance*, fortuitously paired for a number years beginning in 1933. Montana (1908–96) was born Ruby Blevins in Arkansas and arrived in Chicago after stints in Los Angeles and Shreveport. The Ramblers (originally Kentucky Ramblers: Tex Atchison, fiddle; Chick Hurt, mandolin/tenor banjo; Jack Taylor, bass; and Salty Holmes, guitar) were initially an eclectic Kentucky string band, but took on a western identity upon moving to Chicago. They moved increasingly towards western swing with later additions like fiddlers Alan Crockett and Wade Ray, and guitarist Bernie Smith. The Ramblers recorded prolifically without Montana, but they gained their greatest fame together with the hugely successful 1935 recording of 'I Wanna Be A Cowboy's Sweetheart'. The Ramblers remained active into the 1950s, while Montana continued to perform into the 1990s, elected to the Country Music Hall Of Fame in the year of her death.

Roy Newman
(Piano, bandleader 1899–1981)

Roy Newman And His Boys was one of the most distinctive pre-war western-swing bands. Based out of Dallas radio station WRR, pianist Newman was even more heavily pop, jazz and blues-influenced than most contemporaries. The band owed its instantly recognizable sound largely to idiosyncratic clarinetist Holly Horton. Other key band members included fiddlers Cecil Brower and Carroll Hubbard, steel guitarist Bob Dunn and guitarists-vocalists Jim Boyd, Gene Sullivan and Earl Brown.

W. Lee O'Daniel
(Bandleader, 1890–1969)

W. Lee O'Daniel rose to fame as the leader and announcer of The Light Crust Doughboys. President of the band's sponsor Burrus Mill, he disliked their music and had little respect for the musicians, but he was ambitious – and used the band as a tool for self-promotion. After being fired by Burrus, he formed his own flour company and a new band, The Hillbilly Boys. He hired Doughboys vocalist Leon Huff and convinced his own sons Pat and Mike to become musicians. O'Daniel used the band as a springboard to political office. He successfully ran for Texas governorship in 1938, then became a US Senator in 1941, maintaining the band throughout. Though his real career as a bandleader was essentially over after 1938 and he was never a musician himself, he nevertheless remains an important figure – not least for his pioneering use of country music as a political vehicle.

Hank Penny
(Vocals, guitar, bandleader, 1918–92)

Hank Penny was, with his Radio Cowboys, the most ardent exponent of western swing in the south-east prior to the

Above
Prolific songwriter and western singer Red River Dave.

Second World War. He relocated to California after the war and led excellent bands, though as time passed he eased towards comedy at the expense of music. He recorded prolifically from 1938 and over the years his groups included such legendary musicians as guitarist Merle Travis and steel guitarists Noel Boggs and Curley Chalker.

Red River Dave
(Songwriter, vocals, guitar, 1914–2002)

Red River Dave McEnery spent most of his long career in his native San Antonio, though he initially rose to fame in New York in the late 1930s. A prolific songwriter, who specialized in event songs like 'Amelia Earhart's Last Flight', in later years he would even tackle such topics as the kidnapping of heiress Patty Hearst and the Manson family murders of 1969. Stylistically his music leaned towards classic cowboy and western swing.

Left
Hank Penny led a series of fine western-swing bands throughout his career.

Jimmie Revard & His Oklahoma Playboys
(Vocal/instrumental group, 1930s–50s)
Jimmie Revard And His Oklahoma Cowboys formed one of the best and most prolific of early western-swing bands. Revard (1909–91) was from Oklahoma but his band was based in San Antonio, Texas; the original band included Adolph and Emil Hofner, among others. In their heyday, the Playboys struggled locally to compete with The Tune Wranglers, despite their records earning them a national reputation. Revard continued to lead bands locally into the 1950s and recorded as late as 1982.

Below

Floyd Tillman possessed one of country's most distinctive voices – a slurring drawl that was both loved and lampooned.

Art Satherley
(A&R man, 1889–1986)
Arthur Satherley was a pioneering A&R man for several important record companies from the 1920s, responsible for scouting and recording a vast array of country and blues performers. Among these were two important figures whose careers the British-born Satherley helped particularly to shape and steer – Bob Wills and Gene Autry. A legend himself by the 1940s, he essentially retired from producing in the early 1950s. He was elected to the Country Music Hall Of Fame in 1971.

The Shelton Brothers
(Vocal/instrumental group, 1934–50s)
The Shelton Brothers (née Attlesey) were Texans who wavered between an old-time duet style and western swing. Joe (1909–83) played mandolin, Bob (1911–80) concentrated mostly on comedy (a third brother, Merle, played guitar). Originally teamed with Leon Chappelear as The Lone Star Cowboys, they went out on their own in 1934. Their swing leanings were largely due to regional tastes, but The Sheltons, who remained active into the 1950s, employed top-notch players like Bob Dunn and Cliff Bruner.

Carl T. Sprague
(Vocals, 1895–1979)
Carl T. Sprague was one of the earliest singing cowboys to record and, like Jules Verne Allen, he was the genuine article, having worked as a cowboy. He began recording in 1925 and 'When The Work's All Done This Fall' sold almost a million copies. His recording career was short-lived and after 1927 he worked outside the music industry until rediscovery in the 1960s, after which he performed occasionally and recorded a final time in 1972.

Floyd Tillman
(Songwriter, vocals, guitar, 1914–2003)
Floyd Tillman is best known as one of the pioneers of modern country songwriting and one of the architects of honky-tonk. His classic songs include 'It Makes No Difference Now' (1938) and 'Slipping Around' (1949) Tillman came out of Houston's lively western-swing scene. Originally, he was a lead guitarist, not a singer or writer, and he was among the earliest to record with an electrically amplified instrument, with The Blue Ridge Playboys in 1936. He gradually evolved from sideman to bandleader, though he didn't hit full stride until after the war. His peak years were 1946–50, not long after which he gave up full-time performing. He played part-time, on his own terms, living modestly off songwriting royalties, until his death. He was elected to the Country Music Hall Of Fame in 1984.

The Tune Wranglers
(Vocal/instrumental group, 1930s–40s)
The Tune Wranglers was one of the most popular and prolific of early western-swing bands. Formed by guitarist Buster Coward and fiddler Tom Dickey in San Antonio, it was also one of the most strongly western orientated groups. They scored several hits, most notably Coward's bluesy cowboy song 'Texas Sand' in 1936, and gradually

developed a smoother, more pop-influenced sound. Despite their considerable success, the Wranglers broke up by the early 1940s.

Cindy Walker
(Songwriter, vocals, 1918–2006)
The sophisticated songs of Cindy Walker were particularly attractive to western-swing performers like Bob Wills, whose recordings helped establish her as one of the top songwriters in country music. From Mart, Texas, Walker also sang, recorded and appeared in films with Texas Jim Lewis. Over time, she concentrated solely on writing and turned out dozens of classics, including 'Dusty Skies',

'Bubbles In My Beer', 'You Don't Know Me' and many more.

Curley Williams & Paul Howard
(Bandleaders, 1940s)
Curley Williams (1914–70) and Paul Howard (1908–84) were – outside of Pee Wee King – the chief exponents of western swing east of the Mississippi during the music's 1940s heyday. Both led excellent, hot bands on the Grand Ole Opry and both found it necessary to leave the Opry in order to play the music they wanted to play on their own terms. Williams co-wrote the classic 'Half As Much', while Howard penned another classic, 'With Tears In My Eyes'.

Above
San Antonio's Tune Wranglers in about 1934. L-r: Eddie Fielding, Tom Dickey, Brooks Teague, Charley Gregg and Buster Coward.

Left
Texas-born songwriting legend Cindy Walker.

Foggy Mountain Breakdown:
Bluegrass Music

before the Second World War, it was possible to live in certain areas of the USA in almost complete isolation. In the time of The Carter Family, many rural residents never travelled more than 80 km (50 miles) from their birthplace.

But that began to change. The First World War, the Great Depression and the Second World War took young men out of their small towns and sent them around the world. New roads and railroads made it easier to come and go from farms nestled in the Virginia mountains or Kentucky pastures. Wind-up Victrolas and battery-powered radio receivers found their places on cabin tables and bungalow counters, bringing the sound of New York, Chicago and Nashville into homes at the ends of narrow dirt roads.

These changes produced a contradictory response. On the one hand, the displaced sons and daughters of the southern Appalachian mountains hungered for a music as fast and precision-engineered as their new lives. On the other hand, they wanted a music that preserved their affectionate connection to the lives they were leaving behind. They wanted the familiar instrumentation of fiddle, banjo, guitar, mandolin and upright bass, which reminded the listeners of the old hillbilly string bands of their youth. But they wanted those instruments played with the drive of a locomotive and the skill of a full-time professional. They wanted to hear lyrics that celebrated the old farmstead, the wise parents and the innocent farm girl, but they wanted those lyrics delivered with modern, sophisticated harmonies and with a 'high, lonesome' ache that implied that past was slipping away.

Bluegrass answered all these needs. It began as Bill Monroe's new twist on the old string-band sound, but it was so effective at meeting a great need that it soon became its own genre.

Key Artists
Flatt & Scruggs
Jimmy Martin
Bill Monroe
The Stanley Brothers

Influences & Development

'I was determined to carve out a music of my own. I didn't want to copy anybody.'

Bill Monroe

The temptation is to think of bluegrass as an ancient music, for its repertoire and instrumentation stretch back into the shadowy mists of the nineteenth century. But in many ways bluegrass was a radical innovation, a music of the modern world, a sound invented just a decade before rock'n'roll. It was a new/old music, and that central paradox has shaped the music ever since.

Emergence Of A New Style

When Bill Monroe (1911–96) and The Blue Grass Boys made their debut at the Grand Ole Opry on 28 October 1939, the quartet played 'Mule Skinner Blues', a swaggering working-man's boast, first made famous by Jimmie Rodgers (1897–1933), the 'Father of Country Music'. It was an old song, but it had never been played like this.

The band not only sped up the tempo but also punched out the beat so emphatically that the song developed a momentum Rodgers had never imagined. Fiddler Art Wooten added quicksilver single-note runs, and Monroe himself cried out the lead vocal with a high-pitched urgency. The effect was so unprecedented – so modern – that fellow performers such as Roy Acuff (1903–92) and Uncle Dave Macon (1870–1952) gasped in astonishment and the audience demanded three encores.

When Monroe recorded his first sides for Victor the following year, he drew from old folk songs and material by Rodgers and Bob Wills (1905–75), but he rearranged everything so his well-rehearsed band could play fast, hard and in unison. The lyrics may have referred nostalgically to the old homestead, but this was commercial music made by professionals willing to go anywhere and do anything to grasp their ambitions.

Ancient Tones

But the music they adapted was imbued with what Monroe called 'ancient tones'. The same geographic isolation that had cut off the upper South from the modern economy had also allowed the region to preserve a strain of eighteenth-century Anglo-Celtic music that had died out everywhere else, even in the British Isles. With its modal harmonies and stories of death and desperation, this musical heritage – modified by African-American neighbours and the hard life of the mountains – came from a different world than the Tin Pan Alley show tunes of Broadway and Hollywood.

Those 'ancient tones' benefited from a raw spontaneity on the early recordings by The Carter Family, the old-time string bands, the brother duos and the fiddle contests. Monroe wanted to prove that the sound could be turned into performances as brisk, snappy and polished as those of the latest jazz band.

He didn't fully realize that goal until September 1945 when he auditioned a 21-year-old moon-faced kid from

Below

Uncle Dave Macon and his son strum the guitar and banjo. Macon was one of the old-school country musicians who was astonished when Monroe launched the fast-paced style that became known as bluegrass.

It was, by almost universal consensus, the greatest bluegrass band ever assembled. It lasted little more than two years, but it recorded 28 songs that created the template against which every subsequent bluegrass project was measured. Those recordings established the classic instrumentation (mandolin, fiddle, guitar, banjo and bass), the vocal style (pitched high with nasal accents and close-interval harmony) and the repertoire (a mix of instrumental 'breakdowns', breathless 4/4 vocal numbers, sentimental waltzes, gospel hymns and swaggering blues).

The Birth Of Bluegrass

There is much debate about the true birth of bluegrass. Was it the 1939 debut of Bill Monroe And The Blue Grass Boys on the Opry? Was it the band's 1940 recording of 'Mule Skinner Blues'? Was it the band's 1943 tent-show tour? Was it Monroe's hiring of Earl Scruggs in 1945? Any of these dates is plausible, but there is no debate that the genre was single-handedly defined by Monroe – so much that it took its name from his band. The Blue Grass Boys were never actually based in Kentucky, the 'bluegrass' state and Monroe's birthplace, but this was a genre that often looked back wistfully at homes that had long been left behind.

North Carolina. Earl Scruggs (b. 1924) had perfected the new Carolina technique of playing the banjo with a three-finger roll (thumb, index and middle) that created tumbling arpeggios that lent a terrific momentum to the music. Combined with Monroe's mandolin chop and the guitar 'G run' that Monroe had taught to Lester Flatt (1914–79), this string-band music had an unprecedented drive. Within a few months, The Blue Grass Boys featured Monroe, Scruggs, Flatt, fiddler Chubby Wise (1915–96) and bassist Cedric Rainwater.

Left
Lester Flatt and Earl Scruggs – two of the key players in ensuring the success of bluegrass.

Below
Bluegrass was the music of the front porch and the rocking chair – of the quintessential rural American way of life.

Innovators & Imitators

Monroe didn't think he was inventing a new genre; he was just carving out an individual identity in a crowded marketplace. But his music was so appealing that when the Grand Ole Opry show went out over the airwaves of WSM, young, restless country boys did what anyone does when they fall in love with a new sound. They imitated it. When they did, Monroe reacted furiously; he felt he had invented the style and no one else should use it. He lashed out at The Stanley Brothers when they recorded his song 'Molly And Tenbrooks' and refused to speak to Earl Scruggs for the rest of his life after Flatt and Scruggs left The Blue Grass Boys to form their own band with the same sound.

You can copyright a song, but you can't copyright a sound. Monroe was a victim of his own success; his new version of the old music was so widely imitated that by the end of the 1940s it was obvious hc had founded a whole new genre. At first it was referred to as rural, backwoods or mountain music, an offshoot of country; it wasn't until the mid-1950s that the term 'bluegrass' was widely used. Flatt and Scruggs would refuse requests to play their old 'Monroe songs', but they would play their old 'Blue Grass Boys' songs and the name stuck.

Bluegrass Musicians

By that time, the first generation of bluegrass greats had emerged, and most of them had been Blue Grass Boys at one point or another. But they did more than merely copy the master. Carter Stanley, his brother Ralph and their Monroe-like mandolinist Pee Wee Lambert perfected a kind of close, three-part harmony that made their vocals even higher and 'lonesomer' than their role model. Don

Below
*Jimmy Martin (left),
Bill Monroe (centre) and
Sonny Osborne (right)
take to the stage.*

Reno refined the Scruggs style of banjo playing by adding guitar-like runs on the instrument. Jesse McReynolds (never a Blue Grass Boy) adapted the Scruggs roll to the mandolin with his innovative 'cross-picking' style.

Benny Martin, Vassar Clements and Kenny Baker added harmonic embellishments to their fiddling that owed as much to jazz as to country music. Flatt and Scruggs added Josh Graves on the dobro, a resophonic guitar played with the strings facing up and fretted with a metal cylinder. With its weeping, bluesy sound, the dobro became the last instrument widely accepted in bluegrass.

By the late-1950s, however, country music was reeling from the shockwaves of the rock'n'roll revolution. Work was drying up, and bluegrass faced the same kind of extinction that had pushed western swing and cowboy songs off the country charts. Several acts – most notably Jimmy Martin, The Osborne Brothers and Jim And Jesse – responded by moving closer to the country mainstream. Adopting warmer vocals, fuller harmonies, a bigger bottom and songs about truck driving, hillbilly radio and unfaithful women, they didn't just save bluegrass – they put it back on the country charts.

Bluegrass Goes To Hollywood

When Hollywood wanted a shorthand to rural southern life, they found that bluegrass worked like a charm. Thus Flatt and Scruggs were hired to provide the music for the early-1960s' television shows *The Beverly Hillbillies* and *Petticoat Junction* and the 1967 film *Bonnie And Clyde*. The Osborne Brothers appeared in 1967's *The Road To Nashville*, while Eric Weissberg and Steve Mandell adapted Don Reno's 'Feuding Banjos' into 'Duelin' Banjos' for the 1972 movie *Deliverance*. These shows often cast rural southerners in a less-than-flattering light, but the music proved so intoxicating that a whole new audience began searching out bluegrass recordings and shows.

Meanwhile, the folkies who played acoustic guitar or banjo and sang old ballads and laments went looking for past masters. Most old-time musicians were no longer professionals and were ill-prepared to respond, but bluegrass musicians were hardworking pros and ready to play any festival or college concert where the money was right. The working-class bluegrassers and the middle-class bohemians were wary of one another, especially as the turmoil of the 1960s heated up, but they found common

ground in the music. The folkies gained much-needed skills and tradition, and the bluegrassers gained much-needed work.

This back-and-forth led the more adventurous members of both camps – such as Earl Scruggs, Vassar Clements (1928–2005) and The Country Gentlemen on the southern side and Peter Rowan, David Grisman and Sam Bush on the northern side – to imagine a different kind of bluegrass, one with more personal, more ironic lyrics, freer chord changes and longer solos – new grass.

Above
Eric Weissberg (right), responsible for adapting bluegrass songs for the movies.

Hillbilly Jazz

Right
Jazz musician and inventor of the solid-body electric guitar Les Paul (left) earned his wings as a country artist.

Below
Hillbilly Jazz *was released on the Flying Fish label in 1975 and openly fused the two musical genres.*

When Vassar Clements formed a band called Hillbilly Jazz in 1975, Bill Monroe's former fiddler pulled the cover off the hidden connection between country music and jazz. The two genres had more in common than most people thought. After all, Jimmie Rodgers recorded with Louis Armstrong early in their careers; jazz legend Charlie Christian debuted on Bob Wills' radio show; Les Paul (then known as Rhubarb Red) was a country guitarist before he became a jazz and pop hero; steel guitarist Wesley 'Speedy' West earned his nickname for his blistering jazz-like solos; top Nashville session guitarist Hank Garland moonlighted as a jazzer; Miles Davis titled one of his songs 'Willie Nelson'; and Nelson made a jazz record with guitarist Jackie King.

Cowboy Jazz

Nowhere was the skill of country instrumentalists more obvious than in western swing and bluegrass. Two of the first three songs on the two-LP album *Hillbilly Jazz* came from the songbook of Bob Wills, the Texas bandleader who had devoted his career to showcasing fiddle, steel and mandolin soloists on jazzy swing arrangements. When a western-swing revival band formed in Maryland in the 1980s, the new group summed up the genre's long history of improvising genius by choosing the name Cowboy Jazz.

And when Bill Monroe transformed string-band music into bluegrass in the 1940s, he was unleashing a new kind of solo in much the same way that Louis Armstrong had when he transformed ragtime and Dixieland into modern jazz.

The fiddle had set the standard for virtuosity in country music ever since Eck Robertson (1887–1975) made one of the first country records in 1922 and inspired fiddle contests from Appalachia to Texas. But Monroe demanded that every instrument in his band be as fast and fluid as the fiddle, and he set an example by transforming his own mandolin from a rhythmic timekeeper to a freewheeling explorer of themes and variations. Before long, the banjo was similarly liberated by Earl Scruggs, the dobro by Josh Graves and the guitar by Doc Watson (b. 1923). To make sure all the instruments could play together at the breathless speeds he had in mind, Monroe drilled his bands to play with an unprecedented precision of tempo and intonation.

New Interpretations

Suddenly there was a chance to play difficult passages on string-band instruments with the same velocity and accuracy as jazz musicians. Astonishing pickers crawled out of the hidden corners of rural America to meet the challenge. Fiddlers such as Clements, Kenny Baker (b. 1926), Bobby Hicks and Benny Martin were one-upping each other by working swing syncopation, blues licks and quicksilver grace notes into their solos. Mandolinists such as Jesse McReynolds, Frank Wakefield and Bobby Osborne (b. 1931) invented new licks that even Monroe hadn't thought of. Banjoists such as J. D. Crowe (b. 1937), Eddie Adcock, Bill Keith (b. 1939), Don Stover and Sonny Osborne (b. 1937) all found ways to add different rhythm accents to Scruggs' three-finger roll.

Like the early hot-jazz and swing players, these early bluegrass musicians were working with the kinds of tunes that their listeners could play along with at home, even if the amateurs could never match the tempos or trickery of the pros. But just as the beboppers in the 1940s declared that it didn't matter if the folks at home could play along or not, the newgrassers in the 1970s declared that all chords and rhythms were fair game.

It was as if a lid had come off. Musicians such as Clements, David Grisman, Mark O'Connor, Bela Fleck, Edgar Meyer, Richard Greene, John Hartford, Sam Bush, Tony Rice and Jerry Douglas were soon interpreting and composing jazz pieces and collaborating with such jazz musicians as Wynton Marsalis, Stephane Grappelli, Keith Jarrett, Gary Burton, Chick Corea, Dave Holland, Branford Marsalis and Bill Frisell. After a while, you couldn't tell if the hillbillies were playing jazz or the beboppers were playing bluegrass.

Below
Although ostensibly a country musician, Mark O'Connor crossed the divide, to include jazz influences in his performances.

Flatt & Scruggs

Key Artist

'What got me was when my oldest brother got a Flatt & Scruggs record. I was about 11 at the time and, boy, when I heard Earl Scruggs, that was it…. That's when I said, "That's what I want to do".' **Del McCoury**

Below
Flatt, Scruggs and The Foggy Mountain Boys pose outside their bus – advertising their sponsor, Martha White Flour.

Lester Flatt (1914–79) was relieved when Dave 'Stringbean' Akeman left Bill Monroe's Blue Grass Boys in 1945, for Flatt felt the group was better off without a banjo, which had been hindering their efforts to play faster and cleaner than anyone had before. But Monroe agreed to audition a 21-year-old banjoist from western North Carolina, and Earl Scruggs (b. 1924) played the old fiddle tune 'Sally Goodin' with the Carolina three-finger roll that no one in Nashville had heard before. It transformed the banjo from a brake on the music into a gas pedal.

The Biggest Bluegrass Duo

Monroe hired him, and thus began the partnership between Lester Flatt and Earl Scruggs that lasted 24 years and gave them more hit singles than any act in bluegrass history. Scruggs was a musical revolutionary, but he needed Flatt as much as Flatt needed him. The older man lent a warm, inviting voice to the young banjoist's radical inventions and made them accessible to the broader audience that needs a familiar story and a reassuring face attached to musical experiments.

After two-plus years as the lead vocalist and instrumental star of The Blue Grass Boys, Flatt and Scruggs figured, not unreasonably, that they deserved

more than the meagre wages Monroe was paying them. So, in January 1948, Flatt, Scruggs and Cedric Rainwater left to form their own band, The Foggy Mountain Boys. Blackballed from the Opry by an aggrieved Monroe, they recorded briefly with Mercury, but struggled until they signed with Columbia Records in 1950, then enjoyed a Top 10 country hit with 1952's ''Tis Sweet To Be Remembered'. Their big break came in 1953, when they picked up a powerful sponsor, Martha White Flour, which put the duo back on the Opry and booked them for tours and television shows.

New Sounds In Country Music

By 1956, Flatt & Scruggs had clearly differentiated themselves from their ex-employer. Through emphasizing Scruggs' banjo, deemphasizing the mandolin and adding Josh Graves on dobro, they created a different instrumental sound. By having Flatt sing lower and warmer than before, they created a different vocal sound. By writing and borrowing new tunes, they created a different repertoire.

Though he never went to college, Scruggs was a natural intellectual who read widely and sought out new experiences. His wife, the former Louise Certaine, became Flatt And Scruggs' booking agent and manager and proved as ambitious as her husband was inquisitive. She pushed the band beyond the traditional bluegrass circuit to play the Newport Folk Festival in 1959, to record *Live At Carnegie Hall* in 1962, to play San Francisco's Avalon Ballroom at the height of hippiedom in 1967 and to tour Japan in 1968. She won Flatt And Scruggs the jobs of playing the soundtrack on the movie *Bonnie And Clyde* and the television shows *The Beverly Hillbillies* and *Petticoat Junction*.

Flatt was less enthusiastic about all these moves away from traditional bluegrass, and the tensions eventually led to a less-than-amicable split at the end of 1969. One result was Lester Flatt And The Nashville Grass, a traditional band that returned to the Monroe style with help from Graves, fiddler Paul Warren, banjoist Vic Jordan, mandolinist Roland White and a very young Marty Stuart. The other result was the Earl Scruggs Revue, an innovative bluegrass-rock band featuring Graves, fiddler Vassar Clements and Earl's three sons: Randy Scruggs (vocals, guitar, b. 1953), Gary Scruggs (vocals, bass, b. 1949) and Steve Scruggs (vocals, piano, 1958–1992).

Classic Recordings

At Carnegie Hall (1963)
*'Flint Hill Special',
'Hot Corn, Cold Corn',
'Salty Dog Blues',
'Let The Church Roll On'*

The Essential Flatt & Scruggs: 'Tis Sweet To Be Remembered (1997)
''Tis Sweet To Be Remembered', 'Foggy Mountain Special', 'Earl's Breakdown'

Country Legends: Lester Flatt (2003)
'It's Sad To Be Alone', 'Pickin' Away'

The Complete Mercury Recordings (2003)
'Salty Dog Blues', 'Down The Road', 'Pain In My Heart', 'God Loves His Children'

The Essential Earl Scruggs (2004)
'Foggy Mountain Breakdown', 'Roll In My Sweet Baby's Arms', 'Flint Hill Special'

Above

Bill Monroe at first ensured that Flatt & Scruggs were kept away from the Opry, but by 1953 they were regulars on the show.

Left

Together and separately, Lester Flatt and Earl Scruggs guaranteed a worldwide following for bluegrass music.

B 2823 **LESTER FLATT AND EARL SCRUGGS**
HALL OF FAME series
JIMMIE BROWN, THE NEWSBOY • MOTHER PRAYS LOUD IN HER SLEEP • I'LL GO STEPPING TOO • RANDY LYNN RAG

Key Track

'Foggy Mountain Breakdown' (1949)

It was never a hit single and it doesn't feature Lester Flatt's honeyed tenor, but it is the most universally recognized bluegrass ever recorded. Thanks to an Earl Scruggs banjo figure that was both infectiously melodic and dizzyingly quick, this theme from the *Bonnie And Clyde* movie became the first track most people play when they want to give an example of bluegrass.

Jimmy Martin

Key Artist

Below

Controversial bluegrass star Jimmy Martin.

Even when he was sober, Jimmy Martin (vocals, guitar, 1927–2005) was willing to tell anyone who would listen why he was the 'king of bluegrass'. After all, didn't Bill Monroe's sound change dramatically when Martin joined The Blue Grass Boys in 1949? Didn't Martin create a brand new honky-tonk/bluegrass hybrid on his great Decca recordings of the 1950s and 1960s? Wasn't that why they called him 'Mr. Good'n'Country'? Wasn't he a crucial figure on the 1972 *Will The Circle Be Unbroken* album?

A Controversial Musician

All these claims were true, but the way they were presented often rubbed people the wrong way and made Martin one of the most controversial figures in country music. He was the Jerry Lee Lewis of bluegrass – an indisputable genius, an over-the-top personality and an undeniable pain in the neck. How else do you explain his failure to become a member of the Grand Ole Opry or the Country Music Hall Of Fame while he was alive, despite achievements that dwarfed many other members?

> *'We were poor and had no electricity, but we had a battery radio. On Saturday I would listen to the Grand Ole Opry and try to sing like Roy Acuff and try to sing Bill Monroe's songs.'*
>
> **Jimmy Martin**

He grew up in poverty in the East Tennessee mountains, listening to Bill Monroe on the radio and practising those songs beneath a tree. Martin finally travelled to Nashville in 1949, accosted his hero at the backstage entrance and asked if he could sing a few songs with Monroe. After three songs, Monroe asked Chubby Wise what he thought, and the fiddler said, 'Oh, Lordy, son, he's flat got it, ain't he?'

He did. As Monroe's new singer-guitarist, Martin provided a louder, higher voice than Lester Flatt or Mac Wiseman and convinced Monroe to raise the pitch on many of his songs, making them even higher and more lonesome than before. And Martin's guitar work had a pulsing bounce that gave the band a different rhythm. Martin sang all or part of the lead vocals on such Monroe classics as 'In The Pines', 'Walking In Jerusalem' and 'Uncle Pen'.

The Martin Boot-Camp

Martin left Monroe for good in 1954 to pursue his dream of forming a band with Bobby and Sonny Osborne. They recorded the regional hit '20/20 Vision' and seemed on their way when Martin's outsized personality alienated the brothers and caused a split in 1955.

A year later, the classic version of Jimmy Martin and the Sunny Mountain Boys was assembled, with Paul Williams on mandolin and a 19-year-old, skinny J. D. Crowe on banjo. Much like a movie drill sergeant, Martin rehearsed them mercilessly till both the vocal harmonies and instrumental rhythms were to his exacting standards. Many musicians, before and after, fled Martin's boot-camp practices, but Williams and Crowe stuck it out and helped create – with various fiddlers and bassists – one of the greatest bluegrass bands of all time.

On recordings such as 'You Don't Know My Mind', 'Sophronie' and 'Rock Hearts', it is obvious how all that rehearsal paid off in seamless arrangements and an unprecedented toughness. Martin's in-your-face assertiveness had more in common with honky-tonk singers like Webb Pierce and Lefty Frizzell than the lonesome fatalism of most bluegrass singers. Martin never accepted that bluegrass was separate from mainstream country, and he sang about cheating women, country stardom and freewheeling truck drivers as if it didn't matter that he used mandolin and banjo rather than piano and steel guitar.

Above
Martin grew up in the Cumberland Mountains of Tennessee, and it was here that he first heard Bill Monroe on the radio – the man who would inspire him to a musical career.

Left
It took a lot to meet Martin's high standards – not many survived his 'boot-camp' but those that did became members of one of the most influential of all the bluegrass bands.

Key Track

'Sunny Side Of The Mountain' (1961)
In both its idyllic Appalachian lyrics and its lilting three-finger banjo roll, this song harkens back to Martin's days with Monroe. It was such a quintessential bluegrass song that it has been recorded by The Stanley Brothers, The Osborne Brothers and Flatt & Scruggs, but it was also recorded by Hank Snow and Porter Wagoner and became a highlight of the Nitty Gritty Dirt Band's *Will The Circle Be Unbroken* (1972).

Bill Monroe

Key Artist

'I'm a farmer with a mandolin and a high tenor voice.' **Bill Monroe**

Few genres are as closely identified with one person as bluegrass is with Bill Monroe (vocals, mandolin, 1911–96). Monroe not only defined the style's instrumentation, style and repertoire, he also hired most of its major figures and gave the music its name – taken from his group, The Blue Grass Boys.

Below

The father of bluegrass, Bill Monroe, at Nashville's WSM radio station.

Kentucky Roots

Raised on his father's 650-acre farm in western Kentucky, Bill Monroe was a shy boy, thanks to his poor eyesight and

dominating older brothers. When the family played together, little Bill was stuck with the mandolin – the small, eight-string Italian instrument – because the more popular fiddle and guitar were already claimed.

But Bill would switch to guitar when he accompanied the fiddling of his uncle, Pendleton Vandiver, or local coal miner Arnold Schultz at local dances. From his 'Uncle Pen' (later the title of one of Monroe's most popular songs) the youngster learned the Anglo-Celtic repertoire of local whites and from Schultz the blues repertoire of local blacks.

Like many young men of their generation, Bill Monroe and his brothers Birch (fiddle, 1901–82) and Charlie (vocals, guitar, 1903–75) left the farm during the Great Depression to move north. After work at an oil refinery near Chicago, they performed as dancers and musicians for their fellow immigrants from the rural South. Charlie was the leader, and he modelled the group on his favourite string bands and brother duos of the 1920s and 1930s. But his kid brother was not content to merely strum rhythm; Bill poured all his frustrations (orphaned at 16, displaced from home at 18, overshadowed by his brothers) into a mandolin style so fast and so aggressive that it was unprecedented.

Blue Grass Boy

Birch dropped out in 1934, but Charlie and Bill continued as The Monroe Brothers, recording some memorable sides for Bluebird Records. By 1938, however, the act could no longer accommodate the heated sibling rivalry, and Bill ventured out on his own. The following year, he debuted his quartet, Bill Monroe And The Blue Grass Boys, on the Grand Ole Opry in Nashville. By 1945 he had assembled the line-up of banjoist Earl Scruggs, singer-guitarist Lester Flatt, fiddler Chubby Wise and bassist Cedric Rainwater, a quintet that changed the history of country music. Monroe scored seven Top 20 country hits between 1946 and 1949.

He never lost his unerring ear for good musicians. After Flatt And Scruggs departed acrimoniously in 1948, Monroe hired one virtuoso after another. Carter Stanley,

The Essential Bill Monroe And His Blue Grass Boys, 1945–1949 (1992)
'Rocky Road Blues', 'Footprints In The Snow', 'Blue Moon Of Kentucky', 'Little Cabin Home On The Hill'

Live Recordings 1956–1969 Off The Record Volume 1 (1993)
'Fire On The Mountain', 'Blue Grass Breakdown', 'Blue Grass Stomp'

The Music Of Bill Monroe From 1936–1994 (1994)
'My Long Journey Home', 'Muleskinner Blues', 'Uncle Pen', 'I'm Going Back To Old Kentucky'

16 Gems (1996)
'Kentucky Waltz', 'Summertime Is Past And Gone'

Left
L–r: Bill Monroe, Chubby Wise, Cousin Wilbur, Lester Flatt and Earl Scruggs – the winning line-up of The Blue Grass Boys.

Jimmy Martin, Benny Martin, Vassar Clements, Mac Wiseman, Sonny Osborne, Bobby Hicks, Don Reno, Don Stover, Kenny Baker, Buddy Spicher, Peter Rowan, Del McCoury, Bill Keith, Richard Greene, Jim Eanes, Carl Story, Roland White, Lamar Grier, Byron Berline, Butch Robins and Glen Duncan all served an apprenticeship with the 'father of bluegrass' before venturing out to establish their own careers.

He mellowed in the 1980s and 1990s as he relaxed into the role of living legend and elder statesman. He made a series of records that were always respectable if not as staggering as his masterpieces of the 1940s and 1950s. He became the subject of innumerable books, films and television specials, and was a favourite of the folk festivals that

arose in the late 1950s and of the bluegrass festivals that flourished in the late 1960s; he even founded his own – the Bean Blossom Bluegrass Festival, in Indiana. 'I thought bluegrass would get no further than the farmer,' Monroe admitted. 'I'd designed it the way I thought he would like it, because that's where I was raised. Since then it's spread … all over the world.'

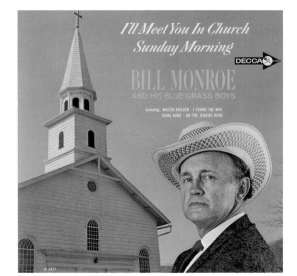

Left
I'll Meet You In Church Sunday Morning (1964), contained several Monroe standards, and featured the talents of Kenny Baker, Benny Williams and Del McCoury, among others.

Key Track

'Blue Moon Of Kentucky' (1946)
Monroe first cut his signature song with the classic quintet of Scruggs, Flatt, Wise and Rainwater as a heartbroken waltz. It's a lament for the girl that left, but the aching vocal and trilling mandolin hint at a bit of homesickness too. When Elvis Presley made the song one of his first rock'n'roll tracks, Monroe cut a driving, 4/4 version for Decca in 1954.

The Stanley Brothers

Key Artist

Bill Monroe invented the 'high, lonesome' sound of bluegrass vocals, but The Stanley Brothers perfected it. Ralph and Carter Stanley refined those vocals into close, three-part harmonies that were unprecedented at the time and which have had a lasting influence ever since. If Bill Monroe And The Blue Grass Boys set the standard for bluegrass picking, The Stanley Brothers set the standard for bluegrass singing.

Barefoot Country Boys

Carter (vocals, guitar, 1925–66) and Ralph Stanley (banjo, vocals, b. 1927) grew up in south-western Virginia, 'way back in the sticks where there were no bathrooms', Ralph later recalled. 'We got a radio in 1936, which is how we first heard records. We were just two barefoot country boys who walked three miles to school each day.' They grew up hearing fiddle tunes, string-band dance bands and brother duos on Saturdays and shape-note and lining hymns on Sundays.

Both boys were fresh out of the service in 1946, when they first formed The Stanley Brothers with fiddler Leslie Keith and mandolinist Pee Wee Lambert. Their first 78s betrayed how closely they copied their hero Monroe, but they soon came up with a unique twist on mountain harmony singing. Instead of a baritone harmony below the lead vocal and a tenor harmony above the lead, Lambert would raise the lower part an octave and sing a 'high baritone' harmony. The effect was thrilling and enabled the Stanleys to carve out their own identity amid the growing numbers of Monroe imitators.

It helped that the leads were sung by Carter, a powerful storyteller both as a songwriter and vocalist. The singles the brothers made for Rich-R-Tone Records (1947–48), Columbia Records (1949–52), Mercury Records (1952–58) and Starday/King (1958–66) were marked by descriptions of death, displacement and romantic betrayal framed by memories of childhood and hopes for an afterlife. The result was a richly melancholy music whose

> *'I've always called my music old-time mountain music or old-time country music. I've never really called my music bluegrass.'*
>
> **Ralph Stanley**

echoing harmonies suggested that the sorrows were shared. Carter was a charismatic stage presence both as a singer and an emcee, so when he died in 1966 from a lifetime of drinking, he left his shy, younger brother in a quandary.

The Clinch Mountain Boys

'It was really hard when my brother passed away,' Ralph explained. 'I didn't really know if I could go on without him. He'd always done the emcee work; he took most of the lead vocals and wrote more songs than me. I didn't know if I could get someone to take his place.'

The fans begged Ralph to go on, so he formed Ralph Stanley And The Clinch Mountain Boys. Over the years, the band included Larry Sparks, Roy Lee Centers, Charlie Sizemore, Joe Isaacs and, in 1970, two East Kentucky teenagers named Ricky Skaggs and Keith Whitley. These musicians carried on The Stanley Brothers tradition and allowed Ralph to age gracefully into a living legend who played a big part in the movie *O Brother, Where Art Thou?* and who sang duets with everyone from Jimmy Martin and Alison Krauss to Emmylou Harris and Bob Dylan.

'I still like singing more than picking,' Ralph said recently. 'There are plenty of good musicians, but singers are scarce. That high, lonesome sound we do goes back to ... those old Baptist churches where they didn't allow any instruments. We learned to sing without any backing. In 1970, I became the first person to sing bluegrass *a cappella*. Now they're all doing it.'

jimmy martin ◉ 80 bill monroe ◉ 82 ricky skaggs ◉ 250

Classic Recordings

Saturday Night And Sunday Morning (1992)
'Miner's Prayer', 'Mountain Folks', 'Great High Mountain'

The Early Starday-King Years 1958-1961 (1993)
'Wild Side Of Life', 'Little Maggie', 'Holiday Pickin'', 'I'll Meet You In Church Sunday Morning'

Angel Band: The Classic Mercury Recordings (1995)
'Angel Band', 'Memories Of Mother'

The Complete Columbia Stanley Brothers (1996)
'The White Dove', 'Gathering Flowers For The Master's Bouquet', 'Pretty Polly', 'I'm A Man Of Constant Sorrow'

Earliest Recordings: The Complete Rich-R-Tone 78s (1997)
'Molly And Tenbrook', 'The Rambler's Blues'

Clinch Mountain Country (1998)
'Pretty Polly', 'The White Dove', 'My Deceitful Heart'

Above
The first Stanley Brothers line-up: Pee Wee Lambert, Leslie Keith, Carter and Ralph.

Left
After Carter's death, Ralph formed The Clinch Mountain Boys. Cry From The Cross *remained true to the bluegrass style.*

Key Track

'Angel Band' (1955)
After a tingling mandolin intro, Carter lulls the listener with the melancholy fatalism of a man awaiting his imminent death. But when he sings of the angels descending to his bed to carry him off to heaven, Ralph comes in with a hair-raising high tenor that suggests both the terror of death and the hope for salvation. When this recording was recycled for *O Brother, Where Art Thou?*, it was the jewel in the crown.

A-Z of Artists

Above
Norman Blake has
remained true
to his bluegrass roots
throughout his career.

Red Allen
(Vocals, guitar, 1930–93)
After three years of pioneering three-part 'high-lead' harmonies with The Osborne Brothers, Red Allen split with his Ohio pals, convinced he could be a bluegrass star in his own right. He and another Dayton friend,

mandolinist Frank Wakefield, moved to Washington in 1960 and recorded with musicians such as Chubby Wise and Don Reno. None of the albums sold very well at the time, but they contain some of the finest bluegrass singing ever recorded.

Kenny Baker
(Fiddle, b. 1926)
Bill Monroe often introduced Kenny Baker onstage as 'the greatest fiddler in bluegrass music'. It was no exaggeration, for Baker, a third-generation fiddler from Kentucky, was capable of blistering breaks, elegant, long-bow phrases and swinging syncopation. He joined Monroe in 1956 and played with him off and on for more than 30 years.

Norman Blake
(Guitar, vocals, b. 1938)
Blake grew up as a traditional bluegrass musician in Georgia, but in 1963 he moved to Nashville, where he joined *The Johnny Cash Show* and recorded with Bob Dylan and Kris Kristofferson. His combination of virtuoso skills, a traditional background and collaborations with innovators led to dozens of albums under his own name, often with his wife Nancy.

The Bluegrass Cardinals
(Vocal/instrumental group, 1974–97)
When Kentucky's Don Parmley (banjo, vocals, b. 1933) found himself in Los Angeles in the early 1960s, he subbed for Earl Scruggs on *The Beverly Hillbillies*.
In 1974, he formed The Bluegrass Cardinals with his son David Parmley (vocals, guitar, b. 1943) and mandolinist Randy Graham. The two youngsters were such terrific singers that the group soon became a favourite on the bluegrass circuit, especially when it moved back East to Virginia in 1976. In 1993, David Parmley formed his own band, Continental Divide, where he was eventually rejoined by Graham.

Hylo Brown
(Vocals, guitar, 1922–2003)

In an era when every other singer was trying to sound like Bill Monroe or Carter Stanley, Hylo Brown sounded like no one else. An Ohio defence plant worker who moonlighted at hillbilly bars during the Second World War, Kentucky's Frank Brown Jr. became renowned for a vocal range that went from a warm baritone to a dizzying falsetto, and a local dj dubbed him Hylo Brown. He moved to Nashville in 1954, joined Flatt And Scruggs as a featured vocalist in 1957 and then formed his own quintet, The Timberliners – one of the finest bluegrass outfits of the era.

Vassar Clements
(Fiddle, 1928–2005)

Vassar Clements was just 14 years old when he joined Bill Monroe And The Bluegrass Boys in 1949. His virtuosic fiddling won him jobs with Jim And Jesse in 1958 and Jimmy Martin in 1967, but it was Clements' emergence as a key figure on 1972's *Will The Circle Be Unbroken* album that led him to the new-grass movement. He co-led the *Hillbilly Jazz* album in 1974, and that title described the fusion he pursued for the next 30 years.

The Country Gentlemen
(Vocal/instrumental group, 1959–1990s)

After a few tentative starts, The Country Gentlemen settled on their classic line up in 1959: Charlie Waller (vocals, guitar, 1935–2004), John Duffey (mandolin, vocals, 1934–96), Eddie Adcock (banjo, vocals, b. 1938) and Tom Gray (bass, b. 1941). They were all great bluegrass pickers, but Duffey's urban brand of humour and the group's taste for songwriters such as Bob Dylan and Paul Simon separated them from the pack. After the others left, Waller carried on the band and its sound with such notable partners as Ricky Skaggs, Jerry Douglas, Jimmy Gaudreau, Mike Auldridge, Bill Emerson and Doyle Lawson.

J. D. Crowe
(Banjo, guitar, vocals, b. 1937)

James Dee Crowe was just a 19-year-old kid from Kentucky when he was hired by Jimmy Martin in 1956. By 1966 he had developed a banjo style that combined Earl Scruggs' tumbling roll with Martin's bouncy pulse. The line-up of Crowe, Bobby Slone, Tony Rice, Ricky Skaggs and Jerry Douglas made only one album, 1975's *J. D.*

Crowe And The New South, but it was an influential classic that introduced three of the most important pickers of the next generation and a new blend of bluegrass, folk-rock and country-rock. Crowe has pursued that new/old blend ever since.

Hazel Dickens
(Vocals, guitar, b. 1935)

Bluegrass was an all-boys club when Hazel Dickens came along from the coalfields of West Virginia with a 'high, lonesome' soprano that grabbed the attention of anyone who tried to ignore her. Her singing was powerful enough, but she also developed into a terrific writer of songs about coalmining tragedies and mistreated women, which were recorded by the likes of Dolly Parton and Lynn Morris.

Below

Hazel Dickens was working in a factory in Baltimore when folklorist Mike Seeger 'discovered' her at a house party.

Josh Graves
(Dobro, b. 1925)

The dobro was pretty much a novelty instrument before Josh Graves established it as one of the most crucial voices in bluegrass. Graves had played with Mac Wiseman and Wilma Lee And Stoney Cooper before joining Flatt & Scruggs in 1955, but it was with that duo that he made his biggest impact. He was prominently featured on their hit singles and albums for Columbia, and stayed with the group until it disbanded in 1969. He went on to play with Lester Flatt And The Nashville Grass, The Earl Scruggs Revue, The Masters and Kenny Baker.

John Hartford
(Vocals, banjo, guitar, fiddle, 1937–2001)

Hartford is best known as the writer of 'Gentle On My Mind', a pop and country hit for Glen Campbell and much-recorded standard, but he was a gifted and devoted bluegrass musician who helped launch the new acoustic music movement with his 1971 album *Aero-Plain*. He celebrated America's rivers as both a songwriter and ship pilot, and he developed a popular solo act that combined storytelling, singing, picking and clogging.

Jim & Jesse
(Vocal/instrumental duo, 1945–80s)

In much the same way that Earl Scruggs revolutionized the banjo with his three-finger roll, Jesse McReynolds (vocals, mandolin, b. 1927) transformed the mandolin with his pioneering cross-picking and split-string innovations. Like Scruggs, he was lucky to have a partner with an appealing tenor voice to make it easier for the public to embrace these instrumental innovations. His brother Jim (vocals, guitar, 1927–2002) sang lead and Jesse harmonized in the

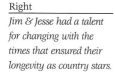

Right

Jim & Jesse had a talent for changing with the times that ensured their longevity as country stars.

old brother-duet style, even when they tackled everything from honky-tonk laments to a Top 20 single about truck driving (1967's 'Diesel On My Tail').

The Johnson Mountain Boys
(Vocal/instrumental group, 1975–95)

In the middle of the new-grass revolution, five young East Coast musicians swam against the tide by forming a hardcore traditional bluegrass quintet called The Johnson Mountain Boys. Led by Dudley Connell (vocals, guitar, b. 1956) and Eddie Stubbs (fiddle, b. 1961), this band from the D.C. suburbs revitalized Monroe's tradition from 1975 through 1995 with help from the likes of bassist Marshall Wilborn, and banjoists Tom Adams and Richard Underwood. Connell became lead singer of The Seldom Scene and Stubbs became the radio emcee of the Grand Ole Opry.

Bill Keith
(Banjo, pedal steel guitar, b. 1939)

Keith grew up in Boston, but he fell in love with bluegrass and mastered the Scruggs roll so well that he could play fast, fluid fiddle tunes on the banjo. He founded a duo with college roommate Jim Rooney (vocals, guitar, b. 1938) and in 1963 joined Bill Monroe. Keith went on to become a much-in-demand session musician and new-acoustic-music pioneer, recording with Judy Collins, Jonathan Edwards, Jim Kweskin, David Grisman, Bela Fleck and others.

Doyle Lawson
(Vocals, mandolin, b. 1944)

Doyle Lawson established a reputation as a terrific mandolinist in the style of his hero Bill Monroe during stints with J. D. Crowe And The New South (1966–71) and The Country Gentlemen (1972–79). But when the eastern Tennesseean started his own band, Doyle Lawson And Quicksilver, in 1979, he took bluegrass in a new direction. Lawson applied the moving, counterpoint harmonies of his favourite gospel quartets to Quicksilver's bluegrass songs and he made their second album, 1981's *Rock My Soul*, the first of many all-gospel projects.

The Lilly Brothers
(Vocal/instrumental duo, 1938–80)

Boston became an unlikely hotbed of bluegrass and old-time music, thanks in large part to The Lilly Brothers – West Virginia's Mitchell Burt 'Bea' Lilly (vocals, guitar, 1921–2005)

and Charles Everett Lilly (vocals, mandolin, b. 1924). They moved there in 1952 and played at a city bar called the Hillbilly Ranch for the next 18 years. Living so far from the south-east, the centre of bluegrass activity, The Lilly Brothers were under-recorded and under-appreciated, but they inspired a whole generation of Boston bluegrass fans.

Del McCoury
(Vocals, guitar, b. 1939)

Del McCoury dominated bluegrass music between 1994 and 2004, winning the International Bluegrass Music Association's Entertainer Of The Year award eight times. His band included two of his sons – mandolinist Ronnie and banjoist Rob – trained almost from birth to play with the hard, driving rhythm and to sing in the high, lonesome wail of their father. Del learned those traits from his brief stint with Bill Monroe in the 1960s and from his decades of toiling in obscure bands. When he finally emerged, however, people couldn't get enough of him. Steve Earle shared the credit with The Del McCoury Band on the 1999 bluegrass album *The Mountain*, and McCoury recorded with everyone from Leftover Salmon and Dierks Bentley to David Grisman.

Above
The line-up of The Johnson Mountain Boys changed over the years, but their true bluegrass sound remained consistent

The Osborne Brothers
(Vocal/instrumental group, 1953–90s)

The Osborne Brothers were well versed in traditional bluegrass but they made their biggest impact by experimenting with pop-country material and arrangements. Before they formed their partnership in Dayton, Ohio, in 1953, Bobby Osborne (vocals, mandolin, guitar, b. 1931) had apprenticed with The Stanley Brothers and Sonny Osborne (vocals, banjo, b. 1937) with Bill Monroe. They recorded the regional hit '20/20 Vision' with Jimmy Martin in 1954; they hired Red Allen as lead singer and recorded 'Once More' with him in 1958. But it was when they signed with Decca in 1963 and joined the Grand Ole Opry the following year that they added electric pick-ups to their instruments and the occasional piano or drums to their arrangements. Purists were horrified but audiences loved the combination of string-band picking and modern rhythm. They were voted CMA Vocal Group Of The Year in 1971.

Far Right
Father and son team Doc and Merle Watson.

Right
Reno And Smiley's Civil War Folk Songs.

Reno & Smiley
(Vocal/instrumental duo, 1949–65)

Of all the banjoists that Bill Monroe hired to fill the shoes of the departed Earl Scruggs, Don Reno (banjo, vocals, guitar, 1927–84) came closer than any. Reno developed his own style by playing single-string guitar-like runs on the banjo. He also found his own equivalent of Lester Flatt when he met Arthur 'Red' Smiley (vocals, guitar,

Right
A fresh-faced Larry Sparks with his Lonesome Ramblers on the album Bluegrass Old And New.

1925–72) after leaving Monroe. They formed Reno & Smiley And The Tennessee Cut-Ups in 1949, with Reno's instrumental invention and piercing high-tenor harmony contrasting with Smiley's disarming, welcoming baritone. They stayed together until 1965, recording a series of classic sides for King Records.

The Seldom Scene
(Vocal/instrumental group, 1971–present)

Three former members of The Country Gentlemen – John Duffey, Tom Gray and Mike Auldridge (dobro, b. 1938) – co-founded The Seldom Scene in 1971 with John Starling (vocals, guitar, b. 1940) and Ben Eldridge (banjo, b. 1938). Several of them had white-collar careers so they could play infrequently (thus the name) and whatever they wanted. They refined the Gentlemen's new-grass sound with more urbane, song-oriented arrangements and soon found themselves more in-demand than they had anticipated. Neither their quality nor their popularity suffered as they replaced different founding members with the likes of Dudley Connell, Lou Reid, Phil Rosenthal and T. Michael Coleman.

Larry Sparks
(Vocals, guitar, b. 1947)

Not many men could have replaced Carter Stanley after his death in 1966, but Larry Sparks had the high, lonesome

edge, the personal intimacy and the songwriting skills to do so. He had been a harmony singer in The Stanley Brothers since 1964, and became the lead singer of The Clinch Mountain Boys in 1966. He left in 1969 after five classic albums to form Larry Sparks And The Lonesome Ramblers.

Doc Watson

(Vocals, guitar, b. 1923)

Arthel 'Doc' Watson was a blind, 37-year farm worker who was playing old-time country and rockabilly on weekends when folklorist Ralph Rinzler came across him in the North Carolina mountains in 1960. Recognizing Watson as one of the most dazzling guitar virtuosos of his generation, Rinzler soon convinced him to perform and record as a solo acoustic guitarist. Since the early 1960s, he has toured and recorded continually, winning five Grammy Awards. His son Merle Watson (guitar, 1949–85) was his partner from 1965 until his tragic death. Doc carried on his career, founding an annual acoustic-music festival in North Carolina that he named Merlefest after his son.

The Whites

(Vocal/instrumental group, 1966–present)

Buck White (vocals, mandolin, b. 1930) was an Arkansas pipe fitter in 1966 when he formed a family bluegrass band with his wife Pat and their daughters Sharon (vocals, guitar, b. 1953) and Cheryl (vocals, bass, b. 1955). Buck's Monroe-like mandolin and his daughters' pretty harmony soon made The Whites a popular fixture on the bluegrass circuit. Sharon married Ricky Skaggs, who helped The Whites score several hit singles with a country/bluegrass fusion similar to his own.

Mac Wiseman

(Vocals, guitar, b. 1925)

Mac Wiseman was a featured singer for Flatt And Scruggs in 1948 and for Bill Monroe in 1949, and when he headed up his own group, The Country Boys (featuring Eddie Adcock and Scotty Stoneman), he kept his warm, friendly tenor and his taste for Carter Family-like songs at the forefront. Wiseman pioneered twin fiddles on bluegrass recordings – an innovation quickly adopted by Monroe – and enjoyed mainstream country hits with 'The Ballad Of Davy Crockett' (1955), 'Jimmy Brown the Newsboy' (1959) and 'Johnny's Cash And Charlie's Pride' (1970).

Tonight We're Settin' The Woods On Fire:
The War Years

during the 1940s and 1950s country music coalesced from various and disparate sub-styles of regional music and emerged as a distinct genre. Nashville's Grand Ole Opry was central to this newfound sense of identity, as it rose in popularity from an obscure local radio broadcast to a national entertainment institution. For decades, beginning in the 1930s, country music became almost synonymous with the Grand Ole Opry, as its weekly broadcast became a stepping-stone and platform for some of rural music's leading figures, including Uncle Dave Macon, Roy Acuff, Bill Monroe, Ernest Tubb and a host of other artists representing a variety of rural musical styles.

It was in the early 1940s that *Billboard*, the music industry's leading trade publication, first begrudgingly acknowledged country music's emerging popularity. The magazine's first chart devoted to country was instituted in 1942 and called, somewhat improbably, the 'Western And Race' charts. Later that year, country releases were lumped into a chart called 'American Folk Records'. It wasn't until 1949 that *Billboard* created its first dedicated 'Country And Western' chart. Bluegrass (and its precursor, mountain string-band music), honky-tonk and even occasional strains of early country-pop, were just a few of the disparate sub-styles that began to fold into and shape this relatively new genre, which was dramatically on the rise by the late 1940s. By the mid-1950s, Nashville's country-record industry finally reached critical mass in the national marketplace and started to put its own imprimatur on country music, while shaping and promoting it with a self-conscious finger on the pulse of changing national tastes and trends. Along with the music industry's increased commercial self-consciousness came the inevitable tensions between traditionalism and progressivism, rural and urbane.

Key Artists

Eddy Arnold

Lefty Frizzell

The Louvin Brothers

Ernest Tubb

Hank Williams

Influences & Development

One of the boldest innovations to coalesce in the 1940s was honky-tonk, a style that not only endures but continues to flourish in contemporary country music. Honky-tonk is a state of mind as well as a distinct musical style. Its roots extend back to the 1930s, though it was in the late 1940s and early 1950s that it came to its fruition.

The Arrival Of Honky-Tonk

The catch phrase 'honky-tonk', as near as anyone has been able to determine, first began to insinuate itself into the unofficial American musical lexicon in 1891. That's when a newspaper in Carter County, Oklahoma reported that 'the honk-a-tonk last night was well attended by ball-heads, bachelors and leading citizens'. It fell to Texas artist Al Dexter (1902–84) to formally introduce the phrase – which had already found currency in blues music – to country listeners. He did this with 'Honky-tonk Blues', recorded for Vocalion in 1936. Before long, honky-tonk's recognition had grown from an ill-defined figure of speech to the demarcation of an exciting new and emerging musical form.

Prior to honky-tonk, the dominant themes in country music were, as often as not, celebrations of bedrock rural values like family, faith, fidelity and the redeeming powers of love and honest labour. Early country offered listeners familiarity, reassurance and a soothing sense of place, often expressed through a prism of comforting nostalgia.

'You got to have smelt a lot of mule manure before you can sing like a hillbilly.'

Hank Williams

But honky-tonk, which first arose in Texas and Oklahoma saloons and dance halls (often called honky-tonks), marked the advent of a new and more tumultuous and rootless era and its attendant discontents as the USA's long, uneasy rural-to urban cultural transition accelerated.

The unease of this demographic shift was especially felt in the rough and tumble, transient Second World War-era oilfield, factory and shipyard settlements in Texas and the great American Southwest. This increasingly strident, electrified and often recklessly celebratory and world-weary music often captured the dislocation and insecurity of the people who lived and worked in these transient

settlements. Honky-tonk's prevailing ethos was a live-for-today commingling of carefree, late-night celebration with the stark realism, despair, and disillusionment of unsettled lives lived from paycheck to paycheck.

The Wild Side Of Life

Unlike the earlier traditional country music of artists such as The Carter Family, honky-tonk tended to be devoid of moral instruction. In its more graphic strains, it celebrated the wilder side of life – alcoholism, infidelity, betrayal – while also lamenting its consequences.

In large part, honky-tonk is a worldly music whose provocativeness and dramatic tension often reside in the way a great honky-tonk song can steep listeners in equal portions of light-hearted abandon and booze-soaked celebration with countervailing emotions of despair, guilt, contrition and even fatalism.

Popular song titles like 'Born To Lose' (Ted Daffan, 1912–96), 'The Wild Side Of Life' (Hank Thompson, b. 1925), 'Slippin' Around' (Floyd Tillman, 1914–2003), 'Divorce Me C.O.D.' (Merle Travis, 1917–83) and 'Drivin' Nails In My Coffin' (Ernest Tubb, 1914–84) reflect the thematic U-turn that honky-tonk signified in the hands of 1940s artists such as Cliff Bruner (1915–2000), Daffan, Dexter and Texas honky-tonk king Tubb.

Talented singers and bandleaders like Louisiana-born Buddy Jones and Jimmie Davis (who would later become a two-term Louisiana governor); along with Texans Tillman and singer/piano-thumper Moon Mullican (1909–67), would also become central players in honky-tonk's 1940s' ascendance.

The first major star to arise in the genre was Texas-born Ernest Tubb, whose illustrious recording career stretched from the early 1940s into the 1960s. A gruff-voiced, yet plaintive singer, Tubb started out in the 1930s as an earnest disciple of Jimmie Rodgers (1897–1933). But he found his own voice with early honky-tonk anthems like 'Walkin' The Floor Over You', 'Wastin' My Life Away', 'Warm Red Wine' and his robust revival of Rodgers' 'Waitin' For A Train'. Tubb would further widen honky-tonk's audience in the early 1940s when he became a member of Nashville's Grand Ole Opry.

Other noteworthy honky-tonk artists, like Lloyd 'Cowboy' Copas ('Filipino Baby') and Pee Wee King And The Golden West Cowboys ('Tennessee Waltz'), would also become Opry members during the 1940s.

ernest tubb ⊙ **106 ted daffan** ⊙ **111 al dexter** ⊙ **111**

Above

The Drifting Cowboys were the original backing band for Hank Williams.

Foot-Tapping And Bottle-Bouncing

Many of the earliest honky-tonk songs were lighthearted and whimsical, especially when contrasted with the despairing heartbreak ballads popularized by Hank Williams (1923–53) and Lefty Frizzell (1928–75), who in the early 1950s more or less set the standards for contemporary honky-tonk. But even in its darkest moments honky-tonk also conveyed a newfound sense of freedom, though it was often laced with unease. As such, it forever loosened and broadened country music's staid emotional and thematic parameters. Many of Frizzell's and Williams' classic recordings – including Frizzell's 'If You've Got The Money I've Got The Time' and 'I Never Go Around Mirrors' and Williams' 'Honky Tonkin' 'Cold, Cold Heart' and 'I'm So Lonesome I Could Cry', have become signature songs of the style.

Honky-tonk's emphasis on electrification (via the guitar) and beat (usually provided by stand-bass and drums) also marked a departure from the gentler acoustic-based sound of traditional country music. Honky-tonk's heavy beat not only captured the *zeitgeist* of precarious times; it also enabled the musicians to be heard over the late-night din of the oilfield and factory-town bar-rooms where it was played. Honky-tonk made the bottles bounce on the table and made people get up and dance.

In some ways, honky-tonk was also a first cousin to western-swing music, which also arose from the dancehalls of the south-western USA in the 1930s and early 1940s. A few noteworthy honky-tonkers from this time – Cliff Bruner and later Hank Cochran (b. 1935) among them – had their feet planted in both styles. Quite a few honky-tonk bands were, in fact, former western-swing bands with their instrumentation trimmed down in order to play in small honky-tonk bar-rooms instead of large dancehalls.

The Ray Price Beat

While singers like Ernest Tubb, Hank Williams and Lefty Frizzell brought definitive, rough-hewn vocal majesty and starker thematic dimensions to honky-tonk, it was Texas singer/bandleader Ray Price (b. 1926) who did much in the 1950s to give honky-tonk a new level of musical sophistication and a distinct musical signature that in large part persists to this day. It is a measure of his influence that the 4/4 shuffle beat often heard in honky-tonk was for years merely referred to as 'the Ray Price beat'.

Price started out singing as a sideline while studying to be a veterinarian at North Texas Agricultural College. Around 1950, he gravitated to Dallas, where he made his first recordings and sang on *The Big D Jamboree*, a popular local radio show. Price was befriended by Hank Williams in 1951 and soon began touring with him and using Williams' band, The Drifting Cowboys, as his own backup band. After Williams' death in 1953, Price took over The Drifting Cowboys. By then, he was already enjoying early hits such as 'Talk To Your Heart' (1952) and 'Don't Let The Stars Get In Your Eyes' (1952).

But Price was intent on injecting his music with a more pronounced western-swing feel, and in 1954 organized his own band, The Cherokee Cowboys. During the next few years, a number of influential musicians – Willie Nelson (b. 1933), Roger Miller (1936–92) and Johnny Paycheck (1938–2003) among them – would serve apprenticeships in the band.

An Enduring Genre

As the popularity of other styles, western swing and country-pop in particular, have ebbed and flowed from one decade to the next, honky-tonk's appeal has endured.

Ushered in by the likes of Al Dexter and Ted Daffan in the late 1930s and refined over the decades by masters such as Tubb (in the 1940s), Williams and Frizzell (the 1950s) and George Jones (b. 1931) and Merle Haggard (b. 1937) in the 1960s and '70s, honky-tonk remains alive and well.

Throughout the final two decades of the twentieth century and into the twenty-first, innumerable, innovative new artists found either fleeting or lasting popularity by revisiting honky-tonk's stylistic and emotional well for their inspiration—Moe Bandy (b. 1944), Gary Stewart (1945–2003), Mel Street (1933–78) and Keith Whitley (1955–89) are just a few among many. Alan Jackson (b. 1958) and Brooks And Dunn are merely two of many contemporary stars who delve frequently into honky-tonk by reviving honky-tonk classics of yore or by introducing new songs written resolutely in the honky-tonk vein.

Left
Popular legend has it that Al Dexter coined the expression 'honky-tonk', although it was actually in use before he started playing in this style.

Below
Brooks And Dunn are one of the many bands keeping the honky-tonk style alive in the twenty-first century.

The Grand Ole Opry

Nashville's Grand Ole Opry is the oldest continuously broadcast live music programme in the world. Since it hit the airways in 1926, it has served as a springboard for dozens of key artists' rise to national fame. Its presence in Nashville was central to the growth of the city's music industry.

Opry Origins

The Opry started almost by accident one day in 1926 when George D. Hay – station director at Radio WSM – made a last-minute decision to substitute Uncle Jimmy Thompson, a local fiddle player, for a preacher who failed to show up for his daily programme. Listener response was immediate and favourable. Soon Hay expanded the programme with other local musicians, including banjo player and raconteur Uncle Dave Macon (1870–1952), a string band called The Possum Hunters and a gifted black harmonica player named DeFord Bailey.

The Opry was actually pre-dated by other popular radio 'barn-dance'-style shows with a country format.

Foremost among these were Shreveport's *Louisiana Hayride*, Chicago's *National Barndance* and Wheeling, West Virginia's *Wheeling Jamboree*. But the Opry soon took on a personality all its own and gradually achieved a national popularity that eclipsed all its radio rivals. By the early 1930s, WSM had boosted its signal to a powerful 50,000 watts that by night was heard in 30 states and parts of Canada. The Saturday evening live music and comedy presentation was gradually expanded to three hours.

The Ryman Auditorium

In the early 1940s, the Opry began broadcasting from what is still called 'The Mother Church Of Country Music': the *c.* 1889, 3,000-seat Ryman Auditorium, in downtown Nashville. By the early 1940s, the Opry – by then in its second decade – had also dramatically expanded and diversified its artist roster to include everything from comedy and old-time string-band music to early honky-tonk and western swing.

By the late 1940s, the Opry had begun to overtake in popularity similar regional country radio shows in Chicago, Wheeling, Shreveport and elsewhere. Gradually it was becoming a musical institution whose name was almost synonymous with country music. As result, the Opry became a magnet and a springboard for many of the era's most talented and original young artists, ranging from smooth, middle-of-the-road singers like Red Foley (1910–68) and hardcore country singers like Roy Acuff (1903–92) to bluegrass music king Bill Monroe (1911–96). Some, like Hank Snow (1914–99), came from as far away as Canada's Maritime Provinces to be part of the show.

Nashville's Finest

The rise of the Opry was also a major factor in the gradual concentration and growth of the Nashville music industry, as more and more record labels, publishing companies, managements and booking agencies began to set up operations in the city. Thus, by the early 1960s, Tennessee's state capital had also become a worldwide music capital, known far and wide as 'Music City'.

Over the years, a host of country greats – Acuff, Williams and Snow among them – have parlayed their status as Opry cast members into national fame. By the 1980s, the Grand Ole Opry's relevance to contemporary country music had waned considerably and most of its headlining artists were long past their commercial heydays. But since then, the Opry's management has made earnest and impressive efforts to re-establish the Opry's currency by recruiting a new generation of popular young artists who share a healthy reverence for the tradition that country music's greatest radio show has embodied for over three-quarters of a century.

Eddy Arnold

Key Artist

Born in Henderson, Tennessee, in 1918, Eddy Arnold has not only shown remarkable longevity as an artist (his career spans seven decades and he has sold more than 80 million records); he was also a pivotal figure in country music's dramatic stylistic shift during the 1950s from rough and rural to urbane and sophisticated.

'I'm trying to sell every audience something. That something is me.'
Eddy Arnold

Speaking Through Song

A farmer's son, Arnold discovered his penchant for singing at a very early age when he listened to the records of stars of the day like Gene Autry, Bing Crosby and Jimmie Rodgers. He often sang at school and at church functions, accompanying himself on a cheap Sears

Roebuck Silvertone guitar. Years later, Arnold recalled the musical epiphany he experienced as a youngster – one that stuck with him over the decades: 'I discovered I could speak to people through songs in a way I never could by just talking.'

The dollar a night he could earn at age 11 as a singer at local ice-cream socials and barbeque picnics came in handy after his father died and the family lost its farm. Within a few years, Arnold moved on to Jackson, Tennessee, where he sang in bars and on local radio stations while also driving for an undertaker. He soon moved on to Memphis and St. Louis, where he sang and also performed down-home comedy on radio.

Big Break

Arnold's big break came in 1940 when he was hired as the featured singer in Pee Wee King's Golden West Cowboys, a popular band of the day. The exposure he gained playing with the Golden West Cowboys on the Grand Ole Opry and elsewhere gave Arnold the confidence to embark on a solo career in 1943. Soon he was performing on the Opry on his own and in December 1944, he had his first recording sessions for RCA in the studio of WSM Radio in Nashville.

Almost from the start, Arnold's releases sold well and for the remainder of the 1940s he rode the top of the charts with hits like 'That's How Much I Love You' (1946), 'Anytime' (1948) and 'Bouquet Of Roses' (1948). Arnold's warm, plaintive vocal style also warmed hearts among pop listeners and as early as the 1940s, his records began crossing over into the pop charts.

Tennessee Plowboy

By the 1950s, Arnold, with methodical and ambitious deliberation, gradually expanded his crossover appeal while opening new avenues both for himself as a singer and for country music in general. In the early 1950s, he was one of the first country performers to play Las Vegas – a city that today is one of country's most lucrative

Below
Eddy Arnold (left) with dj Alan Freeman.

Cattle Call/Thereby Hangs A Tale (1990)
'Cattle Call', 'Cool Water', 'Tennessee Stud'

Standards By Eddy Arnold (1997)
'Scarlet Ribbons', 'The Glory Of Love', 'I Only Have Eyes For You'

RCA Country Legends (2000)
'What's He Doing In My World', 'Make The World Go Away', 'There's Been A Change In Me'

Left
The famous Studio B in Nashville, where Eddy Arnold recorded during his 1960s heyday.

performance venues. He also branched out into television, appearing first on *The Milton Berle Show* and later hosting shows of his own in the mid-1950s. All the while, Arnold, who had actually ploughed with a mule as a kid and later billed himself as 'The Tennessee Plowboy', began cultivating a musical style and a public persona that was increasingly buttoned down, urbane and sophisticated – albeit in a country sort of way.

During the late 1950s, when rock'n'roll was all the rage, Arnold's career cooled somewhat – as did the careers of many of his Nashville contemporaries. He briefly considering retiring from music and instead devoting himself to his real-estate portfolio and other extensive non-musical investments. But he soon bounced back with another wave of mellow, easy-listening hits, including many of the songs for which he remains best known. These include 'Cattle Call' (1955, a cowboy song, which he recorded in a plaintive pop mode, backed by a full orchestra), 'What's He Doing In My World' (1965) and 'Make The World Go Away' (1965).

Key Track

'Cattle Call' (1955)
Arnold set the tone for the new stylistic direction in which he would mine future gold by releasing this lush, pop version of a western classic, which he had initially recorded in 1947. The new version featured orchestral strings and was noticeably lacking a steel guitar. It topped the country charts and also made a minor stir in the *Billboard* pop charts.

Lefty Frizzell

Above
Troubled honky-tonk star Lefty Frizzell.

Right
Like so many other country artists, Frizzell's earliest influence was the music of Jimmie Rodgers.

'Travelin' Blues'– created a template for honky-tonk that endures. Merle Haggard and George Jones are two of many latter-day honky-tonk stars who evince the Frizzell influence with nearly every note they sing.

Troubled Youth

Like many singers of his generation Frizzell was heavily influenced by the music of Jimmie Rodgers and Ernest Tubb as a youth. By age 12, he had his own radio show on a station in El Dorado, Arkansas, where his family lived briefly. In the late 1940s, he began singing in clubs and on radio stations in Paris and Big Spring, Texas, Roswell, New Mexico and elsewhere. He built a particularly large local following with his regular appearances at a dancehall in Big Springs called The Ace Of Clubs.

As a youngster, Frizzell earned the nickname Lefty for his prowess with his fists, and from an early age, he was no stranger to hard living – something that later caught up with him and undermined both his career and creativity. In 1947, he was charged and convicted of statutory rape and served six months in a New Mexico jail.

Frizzell was signed to Columbia Records in Nashville, in 1950, by producer Don Law. Within a single month – October 1951 – he made musical history when four of his single releases simultaneously reached *Billboard*'s country Top 10. For the next couple of years, nearly every record he released made the country Top 10, including classics like 'Mom And Dad's Waltz', 'Forever', 'Always Late' and his rendition of Jimmie Rodgers' 'Travelin' Blues'.

But Frizzell's chart dominance and his stint with the Grand Ole Opry were cut short, largely

Corsicana, Texas-born William Orville 'Lefty' Frizzell (1928–75) was the son of an oilfield worker who grew up in various 'oil patch' settlements in East Texas, Louisiana and Arkansas. His clenched-note, note-bending vocal style (characterized by a penchant for stretching and rephrasing individual words and lyric passages for heightened emphasis) and chart-topping early 1950s hits – 'If You've Got The Money I've Got The Time', 'Always Late' and

Left
George Jones is one of the many modern artists who have been influenced by Lefty Frizzell.

due to his alcoholism and accompanying legal and financial problems. In the summer of 1951, he was arrested backstage at the Opry on charges of contributing to the delinquency of a minor. Though he was never prosecuted, he also became mired in a succession of contractual disputes and lawsuits that often hampered his recording and performing career.

It Hurts To Face Reality

Though his popularity, like that of many of his honky-tonk contemporaries, was also thwarted by the advent of rock'n'roll in the mid-1950s, Frizzell bounced back in 1959 with his recorded version of Marijohn Wilken' 'Long Black Veil'. In 1962, he recorded a signature story-song called 'Saginaw, Michigan', which was also his final No. 1 single.

During his last years, Frizzell had the occasional hit and also wrote and recorded two more enduring honky-tonk classics: 'That's The Way Love Goes' and 'I Never Go Around Mirrors'. But his personal life often remained in turmoil. Though he suffered from high blood pressure, he eschewed medical treatment and medication and continued to drink heavily. In 1975, while preparing to go on tour, he died of a massive stroke. He was 47 years old. He was inducted into the Country Music Hall Of Fame in 1982.

A song that Frizzell wrote sometime during his final years called 'It Hurts To Face Reality' expressed the despair that seemed to dog Frizzell for too much of his relatively short life. Though he never got around to recording the song himself, it became the theme song for *Tender Mercies*, an Academy Award-winning 1983 feature film starring Robert Duvall.

Key Track

'If You've Got The Money I've Got The Time' (1950)
Frizzell wrote this classic good-timey anthem when he was still playing the saloon and dancehall circuit in Texas. A demo he recorded of the song in Dallas landed him a contract with Columbia Records, and his master recording of 'If You've Got The Money' became the first of five No. 1 records he would rack up over the next two years.

The Louvin Brothers

Key Artist

Above

The Louvin Brothers were one of country music's definitive bluegrass- and gospel-style close-harmony duos.

The Radio Twins

Brothers Ira Lonnie (1924–65) and Charlie Elzer Loudermilk (b. 1927) began life in rural poverty on a farm near Section, Alabama, and began singing together as children. They steeped themselves in the close-harmony style they heard on the records of early brother harmony duos: The Delmore Brothers (also from Alabama), The Monroe Brothers (Bill and Charlie) and The Blue Sky Boys. While both learned guitar, Ira also took up mandolin so they could recreate the guitar-mandolin interplay they thrilled to on these records.

'Ira would never preach to an audience, but he could get through the most sentimental recitation and never lose it, always keep a straight face.'

Charlie Louvin

After performing as teenagers in their home region, they moved on to Chattanooga, Tennessee, and in 1942 began performing on a Knoxville radio station with The Foggy Mountain Boys, calling themselves The Radio Twins.

Charlie joined the army in 1945, and for a while Ira worked with Charlie Monroe until the following year when the brothers got back together and began calling themselves The Louvin Brothers. In the late 1940s, they worked at radio stations and at other venues in and around Knoxville, Tennessee. The brothers made their earliest recordings for the Apollo, Decca and MGM labels, though their musical activities were limited by Charlie's military service, which included a stint in Korea.

The Louvin Brothers followed in the footsteps of The Blue Sky Boys, one of the most influential close-harmony groups of the 1940s, and they paved the way for The Everly Brothers, kings of the 1950s and 1960s brother harmony duos. Though The Louvin Brothers' commercial heyday was a relatively brief half-decade in the 1950s, their powerful, definitive harmonies have had a profound influence on several generations of younger artists.

Commercial Heyday

The brothers joined the Grand Ole Opry in 1955. After recording for various labels with sporadic success in the late 1940s and early 1950s, their commercial heyday came in the mid to late 1950s on Capitol Records. It was during this period that they released definitive harmony hits such as 'When I Stop Dreaming' (1955), 'I Don't Believe You've Met My Baby' (1956) and 'You're Running Wild' (1956).

Many of their releases from this vintage period were boldly retrospective in terms of style. Marked by high-lonesome vocal harmonies, Ira's mandolin solos and often no drums, they were more reminiscent of country music of the 1930s than either the honky-tonk or rockabilly styles that were all the rage in Nashville at that time.

By the late 1950s, The Louvin Brothers' popularity and creative inspiration had begun to wane, and the always-tempestuous Ira's behaviour became even more temperamental. They had their final Top 10 chart hit with 'My Baby's Gone' in 1959. Ira and Charlie parted ways to pursue respective solo careers in 1963. Ira completed a solo album, *The Unforgettable Ira Louvin*, in 1964. The following year he was killed – along with his wife and two associates – in a traffic accident in Missouri.

Charlie has continued to record (for Capitol, United Artists, Little Darlin' and other labels) and to perform in the decades since his brother's death, but he has only enjoyed the occasional Top 10 record. In 1979, Emmylou Harris paid a tribute to The Louvin Brothers' harmonies by recording a duet with Charlie, who also recorded a 1989 duet with Roy Acuff of the classic 'Precious Jewel'. He recorded duets with former George Jones singing partner Melba Montgomery and performed and toured briefly with The Whitstein Brothers, a short-lived bluegrass brother harmony group that brilliantly revived Louvin-style harmonies. During the last three decades of the twentieth century, however, he enjoyed sustained popularity with his regular appearances on the Grand Ole Opry.

Classic Recordings

***Close Harmony* (1994)**
'Alabama', 'Cash On The Barrelhead', 'When I Stop Dreaming'

***20 All Time Greatest Hits* (2002)**
'I Don't Believe You've Met My Baby', 'You're Running Wild', 'Hoping That You're Hoping'

***Tragic Songs Of Life* (2003)**
'Kentucky', 'In The Pines', 'Knoxville Girl'

Above

Melba Montgomery, who recorded the album Something To Brag About *with Charlie Louvin in 1971.*

Left

The influence of The Louvin Brothers can be seen in later brother harmony duos like The Everly Brothers.

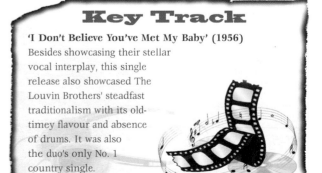

Key Track

'I Don't Believe You've Met My Baby' (1956)
Besides showcasing their stellar vocal interplay, this single release also showcased The Louvin Brothers' steadfast traditionalism with its old-timey flavour and absence of drums. It was also the duo's only No. 1 country single.

Ernest Tubb

Key Artist

One of honky-tonk's most enduring and beloved figures, Ernest Tubb (1914–84) was born near Crisp, Texas, one of five children from a broken home. He began his career singing at local radio stations and working a string of day jobs – among them a ditch digger, drugstore clerk and brewery worker. As a young man, in 1928, he fell under the spell of white country-blues master Jimmie Rodgers and listened incessantly to his records.

Under The Widow's Wing

Legend has it that Tubb began singing and got his first guitar in 1933 – the year that Jimmie Rodgers died of tuberculosis. While working on a road crew by day, he would teach himself Jimmie Rodgers songs at night. By 1934, he had married his first wife and moved to San Antonio, Texas, where he began singing on the radio.

When Tubb made his earliest recordings in the mid-1930s, he was little more than an accomplished Jimmie Rodgers imitator. Yet he was sufficiently talented for Rodgers' widow (who lived in San Antonio) to take him under her wing in 1934 and bring him to the attention of RCA – the label for which Rodgers had recorded. Tubb was not to enjoy the instant success of his role-model though. These early recordings met with little success and showed that the world had only a passing interest in his earnest recreation of the Jimmy Rodgers sound. It was actually a stroke of luck that a 1939 tonsillectomy robbed Tubb of his ability to yodel and lowered his vocal range to a droll yet warm, gut-bucket growl that would become his musical signature.

'I've never been able to hold one note more than one beat…. My voice comes on the jukebox and [guys] say "I can sing better than that" and in about ninety percent of the cases they are right.'

Ernest Tubb

Getting Along Somehow

Tubb had his first taste of commercial success, with a pair of songs – 'Blue Eyed Elaine' and 'I'll Get Along Somehow' – that he recorded for Decca Records in 1940. (The latter song was later covered by singing cowboy Gene Autry.)

Much-Loved Star

Over the years, Tubb recorded duets with numerous artists, including The Andrews Sisters, Red Foley, The Wilburn Brothers and Loretta Lynn. In 1943, Tubb joined the Grand Ole Opry and remained one of its most popular figures for nearly four decades. Aside from his rugged, unadorned vocal style, Tubb is also remembered as one of country music's kindest stars. Hank Snow, Hank Williams, Carl Smith and Loretta Lynn are just four of the many artists to whom he extended a helping hand when they were struggling.

Tubb continued recording for Decca Records until the mid-1970s, though by then changing times and changing musical tastes had passed him by. At that time Nashville producer/steel guitarist Pete Drake, out of great affection for the artist, signed him to his First Generation label.

All throughout his career, until he was sidelined by emphysema in 1982, two years before his death, Tubb toured almost constantly. His devotion to performing, along with his warmth and sincerity, made him dearly loved by his fans.

During this time most of Tubb's popularity – and most of his shows – were still in the Lone Star State until 'Walkin' The Floor Over You', a song he wrote and recorded for Decca, became what would prove to be a million-seller and his all-time biggest career hit in 1942. Tubb was soon singing songs in Hollywood western films and touring the south-eastern USA on package shows with stars of the day such as Grand Ole Opry Star Roy Acuff and western-swing king Bob Wills.

It was during the 1940s that Tubb recorded most of the songs for which he is still remembered: 'Soldier's Last Letter' (1944), 'Tomorrow Never Comes' (1945), 'Rainbow At Midnight' (1946) and 'Filipino Baby' (1946). They also defined Tubb's signature style, which was austere and rough-hewn yet deeply personal and often adorned with only minimal instrumental accompaniment – often an electric lead guitar giving a straightforward re-reading of the song's melody.

Classic Recordings

The Complete Live 1965 Show (1998)
'Thanks A Lot', 'Soldier's Last Letter', 'Blue Eyed Elaine'

Waltz Across Texas (1999)
'Mr. & Mrs. Used To Be', 'With Tears In My Eyes', 'Precious Little Baby'

The Country Music Hall Of Fame – Ernest Tubb (2000)
'Walkin' The Floor Over You', 'It's Been So Long, Darling', 'Waltz Across Texas'

Left
As a vocalist, Tubb was limited – something that ultimately proved as much a strength as a weakness.

Far Left
Genial country singer Ernest Tubb was much loved by his peers and fans.

Left
Tubb's record shop in Nashville still flourishes. There are four outlets in Tennessee and Texas.

Key Track

'Walkin' The Floor Over You' (1941)
Reacting to complaints from jukebox operators that his records couldn't be heard above the din of the bar-room crowd, Tubb enlisted guitar player 'Smitty' Smith to play on the 1941 Dallas recording session. Unaccustomed to playing without written music, Smith merely reiterated the song's melody in his guitar solo, setting a style that would become Tubb's trademark for the next 40 years.

Hank Williams

Key Artist

Musical Rendezvous

Williams was born in Mount Olive, Alabama, in 1923, the son of a log truck driver who suffered from shell shock after the First World War. The family lived in relative poverty and Williams was plagued by health problems throughout his entire life. His parents separated when he was six years old. His father Lon was confined to a veterans' hospital while young Hank moved several times with his mother Lillie, finally landing in Montgomery, Alabama, in 1931.

'I was a pretty good imitator of Roy Acuff, but then I found out they already had a Roy Acuff, so I started singin' like myself.'

Hank Williams

Rural Alabama-born Hiram Williams (1923–53) has emerged in the half-century since his death – at age 29 – as the archetypal honky-tonk artist and arguably the single most influential artist in modern country music. The songs that Williams wrote and sang in the course of his short and none-too-sweet life – 'Hey Good Lookin'', 'I'm So Lonesome I Could Cry', 'Cold Cold Heart', 'Lost Highway', 'I Can't Help It'– have been covered countless times over the years by country and pop artists alike. The power of Williams' music lies in its unadorned emotional sincerity, plainspoken poeticism and his uncanny knack for turning his personal despair into music that has proven universal and enduring.

Above

Hank with his wife Audrey, her daughter from a previous marriage, and their son, Hank Williams Jr.

Williams was an indifferent student, but even as a youngster he was consumed by music. He spent hours listening to records and learning the songs of Jimmie Rodgers and Roy Acuff. After he won a local talent contest in 1937 – singing a song he wrote called 'W.P.A. Blues' – there was no turning back. He soon had his own radio show on a Montgomery station and had developed a small but devoted cadre of local fans.

In 1942, he volunteered to serve in the wartime army but was turned down because of a back disorder – a congenital spine defect that caused him pain and discomfort his entire life. He ended up working in the shipyards in Mobile, Alabama and began assembling a core of talented backup musicians who would later become The Drifting Cowboys, his permanent band.

Williams' star-crossed rendezvous with musical history began in September 1946 when he got an audience with legendary Nashville songwriter and publisher Fred Rose. Rose immediately grasped the scope of Williams' raw talent. Just two months later, Rose produced Williams' earliest master recordings for the Sterling record label.

Williams' Sterling records earned a positive enough reception to land him a contract with the newly formed MGM Records. And in 1947, he recorded and released 'Move It On Over', which turned even more heads toward the wayward young singer, who was already developing a reputation for hard drinking, emotional instability and undependability.

Around this time, he also began appearing on the *Louisiana Hayride* and was soon one of the most popular performers on the show.

Hank's Last Ride

Shortly afterward, he recorded one of his first chart-topping hits, 'Lovesick Blues' – his honky-tonk reprise of an old pop song previously recorded in the 1920s by Emmett Miller. An invitation to make a guest appearance on the Grand Ole Opry soon followed. The six encores that he earned at his Opry debut was a harbinger of the success that was just around the corner.

Hank Williams
MEMORIAL ALBUM
M-G-M Long Playing 33⅓ r.p.m. Record

Above
The Hank Williams Memorial Album *was released in 1955 and contained a collection of his most popular songs.*

Left
The boyhood home of Hank Williams has now been turned into a museum to honour one of the shortest-lived but brightest stars of country music.

In the late 1940s, Williams joined the Grand Ole Opry. For a two-year period, Williams dominated the charts and was one of the most popular touring artists of the day. But by 1951, as he became increasingly plagued by binge drinking, marital problems and intense pain from his spinal disorder, Williams seemed to lose interest in his career and became increasingly unreliable. In 1952, he was fired from the Grand Ole Opry. At one point, he ended up back in Montgomery, Alabama, living in the boarding house run by his mother. Drinking heavily, he often mixed alcohol with chloral hydrate, which he took for chronic back pain.

The singer died on New Year's Day, 1953, in the back of his Cadillac, en route to personal appearances in Charleston, West Virginia and Canton Ohio.

Key Track

'Your Cheatin' Heart' (1953)
Williams wrote this mournful ode of recrimination to his ex-wife Audrey and recorded it at his final recording session in 1952. Released posthumously the following year, it has since become one of honky-tonk's most enduring anthems of heartbreak and despair.

A-Z of Artists

The Bailes Brothers
(Vocal duo, 1944–49)

This popular vocal duo was actually comprised at various times of changing configurations of four brothers: Kyle, John, Walter and Homer Bailes, who were all born in Kanawah County, West Virginia, between 1915 and 1922. The Bailes Brothers' peak years were from 1944 to 1949, when they disbanded. During those four years, they were members of the Grand Ole Opry before moving on to the *Louisiana Hayride*.

Tex Banes
(Vocals, guitar, 1915–2005)

Born in Carlton Victoria, Australia, Burt 'Tex' Banes grew up in an orphanage with Smoky Dawson, another legendary figure in Australian country music. An old-timey singer in the Jimmie Rodgers style, Banes and his long-time band, The Hayseeds, performed extensively in Australia and occasionally in the USA.

Above

Canadian Wilf Carter (aka Montana Slim) was one of the pioneers of singing cowboy music and yodelling.

Rod Brasfield
(Comedian, 1910–58)

Rodney Leon Brasfield, born in Smithville, Mississippi, was one of country music's most beloved comedians and a long-time favourite of Nashville's Grand Ole Opry, where he performed from 1944 until his death. He often teamed with fellow Opry comedienne Minnie Pearl and later with singer-comedienne June Carter Cash.

Jerry Byrd
(Steel guitar, 1920–2005)

One of country music's most influential steel guitar players, Gerald Lester Byrd was born in Lima, Ohio. He started out on the *Renfro Valley Barn Dance*, where he backed singers such as Red Foley and began experimenting with various innovative tunings and playing techniques. In Nashville in the late 1940s and 1950s, he played on recording sessions with dozens of stars of the day.

Wilf Carter (Montana Slim)
(Vocals, 1904–96)

Carter, the son of a Baptist minister, was born in Nova Scotia, Canada, and in his youth worked as a rodeo performer in Canada's western provinces, as well as sang on radio shows. Recording for RCA Records for 50 years, Carter was central to the popularity of cowboy music in the 1930s and 1940s.

Wilma Lee & Stoney Cooper
(Vocal/instrumental duo, 1940s–77)

This West Virginia-born husband and wife team was a popular duo from the late 1940s until Stoney's death. Favouring the acoustic backing of dobro, fiddle and mandolin, Stoney (1918–77) and Wilma Lee (b. 1921) were stalwart champions of old-time country music who performed on *The Wheeling Jamboree* and the Grand Ole Opry. Their biggest hits included 'Come Walk With Me' and 'Big Midnight Special'.

Cowboy Copas
(Vocals, guitar, 1913–63)

A talented Ohio-born singer and flat-top-style guitarist, Lloyd Copas was a regular performer on the Grand Ole

Smoky Dawson
(Vocals, b. 1913)

Australia's first nationally famous cowboy singer was also a country-music pioneer in his home country. Dawson was born in Warrnambool, Victoria. He first recorded in 1941 and is best known for the song, 'I'm A Happy Go Lucky Cowboy'.

Jim Denny
(Music publisher and agent, 1911–63)

During the 1940s and early 1950s James R. Denny, born in Buffalo Valley, Tennessee, was crucial in transforming Nashville's Grand Ole Opry from a regional barn dance-style radio show into a star-studded national programme. Denny was also central to the growth of Nashville's music industry in the 1950s and early 1960s through his resounding success as a publisher and talent agent.

Left
Popular in the 1940s, Cowboy Copas made a comeback shortly before his death in 1963.

Al Dexter
(Vocals, songwriter, 1905–84)

Born Clarence Albert Poindexter, in Troup, Texas, Dexter recorded a string of hits that were part of the early foundation of honky-tonk, including 'Pistol Packin' Mama' (1944), 'So Long Pal' (1944), 'Guitar Polka' (1946), 'Wine, Women And Song' (1946) and 'Honky-Tonk Blues' (1936).

Below
Australian country singer, yodeller and rodeo rider, Smokey Dawson.

Opry from 1944 until his death in the same plane crash that killed Patsy Cline. Copas is best known for honky-tonk hits like 'Filipino Baby' and 'Tragic Romance'.

Ted Daffan
(Vocals, songwriter, bandleader, 1912–96)

Louisiana-born Theron Eugene Daffan was a noted songwriter and popular bandleader who helped pave the way for honky-tonk music's emergence in the 1940s. Daffan started out in the mid-1930s as part of The Blue Ridge Playboys and The Bar X Cowboys – a pair of regionally popular bands of the day. In 1941, Daffan formed his own band, The Texans, and developed a distinctive sound built around an accordion and Buddy Buller's electrified lead guitar. A few of Daffan's mid-1940s hits, such as 'No Letter Today' (1944), 'Born To Lose' (1944) and 'Headin' Down The Wrong Highway' (1945) are considered cornerstones of early honky-tonk.

Above
Slim Dusty was the most prolific of Australia's country-music stars.

Little Jimmy Dickens
(Vocals, b. 1920)
West Virginia-born James Cecil Dickens was a long-time fixture on the Grand Ole Opry and is best known for the novelty hits he released in the late 1940s and early 1950s, including 'Sleepin' At The Foot Of The Bed', 'I'm Little But I'm Loud' and 'Take An Old Cold Tater And Wait'. Dickens was inducted into the Country Music Hall Of Fame in 1983.

The Duke Of Paducah
(Banjo, comedian, 1901–86)
DeSoto, Missouri-born Benjamin Francis 'Whitey' Johnson was, for decades, one of country music's most popular comedians. He appeared on the *Renfro Valley Barn Dance*, in Kentucky in the late 1930s and starred on an NBC network radio show called *Plantation Party* in the early 1940s. He also appeared frequently on the Grand Ole Opry over the years and hosted a Nashville television show named *Country Junction* in the late 1950s and early 1960s.

Right
The dapper Hawkshaw Hawkins was hugely popular through his appearance on radio shows, despite little recording success.

Slim Dusty
(Vocals, 1927–2003)
David Gordon Kirkpatrick, born near Kempsey, New South Wales, was one of Australia's most popular country artists from the 1950s until his death. He sold in excess of five million records in his home country with hits such as 'A Pub With No Beer' (also a Top 3 success in the UK) and 'Lights On The Hill'.

Red Foley
(Vocals, guitar, harmonica, 1910–68)
Clyde Julian 'Red' Foley was born in Blue Lick, Kentucky, and was central to the surge in country music's popularity in the 1940s and early 1950s with hits like 'Smoke On The Water' (1944), 'Tennessee Saturday Night' (1948), 'Chattanoogie Shoeshine Boy' (1950) and 'Birmingham Bounce' (1950). For three decades, Foley headlined on various popular radio barndance shows, including the *Renfro Valley Barn Dance* in Kentucky, the Grand Ole Opry and the *Ozark Jubilee*, in Springfield, Missouri.

Rex Griffin
(Vocals, songwriter, 1912–58)
Though he died in poverty and obscurity in a New Orleans charity hospital and is little remembered today, Griffin's singing strongly influenced a number of major artists, including Ernest Tubb and Hank Williams. Born in Gadsden, Alabama, Alsie 'Rex' Griffin sang and yodelled in the style of Jimmie Rodgers. He recorded for Decca Records in the mid- and late-1930s, performed on radio stations in Alabama and Texas, and wrote the poignantly mournful 'The Last Letter'.

Hawkshaw Hawkins
(Vocals, guitar, 1921–63)
Harold Franklin Hawkins was born in Huntington, West Virginia, and is best remembered for the 1966 honky-tonk hit shuffle 'Lonesome 7-7203'. He joined the Grand Ole Opry in

1955. His promising career was cut short when he was killed in the same 1963 plane crash that took the life of Patsy Cline and Cowboy Copas.

Johnnie & Jack
(Vocal duo, 1938–63)

One of the most accomplished and influential vocal duos of the 1940s and 1950s, Johnnie Robert Wright (b. 1914) and Jack Anglin (1916–93) joined the Grand Ole Opry in 1947, but soon moved on to Shreveport's *Louisiana Hayride*. The duo is best known for its 1950s hits, including 'Poison Love', 'Cryin' Heart Blues' and 'Goodnight, Sweetheart, Goodnight'.

Grandpa Jones
(Vocals, banjo, 1913–98)

Born in Niagara, Kentucky, Louis Marshall Jones was one of the Grand Ole Opry's most beloved figures for more than 50 years, as well as a popular cast member of *Hee*

Haw, a nationally syndicated country music television comedy show that aired from 1969 to 1994.

Lonzo & Oscar
(Comedy duo, 1945–85)

This popular musical comedy duo went through several personnel changes during its four decades on the Grand Ole Opry. The original Lonzo And Oscar comprised two Kentucky-born brothers, Johnny (1917–67) and Rollin Sullivan (b. 1919). The Sullivans began performing on a Jackson, Tennessee radio station, and in 1945 started working as stage and studio back-up musicians for Eddy Arnold. In 1947, Rollin Sullivan began appearing with Lloyd Leslie George (1924–91), another Arnold backup musician, on the Grand Ole Opry as Lonzo And Oscar. In 1950 Johnny Sullivan rejoined his brother when George left for a solo career. When Johnny died in 1967, Rollin hired Dave Hooten (b. 1935) as his replacement and the two continued performing until Sullivan retired in 1985.

Below

Grandpa Jones was inducted into the Country Music Hall Of Fame in 1978.

Moon Mullican
(Vocals, piano, 1909–67)

Corrigan, Texas-born Aubrey Wilson Mullican often billed himself as 'the king of hillbilly piano players'. Mullican was an accomplished musician with a strong grounding in pop, jazz and blues, and was central in carving out a role for the piano in honky-tonk music.

Molly O'Day
(Vocals, 1923–87)

Kentucky-born Lois LaVerne Williamson had one of the most powerful and emotional voices of any traditional female singer to emerge in the 1940s. In May 1945, O'Day and her husband, guitarist Lynn Davis, became headliners on the *Midday Merry-Go-Round*, a popular radio show broadcast by Radio WNOX in Knoxville, Tennessee. At the urging of songwriter/music publisher Fred Rose, O'Day was signed to Columbia Records by producer Art Satherley. Her notable recordings include 'Tramp On The Street', 'At The First Fall Of Snow' and 'Don't Sell Daddy Any More Whiskey'.

James O'Gwynn
(Vocals, songwriter, b. 1928)

Mississippi-born singer O'Gwynn grew up listening to and emulating Hank Williams and Jimmie Rodgers. During the mid-1950s, he was a feature performer on the *Louisiana Hayride* and was a regular on the Grand Ole Opry for a few years in the early 1960s. He is most often remember for minor hits such as 'Talk To Me Lonesome Heart', 'Blue Memories', 'Easy Money' and How Can I Think of Tomorrow'.

Leon Payne
(Vocals, songwriter, 1917–69)

Born in Alba, Texas, Payne is best known as the writer of 'Lost Highway', which became an enduring classic after it was a hit for Hank Williams in 1949, and 'I Love You Because' (Jim Reeves, 1958), alongside many others. As a recording artist, he had a No. 1 hit in 1949 with his own version of 'I Love You Because'. During the 1930s, Payne sang with various south-western bands, including Bill Boyd's Cowboy Ramblers. After a stint in the 1940s on the *Wheeling Jamboree*, he moved on to Nashville's Grand Ole Opry in 1949.

Minnie Pearl
(Comedian, 1912–96)

Often called 'The Queen of Country Comedy', Sarah Ophelia Colley brought smiles of warmth and endearment to several generations of Grand Ole Opry fans in the comic guise of Minnie Pearl. She was a fixture on the Opry for over half a century.

Webb Pierce
(Vocals, 1921–91)

Louisiana-born Webb Pierce was one of the most popular honky-tonk singers of the post-Hank Williams zenith of the style in the 1950s. Throughout this decade, he dominated the

Far Right
Ray Price was a controversial figure in country music, as he embraced changing trends.

Below
Webb Pierce enjoyed more country No. 1 singles than many artists, including Hank Williams and Eddy Arnold.

charts with hits such as 'Back Street Affair' (1952), 'There Stands The Glass' (1953), and 'Honky-Tonk Song (1957).

Ray Price

(Vocals, bandleader, b. 1926)

One of the most important singers and innovators of the 1950s and 1960s, Perryville, Texas-born Ray Price introduced a more rhythmic and modernized variation of honky-tonk in the 1950s. In the early 1960s Price alienated some honky-tonk fans when he embraced the pop influences of the Nashville Sound, with easy-listening hits like 'Danny Boy' (1967), which featured sophisticated background vocals and occasionally even orchestral backings.

Fred Rose

(Music publisher, songwriter, 1898–1954)

Born in Evansville, Indiana, Fred Rose was a key figure in Nashville's rise from a provincial backwater to an international musical capital. Rose penned a number of country standards, including 'Wait For The Light To Shine' and 'Blue Eyes Cryin' In The Rain'. He began his career in Chicago as a jazz songwriter. In 1933, he moved to Nashville, where he continued to write pop and jazz songs, along with popular western hits, including 'We'll Rest At The End Of the Trail'. He also spent time in Hollywood writing songs for Gene Autry, Roy Rogers and other cowboy film stars. In Nashville, he partnered with Grand Ole Opry star Roy Acuff to found Acuff-Rose, one of Nashville's most successful and influential music-publishing firms. Rose discovered Hank Williams in the late 1940s and helped launch his remarkable career.

Jean Shepard

(Vocals, b. 1933)

Born Ollie Imogene Shepard, in St. Paul's Valley, Oklahoma, Shepard was a pioneer whose honky-tonk earthiness and musical topicality broke new ground in the 1950s. A long-time member of the Grand Ole Opry, she first broke into the charts with 'A Dear John Letter' in 1953 and followed this with a string of honky-tonk hits, including 'A Satisfied Mind' (1955) and 'Beautiful Lies' (1955).

Jimmie Skinner
(Vocals, songwriter, 1909–79)
Born in Blue Lick, Kentucky, James Skinner performed on radio stations in Knoxville, Tennessee, Huntington, West Virginia and elsewhere, worked in Nashville as a successful songwriter and also owned and operated a popular record store in Cincinnati, Ohio, for years.

Carl Smith
(Vocals, b. 1927)
Born in Maynardville, Tennessee, Smith's earliest hits – including 'Let's Live A Little' (1951), 'Let Old Mother Nature Have Her Way' (1951), '(When You Feel Like You're In Love) Don't Just Stand There' (1952) and 'Hey Joe' (1953) – came in the early and mid-1950s. As a singer, Smith started out in the honky-tonk mode of Ernest Tubb

Below
Carl Smith was inducted into the Country Music Hall Of Fame in 2003.

and his friend Hank Williams, but eventually matured into a smoother style that presaged the Nashville Sound. As the 1950s became the 1960s, Smith emerged as a pivotal figure in this transitional period.

Hank Snow
(Vocals, 1914–99)
This Nova Scotia-born singer was one of country music's most popular figures in the 1950s and 1960s, and a Grand Ole Opry headliner for a half century. He recorded over 100 albums and had nearly as many chart singles. For more than a decade he recorded for the Canadian Bluebird label before breaking through in the USA in the early 1950s with hits like 'I'm Moving On' (1950), 'The Golden Rocket' (1950) and 'The Rhumba Boogie' (1951).

Buddy Starcher
(Vocals, multi-instrumentalist, 1906–2001)
Born near Ripley, West Virginia, Oby Edgar Starcher performed on radio stations in Baltimore and elsewhere. From the 1940s until the late 1960s, he recorded for various labels and wrote songs such as 'You've Still Got A Place In My Heart' and 'I'll Still Write Your Name', many of which were popularized by other singers.

Grant Turner
(Radio emcee, 1912–91)
The Texas-born 'Voice of the Grand Ole Opry' served as an announcer on the famed Nashville radio show for nearly 50 years – an accomplishment that led to his becoming the first radio personality to be inducted into the Country Music Hall Of Fame (in 1981).

T. Texas Tyler
(Vocals, 1916–72)
Born David Luke Myrick, in Mena, Texas, Tyler first rose to prominence as a member of the *Louisiana Hayride* and later recorded a string of sentimental hits, including 'Filipino Baby' (1946), 'Deck Of Cards' (1948), 'My Bucket's Got A Hole In It' (1949) and 'Bummin' Around' (1953).

Kitty Wells
(Vocals, b. 1919)
Born Muriel Deason, in Nashville, Tennessee, Kitty Wells was one of the first women to achieve stardom in country music. Wells began singing in the 1930s with her cousin

Faron Young

(Vocals, 1932–96)

Young reigned as one of country music's most popular figures, frequently topping the charts with honky-tonk anthems like 'Live Fast, Love Hard, Die Young' (1955), 'I've Got Five Dollars And It's Saturday Night' (1956) and the Willie Nelson-penned 'Hello Walls'. In the late 1960s and early 1970s, he also had success with mellow Nashville Sound hits like 'Wine Me Up' (1969) and 'It's Four In The Morning' (1971).

Left
Honky-tonk angel Kitty Wells was married to Johnnie Wright, of Johnnie And Jack.

Below
Faron Young had a long and prolific career, later embracing several pop-crossover tunes.

Bessie Choate as The Deason Sisters. In 1938, she married singer Johnnie Wright, who would later partner with Jack Anglin in the popular vocal duo, Johnnie And Jack. After singing for a while with her husband and making a few gospel recordings, Wells decided to leave music behind and raise a family. But in 1952, around the time that Johnny And Jack joined the Grand Ole Opry, Paul Cohen, an A&R man at Decca Records, paired Wells with a song called 'It Wasn't God Who Made Honky Tonk Angels', written as an 'answer' song to Hank Thompson's 1952 chart-topper 'The Wild Side Of Life'. Ultimately, Wells' song became nearly as big a hit as Thompson's. The single was No. 1 for six weeks in the summer of 1952, sold 800,000 copies – and even spilled over into the pop charts.

Doc & Chickee Williams

(Vocal duo, 1930s–60s)

For years, husband and wife vocal team Andrew John Smik (b. 1914) and Jesse Wanda Crupe (b. 1919) sang on *WWVA Jamboree*, in Wheeling, West Virginia, and earned regional popularity within that radio show's wide broadcast area. The Williamses were champions of old-time country music and their band The Border Riders created a unique sound that relied heavily on fiddle and accordion.

ernest tubb ⊙ 106 **hank williams** ⊙ 108 **johnnie & jack** ⊙ 113

There's A New Moon Over My Shoulder:
The West Coast Scene

althugh one tends to think of Nashville as the primary source for country music, many other regions contributed to this music's growth, especially the West Coast, where migrant workers from Oklahoma, Texas and other regions of the Southwest played a vital role in putting California on the country-music map.

With Los Angeles as its focal point, the Golden State's country-music scene blossomed. This was due to a number of factors: the singing cowboys of the Hollywood movies; the influx of the western-swing bands and other artists; the boom business of the ballrooms and dancehalls; the radio stations and, later, television shows programming country; the development of recording studios, which moved sessions away from places such as Dallas, Nashville and Chicago; and the creation of Capitol Records, which would – in a few short years – be a giant among the independents and challenging the majors at their own game.

At the same time, Bakersfield – a small town situated some 160 km (100 miles) away from Los Angeles – was fostering a new breed of musician that would provide an alternative to the smooth countrypolitan sounds that were streaming out of Nashville in the late 1950s. Sporting its own roster of local artists, with the likes of bandleader Bill Woods and entrepreneur Herb Henson as catalysts, it created a new, edgy, vibrant sound and introduced two entertainers who would become icons – Buck Owens and Merle Haggard.

The West Coast, with Los Angeles and Bakersfield as the main hubs of activity, gave Nashville a run for its money, but it was relatively short-lived, as Tennessee's Music City gained clout with an abundance of artists and executives, recording studios and record labels.

Key Artists
Merle Haggard

Buck Owens

Tex Ritter

Merle Travis

Influences
& Development

'I got to realizing that I wanted to record, I wanted to experiment. And doing those same old songs the same old way – I said, "I think it's time for me to have some fun"'.
Buck Owens

Below
Wesley Tuttle – one of the changing faces of The Beverly Hill Billies.

Like the USA itself, country music in California was built upon migrant forces, in relation to both musicians and audiences. Unlike Nashville, whose growth was mainly dependent upon local musicians, the Golden State scarcely produced any homegrown talent but, rather, was dependent upon the influx of migrant workers from other states. The greater number of these arrived from

Oklahoma's poverty-stricken Dust Bowl region and all settled in California in search of a better life, many finding work in the munitions plants during the war years. Hot on their heels came the artists, assured of an audience ready for their stylings of hillbilly, honky-tonk and western swing. So, while Tennessee and the Southeast had their own brand of country music, so did the West Coast. To many it became known as 'Okie' music.

Californian Country

Californian country was very different from the music coming out of Nashville, and was uninhibited in content and presentation. It tackled subjects that would have been scorned in the Southeast's Bible Belt and presented it in a louder, looser and, often, rowdier fashion. Although old-time Appalachian fiddlers played at dances, much of the music of the Southeast was a 'listening' music, performed in family circles, churches and other, generally more refined, establishments, the West Coast's music originated from bands used to playing dancehalls, where the music had to compete with noise from raucous crowds.

California had never been completely devoid of country music, though. In common with the eastern regions, it grew out of the fiddle music of the earliest settlers and was complemented by instruments such as the guitar (and its variants, the steel guitar and the dobro), banjo, mandolin and accordion – all from diverse sources. The material of the early country performers was similarly widespread, with traditional folk songs and vaudeville just two of its early sources.

The Crockett Family and The Beverly Hill Billies are credited as being among California's first country-music acts. The first, a genuine family act originally from West Virginia, performed western songs and popular hillbilly fare during the 1930s, moving from local Fresno radio to top status in Los Angeles and New York. Son Johnny Crockett also enjoyed great success as a songwriter. The better-known Beverley Hill Billies were the creation of radio-station (KMPC) manager Glen Rice, who took professional entertainers Leo ('Zeke Craddock') Mannes, Tom Murray and Cyprian ('Ezra Longnecker') Paulette – quickly joined by Henry ('Hank Skillet') Blaeholder and Aleth ('Lem H. Giles, H.D. [Horse Doctor]') Hansen – and attired them as a novelty hillbilly act. The success of the venture made them one of the most popular acts of the 1930s and ensured that the group (with changing personnel, among them Stuart Hamblen, Elton Britt and Wesley Tuttle) remained in business for a further 30 years. The last-known incarnation successfully won a lawsuit against the producers of the television series *The Beverley Hillbillies* for infringement of their name in 1963.

The Singing Cowboy Craze

With radio providing the first opportunities for country music, Hollywood quickly provided the next with the 'singing cowboys'. Cowboys provided a genuinely popular image. Originally read about in dime novels, they came to life in the movies – and music gave them another, equally popular, dimension. As they were real-image figures, the likes of Gene Autry (1907–98) and Roy Rogers (1911–98) used their own names as the characters they portrayed in their movies. Horse operas became big business and the studios

desperately sought out actors who could sing, or vice versa, to meet the endless public demand. By the decade's end, virtually every studio possessed its own singing cowboy.

By the early 1940s Hollywood had become a Mecca for country music, not only for the endless parade of 'singing-cowboy' horse operas, but also for several Nashville country-music stars keen to further their careers with a headlining role in a low-budget 'B' movie. Originally the domain of the poverty-row studios, even the majors soon saw the opportunity to make additional dollars by putting the likes of Roy Acuff (1903–92), Ernest Tubb (1914–84) or Eddy Arnold (b. 1918) – often supported by a familiar line-up of other country artists – in front of the cameras. The acting and the plots might have left something to be desired, but the popularity of the music overcame such shortcomings.

Above

Fiddle player and music publisher Roy Acuff was one of the many to find a place in front of the camera during the singing cowboy craze.

Left

Gene Autry and Roy Rogers – the two most famous singing cowboys.

Above
Spade Cooley And His Orchestra played a significant role in bringing the country music of the West Coast to the public eye.

The Success Of Capitol

Equally vital in the development of California country music were the western-swing bands, including Bob Wills And His Texas Playboys, Spade Cooley And His Orchestra and, later, breakaway Cooley vocalist Tex Williams (1917–85), who headed up his Western Caravan. All attracted sellout crowds at a number of vast dancehalls, such as the Venice Pier, Santa Monica Ballroom and Riverside Rancho in Los Angeles, the Big Barn in Fresno or, in Wills' case, his own Wills Point, located in Sacramento.

It was under such favourable conditions – which outweighed the problems of a shellac shortage – that pop songwriter Johnny Mercer, businessman Glenn Wallichs, and movie producer Buddy De Sylva joined forces to form a new independent label, Capitol Records, on 8 April 1942. With their sights first set on the pop market, they were not foolish enough to overlook the country audience that existed in their own backyard. A country-music department was set up under the direction of Lee Gillette, with Cliffie Stone and Ken Nelson (who took over A&R operations in 1951) playing key roles. Tex Ritter (1907–73) became the first country artist signed to the roster and gave the fledgling label its first country hit with 'Jingle Jangle

Jingle' (1942). Five years later Tex Williams gave the label its first million seller, 'Smoke Smoke Smoke' (1947). Although a number of its initial artists had movie connections, Capitol soon mounted a substantial country roster, with artists such as Merle Travis (1917–83), Ferlin Husky (b. 1927), Faron Young (1932–96) and Hank Thompson (b. 1925). Soon the major labels found themselves facing serious competition from their small independent rivals.

Right
Hank Thompson was one of many artists to ride on the wave of Capitol's interest in country music.

New Media

Country music gained further attention thanks to television. Just as radio had brought the music to mass audience during 1930s, with Stuart Hamblen (1908–89) among the medium's most popular personalities, so television began to make its mark in the post-war years. A major reason for the demise of the ballrooms, television gave Los Angeles' audiences their first taste of country music with *Hometown Jamboree* (1948–59), hosted by the ubiquitous Cliffie Stone (1917–98). Another favourite was *Hollywood Barn Dance*, developed from the radio show that commenced in 1932, though it was *Town Hall Party* (1952–60) that proved the real winner. With Tex Ritter and Jay Stewart among its hosts, this three-hour Saturday-night series was broadcast live from the Town Hall dancehall in Compton, a Los Angeles suburb, and featured a regular lineup alongside guests. Soon sections of the show were picked up for national transmission, while an offshoot, *Western Ranch Party*, commenced in 1957.

The Bakersfield Scene

Around the same time, some 160 km (100 miles) north-east of Los Angeles, a fresh country sound was being heard in Bakersfield. This small Kern County township had its share of bars, clubs and dance halls, but here the music – like the nightspots – were raw and gritty, unlike Los Angeles' more up-market establishments. Several people were responsible for the music's popularity. One was the entrepreneurial Jimmy Thompson, who booked talent into the area. Another was Herb Henson, who was always keen to present new artists on his highly popular television shows. In many people's opinion, though, local bandleader Bill Woods (1924–2000) was the real catalyst, initially employing both Buck Owens (1929–2006) and Merle Haggard (b. 1937) in his outfit, The Orange Blossom Playboys.

Another Bakersfield founding father, Wynn Stewart (1934–85), gave Haggard his first band job. By the early 1960s, Owens, who had successfully fused country with rock'n'roll, had firmly put Bakersfield on the international map, though his reign was soon to be challenged by Haggard.

Capitol was there to sign the Bakersfield artists and Ken Nelson gave many of them the artistic freedom to arrange and use their own bands on the recording sessions. The result was a sharper, more edgy sound, which greatly contrasted with anything coming out of Nashville, especially as Music City was then in its first stages of chasing the pop crossover market and winning new record buyers with its clean cut 'Nashville Sound'.

Sadly, it was Nashville that held the winning hand. Although the West Coast country industry formed its own trade organization, the Academy Of Country Music, created in 1964 to best serve the area's industry needs, the majority of country artists were soon recording in Nashville – even those Capitol acts that had built careers through the West Coast sessions. By then the popularity of the dancehalls and the western-swing bands had diminished, and the singing cowboys had ridden into the sunset, leaving Nashville to become the home of commercial country music.

Below

Wanda Jackson – a key artist to come out of the West Coast scene.

Country Music On The Silver Screen

The singing cowboys did not have the monopoly on country music on the silver screen, although it was their breed that first caught Hollywood's attention. By the time the 1940s rolled around, several of Nashville's top stars found that they could expand their careers by bringing their talents to the vast new audiences.

Singing Stars

In the earlier decade Gene Autry – generally credited as the first singing cowboy – brought his music to the silver screen in *Tumbling Tumbleweeds*, released by Republic in 1935. He wasn't actually the first, though. Ken Maynard, initially seen in silent movies, sang occasionally when sound found its way into film, though the authenticity of John Wayne's vocals have been questioned when he appeared as 'Singing Sandy' in one of his numerous Lone Star productions.

But Autry's role as the 'first' may not have even happened if Warner Bros. hadn't delayed the release of Dick Foran's *Treachery Rides The Range* (1936). Then the floodgates were opened and every studio searched for their own singing cowboy. Roy Rogers came to Republic, the studio with the greatest western output, as a replacement for their star Autry following a studio dispute (Rogers was later joined by his wife Dale Evans in several movies and a long-running 1950s television series). Tex Ritter signed up with the poverty-row outlet Monogram Pictures. Among the many others were Eddie Dean, Jimmy Wakely, Monte Hale and Ray Whitley, the writer of Autry's theme song 'Back In The Saddle Again', while Rex Allen was the last of the breed. Throughout, there was always a mass of West Coast singers and musicians available for support roles. There was also a black singing cowboy, Herb Jeffries (b. 1911); a singing cowgirl, Dorothy Page (1904–61); and Mexican interpretations, like 'Pedro Infante'.

Roy Acuff and Ernest Tubb were the first from Nashville to take a trip to Hollywood, making their sporadic film debuts in *Grand Ole Opry* (1940) and *The Fighting Buckaroo* (1943) respectively. The former also boasted the only screen appearance by the iconic Uncle Dave Macon and his son Dorris. Eddy Arnold, who virtually took over the country charts in the post-war years, made a handful of films beginning with *Feudin' Rhythm* (1949), before hosting one of the earliest television series *The Eddy Arnold Show* (1952).

Walking The Line

Then, in the 1950s, as rock'n'roll found screen time via low budget 'B' movies, similarly so did country music. Ferlin Husky made a handful of movies commencing with *Country Music Holiday* (1958), while such productions as *Hootenanny Hoot* (1963), *Country Music on Broadway* (1965), *Forty Acre Feud* (1965) and *The Road To Nashville* (1967) were little more than an excuse to see a surfeit of artists performing. Marty Robbins and Johnny Cash sought

Below

Ernest Tubb and Sissy Spacek star in Coal Miner's Daughter.

included the rock remake of *A Star Is Born* (1976) with Barbra Streisand. In 1992 Texas honky-tonk superstar George Strait starred in a movie, *Pure Country*. And, more recently, Randy Travis has been building a positive reputation as an actor.

Country music has frequently been found on soundtracks, none more effectively than the plaintive sound of Hank Williams adding to the imagery of Peter Bogdanovich's *The Last Picture Show* (1971). The music found great allies in Clint Eastwood and Burt Reynolds, both featuring country songs and artists in several of their movies, with the latter building a friendship with singer/songwriter Jerry Reed, himself enjoying a flurry of film roles in the 1980s.

out more precise movie careers, with the former complementing his distinctive vocals with dramatic roles that included *Hell On Wheels* (1967) and the western *Guns Of A Stranger* (1973). Robbins also produced a television series, *The Drifter*, which never found its way on to the screen. Cash, whose dramatic debut was in the best-forgotten *One Minute To Live* (1958), developed a fairly substantial career as a film actor, with one of his best performances witnessed in *A Gunfight* (1971) opposite Kirk Douglas. A biopic, *Walk The Line* (2005), featured Joaquin Phoenix as the late superstar and Oscar-winner Reese Witherspoon as his wife June Carter.

Other movies that detailed country stars' trials and tribulations have included *Coal Miner's Daughter* (1980) (in which Sissy Spacek gave an Oscar-winning performance as Loretta Lynn) and *Sweet Dreams* (1985) (Beverly D'Angelo as Patsy Cline). There have also been television movies on the lives of The Judds, Dottie West and Tammy Wynette, among others, while the tragic tale of Spade Cooley hasn't yet progressed beyond the drawing board.

Arguably the most successful of the country-music fraternity to make it into movies was singer-songwriter Kris Kristofferson who, after debuting in Dennis Hopper's *The Last Movie* (1971), moved on to major roles that

Merle Haggard

Key Artist

young son – after the death of his father – frequently saw the inside of juvenile homes and prisons as he paid the price for his lawless aggression.

Misspent Youth

At the same time, Merle Haggard possessed a deep passion for country music, and started playing guitar at the age of 12, encouraged by the recordings of his idols Bob Wills, Hank Williams and Lefty Frizzell. Frizzell in particular offered encouragement and welcomed Haggard to his stage. The positive audience reaction persuaded Haggard to think seriously about a music career but, as his criminal records increased, he eventually served time in San Quentin. It was there that he realized that he could not continue his life as it was and, after a period of rehabilitation, he was granted parole in 1960.

Initially he returned to his earlier, pre-prison occupation of digging ditches, but soon found that the income from playing local venues was enough to make ends meet. His situation was made even more secure when he joined Wynn Stewart's band as bassist in 1962. Around the same time, he came to the attention of Fuzzy Owen, who offered him a deal on Tally Records, a small label that he co-owned with his cousin Louis Talley.

Wynn Stewart provided the right ingredient, 'Sing A Sad Song' (1963), and Haggard debuted in the nation's Top 20 with this, his first single. Three releases later he went Top 10 with a Liz Anderson song '(My Friends Are Gonna Be) Strangers' (1965) and Capitol Records bought up the Tally contract.

'If ever there was a poet for the working class … Merle Haggard would be my nomination.'
David Allen Coe

Above
Merle Haggard threw off his early reputation as a bad boy to become one of country music's best-loved artists.

In the Bakersfield family tree, the likes of Bill Woods and Wynn Stewart set the stage, Buck Owens put the town on the map, and Merle Haggard was the heir apparent. 'The Hag', as he is often known, also had the distinction of actually being born in Bakersfield, on 6 April 1937. His parents, James and Flossie Haggard, were victims of the Depression and moved to California from Oklahoma in search of the better life, while their

Classic Recordings

Sing Me Back Home (1968)
'Sing Me Back Home', 'Wine Takes Me Away', 'Mom and Dad's Waltz'

Big City (1981)
'Big City', 'My Favorite Memory', 'Are The Good Times Really Over'

Pancho & Lefty (1983)
'Pancho & Lefty', 'Reasons To Quit'

Untamed Hawk (1995)
5-CD box set featuring early recordings 1962–68

If I Could Only Fly (2000)
'Wishing All These Old Things Were New', 'If I Could Only Fly', 'Proud To Be Your Old Man'

Left

Even in the twenty-first century, Merle Haggard's songs and recordings show no signs of dating.

Once on the major label, Hag's songwriting came to the fore and, by late 1966, he was riding towards his first No. 1 with 'The Fugitive', a reflection of past bad times, and a career that would realize over 100 chart records, flirtations with other labels after Capitol (to which he returned in 2005), and the establishment of iconic status furthered by induction into the Country Music Hall Of Fame in 1994.

The Secret Of Hag's Success

Merle Haggard's great success was dependent upon a number of factors, primarily his interest in music derived from a melting-pot of sources and distinctive vocal skills reflective of artists such as Frizzell and Stewart. His album catalogue is highly original and includes concept tributes to Bob Wills and Jimmie Rodgers, Dixieland jazz and religion. He was acknowledged as a 'poet of the common people', with his songs telling of man's toil, trials and tribulations, with equal adroitness displayed in his political comments, representing the right with 'Okie From Muskogee' (1969) and 'The Fighting Side Of Me' (1970). He is also a masterful arranger and musician and when on stage with his band, The Strangers, mixes his classic songs with skilful guitar work and the occasional breakdown on a fiddle left to him by Bob Wills. He acknowledges that much of the success of his early, ground-breaking recordings was due to Ken Nelson, a producer who took a 'hands-off' studio approach, leaving Haggard to his own inventiveness and intuition.

Far Left

Merle Haggard's lasting popularity is attributed to his diverse influences and his masterful arrangements.

Key Track

'Okie From Muskogee' (1969)
The song that cemented Haggard's stardom although, at the time, caused a certain amount of controversy, allying the singer to America's right in support of the Vietnam War and condemnation of hippie culture. Some sources subsequently revealed that Haggard said it had been written 'with tongue in cheek'.

Buck Owens

'I always had a lot of driving-type music in my bones. I always loved music that had lots of beat. I always wanted to sound like a locomotive comin' right through the front room.' **Buck Owens**

Although Bakersfield had already played host to a number of country-music artists, it was Buck Owens (1929–2006) who not only put it on the map, but also spread its name around the world. So great was his impact, some even called it 'Buckersfield'.

Below
Buck Owens was a leading light in the Bakersfield Scene.

The Road To Bakersfield

Hailing from Sherman, Texas, and born Alvis Edgar Owens on 12 August 1929, his family moved to Mesa, Arizona, when he was a child. There he learned to play the guitar, eventually performing on local radio stations and working the honky-tonks and clubs around Phoenix. He married Bonnie Campbell and, with two children, moved to Bakersfield in 1951, where he eventually became the lead singer and rhythm guitarist in Bill Wood's Orange Blossom Playboys. With his reputation growing, he formed his own band, The Schoolhouse Playboys, and started playing on recording sessions for Capitol, commencing with Tommy Collins' 'You Better Not Do That'. More work followed during the mid-1950s, as producer Ken Nelson hired him to back up both country and pop artists including Wanda Jackson, Tommy Sands and Faron Young.

on the map. It was around that time that Owens formed his own band, The Buckaroos, and thanks to the freewheeling approach of producer Ken Nelson, the group was soon accompanying their boss on his recording sessions. Owens' first No. 1 came with the Johnny Russell-penned 'Act Naturally' (1963), though Owens carried writer's credit on many of the 15 chart-toppers that followed, including 'Love's Gonna Live Here' (1963), 'My Heart Skips A Beat' (1964), 'Together Again' (1964) and 'Sam's Place' (1967). Nevertheless Chuck Berry did get a look-in with a revival of 'Johnny B. Goode' (1969).

Soon Buck Owens was empire building. By the mid-1960s he had clearly displayed his business acumen as the already successful Blue Book Music (with Howard now bought out) was joined by Buck Owens Enterprises, OMAC Artists Corporation (a booking agency), the ownership of four radio stations and his own weekly, syndicated Buck Owens Ranch television series. By the end of the decade he was operating his own state-of-the-art studio and recording artists that Capitol would promote and market. These included Susan Raye and his son Buddy Alan, alongside his own recordings.

Although the 1980s saw the hits slow down, and a label move from Capitol to Warner Bros., Owens became a television personality when he co-hosted the long running country-comedy series *Hee Haw* with the multi-talented Roy Clark. He made a partial return to recording, thanks to the encouragement of Dwight Yoakam, a committed Buck Owens fan and one of the many contemporary artists he had influenced. He was elected to the Country Music Hall Of Fame in 1998 and died eight years later, on 25 March, following an appearance at Crystal Palace, a nightspot he owned in Bakersfield.

Owens made his recording debut in 1956, cutting tracks for the small independent Pep label, including rockabilly tracks under the name Corky Jones. Although unsuccessful, these recordings further increased the interest in Owens, and Ken Nelson, at first unconvinced of Owens' vocal talents, eventually signed him to a deal. His first releases, country-pop and unsuited to the artist's energetic styling, failed to impress. In the meantime, Owens – already a prolific songwriter – had become friends with another young songwriter, Harlan Howard, and together they created their own music operation, Blue Book Music, to publish their songs (and, later, Merle Haggard's earliest titles). It was an Owens' original, 'Second Fiddle', that finally gave him his first chart entry in 1959, with the follow-up, 'Under Your Spell Again' going Top 5 and opening the way for two decades of virtually non-stop chart activity.

The Buck Owens Empire

Buck Owens' success was dependent on a combination of ear-catching songs and a distinctive, twangy approach to honky-tonk, assisted by longtime friend Don Rich (vocals, guitar, fiddle, 1941–74) who added infectious close harmonies. When the two started playing Fender Telecasters, the resultant rock-influenced sound put Bakersfield squarely

Classic Recordings

Buck Owens Sings Harlan Howard (1961)
'I've Got A Tiger By The Tail', 'Above And Beyond', 'Excuse Me (I Think I've Got A Heartache)', 'Foolin' Around'

Buck Owens Sings Tommy Collins (1964)
'If You Ain't Livin' (You Ain't Lovin')', 'High on A Hilltop', 'Whatcha Gonna Do Now'.

Together Again/My Heart Skips A Beat (1964)
'My Heart Skips A Beat', 'Save The Last Dance For Me', 'Together Again'

Open Up Your Heart (1967)
'Open Up Your Heart', 'Think Of Me', 'Sam's Place'

The Buck Owens Collection (1959–1990) (1992)
All the classics in a 3-CD box set

Above
In later years, Buck Owens was encouraged back into the recording studio, where he proved his talents hadn't waned.

Left
One of Owens' earliest associations was with 'the Sherriff' – Faron Young.

Key Track

'Act Naturally' (1963)
A hit that Buck Owens didn't write – it was penned by Johnny Russell – but it gave him his first No. 1 and was later covered by The Beatles. He re-recorded the song as a duet with Ringo Starr at London's Abbey Road Studios in 1989.

Tex Ritter

Key Artist

Singing cowboy Tex Ritter enjoyed two distinctive careers, the first as 'America's most beloved cowboy' (a title bestowed on him by a Hollywood publicist), and second as a recording artist and stage performer, albeit still making occasional film appearances. He also recorded one of the most memorable western themes of all time – 'High Noon'.

A Screen Icon

Born Maurice Woodward Ritter in Panola County, Texas, on 12 January 1907, his musical career commenced while studying law at the University of Texas. There he created a lecture and song programme, *The Texas Cowboy And His Songs*, which led to touring and radio spots and, in 1931, a role in the Broadway production of *Green Grow The Lilacs* (later revised by Rodgers & Hammerstein as *Oklahoma*). With more stage work and radio performances behind him,

'Tex Ritter bought me my first gunbelt because I loved quickdraws.'
Dick Dale

Ritter approached Art Satherley at ARC, and the producer – obviously aware of Ritter's fine deep voice and his penchant for cowboy songs – set up a recording session that included the traditional 'Rye Whiskey' (1932), which would become a *tour-de-force* showcase song for Ritter in subsequent years when he re-recorded it. Further sessions followed, but none created too much interest and he continued with his radio and stage work. When he returned to the recording studios – this time for Decca – his career had begun to move in a different direction, having come to the attention of Ed Finney, a publicist at the newly formed Grand National Pictures. The result was *Song Of The Gringo* (1936), a movie that marked the commencement of a two-year, 12-picture connection with the company. He subsequently made movies for Monogram, Columbia, Universal and PRC, notching up a staggering 58 productions in nine years – more than any other of his silver-screen compatriots – and exited from the genre with *The Texas Rangers* (1945).

Musical Success

On the music front, Tex Ritter formed a group in the late 1930s. He first called it The Texas Tornadoes then, later, more simply, Texans. They featured on several of his Decca recordings but, once again, the reaction was lukewarm and it wasn't until he became one of the first artists to sign with the newly launched Capitol Records that his fortunes changed. He debuted with '(I've Got Spurs That) Jingle Jangle Jingle' in 1942, and quickly topped the charts with 'I'm Wasting My Tears On You' (1944). 'You Two-Timed Me One Time Too Often' (1945) was his biggest country hit, remaining at the top of the charts for 11 consecutive weeks, firmly strengthening the Ritter-Capitol relationship that would last until his death, over 30 years later. His many albums covered diverse material, from western and folk songs to gospel, from patriotic salutes to narrations, children's songs and straight country yet, strangely, the theme song from the movie *High Noon* (1952) was never a chart success, although it became synonymous with the singer.

After the singing-cowboy movies, Tex Ritter supported his successful recording career with touring, television and the occasional film role, with the West Coast *Town Hall Party* and *Ranch Party* television shows ensuring prime visibility. He was inducted into the Country Music Hall Of Fame in 1964 and, the following year, moved to Nashville, where he joined the Grand Ole Opry and held down a two-year presidency of the Country Music Association, the trade organization that he helped form. He even made a bid, though unsuccessful, for the US Senate in 1970. Four years later, on 2 January 1974, he died from a heart attack while bailing a band member out of jail (for non-payment of alimony).

Tex Ritter's legacy was carried on by his wife, the former actress Dorothy Fay (1915–2003), who became a goodwill ambassador for both Tennessee and the Grand Ole Opry, and son John Ritter (1948–2003), the actor who made his mark in the *Three's Company* television series.

Classic Recordings

Blood On The Saddle (1960)
'Blood On The Saddle', 'Rye Whiskey', 'Little Joe The Wrangler', 'Boll Weevel'

Hillbilly Heaven (1961)
'I Dreamed Of Hillbilly Heaven', 'High Noon', Deck Of Cards'

Chuck Wagon Days (1969)
'Git Along, Little Doggies', 'Red River Valley', 'Home On The Range', 'A Cowboy's Prayer'

Country Music Hall Of Fame (1991)
Decca recordings: 'Sam Hall', 'Sing Cowboy Sing', 'Boots And Saddles', 'Singin' In The Saddle'

Capitol Collectors Series (1992)
'Jingle Jangle Jingle', 'There's A New Moon Over My Shoulder', 'I'm Wasting My Tears On You', 'You Two Timed Me One Time Too Often'

Above
Ritter stars with Rita Hayworth and Yakima Canutt in 1937's Trouble In Texas.

Far Left
Tex Ritter – the most prolific singing-cowboy movie star of the era.

Below Left
Ritter recorded the famous theme tune to the movie High Noon, *although it was never a commercial success for the star.*

Key Track

'High Noon' (1952)
Officially known as 'Do Not Forsake Me (Oh My Darling)', Tex Ritter was heard on the soundtrack without the steady drum beat that gave Frankie Laine the international hit. Ritter quickly recorded the song again, with drums, in London – but it was too late.

Merle Travis

Above

Travis's distinctive guitar only displayed one side of his considerable talents. He was also a singer, songwriter, author, cartoonist and actor.

'I owe my soul ... to Tennessee Ernie Ford.' **Merle Travis**

Coal-Miner's Son

Travis was born on 29 November 1917 in Rosewood, Muhlenberg County, Kentucky. The life of his coal-mining father and the family's frugal lifestyle provided the source for many of the songs that would later secure his reputation. First learning to play the banjo, then given a guitar when he was 12 years old, he joined Clayton McMichen's Georgia Wildcats in 1937. Shortly afterwards he became a member of The Drifting Pioneers, holding down a permanent gig at Chicago's WLW. He teamed with Grandpa Jones (vocals, banjo, 1913–98) and The Delmore Brothers (Alton: vocals, guitar, 1908–64; Rabon: vocals, guitar, 1916–52) as The Brown's Ferry Four, a gospel quartet, then later with Jones as The Shepherd Brothers, becoming the first act to record for the newly launched King Records. By 1944 Travis had gained a national reputation and headed west to Hollywood, where he made appearances in several low-budget Charles Starrett westerns and performed with Ray Whitley's Western Swing Band.

He signed with Capitol Records and achieved success with his first release, the double-sided hit 'No Vacancy' b/w 'Cincinnati Lou' (1946), which was quickly followed by the No. 1 'Divorce Me C.O.D' (1946). The following year he released the 78-rpm concept album *Folk Songs Of The Hills*, a collection based upon his childhood years and the coal mines. Although it was a commercial failure at the time, it introduced several Travis originals – including 'Sixteen Tons' and 'Dark As A Dungeon', both now regarded as classics, while later interest in the album played a role in establishing the following decade's urban folk movement.

Songwriting Success

As a songwriter he wrote 'Smoke Smoke Smoke' (with Tex Williams recording), giving Capitol Records its first million-seller in 1947. It enjoyed lengthy runs at the top of both the country and pop charts. 'Tennessee' Ernie Ford achieved the same crossover feat eight years

Merle Travis was both a vital cog in the development of the West Coast country scene and a major influence on a whole generation of guitarists. Highly innovative, he had a style of three-finger playing named after him – 'Travis picking' – and the equally skilled Chet Atkins well acknowledged the Travis influence, although the latter modestly shrugged off such compliments, crediting Ike Everly (the father of Don and Phil) and Mose Rager for his own inspiration.

later, with 'Sixteen Tons'. In his own right, Travis scored another No. 1 with 'So Round, So Firm, So Fully Packed' (1947) and, while the chart success of his recordings may have slowed down in the 1950s, he maintained a heavy schedule as a much-sought-after session musician, in particular with longtime friend Hank Thompson. Together they scored a Top 5 hit with 'Wildwood Flower' (1955).

A regular on the *Hometown Jamboree* and *Town Hall Party* television shows, he displayed dramatic flair and change of direction with a supporting role in the Oscar-winning *From Here To Eternity* (1953). But alongside his creativity – which also included devising the first solid-body electric guitar (further developed by Leo Fender, and much used in the early days of rock'n'roll) – there was a wild streak that led to several police arrests on charges of drunk driving (on his motorcycle), narcotics and assault on his wife. Nevertheless, he continued to maintain a regular recording schedule, winning a 1974 Grammy (Best Country Instrumental Performance) for his collaboration with Chet Atkins, *The Atkins-Travis Traveling Show*, and having several albums released by the traditional country label CMH Records.

Merle Travis was elected into the Country Music Hall Of Fame in 1977. He died on 20 October 1983 following a massive coronary attack.

Classic Recordings

Folk Songs Of The Hills (1947)/*Songs Of The Coal Mines* (1965)
'Sixteen Tons', 'Nine Pound Hammer', 'Dark As A Dungeon', 'Barbara Allen'

The Atkins-Travis Traveling Show (1974)
With Chet Atkins: Muskrat Ramble', 'Cannonball Rag', 'I'll See You In My Dreams'

Guitar Rags & A Too Fast Past (1994)
5 CD box set, the complete works 1943–55

Above
Merle Travis's best-known song, 'Sixteen Tons', was a comedy number, but also addressed serious social issues.

Left
Travis spent the final years of his life in Oklahoma with his fourth wife Dorothy, the former Mrs Hank Thompson.

Key Track

'Sixteen Tons' (1946)
Although, arguably, the most famous of all coal-mining songs, Merle Travis didn't take his composition seriously, pointing out its 'mixture of pure drama and absurd imagery'. 'Tennessee' Ernie Ford made it a million-selling country and pop hit in 1955.

A-Z of Artists

Above

Rex Allen's father – a fiddle player – gave him his first guitar when he was 11 years old, intending that his son support him at dances.

Right

On radio, Judy Canova's hillbilly persona attracted over 18 million listeners, and beneath weird facial expressions and yodelling, she possessed considerable business acumen.

Rex Allen
(Vocals, actor, narrator, 1920–99)

The last of the singing cowboys, Arizona-born Rex Allen made 19 movies for Republic before the genre ended with his *The Phantom Stallion* (1954). His powerful voice ensured several chart successes – the highest being 'Crying In The Chapel' (1953) – and a long career as a narrator for several Disney documentaries. The musical tradition has been carried on by his son, Rex Allen Jr. (b. 1947), and they collaborated on the album *The Singing Cowboys* (1995).

Johnny Bond
(Vocals, guitar, 1915–78)

Oklahoma-born Johnny Bond originally formed a trio with Jimmy Wakely and gained national attention on Gene Autry's *Melody Ranch* radio show. He made appearances in several singing-cowboy movies, first as a member of The Jimmy Wakely Trio, then leading his own group, The Red River Valley Boys. A prolific songwriter, he is best remembered for 'Cimarron' (the title he adopted for his own group) and for his comic rendition of '10 Little Bottles' (1965), his most successful chart recording. Steady radio work was followed by a move to television, and he was seen on the *Town Hall Party* as musician, host and scriptwriter. He formed a music-publishing company with Tex Ritter and, after Ritter's death, Bond wrote his biography, *The Tex Ritter Story*.

Judy Canova
(Vocals, comedienne, actress, 1916–83)

Beginning her professional career with brother Leon and sister Diane in Florida, Judy Canova appeared on New York's Broadway in the early 1930s before beginning her 15-year, 17-movie career with *Scatterbrain* (1940). She was Republic Picture's top female attraction, and one of several country-orientated comedy acts to enjoy a substantial film career. Others included The Hoosier Hot Shots and The Weaver Brothers And Elvira.

Zeke Clements
(Vocals, songwriter, 1911–94)

Much underrated and overlooked, Zeke Clements combined cowboy songs with fine yodelling, and moved around the nation's radio stations – WLS (Chicago), WSM (Nashville) and other locations – before arriving in Hollywood and voicing the cartoon character Bashful in Walt Disney's *Snow White And The Seven Dwarfs* (1937). After several movie appearances, he returned to Nashville's WSM, became a member of the Grand Ole Opry, built up a substantial reputation as a songwriter and founded his own record label (Liberty).

Tommy Collins
(Vocals, guitar, songwriter, 1930–2000)

One of the earliest pioneers of the Bakersfield Sound, Oklahoma City-born Tommy Collins (Leonard Raymond Sipes) began activities on the West Coast thanks to the encouragement of dj Ferlin Husky. Securing deals with Cliffie Stone's Central Songs and Capitol Records, he began putting Bakersfield on the map with nationwide humorous hits like 'You Better Not Do That' (1954) and 'Whatcha Gonna Do Now' (1954), and featured Buck Owens as lead guitarist on his recording sessions. After a short spell in the ministry, he returned to songwriting and developed a lasting friendship with Merle Haggard, for whom he provided No. 1 hits with 'Carolyn' (1971) and 'The Roots Of My Raising' (1976). Haggard composed a beautiful tribute in 'Leonard' (1981).

Spade Cooley
(Violin, vocals, bandleader, 1910–69)

When Bob Wills set up business in the San Fernando Valley, he found strong competition from Spade Cooley, an Oklahoma-born fiddle player who initially worked as a singing-cowboy stand-in and musician before becoming bandleader in the Venice Pier Ballroom. There he attracted sell-out business with his band, which numbered 22 members at times. 'Shame On You' (1944) gave him his biggest hit. A masterful arranger, Cooley brought a rich, full sound to his brand of western swing and furthered his popularity with appearances in over three dozen movies and a television show, the *Hoffman Hayride*. Great success was overtaken by even greater tragedy, as he was sentenced to life for the murder of his wife, Ella Mae, in 1961. Eight years later he suffered a massive heart attack and died, after performing at a police benefit.

Above

Spade Cooley was a professionally trained fiddler, and began performing when he was just eight years old.

Carolina Cotton
(Vocals, yodels, 1925–97)

Although she might only be a footnote in country-music history, Arkansas-born Carolina Cotton was a prolific entertainer in the West Coast's post-war era. Known as the 'Yodelling Blonde Bombshell', she first gained attention working with Spade Cooley's Orchestra, then furthered her western-swing association by touring with both Hank Penny's and Bob Wills' bands. She was featured regularly on radio, television shows and soundies, and appeared in over two dozen movies, the last being Gene Autry's *Blue Canadian Rockies* (1952).

Eddie Dean
(Vocals, guitar, songwriter, actor, 1907–99)

Not as famous as his singing-cowboy compatriots, Eddie Dean nevertheless had starring roles in over 20 westerns during the 1940s, as well as his own television series *The Marshall Of Gunshot Pass* (1950). Beginning his career on radio, and one-time member of the WLS (Chicago) *National Barn Dance*, he possessed one of the finest voices of all the cowboys and, as a songwriter, penned the classic 'I Dreamed Of Hillbilly Heaven', a hit for him in 1955 and a bigger one for Tex Ritter six years later.

Tommy Duncan

(Vocals, songwriter, 1911–67)

The first crooner in country music, Tommy Duncan's name remains synonymous with Bob Wills and, for many years, he was the featured singer in The Texas Playboys. Regular quarrels between the two finally resulted in a split in 1948, though – better together than apart – Duncan returned to the fold in the early 1960s when the bandleader signed a deal with Liberty Records. Influenced by diverse sources, ranging from Jimmie Rodgers to the Dixie jazz bands, he possessed the skills to tackle equally diverse material. A significant songwriter who created a handful of country classics ('Time Changes Everything', 'Bubbles In My Beer'), his only chart success came with a Jimmie Rodgers' song, 'Gambling Polka Dot Blues' (1949).

Right

The voice of Depression America, Woody Guthrie wrote songs that reflected the hardships of everyday life.

Below

'Tennessee' Ernie Ford was inducted into Nashville's Country Music Hall Of Fame in 1990.

'Tennessee' Ernie Ford

(Vocalist, comedian, author, 1919–91)

A native of Bristol, Tennessee, Ernest Jennings Ford began his career on the West Coast as a dj after military service,

catching the attention of Cliffie Stone, who made him a regular on the *Hometown Jamboree* radio and television shows. He began recording for Capitol in 1948 and initially made his name with a series of fast country boogies, enhanced by the musicianship of guitarist Merle Travis and steel guitarist Speedy West. But it was Travis's 'Sixteen Tons' (1955) that gave him a million-seller and a worldwide reputation, putting him en route to a prime-time television series and a headlining appearance at the London Palladium. A much-loved performer and television personality, he devoted his later years to sacred recordings – the first being *Hymns* (1959), at one time the biggest-selling album in Capitol's catalogue.

Woody Guthrie

(Vocals, songwriter, author, 1912–67)

Arguably the most influential of all folk singers (Bob Dylan is one of his greatest admirers), Oklahoma-born Woodrow Wilson Guthrie experienced life's adversities in his early years, with his mother committed to an insane asylum, and facing the severity of the Dust Bowl with his father in Texas. Such emotional and environmental surroundings provided the basis for a vast song repertoire that included social comment and protest, hobo lifestyles and cowboy songs, coming to life via the lyrics of such classics as 'This Land Is Your Land' and 'Oklahoma Hills'. The latter was much covered, including a 1945 chart-topping version by cousin Jack Guthrie (with whom Woody worked as a country duo during the 1930s). The imagery of the Dust Bowl is best defined in his classic RCA album *Dust Bowl Ballads* (1940), at which time he departed for New York and commenced his socialist activities.

Stuart Hamblin

(Vocals, songwriter, 1908–89)

An early West Coast mover and shaker, Stuart Hamblin was the first cowboy singer to be heard on Los Angeles radio, appearing on KFI as 'Cowboy Joe'. After a brief spell

with the Beverly Hill Billies, he began a 20-year run on his own *Lucky Stars* show (KFWB) in 1932. Two years later he became the first West Coast artist to be signed to Decca. A prolific songwriter, his biggest successes included 'Remember Me' and 'This Ole House', before moving into gospel music during his latter years following a conversion by the Rev. Billy Graham.

Freddie Hart
(Vocals, songwriter, b. 1926)
A regular on the *Town Hall Party*, Alabama-born Freddie Hart arrived in Los Angeles following a troubled childhood, a couple of years in the Marines (enrolling when he was only 15), and travelling across the nation. His 1950s association with Capitol and Columbia resulted in some fine, though overlooked, country and rockabilly recordings,. His returned to Capitol resulted in the double CMA award winner 'Easy Loving' (1971), a recording success that he never equalled.

Harlan Howard
(Songwriter, vocals, guitar, 1929–2002)
Harlan Howard, inspired by Ernest Tubb, first began reaping his songwriting rewards in the late 1950s. 'Pick Me Up On Your Way Down' (1958) was his first hit when recorded by Charlie Walker, followed by 'Heartaches By The Number' (1959), which covered country and pop by Ray Price and Guy Mitchell respectively. More huge successes came with 'I Fall To Pieces' (Patsy Cline, 1961), 'Busted' (1963, Johnny Cash and, later, Ray Charles) and 'I've Got A Tiger By The Tail' (Buck Owens, 1965) and, by the mid-1960s, he had exited the West Coast and moved to Nashville, where his compositions quickly became much sought-after. The archetypal country songwriter, Howard had over 4,000 titles to his name and although he slowed down in the 1980s, he continued to create top hits, like The Judds' 'Why Not Me' (1984) and Patty Loveless' 'Blame It On Your Heart' (1993). Much beloved, Nashville honoured him with annual 'Harlan Howard Birthday Bash' celebrations during his final years.

Above
Freddie Hart experienced more success as a songwriter for other artists than as a recording artist in his own right in the early years.

with Jean Shepard, provided his first hit though 'Gone' (1957) was his major breakthrough, creating a smooth pop-country sound.

Rose Maddox
(Vocals, 1925–98)

Before rockabilly, hillbilly humour and flashy rhinestone outfits, there was the feisty Rose Maddox and her brothers Cal, Fred and Don. She started singing on radio when she was 11, as part of Maddox Brothers And Rose, gaining popularity with a wild, fast-paced presentation that mixed loud honky-tonk music and almost vaudeville-style humour, and recording for Four Star and Columbia. After the brothers retired in 1957, Rose went solo and moved into the Top 5 with 'Loose Talk' (1961), a duet with Buck Owens. After the higher-placed solo offering 'Sing A Little Song Of Heartache' (1962), she moved into bluegrass music and found a ready audience with the folk revivalists. The change of pace opened up new avenues for touring and concerts, which she concentrated upon during her latter years as well as recording for several small labels.

Above
Ferlin Husky developed a comic alter-ego in 'Simon Crum' and appeared in several movies.

Right
Rose Maddox started as a honky-tonker, but turned to bluegrass in her later years.

Ferlin Husky
(Singer, comedian, dj, actor, b. 1927)

One of the first Bakersfield entertainers, Missouri-born Ferlin Husky moved to the town after serving in the Merchant Marines and first found work as a dj before signing with Four Star and recording as Terry Preston. Cliffie Stone put him on the *Hometown Jamboree* (as a replacement for 'Tennessee' Ernie Ford) and secured him a deal with Capitol. 'A Dear John Letter' (1953), a duet

Joe Maphis
(Guitar, vocals, 1921–86)

Known as 'king of the strings' for his ability to play virtually any string instrument, Joe Maphis was an active session musician, a cast member of *Town Hall Party*, and his inventive skills on the double-neck Mosrite inspired many, including a young Larry Collins (of The Collins Kids). He sang with his wife, Rose Lee (b. 1922), scoring their biggest hit with the self-penned 'Dim Lights, Thick Smoke (And Loud, Loud Music)' (1953), now a honky-tonk anthem, as well as recording traditional and bluegrass music.

Skeets McDonald
(Vocals, guitar, songwriter, 1915–68)

Honky-tonk stylist Skeets McDonald was another of Cliffie Stone's discoveries, who put him on the *Hometown Jamboree* before he became a regular member of the weekly *Town Hall Party*. Stone also signed him to Capitol where he achieved a number one with 'Don't Let The Stars Get In Your Eyes' (1952). He had some minor successes on Columbia the following decade, including 'Call Me Mr. Brown' (1963).

Billy Mize
(Vocals, songwriter, steel guitar, b. 1929)

An integral contributor to the West Coast scene of the post-war years, Billy Mize hosted a variety of radio and television shows, including his own *Chuck Wagon Show* (with songwriting partner and musician Cliff Crawford) where, purportedly, 16-year-old Merle Haggard made his television debut. He was also a featured steel guitarist on the long-running *Town Hall Party*, and, in 1966, received the ACM Award as Top Television Personality.

Ken Nelson
(Record producer, b. 1911)

A major force in country music's development during the postwar years, Minnesota-born Kenneth F. Nelson began his days at Capitol Records on the behest of old friend Lee Gillette, handling transcriptions. When Gillette took over the label's pop division in 1951, Nelson took over the A&R country responsibilities, having first become involved with this music from his time as a programme director on radio station WJJD (Chicago). Among his initial assignments was producing a session with Hank Thompson. This resulted in Thompson's first No. 1 hit, 'The Wild Side Of Life' (1952). Over the years he signed many of country music's

foremost artists to Capitol, including Faron Young, The Louvin Brothers, Wanda Jackson, Tommy Collins, Rose Maddox, Jean Shepard, as well as rocker Gene Vincent and comedian Stan Freberg. He helped develop the Bakersfield Sound, fully supporting Buck Owens and Merle Haggard's creative skills. Ken Nelson was elected into Nashville's Country Music Hall Of Fame in 2001.

*Above
The music of Skeets McDonald helped to bridge the gap between country and rock'n'roll.*

Bonnie Owens
(Vocals, 1932–2006)

One of the Bakersfield Sound's few females, Owens began her career singing with Buck Owens in Mesa, Arizona, and married him in 1948. Three years later they moved to Bakersfield, where she worked as a singer and waitress at the Clover Club, and made her recording debut with 'A Dear John Letter' (1953), on which she dueted with Fuzzy Owen. Later she recorded 'Just Between The Two Of Us' (1964) with newcomer Merle Haggard, with whom she shared two ACM Awards (Top Country Duet) and married in 1965.

Wynn Stewart
(Vocals, guitar, songwriter, 1934–85)
A formative figure of the West Coast hardcore honky-tonk movement, Stewart was a major influence on both Buck Owens and Merle Haggard (the latter played bass in Stewart's band). He was a regular on KWTO in Springfield, Missouri when he was 13, before his family relocated to California. Skeets McDonald helped secure his Capitol deal and he made his chart debut with 'Waltz Of The Angels' (1956), though it was when he resigned from the label that he enjoyed his only No. 1 hit, 'It's Such A Pretty World Today' (1967). In total he chalked up over 30 chart entries, but it was the role he played in helping establish a sound peculiar to the West Coast that will be his lasting glory.

Above
Together with his partner guitarist Jimmy Bryant, Speedy West influenced a generation of country and rock'n' roll musicians.

Cliffie Stone
(Vocals, comedian, record producer, bandleader, 1917–98)
Native Californian Cliffie Stone – the son of country comedian Herman the Hermit (aka Herman Snyder) – was a West Coast, one-man industry during the 1940s. Hard to pinpoint any particular activity, he began to get his name known on Stuart Hamblin's *Covered Wagon Jamboree* before establishing his own radio shows in the early 1940s. He joined Capitol Records later that decade in an A&R capacity and was active in signing several acts, including Merle Travis and 'Tennessee' Ernie Ford, with whom he later took over management duties. He also recorded for the label, with the novelty 'Peepin' Through The Keyhole'

(1948) as his biggest hit. In his later years he mixed radio work with music publishing and established Granite Records, the last home for Tex Williams. Stone was elected into the Country Music Hall Of Fame in 1989.

Jimmy Wakely
(Vocals, guitar, actor, 1914–82)
The Jimmy Wakely Trio was first heard on Oklahoma radio before securing a regular spot on Gene Autry's *Melody Ranch* CBS network radio show. Then the door to Hollywood opened and Wakely starred in 28 movies for Monogram during a five-year period (1944–49). He was also an immensely successful singer, with some two dozen hits on Capitol – the biggest of which was 'Slipping Around' (1949), a No. 1 country and pop duet with Margaret Whiting. During his later years he established Shasta Records, a mail-order business that primarily handled cowboy singers.

Speedy West
(Steel guitar, 1924–2003)
Initially influenced by Earl 'Joaquin' Murphy, Wesley Webb West picked up the nickname 'Speedy' for his skills as a steel guitarist, playing with Spade Cooley and Hank Penny before joining forces with the equally adroit guitarist Jimmy Bryant (1925–80). Together they claimed the title 'The Flaming Guitars'. Besides producing dazzling, 'hard to believe' recordings, they were session musicians to virtually all on the Capitol roster.

Tex Williams
(Vocals, guitar, bandleader, 1917–85)
One-time singer and bass player with Spade Cooley's Orchestra, Sollie Paul 'Tex' Williams' vocals were first heard on the Cooley hit 'Shame On You' (1944). It led to a recording deal with Capitol and, following disagreements with his boss, he was fired from the outfit. Disapproving of the sacking, most of the band followed him and were back in new business as Williams' outfit, The Western Caravan. When Merle Travis wrote a talking blues, 'Smoke Smoke Smoke (That Cigarette)', Williams recorded it and it topped the 1947 country and pop charts, giving Capitol its first gold disc. He departed from Capitol in 1951 but continued recording on a variety of labels, with Cliffie Stone's Granite outlet providing his final chart success, 'Those Lazy, Crazy Days Of Summer' (1974).

Bill Woods

(Musician, bandleader, 1924–2000)

Merle Haggard called him the 'Grandpappy of Bakersfield' and, during his 14 years leading The Orange Blossom Playboys at the town's hottest honky-tonk, the Blackboard, he employed both Buck Owens and Merle Haggard, who were to define the Bakersfield Sound. A Texan by birth, he perfected his musical skills by entertaining fellow workers in the San Francisco shipyards and, later, played in both the Bob Wills and Tommy Duncan bands. Although he recorded sporadically, he achieved a regional hit with 'Truck Drivin' Man' (1963) and Red Simpson wrote a fine tribute song, 'Bill Woods From Bakersfield'.

Sheb Wooley

(Vocals, guitar, comedian, songwriter, actor, 1921–2003)

With a career that cut across the entertainment industry, Oklahoma's Sheb Wooley started out a country singer and songwriter but, with a few acting lessons behind him, arrived in Hollywood and became a much sought-after western character actor. His most famed roles were in *High Noon* and the television series *Rawhide*. Besides his country hits, which included the chart-topping 'That's My Pa' (1962) and comic offerings as parody alter-ego 'Ben Colder', he scored a multi-million seller with the novelty rock'n'roll hit 'Purple People Eater' (1959).

Above
Tex Williams got his start in country music playing with Spade Cooley's Orchestra.

Left
Sheb Wooley had many strings to his bow – singer, songwriter, musician, comedian and Hollywood actor.

All My Friends Are Boppin' The Blues:
Rockabilly

The 1950s was a period of enormous upheaval and social change, as the world slowly recovered from the deprivations of the Second World War. Changes were apparent in every aspect of life, but perhaps the greatest was the rise of the 'teenager' as a distinct socio-economic class. For the first time, young people had money in their pockets and a desire to express themselves through their own music and fashion. They were no longer prepared to be merely younger versions of their parents.

Rock'n'roll became the symbol of youth. The war had brought the black and white populations of America closer together and now the strict segregation of different musical styles would disappear forever. Blues, jazz, big bands, hillbilly, western swing and indeed every strand of popular music became interwoven as rock'n'roll provided teenagers with an exciting alternative to the music of the Establishment. Rock'n'roll, with its repetitive beat, honking saxes, crashing drums and screeching guitars, caught the imagination of practically every young person. Their parents hated it.

The word 'rockabilly' has always lacked a clear and concise definition. Strictly speaking it is a hybrid form of country music, combining hillbilly with the blues, and it was this apparently simple formula that gave rock'n'roll its greatest star, Elvis Presley. For a short period in the mid-1950s, rockabilly became commercially successful and so dominant that it ended the careers of many established country singers and briefly threatened the entire fabric of country music.

The success of Elvis Presley opened the door for others to follow. Young rebels like Carl Perkins, Gene Vincent and Jerry Lee Lewis were country boys brought up on the music of Hank Williams. They added a rock'n'roll tempo, cranked up the volume – and for a while the whole world danced to that rockabilly beat.

Key Artists

Jerry Lee Lewis

Carl Perkins

Elvis Presley

Influences & Development

'Rockabilly is really part of our background.... It's a cousin to the blues and country. And that's important.' **Brian Setzer**

Below

The roots of rockabilly lie in the music of early greats such as Hank Thompson and his band.

The arrival of the rockabilly phenomenon in the mid-1950s can be traced back directly to the rise of Elvis Presley (1935–77) and there is no doubt that he was the dominant influence on most of the young country boys who followed him. The impact of Presley can never be overstated, but at the same time he did not materialize out of a vacuum, and the style of hopped-up country music that he adopted with such extraordinary success had been visible for some time

in the rougher honky-tonks in Texas and Tennessee even before Elvis had found his way to the Sun studio.

The Roots Of Rockabilly

The Carl Perkins Band was playing behind chicken wire in the less-wholesome clubs and bars of Jackson, Tennessee, as early as 1950, and their repertoire contained the same components, the same uneasy mix of black and white, that would eventually surface in their recordings some five years later. Before too long, The Johnny Burnette Trio was brawling its way around the Memphis honky-tonks in much the same way. Rockabilly music was growing naturally, but it was the introduction of Presley that proved to be the catalyst.

The majority of the original rockabilly performers were white and came from the southern states and from rural or small-town communities. They grew up listening to early post-war country music and invariably cited the likes of Hank Snow (1914–99), Lefty Frizzell (1928–75) and Red Foley (1910–68) among their favourites. In Texas, where western swing was so popular, Bob Wills (1905–75) was a big influence, as was Hank Thompson (b. 1925) and the piano style of Moon Mullican (1909–67), which is clearly audible in the recordings of Jerry Lee Lewis (b. 1935).

Bill Monroe (1911–96) and his bluegrass music was certainly an influence on the likes of Charlie Feathers (1932–98) and Carl Perkins (1932–98), and rockabilly versions of his songs 'Blue Moon Of Kentucky' and 'Rocky Road Blues' are rightly perceived as classics. Country boogie in the shape of The Delmore Brothers with 'Freight Train Boogie', Wayne Raney (1920–93) and 'Tennessee' Ernie Ford (1919–91) were already close to the rockabilly formula, and the style of Arthur Smith (b. 1921), with his 1948 hit 'Guitar Boogie', provided much of the rockabilly guitar sound, while the slap bass playing of Fred Maddox (1919–92) was adopted by Bill Black on the Presley recordings.

However, one man must take credit for being the biggest single influence on the rockabilly generation and

Left
Hank Williams is believed to have been the greatest influence on rockabilly music as it emerged in the 1950s.

that is Hank Williams (1923–53). His up-tempo recordings were already close to rockabilly, and it would be hard to argue against the claim that his 1947 hit 'Move It On Over' was the first rockabilly record. Other pre-Presley discs of interest were Bill Haley with 'Rock The Joint' in 1952 and 'Juke Joint Johnny' by Lattie Moore the same year.

Black Meets White

In addition to listening to the Grand Ole Opry on the family radio, country boys were now coming into contact with black music by spinning the dial and hearing the likes of Joe Turner, Muddy Waters and John Lee Hooker. Musical segregation was becoming a thing of the past. It was a song by bluesman Arthur Crudup that was adapted to become Presley's first record, and Arkansas rockabilly legend Ronnie Hawkins adequately summed up the situation when he explained, 'We were just trying to sound like Muddy Waters but couldn't do it and it came out like that', while describing his own efforts on record. Even a teenage Janis Martin found that the raunchy sounds of Ruth Brown were enormously exciting and greatly affected her own approach to making music.

Rockabilly broke nationally in early 1956 when both Carl Perkins and Elvis Presley topped the charts, and this led to a brief period of total dominance. The public's

demand for the new music seemed insatiable, and every country singer had to change or perish. Some, like George Jones, who recorded as Thumper Jones, were able to adapt but many careers were brought to a premature end. The Establishment fought against the changes, but the major record companies had lost control and seemingly every week a new young singer emerged on a small independent label and became an instant star through the power of radio and the enthusiasm of the teenage fans.

Below
Appropriately named the Million Dollar Quartet, Jerry Lee Lewis, Carl Perkins and Johnny Cash gather round Elvis Presley.

hank williams ◉ 108 **jerry lee lewis** ◉ 150 **carl perkins** ◉ 152 **elvis presley** ◉ 154 **the johnny burnette trio** ◉ 156

1 4 5

Above

Rosie Flores is one of the key artists leading the rockabilly revival in the USA.

The Fall And Rise Of Rockabilly

By the end of the 1950s, however, rockabilly music had largely ceased to have any commercial significance in America. The major labels had regained control of the industry and new sounds and new styles were appearing on the charts. In Britain, a minority of enthusiasts stayed loyal to rockabilly through fan clubs and specialist magazines, but it was not until the early 1970s that the record companies woke up to the fact that there was still money to be made from the music.

Louisiana record executive Shelby Singleton had purchased the Sun catalogue in 1969, following which compilation albums were made available for the first time in the UK and Europe, showcasing previously unheard material by the lesser Sun artists. Sales of these Sun albums inspired other labels to lease or re-issue vintage material and within a few years there was a startling array

of rockabilly available in British shops and a new generation were becoming hooked on the music.

In 1976, an obscure and primitive near-20-year-old record, 'Jungle Rock' by Hank Mizell, was released in Britain for the first time and reached No. 3 in the charts. Other authentic rockabilly singles by Don Woody, Peanuts Wilson and Billy Lee Riley (b. 1933) also sold in large quantities, and the underground rockabilly movement took on fresh momentum. There was less interest in the USA, although in California a small record label, Rollin' Rock, did make new recordings by several original rockabilly artists as a result of which albums by the likes of Ray Campi (b. 1934), Mac Curtis and Jackie Lee Cochran became popular in Europe.

There was a blurring of the edges between rockabilly and the punk movement during the late 1970s. Robert Gordon from Washington, D.C. recorded with guitarist Link Wray and had a small hit with Riley's 'Red Hot', while a young American trio, The Stray Cats, became immensely popular with punk audiences performing material by the likes of Gene Vincent (1935–71) and The Johnny Burnette Trio. Neo-rockabilly and psychobilly were extreme examples of this trend.

European Popularity

The plethora of rockabilly records available in the shops in Europe created a demand for personal appearances by the American performers where hitherto only the leading figures like Jerry Lee Lewis and Carl Perkins had toured. the *Sun Sound Show* starring Jack Scott (b. 1936), Buddy Knox (1933-99), Charlie Feathers and Warren Smith (1933–80) brought authentic rockabilly to London in 1977 and from then on European festivals and weekenders played host to increasing numbers of rockabilly artists who had recorded, often unsuccessfully, in the 1950s and were now largely forgotten back in the USA. In Europe they were treated as stars.

The European popularity of acts like Johnny Carroll (1937–95), Sonny Burgess and Ronnie Dawson enabled them not only to tour repeatedly but also to record new albums of rockabilly during the 1980s and beyond, often working with younger European musicians. The search for obscure rockabilly singers sometimes proved far from straightforward, such as in the case of Joe Clay, who

after a five-year search was tracked down driving a school bus in New Orleans. The story of his re-emergence as a European rockabilly star became a major news story in the USA.

Rockabilly Today

Fifty years after the rise of rockabilly, it remains a vibrant and dynamic music operating on the fringes of country music, with specialist festivals all around the world and the original American acts still in demand as headliners. Like the bluesmen before them, the first rockabilly generation has continued to perform into old age, but happily there are younger performers poised to take over from them in the years ahead. Sons of famous fathers include Rocky Burnette (b. 1953), son of Johnny and Stan Perkins, son of Carl, who are continuing the family tradition. Contemporary rockabilly acts within Europe worthy of mention include both Wildfire Willie And The Ramblers and the highly talented Eva Eastwood (b. 1967) from Sweden, the recently defunct Rimshots from Wales and the London band, Paul Ansell's Number Nine, all of whom are writing and recording original rockabilly material.

Finally, the American public is slowly waking up to its forgotten heritage. It has been claimed that rockabilly is the only truly original American music and at last the surviving rockabilly pioneers of the 1950s are receiving some measure of acknowledgement at home. Rosie Flores, Deke Dickerson and the Californian trio High Noon are at the forefront of the contemporary rockabilly movement in the United States. What the music now needs is a new young star to bring rockabilly back to the pop charts again.

Left

Charlie Feathers was extremely popular in the UK, playing in the Sun Sound Show.

Below

The Stray Cats are a punk group who have achieved popularity in the USA revisiting rockabilly material.

Country Meets Sun Records - The Beginnings Of Rock'n'Roll

The legend of Sun Records seems to expand and shine brighter with every passing year, as successive generations discover the almost unbelievable array of musical gems that were created at that modest little studio at 706 Union Avenue, Memphis. Sun was the brainchild of one man and it is no exaggeration to say that without his contribution, not just country music but indeed all facets of popular music would have been very different during the second half of the twentieth century.

Below

Sun producer Sam Phillips (right) with rockabilly legend Jerry Lee Lewis.

A Music Legend

Sam Phillips (1923–2003) was the man who changed the world. Raised on a farm just outside Florence, Alabama, his early ambition to practise law was abandoned through economic necessity, so he drifted into radio and by 1945 was working as an announcer for Radio WREC in Memphis. In January 1950 he opened the Memphis Recording Service, an ambitious and highly risky attempt to establish a studio with the specific intention of recording singers from the Memphis area.

Initially Phillips recorded local blues and gospel musicians and leased the tapes to leading independent labels like Chess and Modern. In March 1951, he cut Ike Turner's Kings Of Rhythm on a frantic R&B stomper 'Rocket 88', which featured vocals by Turner's sax player Jackie Brenston. Issued on Chess it became a No. 1 R&B hit and is considered by some to have been the first rock'n'roll record. Other successes followed with Howlin' Wolf and Roscoe Gordon until, perhaps inevitably, in April 1952 Phillips elected to start issuing his own recordings and Sun Records was born.

Through 1953 Sun's earliest releases continued the same policy and proved an outlet for local black musicians, including Little Milton, Rufus Thomas and The Prisonaires – all of whom benefited from Phillips' unorthodox and innovative approach to recording. By 1954, however, Sun started to record hillbilly acts and although releases by performers such as Hardrock Gunter and Doug Poindexter failed to sell, there was a noticeable blurring of the musical boundaries as Sam started his quest for a white boy with the ability to cross the strict demarcation lines that separated R&B, pop and country music.

Eventually Sam Phillips delegated some of his work load to Jack Clement (b. 1931) and his production skills were another important factor in Sun's success. It was Clement who recognized the raw talent of Jerry Lee Lewis when he arrived to audition towards the end of 1956. This massively talented singer/pianist cut four multi-million selling records at Sun before scandal derailed his career.

The ability to create hits by unknown artists continued as Charlie Rich with 'Lonely Weekends' and Carl Mann's 'Mona Lisa' found fame on Sun's sister label Phillips International, but by the end of the 1950s, the great days had passed and Sun was no longer leading the world. During the 1970s a massive re-issue programme of Sun recordings commenced, which continues to this day. It remains a glorious monument to the vision and genius of Sam Phillips.

Left
Carl Perkins was one of Sun Records' golden boys during its golden era of the 1950s.

Below
Phillips had a knack for taking obscure artists such as Charlie Rich and producing immensely popular songs that brought them instant success.

In July 1954 Sun's recording of 'That's All Right' by Elvis Presley commenced their golden period and within 18 months both Johnny Cash (1932–2003) and Carl Perkins were also creating some of their finest work for Sun. That three such important artists should all emerge from such an unlikely source speaks volumes for Sam Phillips' perceptiveness and understanding of this new style of music, and his ability to create classic recordings that remain timeless and unsurpassed in their brilliance.

The Rockabilly Craze

By early 1956 Sun had forsaken its blues artists and was now at the forefront of the rockabilly craze that was sweeping the USA. Financial pressures had forced Sam to sell Presley's contract to RCA but Perkins gave Phillips his first international hit with 'Blue Suede Shoes' (1956). The quality of the recordings made at Sun over the next couple of years was astoundingly high, and many acts deserving of hit records missed out solely because Sun's budgets did not permit the necessary level of expenditure to ensure chart success. Roy Orbison (1936–88) scored his first hit at Sun with 'Ooby Dooby' (1956), but others like Sonny Burgess, Warren Smith, Billy Riley and Ray Smith missed out, despite creating classic recordings that were totally deserving of hit status.

Jerry Lee Lewis

Key Artist

'Other people - they practice and they practice ... these fingers of mine, they got brains in 'em. You don't tell them what to do – they do it. God given talent.'

Jerry Lee Lewis

If Jerry Lee Lewis had never existed, it seems unlikely that anyone would have had a sufficiently vivid imagination to have invented him. Through a 50-year career, this massively talented, yet infuriatingly self-destructive genius has scaled the heights and plumbed the depths, never for one moment compromising his music or his life. Most people mellow with age. Jerry Lee Lewis just keeps on rocking.

Contender For King

Born in Ferriday, Louisiana, on 29 September 1935, he reportedly first saw a piano at the age of eight, while visiting his aunt, and amazed everyone by sitting down and instantly playing it, thereby inspiring his father to mortgage their home to buy him his own upright. Lewis has usually claimed to have been a true original, his music influenced by no other. Inevitably, though, he absorbed the sounds of post-war country music, especially Hank Williams, on the family battery-operated radio and as a youngster would accompany his cousin, the future television evangelist Jimmy Lee Swaggert, to a juke joint outside town, where they would sneak in and listen to black performers like the teenage B. B. King. By 1949 he started to perform music and to learn his craft in the local clubs and honky-tonks.

In November 1956, Lewis arrived at Sun Records in Memphis and auditioned for Jack Clement, having announced himself as someone who played piano like Chet Atkins. He made an immediate impact and his high-energy rendition of Ray Price's hit 'Crazy Arms' became his first release. It was, however, his second Sun single 'Whole Lotta Shakin' Goin' On' (1957), with its frenzied rock'n'roll beat and mildly suggestive lyrics, that rocketed him to instant stardom, aided by an explosive appearance on television's *Steve Allen Show*. The disc became a major hit in the country, R&B and pop charts, and when first 'Great Balls Of Fire' (1957) and then 'Breathless' (1958) repeated the process, Lewis became a genuine contender for Elvis's crown as 'king of rock'n'roll'.

Into The Wilderness

His fourth major hit, 'High School Confidential' (1958), coincided with a concert tour of Britain during which it became known that Lewis, at the age of 22, had recently married for the third time and that the bride was his 13-year-old cousin, Myra Brown. The horrified British media applied such intense pressure that the tour was abandoned and Lewis returned home in disgrace. The scandal quickly

spread to the USA and before long his records had stopped selling and his career was in ruins.

For the next decade Lewis toured constantly and cemented his reputation as perhaps the greatest live act of the rockabilly generation. He performed at venues large and small and suffered every indignity as he struggled to get his career back on track, but although audiences responded positively to his dynamic shows, it proved a long haul back to the top. During this period he left Sun and recorded for Smash Records in a variety of styles including rock'n'roll, pop, country and soul.

Finally in 1968, he returned to the charts with a series of distinctive country hits, including 'Another Place Another Time' (1968), 'There Must Be More To Love Than This' (1970) and 'Would You Take Another Chance On Me' (1972) and re-emerged as a star once again. He did not abandon his rock'n'roll past, however, and continued to live life his own way. Every show was different – and as unpredictable and exciting as the man himself.

Serious health problems, the battle with drink and drugs, six tempestuous marriages and the odd skirmish with the IRS did nothing to slow him down. Only the arrival of old age has noticeably affected his energy levels.

Classic Recordings

1957
'Whole Lotta Shakin' *Goin' On', 'Great Balls* *Of Fire'*
1958
'Breathless', 'High School *Confidential'*
1961
Jerry Lee's Greatest
1964
The Greatest Live Show *On Earth, Live At The* *Starclub, Hamburg*
1965
Country Songs For City *Folks*
1968
Another Place Another *Time*

Far Left

Wild rockabilly artist Jerry Lee Lewis experienced several ups and downs during his career.

Left

Lewis found his way back to the top after a series of professional drawbacks, and remains active later in his life.

Key Track

'Great Balls Of Fire' (1957)
This track represents Jerry Lee Lewis and Sun Records at their best. It is explosive, exciting and wild. The pounding piano style and unrestrained vocals create one of the classic hits of the 1950s.

Carl Perkins

Key Artist

For a brief period in early 1956, Carl Perkins was the first singer to take a pure rockabilly record – his self-penned 'Blue Suede Shoes' – to the summit of the best-selling charts in the USA. He beat Elvis to the top, but was never a realistic candidate to sustain this early promise because he lacked Presley's film-star looks and was too hillbilly for real pop stardom.

Cotton Fields And Honky-Tonks

Carl Lee Perkins was born in Ridgely, Tennessee, on 9 April 1932. His father was a sharecropper and the family struggled on or below the poverty line. Their home lacked the luxury of electricity, so Carl's musical education comprised such country music as was heard on their battery-operated radio plus hours spent with a black sharecropper called Uncle John, who taught him to pick the blues on a guitar.

Carl and his brother Jay started playing in honky-tonks in 1946 and by 1953 The Perkins Brothers Band comprised Carl on vocals and guitar, Jay on rhythm guitar, younger brother Clayton on bass and W. S. Holland on drums. They developed their unique style by introducing the phrasing and rhythm from black music on to basic country tunes. After hearing Elvis on the radio, performing in similar style, they travelled to Memphis in October 1954 and auditioned successfully for Sam Phillips at Sun Records.

'That rockabilly sound wasn't as simple as I thought it was.'
Carl Perkins

Blue Suede Shoes

Perkins' third record, 'Blue Suede Shoes' (1956), became the biggest of his career and one of rock'n'roll's greatest anthems. It reached No. 1 in both the country and R&B charts, and No. 2 on the pop listings. Just as the record was breaking nationally, Carl was hospitalized following a car wreck and missed out on a national television appearance at a critical time.

Classic Recordings

1955
'Turn Around', 'Gone Gone Gone'
1956
'Blue Suede Shoes', 'Honey Don't', 'Boppin' The Blues', 'Dixie Fried'
1957
'Matchbox', 'Forever Yours'
1958
Dance Album
1967
Country Boy's Dream
1973
My Kind Of Country

Left

Carl Perkins, one of rockabilly's finest and a true country boy, originally wrote the 'Blue Suede Shoes' on a potato sack.

remember him, he was delighted to be treated as a star again and to find that audiences not only remembered but loved his Sun recordings. As an added bonus he was introduced to The Beatles, at that time the biggest act in the world. He found that they were devoted fans of his music. The whole experience in Britain served to revitalize his career and to overcome many of the disappointments of the past.

Carl toured the world for several years as a featured part of *The Johnny Cash Show*. He was popular wherever he appeared, but despite recording both country and rockabilly for a variety of different labels, he never came close to rediscovering the spark of magic which had produced 'Blue Suede Shoes'. In 1975 he split from Cash and the following year introduced the new Carl Perkins Band, which included his sons, Stan on drums and Greg on bass. For the remainder of his life, Carl and his sons performed his rockabilly show to successive generations of fans. His influence on other musicians and the sustained popularity of his songs with the public was enormous and far outweighed his limited chart success. He died on 19 January 1998.

He never recovered this early momentum, despite recording more top-quality rockabilly for Sun. His style was too hillbilly and his whole approach too rural for sustained pop stardom. Subsequent releases that are now rightly perceived as classics all failed to sell in worthwhile quantities. Carl just could not be moulded into a teen idol in the same way that Presley could. Disillusionment soon set in. Jay Perkins died of a brain tumour in 1958, W. S. Holland left to join Johnny Cash and Clayton became a hopeless alcoholic. Carl himself hit the bottle as his career slipped away from him.

Britain And The Beatles

By the end of 1963, Perkins had virtually retired from music when he got a call to tour Britain with Chuck Berry in May 1964. Apprehensive as to whether anybody would

Far Left

Despite early chart success, Carl Perkins was unable to compete with the respectively better-looking and more dynamic Elvis and Jerry Lee Lewis.

Left

For many years, Perkins was part of The Johnny Cash Show, *a role that helped revitalize his popularity.*

Key Track

'Dixie Fried' (1956)
Tough, aggressive lyrics, Carl's biting guitar and a vocal style that was fine-tuned in the roughest Tennessee honky-tonks – this is Carl Perkins at his peak. It was hopelessly inappropriate for Top 40 radio in 1956, but it remains a timeless gem of undiluted rockabilly.

Elvis Presley

Key Artist

'I was bucking a good-looking cat called Elvis, who had beautiful hair, wasn't married, and had all kinds of great moves.' **Carl Perkins**

Elvis Presley was the most important figure in popular music during the twentieth century. His influence was enormous, and remains so, nearly 30 years after his death. The recordings that he made during the first few years of his career inspired a whole generation and the initial impact of a country boy singing black R&B changed forever the strictly segregated nature of the music industry in America.

Hillbilly Cat

Born in a two room shotgun shack in Tupelo, Mississippi on 8 January 1935, Presley moved with his family to Memphis in 1948. His musical influences were many and varied. He enjoyed hillbilly and country boogie, gospel quartets like The Blackwood Brothers, R&B singers including Wynonie Harris and Big Mama Thornton, even pop singers like Dean Martin. He picked a little guitar and would hang around the blues clubs on Beale Street. He even adopted the brightly coloured clothes favoured by the negroes. He was a loner and a drifter – and an unlikely candidate for stardom.

Sam Phillips at Sun Records was the man who spotted the potential in Presley. Accompanied by guitarist Scotty Moore and bass player Bill Black, Presley first recorded on 5 July 195, delivering groundbreaking renditions of Arthur Crudup's 'That's All Right' and the Bill Monroe bluegrass standard, 'Blue Moon Of Kentucky'. Both songs were given a raw, primitive feel and the end product sounded quite different – neither country nor R&B. The style became known as rockabilly.

Presley was not an overnight success. Everything about him – his appearance, his overtly sexual persona and his strange-sounding music – was met with confusion, disbelief and open hostility from the general public to begin with. Slowly however, his teenage support increased sufficiently to drown out the dissenting voices. Sun issued five singles by Presley as his popularity gradually expanded through the South, and his final Sun offering 'I Forgot To Remember To Forget' (1955) broke him nationally when it reached No. 1 on the country charts.

King Of Rockabilly

In November 1955, Sun sold Presley's contract to RCA Victor for the then-substantial fee of $35,000. At the same time, his

Classic Recordings

1954
'That's All Right', *'Blue Moon Of Kentucky'*, *'Good Rockin' Tonight'*
1955
'Baby Let's Play House', *'Mystery Train'*, *'I Forgot To Remember To Forget'*
1956
'Heartbreak Hotel', *'Hound Dog'*, *'Don't Be Cruel'*, Rock 'n' Roll No 1
1957
'All Shook Up', *'Jailhouse Rock'*, Rock 'n' Roll No 2
1958
'King Creole', *'Wear My Ring Around Your Neck'*, Elvis's Golden Records Vol 1
1959
'A Fool Such As I'
1960
Elvis Is Back

Left

The making of a legend – Elvis Presley with producer Sam Phillips, guitarist Scotty Moore bassist and Bill Black.

management was acquired by the Svengali-like Colonel Tom Parker. The move to RCA provided Presley with the financial support and superior distribution network to become an international star, and after a slow start, his debut single 'Heartbreak Hotel' (1956) became a worldwide hit.

Over the next year, Presley evolved from a rockabilly singer into the 'king of rock'n'roll', through a series of million-selling records. In August 1956, he travelled to Hollywood to commence work on his first movie, *Love Me Tender*. Colonel Tom Parker was already shaping the direction that his career would take. Presley was called up to serve in the US Army in March 1958, but even this period out of the limelight in no way affected his enormous popularity – his return to civilian life two years later was probably the peak of his career. Gone, however was any trace of his rebel image, and his recordings became increasingly lightweight. They were all sure-fire

hits, but with very few exceptions, they had moved far from his rockabilly roots.

As the years progressed, less and less care was taken over Presley's career. A seemingly endless series of embarrassingly poor films was only matched by some depressingly bad records. Eventually, in 1968, Presley re-emerged with a much-acclaimed television special, following which the last part of his life was spent entertaining sell-out crowds at venues such as Las Vegas. The most charismatic and innovative singer of the twentieth century died unexpectedly on 16 August 1977.

Far Left

Elvis was responsible for creating the rockabilly style – which came out of his first recording session at Sam Phillips' Sun Studios.

Key Track

'That's All Right' (1954)
This was the song that started a revolution. Despite all that has happened since, it still retains the same freshness and vitality. Presley was raw and inexperienced, but you can always feel the energy. This is classic rockabilly at its finest.

A-Z of Artists

Above
Sonny Burgess And The Pacers began their rockabilly ride in the 1950s. They continue to play the music in the twenty-first century.

music in the 1970s and had several releases on Rollin' Rock, which proved very popular in Europe. He also undertook a lot of session work, backing other rockabilly artists. Campi first toured Britain in 1977 with his Rockabilly Rebels and has stayed loyal to the music ever since, recording and touring continually through the years.

Sonny Burgess
(Vocals, guitar, b. 1931)
Born in Newport, Arkansas, Albert 'Sonny' Burgess cut some of Sun's wildest and most primitive-sounding rockabilly. His growling vocals and heavily R&B-influenced style was too extreme for mass sales, but with his group, The Pacers, he had one of the top rockabilly stage acts in the South during the 1950s. He retired for several years but re-emerged during the 1980s and now tours constantly with his reformed Pacers.

The Johnny Burnette Trio
(Vocal/instrumental trio, 1954–57)
Johnny (1934–64), brother Dorsey (1932–79) and guitarist Paul Burlison (1929–2003) were roughnecks from Memphis who played the local clubs during the early 1950s. They earned a recording contract with Coral after winning a televized talent show in New York, and cut some classic rockabilly before disbanding in 1957. Johnny and Dorsey later enjoyed successful solo careers. Paul toured extensively with a reformed Trio fronted by Johnny's son, Rocky.

Right
The Johnny Burnette Trio – Johnny and Dorsey Burnette and guitarist Paul Burlison – proved to be a highly influential act on artists in the later 1950s and 1960s.

Ray Campi
(Vocals, double bass, b. 1934)
Campi recorded rockabilly in Texas 1956–59, then moved to California and became a school teacher. He returned to

Johnny Carroll
(Vocals, guitar, 1937–95)
Johnny Carroll, from Cleburne, Texas, recorded some wild rockabilly for Decca in Nashville and appeared in the cult movie *Rock Baby Rock It* in 1957. He later toured with Scotty Moore and Bill Black after they left Presley. He nearly died after a nightclub shooting in the 1960s, but he recovered and returned to rockabilly, working extensively

in Europe during the 1980s, where he adopted Gene Vincent's black leather image. He died after an unsuccessful liver-transplant operation.

Big Al Downing
(Vocals, piano, 1940–2005)

One of the few black rockabilly performers, Downing – from Lenapah, Oklahoma – was in fact a musical chameleon who tried just about every style of popular music during his long career. While a member of The Poe-Kats he played piano on several Wanda Jackson rockabilly recordings, as well as cut rockers himself for different labels – without success. He charted in later years after re-inventing himself first as a soul and later a country artist. He died from leukaemia.

Charlie Feathers
(Vocals, guitar, 1932–98)

A cult hero, especially in Europe, Charlie enjoyed no commercial success whatsoever but was revered for his authentic rockabilly sound. Born near Holly Springs, Mississippi, he first recorded for Sun in 1954, but cut his finest rockabilly for King and Meteor. His unusual vocal technique – complete with hiccups and stutters – is instantly recognizable and he was much loved by purists because of his refusal to compromise his primitive style.

Dale Hawkins
(Vocals, guitar, b. 1938)

Delmar Hawkins was born in Goldmine, Louisiana, and is a cousin of Ronnie Hawkins. His biggest success came in 1957 with the self-penned 'Suzie-Q' on Checker which, like most of his rockabilly, reflected the strong blues influence in his music. Dale was the first white singer to appear at Harlem's Apollo Theatre. In the 1960s, he moved into record production with both Bell and RCA. He has recently operated a suicide crisis centre in Arkansas.

Ronnie Hawkins
(Vocals, b. 1935)

A larger-than-life personality and hell raiser who in his younger days had a spectacular stage act, Ronnie Hawkins always attracted the finest musicians into his group, The Hawks. Ronnie was born in Huntsville, Arkansas, but settled in Canada where for more than 40 years he was a leading figure on the club circuit. He cut much of his best work for Roulette, and has continued to record rockabilly throughout his long career.

Buddy Holly
(Vocals, guitar, 1936–59)

Born Charles Holley in Lubbock, Texas, Buddy was one of the biggest names of the rock'n'roll era. Along with his group, The Crickets, he recorded for producer Norman Petty and created a series of instantly recognizable worldwide hits. He came from a strictly hillbilly background but incorporated both R&B and blues into his music with great success. His later work veered towards pop and away from rockabilly. Tragically, he died in a plane crash.

Below

Buddy Holly (top here with his band The Crickets) began his career as a rockabilly artist from Texas. His shift to rock'n'roll was inevitable, as was his legendary status after he died in a plane crash.

Johnny Horton
(Vocals, guitar, 1925–60)

The 'Singing Fisherman' recorded country for Abbott and Mercury with only limited success until, in early 1956, he formed a rockabilly trio and went on to cut several hits for Columbia. Born in Los Angeles, Horton married Hank Williams' widow, Billie Jean. Horton later made the pop charts with a series of pseudo-historical country songs. He died in a car wreck on 5 November 1960. His rockabilly recordings have greatly influenced modern rockabilly bands.

Above

A teenage sensation, Janis Martin was signed by RCA in 1956 and billed as 'the female Elvis'.

guitarist James Burton, left him to join Ricky Nelson, after which he adapted to a pop-rock style and scored his biggest hit with 'Let's Think About Living' (1960). In 1962 he moved to Nashville and went country with some success before dying prematurely of pneumonia.

Janis Martin
(Vocals, guitar, b. 1940)

Born in Sutherlin, Virginia, Janis Martin toured extensively but was too raunchy for mass acceptance, despite a series of outstanding rockabilly recordings. She retired in 1959 to raise her family but re-emerged in the 1980s. Since then she has made numerous live appearances, mainly in Europe, where she has established a loyal following and remains in great demand.

Roy Orbison
(Vocals, guitar, 1936–88)

Orbison, in his distinctive dark glasses, became a major star during the 1960s as a result of a succession of hits in a rock-ballad style that was quite unique – and a contrast to the British beat-group craze of the period. Born in Vernon, Texas, he earlier performed rockabilly with his group The Teen Kings and scored his first hit with the novelty 'Ooby Dooby' for Sun in 1956.

Wanda Jackson
(Vocals, b. 1937)

Born in Maud, Oklahoma, Jackson was discovered by Hank Thompson and first recorded country for Decca in 1954. After appearing on shows with Elvis Presley and a label switch to Capitol, she cut several rockabilly classics. Jackson introduced much-needed glamour to the largely male world of rockabilly, and her rasping vocal style is instantly recognizable. A born-again Christian, she still tours the world performing an authentic rockabilly act.

Buddy Knox
(Vocals, guitar, 1933–99)

Knox came from the tiny west Texas town of Happy. His group, The Rhythm Orchids included future country-music executive Jimmy Bowen on upright bass. Their biggest hit, 'Party Doll' (1957), was recorded at Norman Petty's studio in Clovis, New Mexico. Buddy's style was light and melodic, and less aggressive than his contemporaries. His career extended longer than most as he was able to adapt into both the pop and country markets.

Right

Dogged by personal tragedy, including the death of his wife and two of his sons, Roy Orbison managed to maintain a successful career right up to his death from a heart attack in 1988.

Bob Luman
(Vocals, 1937–78)

Greatly influenced by Elvis Presley, Bob Luman from Kilgore, Texas was a regular on the *Louisiana Hayride*. He recorded rockabilly for Imperial and appeared in the movie *Carnival Rock* (1957). His band, which included

Marvin Rainwater

(Vocals, guitar, b.1925)

Part Cherokee, Rainwater was born in Wichita, Kansas, and was already an established country act before his 1958 rockabilly recording, 'Whole Lotta Woman', gave him a British No. 1. He toured Britain, headlining at the London Palladium, and made further fine rockabilly records for MGM. In the 1960s his career dipped after calluses on his vocal chords badly affected his singing voice, but he recovered and remains active as both a country and rockabilly performer.

Billy Lee Riley

(Vocals, guitar, harmonica, b. 1933)

Riley was born in Pocahontas, Arkansas, and enjoyed seven releases on Sun without ever securing the hit that his finest work undoubtedly deserved. He and his band were often utilized as session musicians and worked with many other Sun artists. A highly versatile artist, he eventually recorded rockabilly, blues, hillbilly and country soul, plus harmonica instrumentals for a host of different labels under numerous aliases. Sadly, real commercial success has always eluded him, though 'Flyin' Saucers Rock 'n' Roll' (1956) will remain a classic.

Jack Scott

(Vocals, guitar, songwriter, b. 1936)

Jack Scafone was born in Windsor, Ontario. He wrote most of his own material and all his recordings are highly distinctive, owing to his bluesy, baritone voice and, in many cases, the vocal harmonies of The Chantones. A shy man, he should have become a major country star after the rockabilly era, but this did not happen. He still managed an impressive tally of hits on Carlton, Top Rank and Capitol, though. He remains a dynamic and intense stage performer.

Warren Smith

(Vocals, guitar, 1933–80)

Smith was born near Yazoo City, Mississippi and recorded rockabilly for Sun. The likes of 'Ubangi Stomp' and 'Rock 'n' Roll Ruby' are now perceived as classics but only the more restrained 'So Long I'm Gone' made the national charts. He moved to California and cut a string of country hits for Liberty in 1960–64, before a car wreck curtailed his career. He re-emerged in Britain singing rockabilly again in 1977, but died of a heart attack three years later.

Gene Vincent

(Vocals, 1935–71)

Despite a leg permanently crippled in a road accident, Eugene Craddock, from Norfolk, Virginia, rocketed to stardom in 1956 with his multi-million seller 'Be-Bop-A-Lula' for Capitol. Other hits and movie appearances followed, and along with his group, The Blue Caps, he developed a wild and highly visual stage act. Vincent's health deteriorated through heavy drinking, and he died prematurely of liver failure in California.

Below

In the 1960s, Gene Vincent lived in the UK, where he was a tremendously popular live performer.

When Two Worlds Collide:
Nashville & Beyond

The 1950s and 1960s were milestone decades for country music. It was during these years that the stylistic tensions between traditional and contemporary, rural and urbane, became sharply delineated and the first ideological and aesthetic battle lines between the traditionalists and modernists were drawn in the sand.

Out of this tension arose bold innovation and refreshing diversity. The 1950s saw the nearly simultaneous rise of styles as divergent as wild and youthful Memphis-style rockabilly and its virtual antithesis: the mellow, refined, pop-influenced Nashville Sound.

At the same time, styles that coalesced in the 1940s, such as honky-tonk and bluegrass, continued to flourish and find new listeners. Thus the country charts during the 1950s included everything from the mountain-style ballads and old-timey train songs of Roy Acuff and Hank Snow to the countrypolitan crooning of smooth operators like Eddy Arnold and George Morgan, and the occasional cowboy ballad by the likes of Marty Robbins or Johnny Cash.

Just as important, though, these two decades marked the rise of the Nashville music industry as an entity separate but never entirely independent of the larger pop industry, centered in New York and Los Angeles. By the end of the 1960s, Music City – as Nashville's record industry has come to be called – would make its influence felt in nearly every corner of the globe. In so doing, it would elevate country music from its secondary status as a regional music to an internationally popular form nearly as central to youth culture as rock or pop.

Radio, of course, was central to the rise of country, since record sales, even today, are highly dependent on the exposure of radio airplay. During the 1960s alone, the number of full-time country radio stations in the USA rose from 81 in 1961 to 525 in 1971. The number had risen to 2,321 by 1996.

Key Artists

Chet Atkins

Johnny Cash

Patsy Cline

George Jones

Jim Reeves

Influences & Development

introduction ⊙ 160 key artists ⊙ 168 a-z of artists ⊙ 178

Below
Patti Page's 1950 recording of Pee Wee King's 'Tennessee Waltz' sold nearly five million copies.

The Nashville Sound, which has been as much praised as maligned, was a classic example of Nashville's burgeoning record industry flexing its newfound muscles and making an intentional grab at the brass ring of increased record sales. Occasionally called 'crossover country', 'easy-listening country' or 'countrypolitan', the Nashville Sound was as much a product of commercial calculation as artistic inspiration. Innovative Nashville producers like Chet Atkins (1924–2001) and Owen Bradley (1915–98) saw it as a vehicle for tapping into the increased record sales afforded by crossover success in the pop-music charts.

Country Crossovers

During the 1940s, there had been occasional cross-pollinations between country and pop music. From the 1930s well into the 1950s, Grand Ole Opry star Red Foley (1910–68) charmed both country folk and urbanites alike with his smooth voice and mellow musical sensibilities. In the 1950s and early 1960s Patti Page, an Oklahoman who cut her teeth singing western swing, had massive pop hits with covers of country tunes. Crooner Bing Crosby even got in on the act with covers of Ernest Tubb's (1914–84) 'Walkin' The Floor Over You', while Tubb had recorded with The Andrews Sisters. The untapped sales potential promised by the huge, beckoning pop market did not go unnoticed by country producers and record executives, and the fledgling country-music industry, though still in its infancy, was poised for a commercial explosion at the dawn of the decade.

'Country songs for the most part have always been heavily rooted in reality. The first artists were the people next door. They would sing on their porch or in their living room or at a barn dance. They sang about what they knew....'
Chet Atkins

An Antidote To Rock'n'Roll

The advent of rockabilly and rock'n'roll in the mid-1950s also helped spur the later 1960s Nashville crossover era. The emergence of Elvis Presley (1935–77), Jerry Lee Lewis (b. 1935) and other rock'n'rollers with early rock hits like 'Hound Dog', 'Jailhouse Rock', 'Whole Lotta Shakin'' and 'Great Balls Of Fire' launched a national craze that for a

The crossover craze was also spurred by the success of Nashville-based artists like The Everly Brothers, Roy Orbison (1936–88) and Brenda Lee – teen rock'n'roll idols who seemed to effortlessly capture the mass market with youth-oriented hits written by Nashville-based songwriters and produced in Nashville studios.

Just as radio was an essential building-block in country music in the 1930s and 1940s, the emerging medium of television was a lesser, but still substantial, ingredient in the music's growth in popularity in the 1950s and 1960s. Throughout both decades, dozens of artists – Eddy Arnold and Johnny Cash among them – had their own regionally or nationally broadcast musical variety shows.

while seriously diminished sales in the country market, particularly of honky-tonk and more traditional styles. This is why even unlikely hard-country and honky-tonk singers such as George Jones (b. 1931) and Faron Young (1932–96) briefly tried their hands at rockabilly and rock'n'roll. It was smoother singers of the era – such as Sonny James (b. 1929), Marty Robbins (1925–82) and Don Gibson (1928–2003) who best weathered the storm and enjoyed late-1950s crossover pop hits with mellow teen ballads like 'Young Love', 'A White Sport Coat (And A Pink Carnation)' and 'Oh Lonesome Me'.

The success of such records was not lost upon Nashville's Music Row. Producers Atkins and Bradley, two widely acknowledged 'fathers' of the Nashville Sound, had long been in search of a formula that would enable Nashville-produced records to jump the fence into the pop charts.

The term 'Nashville Sound' has also come to signify the increasingly regimented, somewhat formulaic approach to hit-making. By the early 1960s, the Music Row studio system had come to be dominated by a relatively small, tight-knit coterie of 'A-Team' session musicians that played on hundreds of sessions, which were recorded and produced with factory-clock precision.

The Countrypolitan Controversy

The resulting countrypolitan music was not well received in all corners. Many loyal fans of traditional and honky-tonk-style country felt betrayed – a feeling that persists to this day as mild animosity toward the Nashville record industry's inclination to 'sell out'. These traditionalists considered the Nashville Sound to be an affront to country music's integrity. It was particularly cloying when even a premier honky-tonk singer such as Ray Price (b. 1926) blithely segued into countrypolitan cushiness with crossover hits like 'Danny Boy' (1967) and 'For The Good Times' (1970).

Some Nashville artists like crooner Eddy Arnold (b. 1918, 'What's He Doing In My World'), Grand Ole Opry star George Morgan and Virginia-born songstress Patsy Cline (1932–63) seemed to find their natural voices in the Nashville Sound setting. Others, such as Price, who began their careers steeped in some form of traditionalism, grew to enthusiastically embrace more modern musical adaptations.

Above

Before her untimely death in a plane crash in 1963, Patsy Cline cracked the pop Top 10 with 'Crazy', 'I Fall To Pieces' and 'Walkin' After Midnight'.

Right

Crooner Eddy Arnold, whose music epitomized the Nashville Sound in the era of the pop crossover.

Far Right

Shania Twain's music is clearly grounded in country, but today she has almost totally moved into the pop arena.

Creating The Nashville Sound

The Nashville Sound was largely an aggressive retrofitting of mainstream country music to make it accessible to pop-radio airplay. The motivation was the music of the ringing cash register: during the 1950s, 25,000 units was deemed respectable sales for a hit country single. At the same time, topping the pop charts could mean sales of a million units or more.

Atkins, Bradley and their contemporaries found tasteful ways to subdue the clatter and clang of country music's raw edges and nudge the overall sound in a more uptown direction. They toned down the vocal twang or eliminated it all together. They replaced raucous fiddles and steel guitars with sophisticated background vocal arrangements, bright sparkling 'slip-note piano' embellishments and snazzy string and horn arrangements.

While the Nashville Sound was certainly a dominant force in the 1950s and 1960s, it was really only one piece of the stylistic puzzle. This was, in fact, an era marked by a degree of diversity, which compared to today's highly regimented and formatted charts and radio formats, seems downright amazing in retrospect. It was truly a time when country music expanded its big tent to cover a potpourri of different styles and sub-styles.

Artistic Explosion

While artists like Eddy Arnold and Jim Reeves were crooning their way to crossover success, more tradition-minded artists like George Jones and Stonewall Jackson (b. 1932) would also rise from obscurity to keep the music's more down-home styles and sensibilities refreshed and revitalized. Others, like Arizona-born Marty Robbins, would blossom into incredibly versatile artists whose hit-making prowess straddled such seemingly disparate styles as straight-ahead country laments, melancholy western songs and even teen pop ballads.

Out of the mid-1950s Memphis rockabilly explosion would arise a coterie of young turks who would later mature and become some of the leading figures in country's mainstream in the 1960s – Johnny Cash, Jerry Lee Lewis and Carl Perkins foremost among them. Similarly, a number of young honky-tonkers segued with varying degrees of grace into a mellower, Nashville Sound style as they matured.

Women would also, as never before, become a vital force in the music mix during these years. Along with the rise of a singer like Patsy Cline, who seemed to effortlessly transcend the hazy boundaries between pop and country, there also arose a number of more tradition-minded singers who would make their marks with less progressive styles.

All the while, Nashville's music industry was growing increasingly sophisticated and market-savvy. Record-company executives and promoters were gradually becoming more adept at employing the mass-marketing strategies used by other industries. In 1958, a handful of Nashville's movers and shakers founded the Country Music Association (CMA), an organization whose efforts were crucial in using the power and persuasiveness of television, radio and other mass media in transforming the music into the national and international cultural and commercial force that it has become today.

The Country Music Hall Of Fame

Below

Bluegrass king Bill Monroe was inducted into the Country Music Hall Of Fame in 1970 and the Songwriters Foundation Hall Of Fame in 1971.

Just as sports have their pantheon of greats, the country-music industry established its own Hall Of Fame in 1961 to honour its most influential figures and deepen public understanding and appreciation of the music's rich heritage and history.

A Pantheon Of Country Stars

As of 2005, 62 artists and industry leaders – starting with Jimmie Rodgers (1897–1933) and songwriter and music publisher Fred Rose, who both were posthumously inducted in 1961– have been enshrined in the Country Music Hall Of Fame.

The Hall Of Fame's membership spans the many genres and subgenres contained within the broad, loosely defined and somewhat elastic rubric of country music. Its roll call of greats encompasses more than three-quarters of a century, from founding figures like Jimmie Rodgers and The Carter Family, to contemporary figures like the country-rock band, Alabama. Bluegrass (Lester Flatt, Earl Scruggs, Bill Monroe), western music (Gene Autry, Roy Rogers, The Sons Of The Pioneers), western swing (Bob Wills), honky-tonk (Floyd Tillman, Ernest Tubb, Lefty Frizzell, Kitty Wells, George Jones), old-time music (The Carter Family, Uncle Dave Macon, Grandpa Jones), outstanding songwriters (Felice and Boudleaux Bryant, Harlan Howard, Cindy Walker) and country comedy (Rod Brasfield, The Duke Of Paducah, Minnie Pearl) and rockabilly (Elvis Presley) are just some of the styles represented in the Hall Of Fame.

Also included are a number of producers, songwriters, executives, entrepreneurs and broadcasters who have had a lasting creative or commercial impact in shaping the music and the underlying industry that makes it, promotes it and distributes it.

Pride Of Nashville

The Hall Of Fame was created by the Country Music Association, the country-music industry's leading professional organization. It went public in 1967, when it opened as a museum and tourist attraction in Nashville. It has since become a national tourist destination for thousands of country fans.

The Country Music Hall Of Fame and Museum operates under the non-profit aegis of the Country Music

Foundation. The foundation also maintains an extensive music archive and research library, along with its own publishing arm and record label, through which it has released a number of valuable historic musical compilations and book-length histories.

Annual selections to the Country Music Hall Of Fame are chosen through a formal process. First, a panel of a dozen industry leaders submits a list of nominees to a group of 300 electors, all of whom are members of the CMA. Final decisions for each year's inductions are made by the electors. Each year, anywhere from one to four new members are elected to the Hall Of

Fame. The only exception was 1963 when none of the nominees garnered sufficient votes for induction.

Each new inductee is honored with a bas-relief portrait cast in bronze that is added to the Hall Of Fame display in the Country Music Hall of Fame Museum, in downtown Nashville. More than 10 million people have visited the museum since it opened (its original location was on Nashville's Music Row) in 1967. The Nashville Songwriters Foundation also has its own Hall Of Fame, devoted exclusively to honouring the best and most oft-recorded country-song scribes of the past 75 years. Its membership includes everyone from A. P. Carter to Dolly Parton.

Left
Honky-tonk queen Kitty Wells was inducted into the Country Music Hall Of Fame in 1976 – just one of many honours accorded her.

Below
The original Country Music Hall Of Fame building on 16th Avenue South.

Chet Atkins

Key Artist

Atkins was given his first guitar by his stepfather and by the age of 10 he could already competently find his way around its fret board. He also taught himself to play fiddle. He was influenced extensively by his older half-brother, Jimmy Atkins, who would later play in legendary guitarist Les Paul's backing trio. But young Chet's life was forever changed one night in the late 1930s when he heard Merle Travis finger picking on WLW, a powerful radio station that broadcast from Cincinnati, Ohio. Atkins was mesmerized and would soon formulate and eventually perfect his own intricate finger-picking method.

After performing as a soloist and back-up musician on radio stations in Knoxville, Tennessee, Cincinnati, Ohio, Raleigh, North Carolina and elsewhere, Atkins' big break came in 1947 when he was working at a station in Denver, Colorado. He got a call from producer Steve Sholes who, after hearing some transcription discs of Atkins' guitar-

'Chet Atkins is probably the best guitar player who ever lived.'
Charley Pride

Above
Chet Atkins started his musical career playing fiddle and guitar with his older brother Jimmy.

Right
Merle Travis had a distinct thumb-picking style on the guitar that hugely impressed the young Chet Atkins, and set him on the path to recording success.

One of modern country music's most remarkable figures, Chester Burton Atkins born in Luttrell, Tennessee, rose from rural obscurity to become one of the world's most celebrated guitarists and one of Nashville's most influential record producers. Atkins' musical vision did much to shape country music during the 1950s and 1960s.

Early Years
Atkins was born on 20 June 1924, the son of a music teacher. He spent his early years in the Clinch Mountain foothills of East Tennessee. As a child, he was stricken with asthma, and when his parents separated it fell to him and his brother to keep the family afloat by working the small, hardscrabble farm that was their sustenance.

playing, signed the young instrumentalist to RCA Records. Thus began Atkins' long relationship with both Sholes and RCA – the label with which he was affiliated for 35 years.

Atkins And The Nashville Sound

Atkins made his debut recording for Nashville-based Bullet Records in 1946, and commenced his first solo recordings for RCA the following year. At that time he was still heavily steeped in the Merle Travis influence, but he gradually emerged with his own distinct style that encompassed elements of country, jazz, pop, rock and even flamenco.

In the late 1940s, he became the featured guitarist with Mother Maybelle And The Carter Sisters and began performing with them on The Grand Ole Opry in 1950. Soon, he was one of Nashville's most sought-after session guitarists.

While making his own solo records, Atkins was also frequently called on to serve as Sholes' Nashville assistant. By the early 1950s, he was leading and occasionally producing record sessions for an array of other RCA artists. By 1957, Atkins was overseeing the label's entire Nashville operations. By the mid-1950s, he had begun expanding his guitar-playing technique to embrace elements of pop and jazz with his intricate finger-picking style. While recording adventurous solo releases, he continued to back bedrock country artists like Webb Pierce, Hank Williams and Mother Maybelle And The Carter Sisters in the studio.

As a producer, Atkins was one of the principal architects of the Nashville Sound, a commercially driven movement that first gathered momentum in the mid-1950s. Yet the long, diverse list of artists that Atkins signed to RCA and patiently nurtured into stars covered the stylistic range from traditional to progressive. These included, among many others, Dolly Parton, Waylon Jennings, Bobby Bare, Jim Reeves, pianist Floyd Cramer, Jerry Reed, Porter Wagoner, Charley Pride (the only black artist to break Nashville's racial barriers and achieve stardom) and Don Gibson.

Atkins' collaborations with other guitar masters were also many and varied – he recorded and performed with everyone from Les Paul, jazz prodigy Lenny Breau and British rocker Mark Knopfler to fellow Nashville guitar wizard Jerry Reed, fellow country guitar legends Merle Travis and Doc Watson and The Boston Pops.

In 1973, Atkins became the youngest artist ever inducted into the Country Music Hall Of Fame. He died of cancer in 2001.

Above
Chet Atkins collaborated with many Nashville greats in his long career.

Key Track

'Yakety Axe' (1965)
Atkins' all-time biggest career hit was his playful guitar adaptation of his friend Boots Randolph's 1963 hit saxophone instrumental, 'Yakety Sax'. 'Yakety Axe' was recorded and released during a period when Atkins, as an RCA executive and producer, was producing many of the other artists on that star-studded label roster.

Johnny Cash

Key Artist

One of the most revered figures in modern country music, Johnny Cash's vast, half-century-long body of work as both a songwriter and singer encompasses an extensive tapestry of musical Americana – everything from prison songs and railroad ballads, to folk-style broadsides and even clever novelty tunes like 'A Boy Named Sue'. As a singer, he immortalized a style that was straightforward and unadorned, yet magisterial in its emotional gravitas, melancholy sonorousness and world-weary earnestness. More than a mere country star, Cash was an American master and one of the true voices of his generation.

'You've got a song you're singing from your gut, you want that audience to feel it in their gut. And you've got to make them think that you're one of them sitting out there. They've got to be able to relate to what you're doing.'

Johnny Cash

Country Heritage

Cash was born into a family of cotton farmers in Kingsland, Arkansas, on 26 February 1932 and was weaned on the gospel music his family sang at church. He was also influenced by the music of an older generation of country artists liked The Carter Family and Hank Snow, who he heard on the radio. His early life was informed by tragedy. An older brother, Jack, was killed in a grisly sawmill accident when Cash was still a child, and he seemed to carry the emotional scars of this incident all through his life.

In 1949, after graduating from high school, Cash briefly worked in an auto body plant in Detroit, Michigan. But he really began writing songs, singing and playing guitar in earnest while serving in Germany with the US Air Force in the early 1950s. Back in civilian clothes in 1954, he married for the first time and worked briefly as an appliance salesman in Memphis, Tennessee. It was here that he teamed up with electric guitarist Luther Perkins and stand-up bassist Marshall Grant and began performing gospel music on a local radio station.

'Folsom Prison Blues' (1960), to dramatic ballads of the Old West ('Don't Take Your Guns To Town', 1959). The social awareness evinced in his music also earned him credibility within the 1960s folk music boom. He occasionally performed and recorded with his friend, Bob Dylan.

After bouncing back from a longstanding addiction to pills, Cash found renewed emotional stability and inspiration with his second wife, June Carter, of the illustrious Carter Family, whom he married in 1968. From 1969 to 1971, his fame was enlarged as he hosted his own weekly, prime time musical variety show on ABC TV, on which he performed, along with an array of other established and up and coming country and folk artists, including Bob Dylan and Kris Kristofferson.

By the time Cash parted ways with Columbia Records in 1986, he'd ceased to be a presence in the music charts. But after signing with American Records, a prestigious California-based independent record label, seven years later, he rediscovered his musical vitality with a series of austere albums that earned him fresh currency with a younger, alternative country' audience and reaffirmed his status as an American folk hero.

Though sidelined from performing by health problems for most of the 1990s, Cash was still making records in the final weeks before his death in 2003 due to complications from diabetes. His early years were retold in the Academy Award-winning 2005 biopic *Walk The Line*.

A Prolific Career

Cash and his new backing duo also auditioned and signed with legendary Memphis producer Sam Phillips, who had recently produced and released Elvis Presley's first hits on his own Sun Records label. From the mid-1950s, until he signed with Columbia Records in 1958, Cash had his initial success with Sun-released hits such as 'Cry, Cry, Cry' (1955), 'I Walk The Line' (1956), 'Ballad Of A Teenage Queen' (1958) and 'Guess Things Happen That Way' (1958).

From the early 1960s until his death, Cash amassed a huge body of recorded work that included excursions into all manner of rural musical idioms and byroads – everything from folksy train and prison songs like 'Orange Blossom Special' (1965) and

Classic Recordings

The Sun Years **(1990)**
'Hey Porter', 'Guess Things Happen That Way', 'Big River', 'Get Rhythm'

American Recordings **(1994)**
'Delia's Gone', 'The Beast In Me'

At Folsom Prison **(reissued 1999)**
'Folsom Prison Blues', 'Orange Blossom Special'

The Legend **(2005)**
'I Walk The Line', 'Cry, Cry, Cry'

Above
From the mid-1980s Cash periodically recorded and performed as part of an illustrious quartet called The Highwaymen, which also included Waylon Jennings and Willie Nelson.

Far Left
Johnny Cash had a huge fan base from a wide range of musical spheres, and found receptive audiences in prisons and at mainstream pop festivals as well as on the country circuit.

Left
Joaquin Phoenix and Reese Witherspoon play the Man in Black Johnny Cash and his wife June Carter Cash in the 2005 biopic Walk The Line.

Key Track

'I Walk The Line'
Cash hurriedly wrote the lyrics to 'I Walk The Line' one night in 1956 in a backstage dressing room in East Texas. When Cash recorded the song (for the first of several times) later that year at Sun Records studio, in Memphis, producer Sam Phillips wedged a piece of wax paper under the strings of his guitar to create a percussive effect.

Patsy Cline

Key Artist

Crossover Diva

Cline was one of the few female artists at the forefront of the emerging Nashville Sound. With her smooth yet intensely emotional vocal style, she almost effortlessly bridged the gap between country and pop audiences. She did this by combining the spunk and fervour of honky-tonk and old-time country with the vulnerability of a pop diva. The best of her music has never gone out of print, and her commercial masterpieces – hit singles such as 'Walkin' After Midnight' (1957), 'I Fall To Pieces' (1961), 'Crazy' (1961), 'She's Got You' (1962) and 'Sweet Dreams' (1963) – sound as timeless today as when they were first released.

First Taste Of The Big Time

Born on 8 September 1932, Patricia Patterson Hensley, in Winchester, Virginia, Cline came from a broken home and was the victim of sexual abuse at the hands of her father, who was a gifted amateur singer. 'Ginny', as she was then called, started out singing at churches and local get-togethers. During her formative years, she was indelibly influenced by older singers such as Kay Starr, Kate Smith, Charline Arthur and 1920s chanteuse Helen Morgan.

'Carnegie Hall was real fabulous, but you know, it ain't as big as the Grand Ole Opry.' **Patsy Cline**

One of country music's most influential and enduringly popular figures, Patsy Cline managed to transcend with seeming effortlessness the uneasy rift between traditional country music and the more urbane Nashville Sound that emerged full-blown in the late 1950s.

Feisty and outspoken, Cline left school at age 15 to begin her single-minded pursuit of a music career. By age 20, she had her first small taste of the big time when she began singing with Bill Peer, a country bandleader who enjoyed regional popularity in northern and central Virginia.

It was around that time that she adapted the stage name, Patsy, from her middle name, Patterson. Before long, she was a regular player in the thriving country music scene that had sprung up in Washington, D.C., by the early 1950s. By late 1954, she was appearing regularly on *Town & Country*, a regional television show created and produced by local music mogul Connie B. Gay, on which other then-local celebrities like Roy Clark and Jimmy Dean also appeared regularly.

Years Of Celebrity

Through contacts made in Washington, Cline landed her first recording contract with the Four Star label, in Pasadena, California. Her debut single release, a mournful ballad called 'A Church, A Courtroom And Then Goodbye' attracted little attention when it was released in July 1955 by Decca Records, in a leasing agreement with Four Star. Her next three singles were also unsuccessful.

By this time, Cline had already been in and out of Nashville several times and had appeared on the Grand Ole Opry. But it was her January 1957 appearance on *Arthur Godfrey's Talent Scouts*, a nationally televised show, that suddenly launched her to stardom. Within weeks she had the No. 2 spot in the *Billboard* country charts with 'Walkin' After Midnight'. The record was produced by Owen Bradley, who would serve not only as Cline's producer but also as a sage mentor and musical advisor all through her short but illustrious career.

After a hiatus, during which she married for the second time and had two children, Cline returned to the charts with her first No. 1 single, 'I Fall To Pieces', in 1961.

Far Left
Despite her untimely death at age 30, Cline has served as a role model for many noteworthy singers – Loretta Lynn, Linda Ronstadt, Wynonna Judd and Trisha Yearwood to name but a few.

Middle
Wynonna Judd was just one of many female country singers who were greatly influenced by the style of Patsy Cline – the mother of modern country music.

Left
Jessica Lange portrays Patsy Cline in the film of the singer's short life, Sweet Dreams (1985).

On 5 March 1963, Cline was returning to Nashville from a benefit performance in Kansas City when the small plane she was riding in crashed near Camden, Tennessee. Singers Hawkshaw Hawkins and Cowboy Copas also died in the accident. Her memory lives on in her best-loved song, 'Crazy', which continues to sell in vast quantities every year.

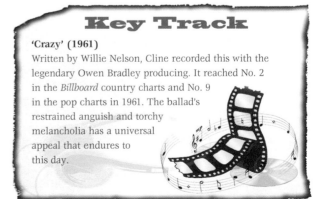

Key Track

'Crazy' (1961)
Written by Willie Nelson, Cline recorded this with the legendary Owen Bradley producing. It reached No. 2 in the *Billboard* country charts and No. 9 in the pop charts in 1961. The ballad's restrained anguish and torchy melancholia has a universal appeal that endures to this day.

George Jones

Key Artist

'Country music to me is heartfelt music that speaks to the common man. It is about real-life stories with rather simple melodies that the average person can follow.' **George Jones**

Below
George Jones has an expansive, soulful, clench-toothed baritone style all his own that repeatedly earned him critical raves as the greatest country singer ever.

Born on 12 September 1931, near Saratoga, Texas, in a remote region of East Texas known as The Big Thicket, George Glenn Jones is widely considered to be country music's quintessential honky-tonk singer and probably the most influential artist to come along since Hank Williams' death in 1953. Throughout his 50 years of record-making, Jones has remained steadfastly faithful to the unadorned 1950s honky-tonk vocal approach pioneered by early 1950s singers like Williams and Lefty Frizzell.

Hard-Living Hero

Like Williams, for much of his career Jones had a strong penchant for honky-tonk style hard living and wild times – something that has merely enhanced his cachet and mystique with fans. Three marriages and divorces, alcoholism and drug addiction were just some of the wages exacted by the near-lethal combination of the stresses and pressures of fame and a tempestuous, volatile personality.

As a youth, Jones grew up in near-poverty in a household fraught by the tension between a hard-drinking, wayward father and a teetotal, churchgoing mother. His father had a mean streak that was often unleashed by alcohol. Sometimes he would come home drunk in the middle of the night, rouse his young son out of bed and command him to sing. Jones has often intimated that this is the source of the stage fright and painful, love-hate ambivalence he has often felt about performing.

When he was young, Jones sang for tips on the streets of Beaumont, Texas, where his father worked in the shipyards during the Second World War and the family lived in a government housing project. After a brief first marriage and a stint in thé US Marines in the early 1950s, he began recording for Starday Records – a fledgling, Dallas-based label – as well as appearing on the *Big D Jamboree*, a local country-music radio show. His earliest hits for Starday (which later linked a brief deal with Mercury Records) included 'Why, Baby Why' (1955), 'Color Of The Blues' and 'White Lightning' (1958).

Honky-Tonk Balladeer

By the early 1960s, Jones was recording in Nashville, where he began to perfect the intense honky-tonk balladry style that became his hallmark. His early flair for this style can be heard on hits like 'The Window Up Above' (1960), 'Tender Years' (1961) and 'She Thinks I Still Care' (1962). In 1969, Jones married his third wife, country singer Tammy Wynette, and joined the Grand Ole Opry. For a few years, Jones and Wynette were something akin to the

Left

George Jones with his then-wife Tammy Wynette. This was the third marriage for both of them; it lasted six years.

Sonny And Cher of country music. They appeared together regularly on the Opry and recorded a string of best-selling duets, including 'Take Me' (1971), ''The Ceremony' (1972) and 'We're Gonna Hold On' (1973).

By the time Jones and Wynette divorced in 1975, Jones was already on a downward spiral of alcoholism and drug abuse, from which he would not emerge for nearly a decade. Yet even during these lost years, he managed to record some extremely moving music. In 1980, he released a mournful, fatalistic ballad called 'He Stopped Loving Her Today', which reached the top of the charts, won the singer both Grammy and Country Music Association Awards, and gave his career renewed momentum.

In the years since, Jones has mellowed into one of country music's distinguished elder statesmen and has continued recording, performing and scoring the occasional hit. In 1992 he was inducted into the Country Music Hall Of Fame.

Left

George Jones accompanies leading female country artists Bonnie Raitt and Linda Ronstadt.

Key Track

'He Stopped Loving Her Today' (1980)
Jones was mired in personal problems when he first heard this song, written by Bobby Braddock and Curly Putnam, and was put off by its self-pitying tone. Nonetheless, producer Billy Sherrill persuaded him to record it in early 1980. Released later that year, it earned a slew of awards, became Jones's first million-selling single, and gave second wind to his career.

Jim Reeves

Key Artist

tonk years), Reeves possessed a warm, reflective baritone that conveyed warmth and earnestness when framed by understated, easy-listening style arrangements of pianos and subdued background vocals.

Early Years

Before embarking on a musical career, Reeves briefly attended the University of Texas on a baseball scholarship in the early 1940s. He dropped out of college to work in the Houston shipyards during the Second World War. After that he played minor-league baseball for several years before injuries sidelined him for good.

Reeves was working as a disc jockey on a radio station in Henderson, Texas, when it dawned on him that he could sing as well as – if not better than – many of the artists of

'After more than forty years, Jim Reeves remains one of the fascinating figures in the history of American entertainment and stands as one of the greatest figures that ever lived.' **Former Grand Ole Opry announcer Kyle Cantrell**

James Travis Reeves, born in Galloway, Texas, on 20 August 1924, was one of the most talented singers to find his voice and define his musical style during the late 1950s' emergence of the Nashville Sound. Like Eddy Arnold and Ray Price (in his post-honky-

the day whose records he was spinning. He made his first recordings in 1949 for a small, local Houston label (Macy's), but they attracted very little attention when released. In April, 1953, his fortunes turned when he recorded a straight-ahead country tune called 'Mexican Joe' for Abbott Records. At the time, he was working as an announcer on the *Louisiana Hayride*. After its release, 'Mexican Joe' hit the top of the charts and when Reeves first performed the song on the *Louisiana Hayride* he garnered six encores. For the next two years, he was one of the live radio show's headlining performers.

By the late 1950s, Reeves had moved on to RCA Victor, where he had a string of Top 10 records. But the sudden rise of rockabilly sapped the record-buying public's enthusiasm for the rustic, steel guitar-and-fiddle honky-tonk sound, and country record sales temporarily plummeted.

As a result, Nashville producers like RCA's Chet Atkins, in search of an antidote, began rethinking their basic approach to hit-making. In Reeves' case, Atkins stripped the fiddle and steel guitar out and instead incorporated less aggressive and subtle rhythm arrangements while relying more heavily on smooth background vocals to fill in the arrangement. Atkins also urged Reeves to sing more softly and stand closer to the microphone, thus imbuing his records with an enhanced sense of intimacy with his listeners.

Crossover Success

Reeves' first flush of success with the Nashville Sound came with 'Four Walls' – a plaintive ballad that reached No. 2 in *Billboard*'s country charts shortly after its early 1957 release. 'Four Walls' also crossed over and climbed to the No. 11 position in *Billboard*'s pop charts. In 1959, Reeves had even more resounding crossover success with 'He'll Have To Go', a lush romantic ballad that topped the country charts and reached No. 2 on the pop charts. Reeves' across-the-board success led to appearances on both the Grand Ole Opry and *American Bandstand*, a television show that largely featured teen rock and pop idols.

By the mid-1960s, Reeves' recording and touring careers were still going strong, even though he had begun to grow weary of the hectic months he was spending on the road. He began cutting back on personal appearances and started to venture into new fields, including acting and real-estate investment. It was one of his land investments that took Reeves (who was also an amateur pilot) on a plane trip to Arkansas in late July 1965. On the return flight to Nashville on 31 July, Reeves and Dean Manuel were both killed when the plane crashed in a thunderstorm near Nashville.

Classic Recordings

Jim Reeves (2000)
'Am I That Easy To Forget', 'I Guess I'm Crazy', 'Am I Losing You'

Jim Reeves – Greatest Hits (2001)
'He'll Have To Go', 'Four Walls', 'Billy Bayou'

Jim Reeves – The Ultimate Collection (2002)
'Mexican Joe', 'Have I Told You Lately That I Love You', 'Adios Amigo'

Left
After his untimely death, the globally popular Reeves was posthumously inducted into the Country Music Hall Of Fame in 1967.

Far Left
Jim Reeves was certainly capable of singing hard-core country tunes, but he made his name as a country-pop balladeer, which appealed to a larger audience share and brought him great success.

Middle Left
Velvet-voiced Reeves hosted the country radio show the Louisiana Hayride; one day, when Hank Williams failed to turn up, Reeves stood in – and was signed immediately by Abbott Records.

Key Track

'He'll Have To Go' (1959)
This Texas-born artist was in the midst of trading his cowboy hat and boots for a sports coat and slacks and fervently embracing up-town-style Nashville Sound when he recorded this smooth lament. It topped the country charts, reached No. 2 in *Billboard*'s pop charts and became the biggest record of Reeves' tragically short career.

A-Z of Artists

Bill Anderson takes centre stage at the Grand Ole Opry in Nashville. He joined the show in 1961, and remained a popular performer there for many years.

Bill Anderson
(Vocals, b. 1937)

Columbia, South Carolina-born James William Anderson emerged as one of Nashville's most celebrated songwriters in 1958, when Ray Price took his 'City Lights' to the top of the charts. Anderson soon signed his own recording contract with Decca Records and joined the Grand Ole Opry in 1961. In the years since he has parlayed his songwriting prowess, whispery vocal style and affable public persona into a resilient and enduring career. His biggest successes as a singer have come with smooth, easy-listening hits like 'The Tips Of My Fingers' (1960), 'Mama Sang A Song' (1962), 'Still' (1963) and 'I Can't Wait Any Longer' (1978).

Right

Boudleuax and Felice Bryant (here with music publisher Wesley Rose) were the most famous songwriting team of the 1940s and 1950s. Together they penned many classic hits.

Bobby Bare
(Vocals, b. 1935)

This gifted Ironton, Ohio-born singer possesses a laconic, empathic baritone voice that has made him one of country's most adventurous and imaginative song interpreters. During the 1960s, Bare found pop chart success and popularity with folk audiences with wistful, pop-flavoured crossover ballads like 'Detroit City' (1963) and 'Streets Of Baltimore' (1966). He was also a minor but important figure in the country outlaw movement of the 1970s.

Owen Bradley
(Producer, record executive, 1915–98)

This influential Westmoreland, Tennessee-born record producer started out as a piano player in pop dance bands before being hired as an assistant to pioneering Nashville producer Paul Cohen at Decca. From the late 1950s until the 1980s, Bradley produced the records and helped shape the musical identities of a host of stars, including Kitty Wells, Patsy Cline, Loretta Lynn, Ernest Tubb, The Wilburn Brothers and, in more recent years, Canadian alt country-pop diva k.d. lang.

Boudleaux & Felice Bryant
(Songwriters, 1940s–80s)

Husband-and-wife songwriting team Boudleaux (1920–87) and Felice (1925–2003) Bryant composed many country classics, including 'Bye Bye Love' (popularized by The Everly Brothers), 'Rocky Top' (first popularized by The Osborne Brothers and covered by dozens of others) and 'Let's Think About Living' (Bob Luman).

Hank Cochran

(Songwriter, vocals, b. 1935)

One-time member of the Cochran Brothers (with rock'n'roller Eddie Cochran, no relation), Isola, Mississippi-born Garland Perry Cochran was one of the most-oft-recorded songwriters of the 1960s and 1970s. 'She's Got You' (a hit for Patsy Cline), 'Make The World Go Away' (a hit for both Ray Price and Eddy Arnold) and Willie Nelson's 1981 hit, 'Angel Flying Too Close To The Ground' are among his best-known titles.

Floyd Cramer

(Piano, songwriter, 1933–97)

This Santi, Louisiana-born pianist was to country piano in the 1950s and 1960s what his mentor Chet Atkins was to guitar. Cramer's distinct 'slip-note' style became a hallmark of the Nashville Sound. As a soloist, he also recorded dozens of albums and scored some crossover pop hits with 'Last Date' (1960) and 'San Antonio Rose' (1961).

Skeeter Davis

(Vocals, 1931–2004)

Davis (real name Mary Frances Penick) began her career in a duo called The Davis Sisters, along with her friend Betty Jack Davis. They had a No. 1 hit for RCA with 'I Forgot More Than You'll Ever Know' in 1953 before Betty Jack was killed in a car crash later that year. On her own, Davis found solo fame with late 1950s and early 1960s hits like 'I'm Falling Too' and 'The End Of The World', which was a hit in both the country and pop charts in 1963.

Jimmie Driftwood

(Vocals, songwriter, folklorist, 1907–98)

James Corbett Morris, born in Mount View, Arkansas, started writing songs for the entertainment and edification of his students when he was a schoolteacher. He later penned some country classics, including 'Tennessee Stud' (a hit for Eddy Arnold in 1959), 'The Battle Of New Orleans' (a No. 1 single for Johnny Horton in 1959). Driftwood was also a recording artist and a popular performer during the 1950s folk music boom.

Dave Dudley

(Vocals, songwriter, 1928–2003)

The king of the country truck-driver song – a melding of honky-tonk and country rock – was born David Pedruska in Spinner, Wisconsin. He started playing guitar at the age of 11, but he really only began to focus on music after an injury put paid to a career in baseball. He rose to fame with the 1965 hit, 'Six Days On The Road'.

Below
Skeeter Davis was a celebrated – and outspoken – member of the Grand Ole Opry.

Above

George Hamilton IV has been responsible for broadening the popularity of the country sound beyond the USAs, touring frequently in the UK and other parts of Europe.

Ralph Emery

(Radio and television personality, b. 1933)

McEwen, Tennessee-born Walter Ralph Emery was for decades country's most popular radio and television host, and he became as famous as many of the stars whose careers he helped launch. A long-time fixture on WSM Radio in Nashville, Emery also hosted various country music television shows in the 1970s, 1980s and 1990s.

Dallas Frazier

(Songwriter, vocals, b. 1939)

Spiro, Oklahoma-born Dallas Frazier was a quintessential honky-tonk songwriter of the 1960s and 1970s. 'If My Heart Had Windows' (a hit for George Jones, 1967), 'I'm So Afraid Of Losing You Again' (Charley Pride, 1969), 'Johnny One Time' (Brenda Lee, 1969) and 'What's Your Mama's Name' (Tanya Tucker, 1973) are among his many compositions.

Connie B. Gay

(Promoter, manager, radio personality, 1914–89)

Working out of Washington, D.C., this North Carolina-born promoter and behind-the-scenes media wizard was a key figure in the rise of country music's popularity in the 1950s and 1960s. Gay was instrumental in the careers of leading artists like Patsy Cline, Roy Clark, Jimmy Dean and Grandpa Jones.

Don Gibson

(Songwriter, vocals, 1928–2003)

This Shelby, North Carolina-born singer and songwriter not only penned hits for others – Patsy Cline's 'Sweet Dreams' and 'I Can't Stop Loving You' (recorded by Elvis Presley, Ray Charles and dozens of other artists) – but also had hits of his own, with such original classics as 'Oh Lonesome Me', 'I Can't Stop Loving You' and 'Blue Blue Day'. Gibson's soulful yet smooth singing style also earned him popularity as a recording artist during the Nashville Sound era.

George Hamilton IV

(Vocals, b. 1937)

While still a student at the University of North Carolina, this smooth singer scored a pop hit with 'A Rose And A Baby Ruth (1956)'. Moving to Nashville, Hamilton had his first country hit in 1963 with the ballad 'Abilene', which also did well in the pop charts. Throughout the 1970s and 1980s, while enjoying only sporadic success in the country charts, Hamilton has remained a popular performer in Europe and Canada.

John Hartford

(Vocals, banjo, songwriter, 1939–2001)

New York City-born, St. Louis, Missouri-raised John Hartford first made his mark in Nashville when he wrote and recorded a whimsical ballad called 'Gentle On My Mind', which became a massive country and pop hit for

Glen Campbell in 1967. In the early 1970s, Hartford gravitated towards bluegrass music and emerged with his own quirky folk acoustic style, exemplified by albums such as 1971's *Aero Plain* and 1976's *Mark Twang*.

Stonewall Jackson

(Vocals, 1932)

Thomas 'Stonewall' Jackson (named after the revered Civil War general) was born in Emerson, North Carolina. He grew up in poverty and suffered physical abuse at the hands of a cruel stepfather. After running away from home at 15 and serving a four-year stint in the US Navy, Jackson worked as a sharecropper in Georgia while saving the money to go to Nashville.

In the autumn of 1956, Jackson literally drove into Nashville and within three days auditioned, was hired and debuted on the Grand Ole Opry. Jackson's first hit came in late 1958, with 'Life To Go', written by his friend George Jones. His career-making record, a stirring saga song called 'Waterloo', was a No. 1 country hit and a Top 5 pop hit in 1959. Jackson had several more big hits in the mid-1960s, including 'A Wound Time Can't Erase' (1962) and 'Don't Be Angry' (1964).

Sonny James

(Vocals, b. 1929)

From the late 1950s through to the early 1980s, Hackleburg, Kentucky-born James Hugh Loden had a long string of chart-topping hits with romantic ballads, starting with 'Young Love', which reached the top of the country and pop charts in 1957. Other big hits for James were 'Need You' (1967), 'Heaven Says Hello' (1968) and 'Running Bear' (1969).

Merle Kilgore

(Songwriter, vocals, 1934–2005)

One of Nashville's most beloved characters, Chickasha, Oklahoma-born Kilgore was best known for penning classics such as 'Ring Of Fire' (a hit for Johnny Cash, 1963), 'Wolverton Mountain' (Claude King, 1962), 'More And More' (Webb Pierce, 1954) and 'Johnny Reb' (Johnny Horton, 1959).

Left
Stonewall Jackson had a heart-wrenching pleading tone in his voice that seemed to reflect his tough upbringing on a North Carolina farm.

Below
As a teenager, Merle Kilgore was a protégé of Hank Williams, and he later toured with and worked for Hank Williams, Jr.

Brenda Lee
(Vocals, b. 1944)

The dynamic, big-voiced Atlanta, Georgia-born Virginia Mae Tarpley sold millions of records during the 1950s, 1960s and 1970s, and had a major impact on both the pop and country market – all the while recording in Nashville. Lee first broke through in the late 1950s as a teen idol. Her signature hits included 'Sweet Nothin's' (1959) and 'I'm Sorry' (1960).

Hank Locklin
(Vocals, b. 1918)

Best known for a pair of late 1950s and early 1960s hits – 'Send Me The Pillow That You Dream On' and 'Please Help Me, I'm Falling' – McLellan, Florida-born tenor singer Lawrence Hankins started singing during a slow recovery from an injury as a child. He has been a fixture on the Grand Ole Opry for decades.

Hubert Long
(Publisher, promoter, executive, 1923–72)

Born in Poteet, Texas, Long was a central figure in the growth of the country-music industry from the 1950s until his death in the early 1970s. His business acumen was manifest in nearly every aspect of the business – everything from artist management and booking, to promotion and advertising. Long was a founding board member of both the Country Music Association and the Country Music Hall Of Fame. He was posthumously inducted into the Hall Of Fame in 1979.

Roger Miller
(Vocals, songwriter, 1936–92)

Born in Fort Worth, Texas, Roger Dean Miller wrote and recorded a string of brilliant novelty hits that earned him 11 Grammy Awards, as well as country and pop stardom during the 1960s. Chief among his self-penned songs are 'Dang Me', 'Chug-A-Lug' – both hits in 1964 – 'King Of The Road' and 'Kansas City Star', hits in 1965. After a stint in the US Army, where he played fiddle in the Special Forces, Miller got his start in Nashville playing the same instrument in Grand Ole Opry commedienne Minnie Pearl's road band. In 1958, he was hired as front man for Ray Price's band and had his first significant success as a songwriter when Price had a big hit with his 'Invitation To The Blues' (1958).

Above

Brenda Lee was a strong presence in the country charts in the 1960s with ballads such as 'Nobody Wins' (1973) and 'Big Four Poster Bed' (1974).

Top Right

Although Roger Miller is best-known for his humorous novelty songs, he was also responsible for several serious country hits.

Don Law
(Producer, executive, 1902–82)

London, England-born Don Law was one of the most influential producers in modern country music. As head of Columbia Records' country division in the 1950s and 1960s, he produced cornerstone artists such as Johnny Cash, Marty Robbins, Ray Price and Johnny Horton. Columbia Records, under Law's tenure, was also at the forefront of the Nashville Sound with an artist roster that included a number of the era's most successful country-to-pop crossover artists.

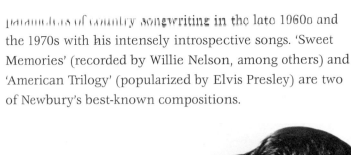

paradigms of country songwriting in the late 1960s and the 1970s with his intensely introspective songs. 'Sweet Memories' (recorded by Willie Nelson, among others) and 'American Trilogy' (popularized by Elvis Presley) are two of Newbury's best-known compositions.

Below
George Morgan took over from Eddy Arnold on the Grand Ole Opry, and in many ways emulated the older star, with his grand country love songs.

Beginning in the late 1950s, Miller recorded for several labels, with limited success. It was only after signing with Smash in 1963 that he scored the first of a long string of crossover hits, starting with 'Dang Me'. Miller also composed the musical score for the 1974 Walt Disney movie version of *Robin Hood*. In 1985, he won a Tony Award for his original score for the Broadway musical, *Big River*, based on the Mark Twain classic, *The Adventures Of Huckleberry Finn*. Miller was inducted into the Country Music Hall Of Fame in 1995.

George Morgan
(Vocals, 1924–75)
Waverly, Tennessee-born George Morgan is best remembered for the smooth, late-1940s, chart-toppers 'Candy Kisses' and 'A Room Full Of Roses' (which also reached the pop Top 30). Morgan was a favourite on the Grand Ole Opry from 1948 until shortly before his death due to complications from open-heart surgery. He was the father of contemporary country singer Lorrie Morgan.

Mickey Newbury
(Songwriter, vocals, 1940–2002)
Houston, Texas-born Milton Sim Newbury Jr. was a contemporary of Kris Kristofferson; and, like Kristofferson, he greatly expanded the thematic and emotional

Below

A sharecropper's son born in Sledge, Mississippi, Charley Pride is the only black singer to break country music's subtle racial barrier and achieve major mainstream stardom.

Jimmy C. Newman
(Vocals, songwriter, b. 1940)

Born in High Point, Louisiana, Newman was one of the first Cajun artists to succeed in country music's mainstream – though his earliest recordings bore few traces of the Cajun influence. In the early 1950s, Newman became a popular performer on the *Louisiana Hayride*

before moving on to Nashville and the Grand Ole Opry. He had his biggest chart successes in the mid-1950s, with hits such as 'Cry, Cry, Darlin' (1954) and 'A Fallen Star' (1957).

Charley Pride
(Vocals, b. 1938)

With his richly textured baritone, Pride had a nearly unmatched string of 29 No. 1 country hits from the mid-1960s until the late 1980s. Perhaps more significantly, Pride is merely the symbolic tip of the iceberg – only the most visible of many gifted but far less celebrated black singers who, just like their white counterparts, grew up listening to the Grand Ole Opry and earnestly emulating the singers they heard there.

As a youth, Pride was heavily influenced by Ernest Tubb, Roy Acuff and Pee Wee King who he heard on the Opry's Saturday night radio broadcasts. Pride played baseball in the American Negro League for several years and served a stint in the US Army before being signed to RCA Records by Chet Atkins. Some of his biggest hits were 'All I Have To Offer You (Is Me)' (1969), 'Kiss An Angel Good Mornin' (1971) and 'My Eyes Can Only See As Far As You' (1976).

Voted Country Music Association's 'Entertainer Of The Year in 1971, Pride joined the Grand Ole Opry in 1993, rather late in his career. In recent years he has recorded sporadically, devoting the majority of his time to substantial real-estate and banking investments in the Dallas, Texas area, where he resides. He was inducted into the Country Music Hall Of Fame in 2000.

Jerry Reed
(Vocals, guitar, songwriter, actor, b. 1937)

A dazzling guitar player, Atlanta, Georgia-born Jerry Reed Hubbard started out in Nashville in the mid-1960s, playing on recording sessions with artists such as Bobby Bare and Porter Wagoner. Later, Reed backed Elvis Presley on guitar when Presley recorded a pair of Reed's original songs in 1968, 'Guitar Man' and 'US Male'. Reed's own biggest hits came during the early 1970s with high-energy novelty songs, including 'When You're Hot, You're Hot' and 'Amos Moses'. The records showcased both his boisterous vocal style and his intricate, finger-picking guitar technique. Reed also co-starred in a number of feature films in the 1970s and early 1980s, most notably with Burt Reynolds in *WW And The Dixie Dance Kings*.

business in 1945 as general manager of Acuff-Rose, the Nashville publishing company co-founded by his father and singer Roy Acuff. Under the younger Rose's steady hand, Acuff-Rose (whose crown jewel was the priceless Hank Williams song catalogue) became one of the world's most successful and powerful music-publishing enterprises in the 1960s and 1970s. A founding member of the Country Music Association, Rose was inducted into the Country Music Hall Of Fame in 1986.

Left

Jerry Reed recorded in a number of styles – from traditional country, through rockabilly, to Cajun music.

Below

Marty Robbins was a consistent hit-maker right up until his death, scoring almost 100 chart singles.

Marty Robbins

(Vocals, songwriter, 1925–82)

One of country music's most versatile singers and energetic stage performers, Martin David Robison, born near Glendale, Arizona, possessed a fluid, empathetic baritone that enabled him to master a variety of music idioms, including country, pop and western (cowboy) songs. One of the most popular figures on the Grand Ole Opry from 1953 until his death from a heart attack nearly three decades later, Robbins topped the charts repeatedly in the 1950s and 1960s with teen pop ballads ('A White Sport Coat And A Pink Carnation'), country odes ('You Gave Me A Mountain') and ballads of the Old West ('El Paso' and 'Big Iron').

Wesley Rose

(Publisher, 1918–90)

The son of legendary songwriter and publisher Fred Rose, Chicago-born Wesley Herman Rose entered the music

Billy Sherrill
(Producer, songwriter, multi-instrumentalist, b. 1936)

One of Nashville's most influential producers during the 1970s and early 1980s, Alabama-born Billy Norris Sherrill started out playing piano at tent shows where his father, an evangelist minister, preached. Later, he played in local rock'n'roll and R&B bands.

When he came to Nashville in 1964, Sherrill brought an outsider's sensibility to his role as a back-line producer at Columbia Records, and held to his iconoclasm even as he rose to head the label's Nashville operations. During the 1970s, he discovered and produced some of the label's biggest stars. As his reputation as a hit-maker grew, his occasionally heavy-handed approach to record-making became even more lavish and extravagant. By adapting rock producer Phil Spector's multi-layered 'Wall Of Sound' approach, Sherrill relentlessly pushed the country-to-pop crossover envelope. His efforts paid off with a string of landmark easy-listening crossover hits, including Charlie Rich's 'Behind Closed Doors' (1973) and David Houston's 'Almost Persuaded' (1966). During the same years, Sherrill also coaxed definitive honky-tonk and hard country records out of traditional artists, including George Jones and Tammy Wynette.

Below

The Statler Brothers are a country institution, having performed together for half a century. They have released more than 40 albums, and received numerous awards, including two Grammys.

Steve Sholes
(Producer, record executive, 1911–68)

Washington, D.C.-born Steve Sholes was a central figure in country music's rise from regional to national popularity in the 1940s and 1950s. Chet Atkins, Eddy Arnold, Hank Snow and Pee Wee King are a few of the numerous artists that Sholes signed, produced and cultivated into stars.

Jack Stapp
(Publisher, radio producer, 1912–80)

Nashville-born Jack Smiley Stapp was the founder and long-time chief executive of Tree International, which during the 1970s and 1980s was one of the most powerful and influential music publishing houses in the world. Prior to founding Tree in 1951, Stapp worked at Nashville's WSM Radio, where he produced the Grand Ole Opry's national network broadcasts. At the Opry during the late 1930s and the 1940s, Stapp also played a role in scouting and signing key artists such as Roy Acuff and Eddy Arnold.

The Statler Brothers
(Vocal quartet, 1955–present)

The Statler Brothers first performed as The Kingsmen, in and around Staunton, Virginia, where the founding members attended high school together. The original Statlers were brothers Harold (b. 1939) and Don Reid (b. 1945), Lew DeWitt (1938–90) and Phil Balsley (b. 1939). When DeWitt was sidelined with illness in 1981, he was replaced by Jimmy Fortune (b. 1955). One of modern country music's most popular and long-running vocal groups, The Statlers brilliantly adapted the gospel-quartet vocal style to secular music and became a force in the country charts and occasionally the pop charts from the mid-1960s until the 1980s. First hitting the charts with 'Flowers On The Wall' (1965), their other best-known, nostalgia-laden odes include 'Do You Remember These' (1972), 'Do You Know You Are My Sunshine' (1978) and 'Elizabeth' (1983).

Porter Wagoner
(Vocals, songwriter, b. 1927)

This Howell County, Missouri-born artist grew up on a farm and worked in a butcher's shop before he began singing on local Missouri radio shows. In 1957, Wagoner moved to Nashville and landed a spot on the Grand Ole Opry. In more recent years, with the deaths of longtime Opry stalwarts Roy Acuff and Hank Snow, Wagoner has emerged as the show's distinguished elder statesman. His hard country hits from the 1950s and 1960s include 'A Satisfied Mind' (1955), 'Misery Loves Company' (1962) and 'The Carroll County Accident' (1968). Wagoner continues to perform and occasionally record. A member of Nashville's Country Music Hall Of Fame (elected in 2002), he also brought Dolly Parton to national attention via his road and television show.

Left
Despite the nickname of 'America's favourite folk singer', Slim Whitman enjoyed greater popularity in Europe for most of his career.

Below
The Wilburn Brothers were the last in the great tradition of brother harmony duos that stretched back to the roots of country music.

Slim Whitman

(Vocals, b. 1924)

Tampa, Florida-born Otis Dewey Whitman Jr. is best known for his warbling, high-falsetto vocal flourishes on sentimental hits like 'Indian Love Call' (1952) and 'Secret Love' (1954). Although Whitman enjoyed only limited success in the United States, he achieved considerable fame in Europe, especially the British Isles. During the 1980s, he experienced resurgence in the USA after years of relative obscurity.

The Wilburn Brothers

(Vocals, songwriters, publishers, 1950s–60s)

Brothers Virgil Doyle (1930–82) and Thurman Theodore (1931–2003) from Hardy, Arkansas, first began performing as children along with three older siblings. In the early 1950s, Doyle and Teddy recorded and toured with Webb Pierce. In 1954, striking out on their own, they signed with the Grand Ole Opry and began recording as a duo for Decca Records. Their commercial heyday came in the 1950s and 1960s with hits like 'Sparkling Brown Eyes' (with Webb Pierce, 1954), 'I'm So In Love With You' (1956) and 'Roll Muddy River' (1963).

Are You Sure Hank Done It This Way?:
Country Rock
& The Outlaws

When Jimmie Rodgers and The Carter Family became country music's first superstars in 1927, their audience was the farmers, miners, wives and other blue-collar workers of the rural South. It was an audience that left school early for a life of hard work in isolated communities. When those men and women gathered at a tavern or schoolroom on a Saturday night, they wanted their music strong and straightforward.

Thanks to the social programmes of Franklin D. Roosevelt's New Deal and Lyndon Johnson's Great Society, however, the grandchildren of that original audience were attending college, watching television and criss-crossing the nation by the end of the 1960s, caught up in the political, cultural and sexual changes of that decade. When they plugged their earphones into the stereo, they wanted a music as irreverent, ironic and erotic as the world around them, but they wanted it in the musical language they had grown up with. They wanted it to sound like country even if it worked like rock'n'roll.

Two camps gave them what they wanted. Certain country performers – especially Texans such as Willie Nelson, Waylon Jennings and Billy Joe Shaver, but also Hank Williams Jr., the heir of country royalty – decided to roughen up their sound with louder drums, wilder guitars and ruder lyrics. They were dubbed the Outlaws.

Meanwhile, folk-rockers such as Gram Parsons, Roger McGuinn, Chris Hillman, Bob Dylan and Neil Young realized that it was a short, natural jump from the Appalachian ballads and reels they already loved to traditional country music. The resulting hybrid was called country-rock, but it was the flip-side of the Outlaws coin. Whether they were honky-tonkers embracing rock or rockers embracing honky-tonk, they created a new kind of country music that resonated with the Confederate Diaspora, the descendants of the rural South who had dispersed throughout the USA, but who had never lost their native tongue – hillbilly songs.

Key Artists
The Byrds
Waylon Jennings
Willie Nelson

Influences & Development

biopic *Your Cheatin' Heart*. Recording for his father's long-time label, MGM, Junior overdubbed duets with Senior and even recorded as Luke The Drifter Junior.

A New Beat

Hank Jr. wasn't the only country artist still imitating Hank Sr. in the early 1970s, nor was he the only one drowning in string arrangements and background singers. Like many of his fellow baby-boomers, Hank Jr. was dissatisfied with a country music that belonged to his parents' generation; he wanted a country music of his own. He wanted a country music as impatient and impulsive as the southern rock he was hearing from such favourites as The Allman Brothers Band, Lynyrd Skynyrd and Charlie Daniels (b. 1936).

So he took Daniels, Marshall Tucker's Toy Caldwell and The Allmans' Chuck Leavell into the studio and made a 1975 album called *Hank Williams Jr. And Friends*. The themes were still country and so was the voice, but the punchy beat and the soaring guitars transformed the sound. Moreover, the swaggering bravado of 'Stoned At The Jukebox' and the personal confession of 'Living Proof' revealed a new brand of songwriting.

When Waylon Jennings (1937–2002), another Nashville insider, added southern rock guitars and drums, he wrote a No. 1 hit in 1975 that asked the question, 'Are You Sure Hank Done It This Way?'. It was an attack on the slick countrypolitan sound that had polished all the rough edges off country music, but it was also an admission that Jennings and his fellow Outlaws had added some rough edges that Hank Sr. had never dreamed of. Jennings didn't sound like Hank Sr. but he was working the same job: providing down-to-earth songs for working-class white southerners. The tools and specs had changed, but the job was much the same.

Outbreak Of The Outlaws

It wasn't just a matter of louder guitars and drums, however. It was also a question of artistic freedom. Rock acts such as The Beach Boys, The Who and The Rolling

'You can tell the difference when a song is written just to get on the radio and when what someone does is their whole life. That comes through in Bob Dylan, Paul Simon, Willie Nelson. There is no separating their life from their music.' **Lyle Lovett**

Hank Williams Jr. (b. 1949) was only three years old when his daddy died, and he barely knew the man who was, arguably, the greatest honky-tonker of them all. But his widowed mother groomed her baby boy to imitate his papa as closely as possible. He was on stage by eight, in the recording studio by 14 and became his dad's voice on the soundtrack to the 1964

Stones had long been able to pick their own songs, choose their own musicians, produce their own albums and fashion their own image; why couldn't country acts do the same? Jennings had had enough hits by the early 1970s to demand the same freedom, and in 1972 he won the right to produce the album *Lonesome On'ry And Mean*, using his own road band and singing songs by such pals as Steve Young, Willie Nelson (b. 1933) and Kris Kristofferson (b. 1936). As Jennings' music got rougher, so did his image; he began to sport a goatee, long hair and a leather jacket.

Nelson hadn't had quite as much success playing by Music Row's rules as his buddy Jennings had, so when Nelson got fed up with business as usual, he moved from Nashville back home to Texas and created an alternative scene there. Freed from restrictions, he was able to follow his songwriting muse in novel directions and to display supple, jazz-like aspects of his singing and guitar-picking. When he noticed that his Texas shows were drawing equal numbers of short-haired country fans and long-haired rock fans, he realized he was on to something.

This new country music pioneered by Hank Jr., Jennings and Nelson soon attracted many fellow travellers: Texas singer-songwriters such as Jerry Jeff Walker (b. 1942), Townes Van Zandt (1944–97) and Guy Clark; older Nashville iconoclasts such as Johnny Cash (1932–2003), Johnny Paycheck (1938–2003) and Tompall Glaser (b. 1933); and unconventional songwriters such as Billy Joe Shaver (b. 1939), Lee Clayton (b. 1942) and Shel Silverstein (1930–99). All the movement needed was a name.

Nashville publicist Hazel Smith, inspired by Jennings' recording of the Clayton song 'Ladies Love Outlaws', had been describing these acts as 'Outlaws'. RCA Records picked up on the phrase when it gathered some previously released tracks by Jennings, Nelson, Glaser and Jennings' wife Jessi Colter (b. 1943) into *Wanted! The Outlaws*, a 1976 album featuring an Old West wanted poster as cover art. The collection captured the public imagination and became the first mainstream country album to ever go platinum (by selling a million copies in the USA). The name stuck.

Above

Waylon Jennings (along with artists Willie Nelson and Kris Kristofferson, also pictured) began to give country music a makeover in the 1970s.

Far Left

Hank Williams Jr. was neither the earliest nor the best of the country-rockers, but no one better personified the passing of generations than this son of Nashville royalty.

The Country-Rock Revolution

Before the Outlaw movement even got rolling, however, two of the world's biggest rock acts came to Nashville in 1968 to make country albums. Bob Dylan (b. 1941), who had earlier cut the rock'n'roll album *Blonde On Blonde* there, returned to make the country-flavoured *John Wesley Harding* with the town's top session players. A few months earlier, The Byrds had been in the city to record the traditional-country project, *Sweetheart Of The Rodeo*. The two LPs would point thousands of young musicians down a new road.

Dylan was coming off the most turbulent period of his life. He had 'gone electric' at the 1965 Newport Folk Festival; he had released the landmark *Bringing It All Back Home*, *Highway 61 Revisited* and *Blonde On Blonde* albums, and he had faced down boos and accusations of being a

'Judas' on his 1966 worldwide tour with The Band. But when he broke his collarbone in a motorcycle accident on 29 July 1966, he retreated from public view to his country home near Woodstock, New York.

Dylan needed a respite from rock'n'roll craziness and he found it in country music. His folk-music heroes such as Woody Guthrie (1912–67) had more than a little country music in their sound, and Dylan had always been a fan of Hank Williams and Jimmie Rodgers (1897–1933). While recuperating, he recorded the country-flavoured *Basement Tapes* with The Band in upstate New York and then travelled to Nashville to record the country-soaked *John Wesley Harding*. When he followed that up with *Nashville Skyline* a year later, he included a duet with Johnny Cash, who had been a friend ever since the 1964 Newport Folk Festival.

Below

Poco took the path that followed the likes of Gram Parsons – towards the country-rock style. Despite this, they did have some success on the pop charts, most notably with 'Crazy Love' in 1978.

The Byrds, led by Roger McGuinn, had already launched two musical revolutions: folk-rock and psychedelic-rock. In 1968, thanks to new member Gram Parsons and founding member Chris Hillman, the band would launch a third: country-rock. *Sweetheart Of The Rodeo* was such an influential album that Vince Gill's wife formed a country band of that name, Emmylou Harris wrote a song about Parsons with that same title, and Parsons and Hillman formed a legendary new band, The Flying Burrito Brothers, to follow up the breakthrough.

stages with the Outlaws. Lynyrd Skynyrd's Ronnie Van Zant wrote some classic country songs such as 'Simple Man' (covered by Hank Jr.) and 'Saturday Night Special' (Jerry Jeff Walker). The Allman Brothers Band's Dickey Betts did the same with such numbers as 'Ramblin' Man' (Gary Stewart) and 'Long Time Gone' (Hank Jr.). Even when they had two or three lead guitars wailing at once, these bands worked from a country foundation that was impossible to ignore. Hank Jr. didn't.

Left

The Nitty Gritty Dirt Band was one of the major groups of the 1970s. While adding a rock flavour to their music, the band still encouraged traditional country sounds – as evidenced by their seminal album Will The Circle Be Unbroken.

Below

David Crosby, Graham Nash and Stephen Stills formed one of the most influential groups of the era, which led the country-rock movement in California.

Major Influences

The country-rock movement followed two paths. Those most influenced by Dylan were the singer-songwriters who wanted to blend traditional country forms with modernist irony and imagery the way their role model had. Falling into this camp were folk-rockers such as Neil Young, Robbie Robertson and Roger McGuinn; Texas songwriters such as Townes Van Zandt, Butch Hancock and Ray Wylie Hubbard; and Nashville literati such as John Prine, Kris Kristofferson and Steve Young (b. 1942).

Those most influenced by Parsons and Hillman were lead singers and guitarists who wanted that same mix of hillbilly harmonies and thumping backbeat. Most of these were based in California, where The Eagles, Poco, Linda Ronstadt, Michael Nesmith, John Stewart, The Dillards, The Nitty Gritty Dirt Band and Crosby, Stills And Nash led a country-rock scene that finally paid off with pop hits for many of the acts.

Meanwhile, the southern-rock scene that so influenced Hank Williams Jr. became a major concert draw, especially in the South, where the

Texas - A Place Apart

songwriter and the dancehall bandleader. Both types valued the footloose-and-fancy-free independence of the cowboy, and both were inevitably influenced by the black blues musicians of East Texas, the German-Czech polka bands of Central Texas and the Tex-Mex conjuntos of South Texas. All these factors made Texas music a world unto itself, and every time the country-music industry in Nashville got too conservative and too formulaic, the Lone Star State's imaginary cowboys had a ready answer in their maverick songs and boot-scooting dance numbers.

That was certainly true in the early 1970s, when Nashville's countrypolitan sound was suffocating beneath its pillowy arrangements. Fresh alternatives could be heard a thousand miles to the south-west, where the Outlaw movement, the Cosmic Cowboy songwriters and the western-swing revival all sprouted from Texan soil.

If they couldn't find the utopian dancehall of their dreams, these Texan musicians would invent one. Luchenbach, for example, was virtually a ghost town in the Texas hill country when local rancher John R. 'Hondo' Crouch bought it up in the early 1970s and turned it into the laid-back small town and anything-goes dancehall of his dreams. Waylon Jennings turned a song about it, 'Luchenbach, Texas (Back To The Basics Of Love)' into a No. 1 country hit in 1977.

Above

Commander Cody And His Lost Planet Airmen were among the groups to take advantage of the new venues to ply their trade – the most popular of which was the Armadillo World Headquarters in Austin.

Almost no Texan musicians have ever herded cattle, but most like to think of themselves as cowboys nonetheless. They imagine themselves pulling out an acoustic guitar after dinner and singing a song about the adventures and frustrations they have known. And not just any old song – it has to be one they wrote and it has to be more original and more memorable than the one sung by the guy sitting next to them at the campfire. And they like to imagine themselves riding back into town on Saturday night, to kick up their boots at a dancehall to a honky-tonk band.

The Cowboys Of Country Music

These persistent fantasies have given rise to two crucial types of Texas musicians: the story-telling singer-

Swinging At The Armadillo

Meanwhile, in nearby Austin – the state capital – some hippies took over an abandoned National Guard armoury in 1970 and transformed it into a concert ballroom like the Fillmore in San Francisco, complete with psychedelic murals on all the walls. They called it the Armadillo World Headquarters and booked fellow non-conformist Willie Nelson as one of the first headliners. 'I got up and picked at the Armadillo one time,' he told his biographer Michael Bane, 'and there was this brand new audience. I discovered that there were young people who liked what I had been singing all my life to people my age or older.'

The Armadillo became a demilitarized zone, where young rock fans and older honky-tonkers could declare a truce and share their enthusiasm for Nelson and such fellow Outlaw acts as Kris Kristofferson and Billy Joe Shaver. The Armadillo also became a centre for the western-swing revival, which brought back to life the hillbilly jazz of Bob Wills and Milton Brown. Commander Cody And His Lost Planet Airmen and Dan Hicks And His Hot Licks both visited the Armadillo from California, but the kings of the revival, Asleep At The Wheel, made Austin their home base in 1974, collaborating with such local Wills alumni as Johnny Gimble.

The Cosmic Cowboys

Houston had already become the state's centre of singer-songwriter folkies. Young artists such as Townes Van Zandt, Guy Clark, K. T. Oslin, Gary White and a transplanted Jerry Jeff Walker were obviously influenced by Bob Dylan, but they gave that approach a distinctively East Texas twist by adding the influence of local bluesmen Lightnin' Hopkins and Mance Lipscomb, a rural balladeer.

Van Zandt was the mentor for the group and on his restless travels he spread the word to such like-minded singer-songwriters as Joe Ely, Jimmie Dale Gilmore, Butch Hancock, Willis Alan Ramsey, Steven Fromholz, Ray Wylie Hubbard and Michael Martin Murphey. Folks began calling them the Cosmic Cowboys after a Murphey song, for their mix of country storytelling and Dylanesque surrealism.

The Cosmic Cowboys found their own campfires when the Kerrville Folk Festival was founded in the central Texas Hills in 1972. Each May, singer-songwriters still gather from all across Texas – and eventually from all across the nation – to sit around real campfires and play their latest songs on their acoustic guitars. It was a scene that put an emphasis on inspiration and craft first and second and stardom a distant third, and was the graduate school for some of the finest country songwriters of the 1970s.

Above

Jimmy Dale Gilmore was one of the many folk artists that made Houston their centre in the 1970s. This group earned themselves the moniker of Cosmic Cowboys.

Left

Asleep At The Wheel play a highly original fusion of country, jazz and swing, but their inherent love of the Bob Wills sound was commemorated on their 1999 album Ride With Bob.

The Byrds

Key Artist

'I followed The Byrds a lot, and then when they did a country styled record it made me curious to know who these people were that they liked.' **Elvis Costello**

The Byrds hired Gram Parsons (vocals, guitar, 1946–73) in 1968 because they needed a guitarist and pianist to fill the instrumental void left by the recent departure of David Crosby (vocals, guitar, b. 1941) and the earlier departure of Gene Clark (vocals, guitar, 1944–91). The remaining Byrds – Roger McGuinn (vocals, guitar, b. 1942) and Chris Hillman (bass, mandolin, guitar, vocals, b. 1944) – also needed something to reawaken their career, which had begun to sputter after their early run of hits.

The Musical Revolution

The Byrds had launched one musical revolution in 1965 by pioneering folk-rock with such hit singles as Bob Dylan's 'Mr. Tambourine Man' and Pete Seeger's 'Turn! Turn! Turn!'. The Los Angeles quintet then launched a second revolution in 1966 by introducing psychedelic-rock through such singles as '5D (Fifth Dimension)' and 'Eight Miles High'. Little did they suspect that hiring Parsons would lead them to launch a third: country-rock.

McGuinn (once known as Jim but now known as Roger), Clark and Crosby had all been members of the early-1960s folk revival, but when they heard The Beatles' first singles they were overcome by the power and elation of the British band. So they took the songs they already knew – folk staples by Dylan, Seeger and others – and arranged them as if they were Beatles singles.

Unlike the others, though, Hillman wasn't an ex-folkie; he had grown up in California, playing in bluegrass and country bands. He knew those old country songs could be as strange and wonderful as anything written by Dylan or inspired by LSD. He brought his teenage pal

through the folk-music revival, Parsons founded his first country-rock group, the International Submarine Band, in Boston in 1965. The group moved to Los Angeles and released their only album in 1968.

Sweethearts Of The Rodeo

By that time, the ambitious Parsons had already signed up with the much better known Byrds, and he and Hillman had convinced McGuinn to devote the next Byrds album to country music. The album that emerged, *Sweetheart Of The Rodeo*, resembled the traditional country music of the 1940s and 1950s more than the country music of 1968, and it didn't sell very well. But the hip, understated, twangy treatment of folk-flavoured songs mixed in with country standards seemed to change the life of everyone who did hear it. Within a few years there were country-rock bands everywhere you turned.

Parsons and Hillman, who had left The Byrds soon after *Sweetheart Of The Rodeo* had flopped, formed The Flying Burrito Brothers, a band that brought out their best songwriting but never quite captured the potential of those songs in the studio. Parsons finally conquered the studio when he made two terrific solo albums with his new harmony singer, an unknown named Emmylou Harris. Hillman eventually went on to join the country-rock bands Manassas and Souther-Hillman-Furay, to make some fine solo bluegrass albums and to co-found the Desert Rose Band, which scored a dozen Top 40 country singles between 1987 and 1991.

McGuinn kept The Byrds going by hiring Clarence White to pursue the country-rock sound even further. But tragedy stalked the dispersed group. White was killed by a drunk driver in 1973, and Parsons died of heroin overdose a few months later. His road manager Phil Kaufmann fulfilled Parsons' request by stealing the corpse and burning it out in the middle of the Joshua Tree desert.

Clarence White into The Byrds' 1967 recording session for *Younger Than Yesterday* to play stinging Bakersfield-country guitar on Hillman's song 'Time Between'.

But Hillman didn't have the country-fan ally he needed until Parsons joined the Byrds. Parsons had grown up in Georgia and Florida, the son of a suicidal father and an alcoholic citrus-heir mother. He loved the southern country music of his youth, especially the way it was given rhythm and swagger by Elvis Presley. Though he took a

Classic Recordings

***Sweetheart Of The Rodeo* (1968)**
'Hickory Wind', 'You Ain't Going Nowhere', 'You're Still On My Mind', 'One Hundred Years From Now'

***The Ballad Of Easy Rider* (1970)**
'Ballad Of Easy Rider', 'Oil In My Lamp', 'Way Beyond The Sun'

Untitled
'Chestnut Mare', 'Just a Season', 'Nashville West', 'Eight Miles High'

Left

Gram Parsons was arguably the most influential figure on the country-rock scene, inspiring everyone from The Rolling Stones to The Eagles. Parsons died tragically young from a heroin overdose, at age 29.

Key Track

'Hickory Wind' (1968)
Gram Parsons co-wrote and sang this song, a lilting waltz that hovers between the singer's fond remembrance of a South Carolina childhood and the melancholy feeling that he'll never be able to follow the wind that's calling him home. It was a highlight of *Sweetheart Of The Rodeo*, Parsons' only album with The Byrds.

Waylon Jennings

Key Artist

'Mainly what I learned from Buddy [Holly] was an attitude.... He loved music, and he taught that it shouldn't have any barriers to it.' **Waylon Jennings**

Above
Jennings is rightfully known as the father of the Outlaw movement – even the name was taken from the title of one of his songs.

That Rhythm Thing

It took a traumatized Jennings six years to get his music career back on track, but when he did, he never forgot the lessons of his brief time with Holly. He never forgot how exciting country music can sound when you add an electric guitar, drums and lusty vocals. He never forgot how Holly insisted on producing his own sessions, picking his own songs and setting his own arrangements. He never forgot how Holly transformed Elvis Presley's rock'n'roll by putting a West Texas country twist on it.

After several dj jobs, a rockabilly band in Phoenix and some pop-folk singles in Los Angeles, Jennings found himself in Nashville in 1965, sharing an apartment with the newly divorced Johnny Cash. Jennings had a Top 40 hit before the year was out and a Top 10 hit the following year. He was singing whatever RCA Records told him to sing – the honky-tonk classic 'The Only Daddy Who'll Walk The Line', as well as songs borrowed from Chuck Berry, Elvis Presley, Bobby Vinton, Richard Harris, Joe Simon and Peter, Paul And Mary – and was singing in whatever way producers Chet Atkins and Danny Davis told him to.

But Jennings, remembering Holly's example, began to assert himself. He started insisting on singing songs by such renegades as Lee Clayton, Hoyt Axton and Tony Joe White in a rougher, less polished way. When his contract came up for renewal in 1972, he had already had 23 Top 40 singles, including eight Top 10 hits. He was in a position to demand artistic control over all aspects of his career – and that's what he got. His first album under the new contract, *Lonesome, On'ry And Mean*, showcased songs by Willie Nelson, Kris Kristofferson and Mickey Newbury.

Father Of The Outlaws

Nine of the 10 songs on the second album, 1973's *Honky Tonk Heroes*, were by the unknown and unconventional Texas songwriter Billy Joe Shaver. From the lean mix of blues harmonica, Texas swing fiddle and Jennings' rockabilly road band to Shaver's celebration of 'lovable

Waylon Jennings (vocals, guitar, 1937–2002) was a teenage disc jockey in Lubbock, Texas, when he first met the hometown hero Buddy Holly (1936–59). Holly produced Jennings' first single, 'Jole Blon', in September 1958, and hired Jennings as his bassist the following January. On 3 February 1959, Jennings was all set to take a charter flight with Holly from Clear Lake, Iowa, to Moorhead, Minnesota, but gave up his seat at the last minute to the Big Bopper. That plane, of course, crashed and killed all on board.

losers and no-account boozers and honky-tonk heroes likc mc', to the front-cover photo of the dishevelled musicians drinking, smoking and grinning in the studio, it was unlike any album Nashville had ever released. The album yielded a Top 10 single, 'You Ask Me To', and seized the imagination of a younger audience hungry for a less tamed kind of country music.

Jennings' long-time pal and fellow Texan Willie Nelson was going through similar changes at the same time and the two forged a partnership in the face of Music Row resistance. Nelson co-produced Jennings' quiet, introspective 1974 album *This Time*, co-wrote the hit single 'Good Hearted Woman' and dueted on such hits as 'Luchenbach, Texas' (1977), 'Mammas Don't Let Your Babies Grow Up To Be Cowboys' (1978), 'Just To Satisfy You' (1982) and The Eagles' 'Take It To The Limit' (1983). Jennings married singer Jessi Colter in 1969 and they often collaborated, scoring hit singles with remakes of Presley's 'Suspicious Minds' (1976) and Hank Thompson's 'Wild Side Of Life' incorporating Kitty Wells' 'It Wasn't God Who Made Honky Tonk Angels' (1981).

Jennings struggled with alcohol, drugs, marital conflict and lack of inspiration, but he often transformed that turmoil into fodder for music that furthered his legend as the father of the Outlaws. After all, that movement took its name from Jennings' recording of 'Ladies Love Outlaws', and when Jennings, Nelson, Kristofferson and Cash formed a vocal quartet late in their careers, they named themselves the Highwaymen after Jennings' 1985 No. 1 hit of that name. But Jennings' original motivation stretched back further than that, and on his 1978 album *I've Always Been Crazy*, he reunited with the surviving Crickets and recorded four of Holly's hits in a medley that displayed the true roots of the Outlaws' attitude.

Above
Willie Nelson and Waylon Jennings – the most wanted men of the Outlaw movement. One of Jennings' best Outlaw statements was the song 'Are You Sure Hank Done It This Way?', a satire on the commercialism of Nashville.

Left
Jennings said: 'Buddy was an enormous influence even after I started cutting country. He always went for the edge, that rhythm thing.'

Key Track

'Good Hearted Woman'
This song captured Jennings' persona so well that he released it twice. It was a No. 3 hit for him in 1972, and three years later the song's co-writer, Willie Nelson, overdubbed a vocal and it became a No. 1 single. It's sung from the perspective of a man who's well aware that he hasn't kept the promises he made to his wife, and the confession is delivered with all the charm and remorse that keeps her around.

Willie Nelson

Key Artist

A few days after Christmas, 1969, Willie Nelson (b. 1933) watched his house outside Nashville burn to the ground. Going up in flames were not only his furniture, guitars and only copies of unpublished songs – but also some of his ties to Music Row.

'I'm a country songwriter and we write cry-in-your-beer songs. That's what we do. Something that you can slow-dance to.'
Willie Nelson

A New Beginning

Nelson had begun the decade as one of the hottest songwriters in town, penning hits for Patsy Cline ('Crazy'), Ray Price ('Night Life') and Faron Young ('Hello Walls'), but his own career sputtered. He had cut some modestly successful singles for Liberty, including a Top 10 duet ('Willingly') with his second wife Shirley Collie, but he never seemed too comfortable in Chet Atkins' polished production or in the spiffy suits he was made to wear for the publicity photos.

He preferred hanging out at Tootsie's Orchard Lounge in his jeans, trading songs with similarly dissatisfied songwriters such as Roger Miller, Waylon Jennings and Tom T. Hall. He was getting a great reaction from the honky-tonk joints he played in Texas, Oklahoma and

Below
Willie Nelson makes time for his many fans in country's capital Nashville. He has been an enduring popular figure on the scene for nearly half a century.

Louisiana, but he couldn't transplant that excitement to Nashville's recording studios. And when his house burned down, he decided, the hell with it; he was going back to Texas.

Unlike most country acts of the time, Nelson carried his own band, despite the cost, and encouraged them to emphasize the swinging rhythms that had more in common with Bob Wills and early Ray Price than with the records Nelson had been making in Nashville. Over this muscular dance beat, he was singing his new songs about stubbornly independent cowboys in a slippery jazz phrasing that had more to do with Frank Sinatra and Ray Charles than anyone he had left behind on Music Row.

Making Texas Fashionable

It was one of the ironies of the Outlaw movement that the old music became the new music. Audiences hungering for a more physical, more honest country music found it buried in the past of Texas dancehalls. But even as Nelson changed the new audience, the new audience changed Nelson. He let his hair grow out into long braids; he sprouted a beard and took to wearing jeans and kerchiefs. He demanded the same freedom as his rock contemporaries and recorded the stripped-down, personal singer-songwriter album *Yesterday's Wine* in 1971, the horn-backed dancehall album *Shotgun Willie* in 1973 and the song suite about a divorce, *Phases & Stages*, in 1974.

The next year Nelson followed up that concept album with another, *Red Headed Stranger*, a collection of interconnected songs about a preacher betrayed by a woman; he saddles a black stallion and wanders across the West in search of redemption. Recorded in Garland, Texas, with Nelson's road band, the album sounded spare and unfinished to the executives at Nelson's new label, Columbia. But the first single, a remake of the old Fred Rose song 'Blue Eyes Crying In The Rain' rose to No. 1 and the album soon followed. It made Nelson an overnight success 15 years after he first moved to Nashville.

Classic Recordings

Shotgun Willie **(1973)**
'Whiskey River', 'Bubbles in My Beer', 'Sad Songs And Waltzes'

Red Headed Stranger **(1975)**
'Blue Eyes Crying In The Rain', 'Time Of The Preacher', 'Bonaparte's Retreat'

Stardust **(1978)**
'Georgia On My Mind', 'Blue Skies', 'Stardust'

Willie And Family Live **(1978)**
'Whiskey River', 'If You've Got The Money (I've Got The Time)'

Tougher Than Leather **(1983)**
'Changing Skies', 'Somewhere In Texas', 'My Love For The Rose'

Teatro **(1998)**
'I Never cared For You', 'These Lonely Nights', 'I've Loved You All Over The World'

He used this new clout to push his artistic freedom even further. He recorded duets such as 'Good Hearted Woman' and 'Mammas Don't Let Your Babies Grow Up To Be Cowboys' with his Texan pal Waylon Jennings; he recorded an album of songs by his songwriting friend Kris Kristofferson; he recorded several albums of Tin Pan Alley standards such as 'Georgia On My Mind' and 'Blue Skies'; he recorded duets with Merle Haggard, Roger Miller, Dolly Parton, Ray Price and Ray Charles; he starred in movies such as *The Electric Horseman* (1979), *Honeysuckle Rose* (1980), *Songwriter* (1984) and *Red Headed Stranger* (1986), creating memorable soundtracks for each.

He became one of the biggest stars country music has ever known, and he did it by taking the big gamble, turning his back on Music Row and placing all his bets on a brand of Texas dancehall music that had gone out of fashion.

Above

Nelson, sporting his now-trademark long hair and beard, sings along with Merle Haggard and Toby Keith.

Left

Willie Nelson gets up close with Amy Irving in the movie Honeysuckle Rose *in 1980.*

Key Track

'On The Road Again' (1980)
This bouncy shuffle with the hypnotic sing-song tune was the theme song from the *Honeysuckle Rose* movie and a No. 1 hit in 1980. It also captured the travelling-circus camaraderie of Nelson and his band, which he called The Family, as they toured one of the best live shows of the 1970s and 1980s.

A-Z of Artists

Asleep At The Wheel
(Vocal/instrumental group, 1970s–present)

The most impressive and most successful of the western-swing revival bands was co-founded by a couple of hippies from the Philadelphia suburbs. Ray Benson (vocals, guitar, b. 1951) and Reuben 'Lucky Oceans' Gosfield (pedal steel guitar, b. 1951) fell in love with the records of Bob Wills and formed the band in 1969, soon adding Chris O'Connell (vocals, b. 1954), rhythm guitarist Leroy Preston and pianist Jim 'Floyd Domino' Haber. After two early albums,

they finally broke through on the country charts with 1975's 'The Letter That Johnny Walker Read'. Members came and went, with the charismatic, six-foot-seven Benson the only constant, but the level of musicianship was always high and the commitment to the Wills sound was unbending. To date, Asleep At The Wheel have won eight Grammy Awards, and its alumni include bassist Tony Garnier, fiddler Link Davis, singer Mary Ann Price and steel guitarist Cindy Cashdollar.

Johnny Bush
(Vocals, guitar, b. 1935)

Bush is best known for writing 'Whiskey River', for Willie Nelson, who used it to open and close every concert from the mid-1970s onwards. But Bush was a favourite of Texas audiences from the early 1950s through to the early twenty-first century with his vigorous dancehall brand of honky-tonk. He played in the bands of Nelson and Ray Price before stepping forward as a lead singer and scoring five Top 20 country singles between 1968 and 1972, including 1969's 'You Gave Me A Mountain'.

Lee Clayton
(Vocals, guitar, b. 1942)

Clayton, a former fighter pilot from Tennessee, was one of the most original songwriters in the Outlaws movement, penning 'Ladies Love Outlaws' for Waylon Jennings, 'If You Could Touch Her At All' for Willie Nelson and 'Lone Wolf' for Jerry Jeff Walker. Clayton's own albums, marked by vivid if unconventional and introspective imagery, flopped commercially but were prized by a cult following, especially in Europe, where U2's Bono fell under his spell.

David Allan Coe
(Vocals, guitar, b. 1939)

Coe broke through first as a songwriter, penning tunes for Tanya Tucker (1973's No. 1 'Would You Lay Me Down (In A Field Of Stone)', Willie Nelson and George Jones. Coe scored

Below

Unlike most of the country-music Outlaws, David Allen Coe had a genuine criminal past, serving hard time in the Ohio Penitentiary before moving to Nashville in 1967.

his own hit with 1975's 'You Never Even Called Me By My Name', followed by five more Top 25 hits, including 'Willie, Waylon and Me'. Coe was never shy about promoting himself, even performing as the sparkly, masked 'Mysterious Rhinestone Cowboy', and he recorded prison songs and pornographic party records in addition to his country fare.

Jessi Colter
(Vocals, b. 1943)

Colter became associated with the Outlaw movement even though her big, pure pop-country voice gave her more in common with Glen Campbell than with her husband Waylon Jennings. She was born Mirriam Johnson in Phoenix, Arizona, where she married rockabilly guitarist Duane Eddy in 1962. After a 1968 divorce, she adopted her new stage name and married Jennings. He produced many of her recordings and often sang duets with her, but Colter's biggest moment was her 1975 No. 1 hit, 'I'm Not Lisa'.

Charlie Daniels
(Vocals, guitar, fiddle, b. 1936)

Daniels was a North Carolina rock'n'roller who had a song cut by Elvis Presley and who played on Bob Dylan's *Nashville Skyline*. Daniels formed his own band in 1972, modelled on the southern rock of The Allman Brothers Band, and had a hit with the 1973 tall tale, 'Uneasy Rider' – the story of a long-haired hippie wandering into the wrong bar. He had his biggest hit in 1979 with 'The Devil Went Down To Georgia'. Daniels gave the southern-rock movement some cohesion with his annual Volunteer Jam charity concerts, but he gradually became more conservative in his music and his politics.

Left
Jessi Colter was the only woman on the 1976 platinum album Wanted! The Outlaws.

The Dillards
(Vocal/instrumental group, 1962–80)

Doug Dillard (banjo, b. 1937) and Rodney Dillard (vocals, guitar, b. 1942) grew up in Missouri's Ozark Mountains but ended up in California where they portrayed Mayberry's local bluegrass band on television's *Andy Griffith Show*. The Dillards, featuring mandolinist Dean Webb and electric bassist Mitch Jayne, soon mixed their bluegrass with Bob Dylan songs and a drummer, paving the way for the California country-rock revolution. Doug left the group in 1967, forming the Dillard And Clark duo with ex-Byrd Gene Clark, and then pursuing a solo career. Rodney kept the Dillards going, mixing art-rock and country-rock in the ornate arrangements of 1968's *Wheatstraw Suite* album and 1971's *Copperfields*.

Below
The Dillards were one of the leading bluegrass bands in the 1960s, but over the years they honed their style and took on a more country-rock style.

Bob Dylan

(Vocals, guitar, b. 1941)

Dylan had already conquered the folk and rock'n'roll fields completely by the time he recorded in Nashville for the first time in 1965. That was for the rock-flavoured *Blonde On Blonde* album, but he was soon back to cut the more obviously country projects *John Wesley Harding* and *Nashville Skyline*, which helped kick off the country-rock movement.

The Eagles

(Vocal/instrumental group, 1971–present)

Bernie Leadon (guitar, mandolin, b. 1947) of The Flying Burrito Brothers and Randy Meisner (bass, b. 1946) of Poco joined Glenn Frey (guitar, b. 1948) and Don Henley (vocals, drums, b. 1947), first as Linda Ronstadt's back-up band and then as The Eagles. Their second disc, 1973's *Desperado*, was a concept album about a hold-out against the decline of the Old West and the title song became a country standard. The 1975 single, 'Lyin' Eyes' broke into the country Top 10. Don Felder (guitar, b. 1947) joined in 1975; Joe Walsh (guitar, b. 1947) replaced Leadon in 1975, and Timothy B. Schmit (vocals, bass, b. 1947) replaced Meisner in 1977. The best-selling 1993 tribute album, *Common Threads*, revealed the huge influence The Eagles had on participating country acts such as Travis Tritt, Alan Jackson, Vince Gill and Brooks And Dunn.

Freddy Fender

(Vocals, guitar, b. 1937)

Fender was born Baldemar Huerta in the southernmost tip of Texas, but adapted his Anglo stage name in the late 1950s as he shifted from the Tex-Mex music he grew up on to rockabilly. After a marijuana conviction, however, he

was reduced to working as an auto mechanic when producer Huey Meaux coaxed him to Houston to make Latin-tinged country records. Their first three singles, 'Before the Next Teardrop Falls', 'Wasted Days And Wasted Nights' and 'Secret Love' all went to No. 1 on the country charts in 1975, thanks to Fender's spectacular tenor and an astute blend of mainstream honky-tonk and Tex-Mex exoticism. Fender stayed on the country charts through to 1979, and he revived his career in 1990 by co-founding the Texas Tornadoes supergroup with Flaco Jimenez, Augie Meyers and Doug Sahm.

The Flatlanders
(Vocal/instrumental group, 1970s–2004)
Joe Ely (vocals, guitar, b. 1947), Jimmie Dale Gilmore (vocals, guitar, b. 1945) and Butch Hancock (vocals, guitar, b. 1945) were teenage pals in the West Texas cotton town of Lubbock when they formed The Flatlanders by combining the music of such local heroes as Buddy Holly and Bob Wills with the songwriting of such adopted heroes as Bob Dylan and Townes Van Zandt. The trio recorded a 1973 album (*One More Road*) that was initially released only on eight-track tape and then splintered into solo careers. Ely had the most success by pursuing a muscular country-rock

that worked equally well as the opening act for The Clash (documented on *Live Shots*) and in a Texas dancehall. Gilmore had the purest voice, a high tenor in the style of his namesake, Jimmie Rodgers. Hancock was the best songwriter, a dazzling wordsmith in the Dylan mode.

Tompall Glaser
(Vocals, guitar, b. 1933)
Glaser was already a successful mainstream-country artist with 13 Top 40 hits to his credit when he joined Willie Nelson, Waylon Jennings and Jessi Colter on the landmark 1976 album *Wanted! The Outlaws*. Tompall had grown up in rural Nebraska with his brothers Jim Glaser (vocals, guitar, harmonica, b. 1937) and Charles Glaser (vocals, guitar, b. 1936); they formed a folk trio and became a mainstream country act under the tutelage of producer Cowboy Jack Clement. Tompall And The Glaser Brothers were the Country Music Association Vocal Group Of The Year in 1970 and scored a Top 10 hit with 'Rings' in 1971. They also formed a recording studio, Hillbilly Central, in 1969 that became the favourite hangout for the Outlaws. Tompall went solo in 1973 and formed the Outlaw Band with members of Bobby 'Blue' Bland's group. Jim Glaser had 10 Top 40 country singles as a solo act.

Above
The members of The Flatlanders remained close friends, often contributing songs, guitar playing and/or vocals to one another's solo records. They finally reunited as a group for albums in 2002 and 2004.

Ray Wylie Hubbard
(Vocals, guitar, b. 1946)

Hubbard made his reputation early on by writing the rousing, tongue-in-cheek sing-along, 'Up Against The Wall, Redneck Mother', which Jerry Jeff Walker turned into his theme song. Alcohol and record-company problems prevented Hubbard from building on that success until the 1990s when he sobered up and emerged as one of the finest singer-songwriters in Texas, a wry, blues-drenched craftsman like his role model Townes Van Zandt.

Kris Kristofferson
(Vocals, guitar, b. 1936)

Kristofferson grew up on country music in Texas, but college in California, a Rhodes scholarship to England and service as an army helicopter pilot convinced him that the times demanded a new kind of country lyric – one that owed as much to Bob Dylan as to Hank Williams. Kristofferson moved to Nashville in 1965 and began to write those lyrics, becoming Top 25 hits for Roy Drusky ('Jody And The Kid'), Johnny Cash ('Sunday Morning Coming Down'), Waylon Jennings ('The Taker'), Roger Miller ('Me And Bobby McGee') and Sammi Smith ('Help Me Make It

Through The Night'). Kristofferson's first two albums, 1970's *Kristofferson (aka Me And Bobby McGee)* and 1971's *The Silver-Tongued Devil And I*, contained his best songs, but he continued to record despite his limited voice.

Lynyrd Skynyrd
(Vocal/istrumental group, 1970s–present)

Lynyrd Skynyrd were finally recognized as the major influence on country music that they were when the tribute album *Lynyrd Frynds* was released in 1994. At last artists such as Alabama, Hank Williams Jr., Travis Tritt, Steve Earle, Charlie Daniels and Wynonna Judd acknowledged how much they had borrowed from the Jacksonville, Florida, band that buried some classic country songwriting beneath their three-guitar onslaught. Lead singer and chief lyricist Ronnie Van Zant (1949–77) wrote about the same kind of blue-collar workers, beer joints and rocky marriages as his fellow southerners in the honky-tonk and Outlaw movements did and with a vividness matched only by a few. Lead guitarists Gary Rossington (b. 1951) and Allen Collins (1952-90) invented fetching hillbilly melodies that turned songs such as 'Free Bird' and 'Sweet Home Alabama' into southern anthems.

Wes McGhee
(Vocals, guitar)

McGhee was England's contribution to the Outlaw movement. Though he grew up in Leicestershire, England, and played in rockabilly legend Gene Vincent's last band, McGhee was such an ardent fan of progressive country that he travelled to Austin, Texas, in 1978 and befriended artists such as Butch Hancock, Jimmie Dale Gilmore, Kimmie Rhodes and Cowboy Jack Clement. With their

introduction ⊙ 188 **influences & development** ⊙ 190 **key artists** ⊙ 196

help he recorded *Airmail In Texas* and with their inspiration, *Long Nights And Banjo Music* in England. He remained based in Britain, but frequent trips to the USA kept him connected to the Outlaw and alt-country scenes there.

Michael Nesmith
(Vocals, guitar, b. 1942)

Former member of The Monkees, Nesmith wrote key hits for Linda Ronstadt ('Different Drum') and the Nitty Gritty Dirt Band ('Some of Shelly's Blues') and formed the First National Band, whose albums demonstrated how country-rock might marry the Americana mythology of the former and the conceptual ambition of the latter. The TV-savvy Nesmith also became a key figure in the nascent music-video revolution.

The Nitty Gritty Dirt Band
(Vocal/instrumental group, 1960s–present)

The Nitty Gritty Dirt Band began as a jug-band revival group in Los Angeles, but evolved into a band that took traditional country music very seriously – so seriously that it organized *Will The Circle Be Unbroken* – the 1972 album that introduced Earl Scruggs, Jimmy Martin, Doc Watson and Maybelle Carter to the rock audience and sold a million copies. Jeff Hanna (vocals, guitar, b. 1947), John McCuen (banjo, mandolin, b. 1945), Jimmie Fadden (vocals, guitar, harmonica, b. 1948) and Les Thompson formed the band (Jackson Browne was a brief, early member) in 1967 and moved to Colorado in 1970, where they added Jimmy Ibbotson (drums, b. 1947). They applied folk-rock and string-band arrangements to both originals and favourite songs by Browne, Kenny Loggins and Jerry Jeff Walker (whose 'Mr Bojangles' became a Top 10 pop hit for the band in 1971).

Poco
(Vocal/instrumental group, 1968–80s)
Poco was formed in 1968 by two former members of the splintered Buffalo Springfield, Richie Furay (vocals, guitar, b. 1944) and Jim Messina (vocals, guitar, b. 1947). They signalled their commitment to the new country-rock sound in Los Angeles by hiring full-time steel guitarist Rusty Young (b. 1946) as well as George Grantham (drums, b. 1947) and Randy Meisner. Though they never matched the pop success and country-music impact of the similar Eagles (the band that hired away not only Meisner but also his replacement Timothy B. Schmit), Poco did release a string of moderately successful pop singles, including 1978's number 17 'Crazy Love'.

John Prine
(Vocals, guitar, b. 1946)
Prine was a Chicago mailman when Kris Kristofferson stumbled across him at a local folk club and recognized him as one of the best lyricists of his generation. A very different lyricist than Bob Dylan, Prine used the unspoken implications of plain, blue-collar speech rather than the dazzle of literary language to make his points, but the monologues he put into the mouths of a Vietnam veteran, an Alabama housewife, a coal-miner's son and an aging couple were so vivid that his 1971 debut album, *John Prine*, became an instant classic. His music was a simple mix of country, folk and rock and his records sold modestly, but his remarkable songs were eagerly recorded by everyone from Tammy Wynette and Johnny Cash to Bonnie Raitt and The Everly Brothers.

Above

Johnny Paycheck's single, 'Take This Job And Shove It', gave a hint about the man himself – feisty and hard-living, he maintained his musical career in between periods in jail.

Johnny Paycheck
(Vocals, guitar, 1938–2003)
Johnny Paycheck was, like David Allan Coe, an outlaw in fact as well as by musical reputation. The former Donald Eugene Lytle was court-martialled from the US Navy in 1956 and served two years in an Ohio prison after shooting a man in a 1985 bar fight. In between he recorded rockabilly as Donnie Young in 1959 and mainstream country as Johnny Paycheck in 1965, scoring hits with 'A-11' and 'The Lovin' Machine'. He wound up on skid row in LA, got signed by Nashville producer Billy Sherrill and recorded a parade of hits for him, including 'Slide Off Your Satin Sheets' (1977) and the No. 1 working-class anthem, 'Take This Job and Shove It' (1977, written by Coe). Four of Paycheck's duets with George Jones became Top 40 singles.

Right

Linda Ronstadt, one of the stars of the Urban Cowboy *soundtrack, shows that she is a country girl at heart.*

Linda Ronstadt
(Vocals, b. 1946)

Linda Ronstadt has had success with many different kinds of music – folk, rock, soul, operetta, show tunes and Tex-Mex – but much of her biggest success is associated with country music and she has been cited as a major influence by such singers as Trisha Yearwood, Patty Loveless and Terri Clark. Ronstadt left her native Arizona to join the folk-revival scene in Los Angeles, and her first band, the Stone Poneys, had a 1968 hit with the country-rock 'Different Drum'. Ronstadt pursued country-rock on her 1969 debut solo album, on 1970's *Silk Purse* recorded in Nashville, and on two more featuring the group that became The Eagles. Her 1975 version of Hank Williams' 'I Can't Help It (If I'm Still In Love With You)' featured harmonies by Emmylou Harris and became a No. 2 country hit. Ronstadt and Harris continued to collaborate and eventually joined forces with Dolly Parton as The Trio; their 1987 album, *Trio*, became a platinum smash that generated four Top 10 country singles.

Billy Joe Shaver
(Vocals, guitar, b. 1939)

Shaver arrived in Nashville in 1968, sold songs to Kris Kristofferson and Tom T. Hall, and wrote all but one song on Waylon Jennings' 1973 album *Honky Tonk Heroes*. That led to Shaver's own debut later the same year with *Old Five And Dimers Like Me*. Shaver had his songs recorded by Elvis Presley, The Allman Brothers, Johnny Cash, Willie Nelson, John Anderson and Asleep At The Wheel, but he didn't hit his stride as a performer until he formed the band Shaver with his son Eddy Shaver (guitar, 1962–2000) in 1993. Eddy's rock guitar added a jolt of excitement to the songs but the son left plenty of space for the father's storytelling; the result was some of the best country-rock of the 1990s.

Above

Billy Joe Shaver lost several fingers and most of his innocence working in a sawmill and rambling around Texas, but he translated those experiences into some of the most memorable songs of the Outlaws era.

'The Taker' for Waylon Jennings (1970), the seductive 'Once More With Feeling' (1979) for Kris Kristofferson and the whole double album, *Lullabies, Legends And Lies* (1974), for Bobby Bare.

James Talley
(Vocals, guitar, b. 1943)
James Talley grew up in Oklahoma near Woody Guthrie's birthplace and carried on Guthrie's legacy with acoustic songs that were tough in their attacks on social injustice, irreverent in their attacks on pomposity and tender in their defence of love. Though he had songs recorded by Johnny Cash, Johnny Paycheck and Hazel Dickens and was lionized by critics, Talley sold few records and turned to selling real estate late in his career.

Jerry Jeff Walker
(Vocals, guitar, b. 1942)
Walker grew up in upstate New York State and wrote his most famous song, 'Mr Bojangles', as a Greenwich Village folkie, but when he moved to Austin in 1972 he embraced the town's cowboy-hippie ethos so wholeheartedly that he became its personification. Backing his singer-songwriter material with a Texas dancehall band transformed his songs into celebrations of life as an ongoing party. Breakthrough albums such as 1971's *Jerry Jeff Walker*, 1973's *Viva Terlingua*

Above

After his musical career, Shel Silverstein went on to pen several bestselling children's books, including A Light In The Attic *and* Where The Sidewalk Ends.

Shel Silverstein
(Vocals, guitar, 1932–99)
Silverstein had just the right irreverent, satirical edge that the Outlaws movement was looking for, thanks to his background as a successful cartoonist for *Playboy* and a semi-successful folk singer. He wrote the comic fable 'A Boy Named Sue' for Johnny Cash (1969), the voodoo tale 'Marie Laveau' for Bobby Bare (1974), the ladies-man boast

and 1975's *Ridin' High* introduced unknown songwriters such as Guy Clark, Ray Wylie Hubbard, Gary P. Nunn and Michael Martin Murphey to the world.

The White Brothers
(Vocal/instrumental group, 1960s)

Clarence White (guitar, 1944–73) and his brother Roland White (vocals, mandolin, b. 1938) grew up in Maine and then California but they called their string band The Kentucky Colonels. That's where Clarence pioneered the concept of lead acoustic guitar in a bluegrass band and became a legend to pickers everywhere. When Clarence switched to electric Telecaster guitar and mainstream country, he was hired to play sessions for the Byrds in 1967–68 and was hired as a full-time member in 1969. He was also part of the new-grass group, Muleskinner, with Peter Rowan, Richard Greene and Bill Keith, but Clarence was killed by a drunk driver in 1973. Roland stayed true to the bluegrass calling, playing with Bill Monroe And The Blue Grass Boys 1967–69, Lester Flatt And The Nashville Grass 1969–73, Country Gazette 1973–86 and the Nashville Bluegrass Band 1989–2000.

Hank Williams Jr.
(Vocals, guitar, b. 1949)

Williams was only three when his famous father died, but the youngster was raised to imitate his daddy's records as closely as possible. He finally rebelled against that formula in 1975 by releasing *Hank Williams Jr. And Friends* with his southern-rock friends. After an injury-induced break, he returned to performing in 1976, picking up his new country-rock sound where he left off. Between 1979 and 1990 his boisterous brand of bravado led to 35 Top 15 singles, including the emblematic 'Whiskey Bent And Hell Bound' (1979), 'All My Rowdy Friends' (1984) and 'Born To Boogie' (1987). His autobiography, *Living Proof*, was turned into a television movie in 1983; he was voted CMA's Entertainer Of The Year in 1987, and he became the official singer of television's *Monday Night Football* in 1989.

Townes Van Zandt
(Vocals, guitar, 1944–97)

Van Zandt, the bohemian son of Texas aristocracy, spent much of his life drifting from place to place and battling alcoholism, but he became a songwriting mentor for Steve Earle, Guy Clark, Susanna Clark, Nanci Griffith, Rodney

Crowell and The Flatlanders. His small, roughened voice limited the appeal of his own albums, but the many gems there were covered by countless artists. Two of his best songs became Top 3 country duets: 'If I Needed You' for Emmylou Harris and Don Williams in 1981 and 'Pancho and Lefty' for Willie Nelson and Merle Haggard in 1983.

Steve Young
(Vocals, guitar, b. 1942)

Young grew up listening to country music in his native Georgia, played folk music in Greenwich Village and recorded early country-rock with Gram Parsons and Chris Hillman in California. He wove these disparate experiences into vivid story songs that were recorded by the Eagles, Waylon Jennings, Hank Williams Jr. and Dolly Parton. Young's own recordings were prized by critics even if they were ignored by the general public.

Above
Townes Van Zandt – 'the best songwriter in the whole world' according to Steve Earle.

Left
Jerry Jeff Walker continues to enchant audiences with his rich, warm voice in the twenty-first century.

Working Nine To Five:
Mainstream Country & The Pop Crossover

major changes occurred in country music during the 1970s and 1980s, and country icons came and went as the music escaped from the stereotypical image of the 1960s, when it had been gingham dresses for the ladies and rhinestone suits for the men. Now country music had a new face: Dolly Parton's extravagant dress sense and the shaggy-haired Outlaw acts, coupled with Loretta Lynn, whose songs spoke of everyday life, which was not how women were used to being perceived by Nashville executives and portrayed in the news media or television. Not since Kitty Wells and 'It Wasn't God Who Made Honky Tonk Angels' (1952) had female acts seen such success as that achieved by Parton, Lynn and Tammy Wynette – all of whom had started out successfully in the 1960s.

The difference lay in the fact that they became superstars, each with their particular type of country music. Acts such as Alabama and the storyteller Tom T. Hall, whose songs Bobby Bare often recorded, were also cut from a different cloth. Singer/songwriter/actor Ed Bruce, Vern Gosdin, John Anderson and John Conlee held tight to tradition, while others who were less committed fell away.

By the end of the 1980s, the compact-disc format had all but taken over from vinyl, and the 'hat' acts arrived, resulting in innumerable videos shown on Country Music Television (CMT), which became a popular, expensive and essential trend.

Major female newcomers included Barbara Mandrell, Canadian songbird Anne Murray and Tanya Tucker, who after having been tempted into the world of pop, returned to a music she had stormed at the age of 13, displaying unbelievable maturity. To paraphrase the title of the Waylon Jennings hit, Hank sure never did it this way.

Key Artists
Alabama

Loretta Lynn

Dolly Parton

Tammy Wynette

Influences & Development

At the beginning of the 1970s, the influences in mainstream country music continued to originate from a wide spread of sources, the most dominant being the Nashville Sound, which now had strong pop overtures alongside a greater distortion of country music itself. On the other hand, an innovative breed of songwriters were about to be heard, bringing fresh lyricism to country music and attracting new audiences. Their presence helped counteract the pop sensibilities now being created by Nashville's industry.

Below

Bobby Bare was one of the first country artists to have a pop crossover hit, with 'The All-American Boy' in 1958. It was the start of a crossover trend that reached its peak in the 1970s.

The New Face Of Country

Heading up this new breed of songwriters was Kris Kristofferson (b. 1936), the son of a US Air Force major general and Oxford Rhodes Scholar, who flew helicopters before arriving in Nashville where he worked as a janitor, among other jobs, while pitching his songs around Music Row. Many people still recall that evening at the 1970 CMA Awards when sections of the audience were aghast as this 'long-haired hippie' took to the stage to collect the Song Of The Year for 'Sunday Morning Coming Down', a No. 1 when recorded by Johnny Cash. Conservatism reigned in Nashville back then: even Waylon and Willie were clean-shaven and short-haired.

'Fads are the kiss of death. When the fad goes away, you go with it.' **Conway Twitty**

Of course Kris Kristofferson wasn't the first to change the method of creating a Nashville song. Back in the mid-1960s an equally innovative free spirit named Roger Miller (1936–92) changed the rigid structure of the country lyric with mapcap wordplay. Kristofferson was much more the sensitive lyricist and Johnny Cash's plaintive vocals ideally complimented the writer's moody 'Saturday Morning Coming Down', though Cash wasn't the first to record a Kristofferson song. That credit is due to Roy Drusky (1930–2004) and Miller, who gave the writer his debut chart appearances with 'Jody And The Kid' and 'Me And Bobby McGee (co-penned with Marijohn Willkin) respectively. Alongside the Cash success, Sammi Smith (1943–2005) created a sensual rendition of 'Help Me Make It Through The Night' and Ray Price (b. 1926) secured one of the biggest records of his post honky-tonk period with 'For The Good Times'. Both records collected Grammy Awards.

Kristofferson's substantial influence cannot be overstated and an influx of young writers, with a new level of adult lyricism, came to the attention of Nashville's music publishers and recording executives. Among them were Guy Clark (b. 1941), Chris Gantry (b. 1942), John Hartford (1937–2001), Mickey Newbury (1940–2002), Billy

Joe Shaver (b. 1939) and Townes Van Zandt (1944–97). As the decade progressed, another important contributor to the this new music growth, Shel Silverstein (1932–99) frequently hung out at Hillbilly Central (aka Glaser Sound Studio) with several of his songs set to contribute to the Outlaw movement. Tompall Glaser (b. 1933), along with brothers Chuck and Jim, had caused attention in Nashville circles by creating their own music publishing and studio complex, business not previously association with an artist.

Crossover And Controversy

While the new breed of songwriters fitted alongside established peers like Harlan Howard, Jerry Chesnutt (b. 1931), Hank Cochran (b. 1935), Dallas Frazier (b. 1939) and Willie Nelson, the mainstream recording industry appeared more even more intent on developing the crossover market. It was well supported by radio, the medium that had always been the prime voice of country music, which totalled 525 stations in 1971. Many of the stations that had switched formats to country from rock still employed the former djs and programmers, and their sensibilities favoured the new rather than the old. As airplays determined the country charts, anomalies such as the Pointer Sisters ('Fairy Tale', 1975), Bee Gees ('Rest Your Love On Me', 1978) and Bonnie

Tyler ('It's A Heartache', 1978) enjoyed country-music success. Fortunately such occurrences were rare.

Billy Sherrill (b. 1936) – songwriter and powerhouse Columbia/Epic producer – accurately assessed the crossover situation with the comment: 'Twin fiddles don't make it country anymore – and not having twin fiddles doesn't make it not country. Country is no longer the basic sound any more than rock'n'roll is. Country is really a state of mind.' Ironically, Sherrill kept the majority of his artists' recordings to more stone country roots, though the exception came with Charlie Rich. A former Sun artist, he sensationally hit the big time in 1973 with the ultra-smooth 'Behind Closed Doors'

and quickly followed up with the equally lushly produced 'The Most Beautiful Girl In The World'. Both singles earned him major crossover positioning and a CMA Entertainer Of The Year accolade in 1974. In some people's opinions such diverse realms did not qualify Rich as a country artist, but such criticism was mild in comparison to that heard when UK-born, Australian-raised pop singer Olivia Newton-John walked away with the 1974 Female Vocalist Of The Year.

The backlash continued with the creation of an organization to protect country music's former values and traditions, Association Of Country Entertainers (ACE), comprising country artists with a screening committee. Stalwart Billy Walker (1929–2006), who started charting in 1954, pointed out that 'outside interests were diluting the music ... we're mainly people who have made country what it is today and trying to project our business.' Nevertheless, ACE was relatively short-lived, its growl worse than its bite, and several of its members moved on to the crossover bandwagon themselves, including Dolly Parton who, by the end of the decade, was based in Hollywood and recording rock and disco tracks.

Right
Smooth country crooner Kenny Rogers – a master of the country-pop crossover – sings with the queen of modern country, Dolly Parton.

Below
Billie Jo Spears was part of the travelling music scene of the 1970s, which saw stars touring widely, performing at festivals, and making the most of television appearances. Suddenly country music reached a wider audience than ever before.

Crossover Success Stories

Like it or not, crossover was a fixture of the country landscape and, as the decade progressed, it gained in strength, with its greatest exponents veering towards an MOR (middle-of-the-road) sound. Glen Campbell had begun his ascendancy to eventual 2005 Hall Of Fame induction with 'Gentle On My Mind' and 'By The Time I Get To Phoenix' (both 1967), and continued through the 1970s, hitting the top with 'Rhinestone Cowboy' (1975) and 'Southern Nights' (1977), as well as enjoying further success duetting with Canada's Anne Murray and Bobbie Gentry (b. 1944). There was also John Denver, more a folk artist though he walked away with the 1975 CMA Entertainer Of The Year Award.

Campbell, Murray, Gentry and Denver further added to their sales, chart and award triumphs by establishing a loyal market internationally, a feat also accomplished by Lynn Anderson, who scored the first major crossover hit of the 1970s with the Joe South -penned 'Rose Garden'. Produced by her husband Glenn Sutton (b. 1936), an associate of Sherrill's, it gave the champion horsewoman a ride at the top of the crossover market as well as Top 3 pop success in Britain. Just a few years later several other artists were also riding the crossover bandwagon in both domestic and international terms, headed up by one-time leader of the First Edition, rock artist Kenny Rogers, whose lasting country success was ensured with 'Lucille' (1977) and story songs like 'The Gambler' (1978) and 'Coward Of The County' (1979),

both later adapted for movies. In the 1980s, duets with both country (Dottie West and Dolly Parton) and pop (Kim Carnes and Sheena Easton) artists secured major country-pop successes. The Bellamy Brothers, Howard and David, also moved over from the rock world with 'If I Said You Had A Beautiful Body (Would You Hold It Against Me)' (1979) and established a country credibility that has been particularly rewarding in the European marketplace, while The Charlie Daniels Band put southern country-rock on the crossover map with 'The Devil Went Down To Georgia' in 1979.

Dot Records found success as Donna Fargo collected Grammy and CMA awards with 'The Happiest Girl In The Whole USA' (1972). Crystal Gayle enjoyed a succession of hits on United Artists, the biggest being the Grammy Award-winning 'Don't It Make My Brown Eyes Blue' (1977), while labelmates Billie Jo Spears (b. 1937) and veteran Grand Ole Opry star Jean Shepard tasted one-off success with 'Blanket On The Ground' (1975) and 'Slippin' Away' (1973) respectively. But the most enduring success, especially in the UK, where he's been the recipient of numerous gold and platinum discs, came for Don Williams, whose gentle-voiced collection of hits commenced with 'Amanda' (1973) and 'You're My Best Friend' (1975).

Boom And Bust

By the decade's end further changes were afoot. Wild Country, a self-contained band from Fort Payne, Alabama, paid its dues, changed its name to Alabama and opened the floodgates to other country groups arriving on the scene. Hollywood, which always had associations with country music, moved closer by not only launching Dolly Parton on a fully fledged movie career with *Nine To Five* (1980), in the company of Jane Fonda and Lily Tomlin, but also making a movie of Loretta Lynn's bestselling biography *Coal Miner's Daughter* (1980), securing Sissy Spacek (b. 1949) an Oscar and shortlived country recording career. Lynn herself – among the most grass-rooted of country performers – suddenly shocked audiences when she tackled contemporary subjects in 'Rated X' (1972) and 'The Pill' (1975).

Then John Travolta headlined *Urban Cowboy* (1980), promising to do for country music what *Saturday Night Fever* had done for disco. It did. A massive box-office hit, the soundtrack produced two multi-million-selling albums and the shortlived urban cowboy movement. But the mass public's flirtation with country led to an inevitable boom and bust, only revived by the New Traditionalist movement which, ironically, brought the music back to its roots.

Above
Although at heart a country act, The Bellamy Brothers added elements of rock, pop and reggae to their music that ensured their crossover success.

Precious Memories - The Gospel Influence In Country Music

Country music and gospel have always been close partners, since many gospel acts come from the American South, and Nashville, the home of country music, lies in the heart of Bible Belt. Numerous influences abound within the Church, stretching from traditional shape-note singing that goes back several hundred years, to today's contemporary and Christian music. Primitive and Southern Baptists, and Evangelical Methodists all have a long and fine heritage when it comes to singing, alongside other branches of Christian groups that grew out of the South – all provided an excellent grounding for future country and bluegrass performers.

Country-Gospel In The Charts

Modern America's ever-growing and changing ways took longer to reach the rural South, and because of this, the area has retained many traditional vocal styles. Country music has been a major beneficiary over the years, with gospel music playing a significant part in the lives of country artists. Even the biggest stars over the years have recorded gospel music – and several still do, if not to the same degree as in the past. At one time it was expected that even the biggest stars would record at least one gospel album and the posthumously released *My Mother's Hymn Book* was just one of several in the substantial Johnny Cash catalogue. His 1968 chart-topping single, 'Daddy Sang Bass', featuring The Statler Brothers and The Carter Family, was country gospel, and Skeeter Davis, Connie Smith, Merle Haggard and Bonnie Owens, Dolly Parton, Elvis Presley, Jeannie C. Riley, George Hamilton IV, Vern Gosdin and George Jones head a long list of those who recorded gospel material.

Several veteran acts devoted the latter years of their lives to recording gospel music, among them 'Tennessee' Ernie Ford, whose early collection *Hymns* was, at one time, the biggest seller in the Capitol Records catalogue;

'I Saw The Light' standing well alongside such Albert E. Brumley (1905–77) favourites as 'I'll Fly Away' and 'Turn Your Radio On'. Other songs like 'Amazing Grace' and 'How Great Thou Art' remain among the most performed and recorded items in gospel and country music.

Arguably the most successful contemporary gospel song is 'One Day At A Time' (co-written by Marijohn Wilken and Kris Kristofferson). Originally recorded by Marilyn Sellars (b. 1950) in 1974, it became a chart-topper when covered by Cristy Lane (b. 1940) six years later. It also spawned several international hits, including No. 1s in Scotland and Ireland, by Lena Martell and Gloria respectively, and by 2005 the cover versions had topped the 600 mark. Kristofferson also scored a No. 1 country hit with his original 'Why Me' in 1973. A year earlier, Tom T. Hall scored one of his many chart successes with 'Me And Jesus' accompanied by a Methodist church choir. Also displaying a slightly different slant on the genre, one of Bobby Bare's best-known sounds is 'Dropkick Me, Jesus (Through The Goalposts Of Life)' (1976).

But while gospel music provided part of many country artist's repertoire, it was the complete *raison d'etre* for a multitude of southerners, with many singers forming groups and developing a unique blend of four-part harmonies. The Oak Ridge Quartet was one such group and saw various personnel changes over the years since its formation in 1945, eventually becoming The Oak Ridge Boys in 1962 and then making the move to country music the following decade. Another multi-award winning group, The Statler Brothers, have their vocals deep rooted in gospel music while a multitude of groups have kept their music firmly entrenched in religious and Christian surroundings. Gospel music is, indeed, a realm in its own right and a major music genre to be undertaken separately.

Connie Smith – one of the finest voices in country music – was suited to the richness and sincerity that gospel undertones in country music demanded.

Left
Ferlin Husky's gospel offerings included the evergreen 'Wings Of A Dove'.

Below
The Kendalls (father Royce and daughter Jeannie Kendall) are best known for their 1977 chart-topper (and CMA Single Of The Year), 'Heaven's Just A Sin Away' – a gospel favourite.

western movie favourites Roy Rogers sand Dale Evans; and Jimmie Davis, whose amazing career included being twice elected Governor of Louisiana.

Gospel music was most prevalent in the 1940s and 1950s, prior to which it had been the staple diet of such pioneering country music families as the Carters and Stonemans; The Monroe Brothers (Charlie and Bill) and Bailes Brothers; and several groups that included the Brown's Ferry Four.

Old And New Favourites

Roy Acuff, together with his Smoky Mountain Boys, was the biggest name on the Grand Ole Opry and heard regularly throughout the nation thanks to WSM's powerful 5,000-watt transmitter, would perform such stirring gospel favourites as 'Great Speckled Bird' and 'Were You There When They Crucified My Lord'. Hank Williams, whose shortlived association with the Opry was part of an equally short and tragic life, wrote several enduring gospel songs, with his

Alabama

Alabama, who appropriately came from Fort Payne, in Alabama, emerged into the spotlight in 1980, when 'Tennessee River' topped the *Billboard* country charts. Three group members – Randy Owen (guitar, lead vocals, b. 1949), Teddy Gentry (bass, vocals, b. 1952) and Jeff Cook (keyboards, fiddle, vocals, b. 1949) – were cousins. Country music was going through one of its regular transitional periods, trying to escape from the 'Urban Cowboy' era, a time when the music was heavily diluted for commercial rather than aesthetic reasons, and was hardly recognizable as country. The emergence of the all-conquering Alabama, who merged southern country rock with contemporary sounds, ended the dominance enjoyed by The Oak Ridge Boys and

'The Bowery gave us a great place, a great avenue to be a band and to be able to write and be able to create.'
Randy Owen

Below
Alabama was one of the longest-serving bands in country music. The group was inducted into the Country Music Hall Of Fame in 2005.

The Statler Brothers in both the charts and the annual Country Music Association awards.

The Midas Touch

Formed originally in 1969 as Young Country, then Wildcountry, by Gentry, Cook and Owen plus drummers Bennett Vartanian (until 1976) and Mark Herndon (after 1979, b. 1955), they became Alabama in 1977, towards the end of a seven-year residency at The Bowery in Myrtle Beach, South Carolina, where they played up to 13 hours some days. They had genuinely paid their dues, and were rewarded in July 1980 when they signed a record deal with RCA.

Not renowned for working with country groups, RCA was well served over the next 20 years. By 1993, Alabama had accumulated 32 country No. 1 hit singles, including a

Classic Recordings

My Home's In Alabama **(1980)**
'Tennessee River', 'Why Lady Why', 'My Home's In Alabama', 'Hanging Up My Travelin' Shoes', 'I Wanna Come Over'

Feels So Right **(1981)**
'Feels So Right', 'Old Flame', 'Love In The First Degree', 'Burn Georgia Burn', 'Set The Embers, Feel The Flame'

Mountain Music **(1982)**
'Mountain Music', 'Close Enough To Perfect', 'Words At Twenty Paces', 'Green River', 'Take Me Down'

Closer You Get **(1983)**
'Lay Down On Your Love', 'Alabama Sky', 'The Closer You Get', 'Dixieland Delight', 'She Put The Sad In All His Songs'

Southern Star **(1989)**
'Song Of The South', 'High Cotton', 'Southern Star', "Ole' Baugh Road', 'The Border'

record 21 consecutive chart-toppers, starting with 'Tennessee River' (1980). After that, it seemed everything they touched turned to gold. An Artist Of The Decade award came as no surprise for arguably country music's hardest-working act.

Songs Of The South

Frequently displaying a love of the American South in their songs, as epitomized by 1982's 'Mountain Music' – the title track of an album certified quadruple platinum and the second of three consecutive albums that made the Top 20 of the US pop chart – Alabama could have rivalled The Eagles as a mainstream attraction. However, perhaps songs like 'If You're Gonna Play In Texas (You Gotta Have A Fiddle In The Band)' (1984), 'Song Of The South' (1988), 'High Cotton' and 'Southern Star' (both 1989) seemed a bit provincial to younger, hipper audiences, and prevented Alabama from crossing over into the biggest arena. They did not do badly, though – 15 US pop chart albums by 1992, all gold or better, and three Top 20 singles ('Feels So Right', 'Love In The First Degree' and 'Take Me Down', all in the early 1980s) is an achievement few have bettered.

Their sales are now approaching 60 million, largely due to their annual sell-out tours across North America. Their total absence from the UK pop chart until 1986, when they sang backing vocals on Lionel Richie's 'Deep River Woman' suggests that Alabama were happy with their domestic success and uninterested in conquering Europe.

Alabama became an institution, and were much honoured in the CMA Awards, winning Vocal Group Of The Year in 1981, 1982 and 1983, and Entertainer Of The Year in 1982, 1983 and 1984. They became a fixture in the American Music Awards, where voters are the general public, and won the Favorite Country Band, Duo Or Group category no fewer than eight times during the 1990s. Apart from the Lionel Richie single, their only major collaboration was with K. T. Oslin, who joined them as guest vocalist on their 1988 chart-topper, 'Face To Face'.

Above

Alabama split in 2003, leaving a devastated fan base, which had by then given them 42 country No. 1 hits, and also supported the group's charity work, for which Alabama were noted.

Key Track

'Tennessee River' (1980)
'Tennessee River' was Alabama's first country chart topper in 1980, and comprises two parts. Starting off with a lazy southern brew, simmering on the stove, it first tells of their roots and the pride that goes with it, then Jeff Cook strikes up on fiddle and in an instant, one of the band's most loved and finest songs has paid for its recording time a hundred times over.

Loretta Lynn

Key Artist

Key Artist

Right

The collaboration between Loretta Lynn and Conway Twitty was dynamite – the duo enjoyed an uninterrupted stream of No. 1 hits for nearly five years.

Below

Loretta Lynn sang about real life in her music, and several of her songs – including 'The Pill' and 'One's On The Way' were adopted as anthems for the women's liberation movement in the 1970s.

Country music has spawned numerous superstars, but few can match the impact made by the woman who became known as the Coal Miner's Daughter. Born Loretta Webb on 14 April 1935 in Butcher's Hollow, Kentucky, she married Oliver 'Moonshine' Lynn in 1949. She has been an inspiration and guide to countless aspiring female acts who followed her into country music.

Honky-Tonk Girl

Lynn started her adult life in a greater hurry than even girls of the Deep South. By the time she was 18 and living in Custer, Washington, she already had four children. While doing her daily chores, she kept herself amused by singing.

When time allowed, she played in a band with her brother, Jay Lee Webb. Her younger sisters, Peggy Sue and Crystal Gayle, would later follow her into music and the charts.

In 1959, she signed to Zero Records, where her debut hit single, 'I'm A Honky Tonk Girl', started one of the richest veins in the history of female acts in country music. She and her husband Mooney took the single personally to radio stations, and against all the odds, the independent release reached the Top 20 of the country chart. Impressed by the song, The Wilburn Brothers (Doyle and Teddy) hired Lynn to tour with them, which she continued to do until 1968, when she moved to Nashville.

By this time, she had built up a succession of hits with Decca, the label to which Patsy Cline was also signed, and was produced, like Cline, by Owen Bradley. Lynn topped the country charts for the first time in 1967 with 'Don't Come Home A'Drinkin' (With Lovin' On Your Mind)', and walked away with the CMA Female Vocalist Award that year, while 'Fist City' in 1968 raised Establishment eyebrows for a second time.

'A woman's two cents is worth two cents in the music business.'
Loretta Lynn

Breaking The Nashville Mould

Lynn's expressive and direct style of writing, fashioning songs relating to women, resulted in her winning many admirers, and the autobiographical 'Coal Miner's Daughter' topped the country chart in 1970. Shortly after this, she started recording duets with Conway Twitty. Duets weren't new to Lynn, who had seen some chart success duetting with Ernest Tubb. However, nothing matched the scale of the unbroken sequence of five No. 1 singles between 1971 and 1975 she enjoyed with Twitty. This run included 'After The Fire Is Gone' (1971), 'Lead Me On' (1971) and 'Louisiana Woman, Mississippi Man' (1973). The early 1970s almost belonged to the duo, as awards were bestowed on them like confetti. In 1972, Lynn won both

the CMA Female Vocalist Of The Year (which she retained in 1973) and Entertainer Of The Year Awards, also picking up (with Twitty) Vocal Duo Of The Year Award, which they retained for four years. During this time, Lynn also

stormed to the top of the country singles chart with such classics as 'One's On The Way' (1971) while 'The Pill' (1975) struck home with the Women's Lib movement – hardly what Nashville expected!

A 1980 movie of Lynn's *Coal Miner's Daughter* autobiography was a huge box-office success and Sissy Spacek won an Academy Award for her portrayal of the country superstar. However, declining sales saw Lynn fade from the scene during the late 1980s and early 1990s, until 1993's 'Honky Tonk Angels' project with Tammy Wynette and Dolly Parton, and she also returned in 2000 with 'Still Woman Enough'. In 2004, Jack White (of The White Stripes) produced the Grammy-winning *Van Lear Rose* album, which was a splendid return for Lynn, the legend who was elected to the Country Music Hall Of Fame in 1988.

Left

Tootsie's Orchid Lounge on Broadway, in Nashville, has been the haunt of many country artists since the 1960s – including Kris Kristofferson, Willie Nelson and Waylon Jennings. Some scenes from the Loretta Lynn biopic Coal Miner's Daughter *were filmed here.*

Key Track

'Coal Miner's Daughter' (1970)
An autobiographical creation by Lynn, telling of her simple, but wholesome upbringing and how her father, a coal miner, supported eight children and his wife. Life in rural Butcher's Hollow, Kentucky, was straight from the backwoods and that sticks in the listener's mind, especially when sung by a true country voice. When listening to Loretta Lynn, you are listening to real country.

Dolly Parton

Key Artist

'If you talk bad about country music, it's like saying bad things about my momma. Them's fightin' words.'
Dolly Parton

Dolly Rebecca Parton was born on 19 January 1946, in Locust Ridge, Tennessee. Immediately after graduation in the summer of 1964, she travelled from the Blue Ridge Mountains to Nashville, taking with her dreams of country stardom and little else. Ever since, she has thrilled audiences worldwide. An entertainer extraordinaire, Dolly has also become an icon of country-style glamour and is adored by the public.

Right
The irrepressible Dolly Parton has been charming the music industry for decades, and is still going strong.

Top Right
Parton and Porter Wagoner had numerous hits – their biggest songs were 'Just Someone I Used To Know' (Top 5, 1969), 'Please Don't Stop Loving Me' (No. 1, 1974) and 'Making Plans', which came six years after Dolly had left Wagoner's show.

Early Success

Dolly was one of 12 children born and raised in a wooden shack with newspaper pasted on the inner walls to keep out the cold in winter. Her childhood was simple, but her vivid imagination pictured a world beyond her immediate surroundings. She began making up songs at the age of five – before she could even read. With the help of her uncle, Bill Owens, she got to perform on a local radio station at the age of 11, and made her first record – 'Puppy Love' – on Gold Band, a Louisiana label, that same year. The rest is history. Her bubbly personality, colourful make-up, tight-fitting dresses and extravagant hairdos brought a breath of fresh air to Nashville. She signed with RCA in 1968 after a brief spell with Monument and immediately started to change the way women were viewed in both the microcosm of Nashville and country music in the wider world.

She replaced vocalist Norma Jean on *The Porter Wagoner Show* and became the permanent female singer there in 1967 – a position she held until 1974. Wagoner and Parton took their winning collaboration into the studio as well, making 14 Top 10 singles and winning the CMA Vocal Duo Of The Year Award in 1970 and 1971.

All The Way To Dollywood

Parton's first solo chart-topper came in 1971 with 'Joshua', after which the floodgates opened. She followed this with some of the most homey country songs ever written, including 'Coat Of Many Colors'(1971), 'Jolene' (1973 No. 1, which crossed over into the US pop chart), 1974's 'Love Is Like A Butterfly' and 'I Will Always Love You', written about her association with Wagoner. This charted again – and made No. 1 – in 1982, when Parton performed it in *The Best Little Whorehouse In Texas*, a movie in which she starred with Burt Reynolds. However, it found its greatest success, and brought Parton both recognition and riches, a decade later when Whitney Houston recorded it for the soundtrack to *The Bodyguard*. Houston's version topped the US pop chart for 14 weeks and the UK chart for 10 weeks.

Parton has appeared in a number of notable feature films, including *9 To 5* (with Jane Fonda and Lily Tomlin), *Rhinestone* (with Sylvester Stallone) and the all-star *Steel Magnolias*. She also enjoyed recording success when she teamed up with Emmylou Harris and Linda Ronstadt for two albums as Trio. The first album included the 1987 chart-topping single, 'To Know Him Is To Love Him'. Another of her 24 No. 1 hits was 1983's million-selling duet with Kenny Rogers, 'Islands In The Stream'.

In 1975 and 1976, she was voted CMA's Top Female Vocalist and, in 1978, Entertainer Of The Year. A flirtation with pop followed in the 1980s, with '9 To 5' (from the movie) topping the US pop chart in 1981, and becoming her second gold single. After her 1999 induction into the Country Music Hall Of Fame, she reverted to recording bluegrass and folk albums. These include *The Grass Is Blue* (1999) and *Little Sparrow* (2001), which recalled the music she heard as a child. Dolly Parton has been a major country-music icon for 30 years, and shows few signs of slowing down.

Classic Recordings

Joshua (1971)
'J. J. Sneed', 'Daddy's Moonshine Still', 'It Ain't Fair That It Ain't Right' 'Joshua', 'Chicken Every Sunday', 'Walls Of My Mind'

Touch Your Woman (1972)
'Will He Be Waiting', 'A Little At A Time', 'Mission Chapel Memories', 'Second Best', 'Touch Your Woman'

My Tennessee Mountain Home (1975)
'In The Good Old Days (When Times Were Bad)', 'Old Black Kettle', 'My Tennessee Mountain Home', 'The Wrong Direction Home', 'Dr. Robert F. Thomas'

All I Can Do (1976)
'Boulder To Birmingham', 'Preacher Tom', 'Shattered Image', 'All I Can Do', 'Life's Like Poetry'

The Grass Is Blue (1999)
'Travelin' Prayer', 'Steady As The Rain', Train, Train', 'The Grass Is Blue', 'I'm Gonna Sleep With One Eye Open'

Left

Another aspect of the Parton success story began in 1985, when she opened her theme park, Dollywood, in Pigeon Forge, Tennessee, where she employs many of her relatives.

Key Track

'Jolene' (1974)
Parton's second country chart-topper finds her pleading with another woman not to take her man from her – which would be hard to imagine in real life, taking into account the charm and beauty of Ms Parton. Boasting a simple melody, the timbre of her vocals makes this another classic, indicative of Parton performing at her natural best.

Tammy Wynette

Key Artist

Above

Tammy Wynette always kept her beautician's licence up to date, believing that bubble of fame and fortune could burst at any moment.

Nashville's Number One

When it came to paying her dues, Wynette measured up with the best, combining the duties of a single mother to three daughters, holding down a job and trying to break into the music business. After gaining some exposure on local television while living with relatives in Birmingham, Alabama, she made several trips to Nashville around 1965 and moved there in 1966. She started working as a song plugger, but within a relatively short time she was signed to Epic by producer Billy Sherrill, and it was he who gave Tammy her stage name, signalling the beginning of one of the greatest working relationships in country-music history. During the period of her association with Sherrill, she accumulated 20 chart toppers, three of them duets with her husband, the hell-raising country legend George Jones, whom she married in 1969 and divorced in 1975 (although their final chart-topping duet, 'Golden Ring', came out in 1976).

'A part of me still thinks getting paid to sing's too good to be true.'

Tammy Wynette

Wynette's pure but tearful voice was made for emotion-torn country ballads – songs dealing in heartache and pain. Her first success came in early 1967 with the Top 50 country hit 'Apartment No. 9', which won Wynette her first Grammy. Her second arrived in 1968 for her fifth US

Labelled the 'first lady of country music', Virginia Wynette Pugh was born on 5 May 1942, in Itawamba County, Mississippi. Throughout the early 1960s she worked as a waitress and beautician – among other jobs – and only dreamed of stardom. It was not long coming, but like many of her contemporaries, Loretta Lynn, Connie Smith and Dolly Parton included, Tammy Wynette worked her way up from the bottom.

country No. 1/pop Top 20 smash, 'Stand By Your Man', which she also co-wrote with Sherrill. This classic, since covered by Lyle Lovett and others, immediately followed the similarly striking 'D-I-V-O-R-C-E.' Both singles topped *Billboard*'s country chart for three weeks.

International Success

Wynette swept to the top of the UK pop chart in May, 1975, with 'Stand By Your Man', which made it her career song. It resulted in almost annual tours and appearances at the International Festival Of Country Music at Wembley in London. Her career reached its peak with a run of no less than 10 No. 1 hits as a solo act during the 1970s. The last of these was 1976's 'You And Me' (another crossover hit). Her penultimate US country chart-topper, "Til I Can Make It On My Own', co-written by Sherrill and her manager/ husband, George Richey, was Tammy's all-time favourite.

Her successful public face belied a troubled personal life. She suffered break-ins, vandalism of her home, and an abduction, followed by financial difficulties, all of which contributed to Wynette's health problems during the 1980s and 1990s. Despite this, she published her autobiography, *Stand By Your Man*, in 1979, which was made into a television movie in 1981. Her projects in the 1990s included 'Justified And Ancient', a somewhat unlikely US Top 20/UK Top 3 single in 1992 as guest vocalist with British dance act KLF. In 1995, she recorded a final duet album with George Jones, *One*, and they made a last trip to England together. Soundtracks to the films *Five Easy Pieces* (starring Jack Nicholson and featuring four of her songs) and *Run Angel, Run* also showcased her work. She died in 1998 and was posthumously inducted into the Country Music Hall Of Fame the following year.

A-Z of Artists

Lynn Anderson
(Vocals, b. 1947)

The daughter of songwriter Liz Anderson (b. 1930, whose hits included 'All My Friends Are Gonna Be Strangers' and 'The Fugitive' for Merle Haggard), Anderson enjoyed success in equestrian competitions during the mid-1960s before turning to music. After a dozen hits on Chart Records, she signed to Columbia (1970–80), where she quickly achieved her million-selling hit, 'Rose Garden'. Other No. 1s included 'You're My Man' and 'How Can I Unlove You' (both 1971).

Below
Oklahoma-born Hoyt Axton released his last album, Spin Of The Wheel, in 1990, but his health continued to decline and he was forced into retirement.

Hoyt Axton
(Vocals, songwriter, actor, 1938–99)

Axton's mother, Mae Boren Axton, co-wrote 'Heartbreak Hotel', and Hoyt himself enjoyed his greatest success through other artist's covers of his songs – 'Greenback Dollar' (Kingston Trio), 'Joy To The World' (Three Dog Night) and 'The Pusher' (Steppenwolf). Popular in the UK through his 1979 singles 'Della And The Dealer' and 'A Rusty Old Halo', and in the movie *Gremlins* (one of several acting roles), Axton hardly gained the chart success he deserved. His 1974 Top 10 hits, 'When The Morning Comes' and 'Boney Fingers', were typical of this deep-voiced act.

Glen Campbell
(Vocals, guitar, b. 1936)

Glen Campbell's route to fame took him first to America's West Coast, where he grew to be much in demand as a session musician, earning $50,000 to $70,000 a year. Signing to Capitol in 1962, he became a temporary member of The Beach Boys three years later, and 'By The Time I Get To Phoenix' (1967) started his solo career in earnest. Between 1969 and 1977, he enjoyed five country chart-toppers, and both 'Rhinestone Cowboy' (1975) and 'Southern Nights' (1977) became million-selling US pop No. 1s. He also had major crossover success duetting with Bobbie Gentry and Anne Murray. The 1968 CMA Entertainer of The Year also starred in the films *True Grit* and *Norwood* and hosted his own television show, *The Glen Campbell Goodtime Hour* (1968–72). A hugely talented guitar player, Campbell was elected into the Country Music Hall Of Fame in 2005.

Mary Chapin Carpenter
(Vocals, songwriter, b. 1958)

As a teenager, New Jersey-born Carpenter moved to Washington, D.C., where music became an integral part of her life. Establishing herself on the local folk circuit, she signed with Columbia, resulting in her 1986 debut album, *Hometown Girl*. Produced by guitarist John Jennings, it marked the beginning of a successful and productive relationship. Albums *Shooting Straight In The Dark* (1990), *Come On, Come On* (1992), which sold two million copies, and *Stones In The Road* (1994) saw her gain pop status. 'He Thinks He'll Keep Her' (1993) was peppered with typical Carpenter humour, and 'Shut Up And Kiss Me' (1994) gave this astute songwriter her first No. 1 country hit. Her folk-rock songs and styles broadened country music, and she took the CMA's Female Vocalist Award in 1992 and 1993.

Roy Clark
(Entertainer, b. 1933)

Voted CMA Entertainer Of The Year in 1973, Clark – apart from being a champion banjo player and electric guitarist – appeared regularly in the 1960s television series, *The Beverly Hillbillies*, and was the host of *Hee Haw* from its 1960 beginning. His sparkling show was greatly sought after in the 1970s and he was reportedly the highest-paid act in country music. His biggest songs include 'Yesterday When I Was Young' (1969), 'Thank God And Greyhound' (1971) and 'Come Live With Me' (1973, his only No. 1). In the mid-1980s, he moved to Branson, Missouri, where he headlined at his own theatre.

John Conlee
(Vocalist, b. 1946)

Apparently the only licensed mortician to top the US country charts, the first of Conlee's seven No. 1s was 1979's 'Lady Lay Down', his second hit after his signature song 'Rose Colored Glasses'. His booming voice and blue-collar presentation helped compensate for country music's urban cowboy phase, and chart-topping singles 'Backside Of Thirty' (1979) and 'Common Man' (1983) continued the trend for this Grand Ole Opry member since 1981.

Lacy J. Dalton
(Vocalist, b. 1948)

Pennsylvania-born Dalton (real name Jill Byrem) worked as a folk singer, recorded under the name of Jill Corston, and was part of the rock group Office before emerging in 1979 after producer Billy Sherrill heard a demo tape. Recording gritty, real-life songs, she won respect and a string of Top 20 country hits following her debut release,

'Crazy Blue Eyes' (1979), 'Hard Times' (1980) and Tom Schuyler's songwriter's anthem '16th Avenue' (1982) typified her unshakeable good ol' girl image. She continues to perform and record despite having left Nashville during the 1990s. Song Dog Records released her *The Last Wild Place* album in 2004.

Below
Lacy J. Dalton's vocal style has been compared to that of Bonnie Raitt. Strong and gritty in tone, Dalton has been a country staple since the 1970s.

John Denver had a run of success in the early 1970s and was voted CMA Entertainer Of The Year in 1975. He died piloting a plane that crashed off the California coast.

Mac Davis
(Vocals, songwriter, actor, b. 1942)

Also a television host, composer and one-time representative for Vee-Jay records, Texas-born Davis is responsible for several bestselling songs, including 'In The Ghetto' and 'Don't Cry Daddy', both 1969 US Top 10 hits for Elvis Presley. Davis himself topped the US pop chart in 1972 with the million-selling 'Baby Don't Get Hooked On Me' and made the US pop Top 10 two years later with 'Stop And Smell The Roses'. Fifteen of his 30 US country hits between 1970 and 1986 crossed over to pop, including 1980's humorously egotistical 'It's Hard To Be Humble', and the same year's 'Texas In The Rear View Mirror'. His biggest country hits came in 1981, with 'My Bestest Friend' and 'Hooked On Music'.

John Denver
(Vocals, songwriter, 1943–97)

Born John Henry Deutschendorf in Roswell, New Mexico, Denver worked with folk act The Chad Mitchell Trio between 1965 and 68. He turned from folk to country and pop in 1969 when he wrote 'Leaving On A Jet Plane' (1969) – Peter, Paul And Mary's only No. 1. Signed to RCA, he enjoyed crossover success with his pop/folk material during the 1970s. The million-selling 'Take Me Home Country Roads' was his first US country hit in 1971, also making the US Pop Top 3, while Olivia Newton-John's 1973 cover version was a UK Top 20 hit. 'Back Home Again' was Denver's first country No. 1 in 1974, a year when both 'Sunshine On My Shoulder' and 'Annie's Song', penned for his then wife, were million selling US pop No. 1s; other million selling country/pop No. 1s include 'Thank God I'm A Country Boy' and 'I'm Sorry' (both 1975).

Donna Fargo
(Vocals, songwriter, b. 1949)

Born Yvonne Vaughan in North Carolina, Fargo was a schoolteacher and weekend vocalist. When she and her producer husband, Stan Silver, visited Nashville around 1970, she signed with Dot Records, making a dream start when two of her own songs, 'The Happiest Girl In The Whole U.S.A.' and 'Funny Face', became million-selling US country chart-toppers. Both crossed into the US pop Top 20 in 1972. After three further country No. 1s during 1973–74, she signed for a reportedly substantial advance with Warner Bros. in 1977, when she released her last No. 1 to date, 'That Was Yesterday' – a recitation.

Janie Frickie
(Vocals, b. 1947)

Indiana-born Janie Fricke (as her surname was spelt until the mid-1980s) moved to Nashville after spending time in Dallas, Memphis and Los Angeles. In country's capital, however, she quickly became a much sought-after session and jingle singer, providing backup vocals on hits by Conway Twitty, Elvis Presley, Moe Bandy, Mel Tillis, Vern Gosdin and many others. However, it was her impressive duets with Johnny Duncan on 'Jo And The Cowboy' (1975) and 'Thinking Of A Rendezvous' (a 1976 No. 1) that alerted Duncan's label, Columbia, to her talent. She again sang with Duncan on 'Come A Little Bit Closer' (1977),

partnered with Charlie Rich on the 1978 country chart-topper 'On My Knees' and duetted with Merle Haggard on 'A Place To Fall Apart' (1984).

Crystal Gayle
(Vocals, b. 1951)

Loretta Lynn's younger sister was born Brenda Gail Webb, and her professional career began as part of her older sister's show. After minor success on Decca, she signed with United Artists in 1974, which resulted in an almost-immediate change of fortunes. The lilting Top 10 hit,

'Wrong Road Again' (1975), opened the floodgates, and big, soulful ballads brought her 18 country No. 1s throughout the 1970s and 1980s. 'Don't It Make My Brown Eyes Blue' (1977) ensured her international stardom when it reached the Top 3 on *Billboard*'s pop chart and became a major success story for record producer Allen Reynolds. CMA Female Vocalist Of The Year in 1977 and 1978, Gayle sang on the soundtrack of the 1986 Francis Ford Coppola movie *One From The Heart*, and her 1982 duet with Eddie Rabbitt, 'You And I', was also a country chart-topper. At times, Gayle's hair reaches five feet in length!

Above
Janie Frickie had an extremely successful run of hits with partners such as Johnny Duncan and Merle Haggard, She was voted CMA Female Vocalist Of The Year in 1982 and 1983.

Tom T. Hall is affectionately known as 'The Storyteller' – he has written a novel and children's books, as well as many hit songs. Today, Hall and his English wife, Dixie, lend support to budding bluegrass acts.

Tom T. Hall
(Vocals, songwriter, guitar, b. 1936)

Hall had his own band, The Kentucky Travelers, by the time he was 16. He worked as a commercial DJ and for armed-forces radio in Germany between 1957 and 1961, moving to Nashville in 1964. Hall's career changed overnight in 1968 when Jeannie C. Riley took his song, 'Harper Valley P.T.A.', to the top of both *Billboard*'s country and pop charts. His melodic songs about ordinary people triggered a succession of hits: 'A Week In A Country Jail' (1970, his first US country No. 1), 'The Year That Clayton Delaney Died' (1971) and '(Old Dogs, Children And) Watermelon Wine' (1973) were among his biggest hits recorded for Mercury. His songs 'Ballad Of Forty Dollars' (1968), 'Homecoming' (1969) and 'Salute To A Switchblade Knife' (1970) underlined why Bobby Bare, Dave Dudley and Jimmy C. Newman gravitated to his work.

Barbara Mandrell
(Vocals, bass, steel guitar, banjo, saxophone, b. 1948)

Born in Texas and raised in California, Mandrell is an all-round instrumentalist. Starting in The Mandrell Family Band, she was playing steel guitar in Las Vegas nightspots by the time she was 16 – by which time she had also appeared regularly on the Johnny Cash and Red Foley television shows. Moving to Nashville in 1971, she signed to ABC/Dot, making the US country Top 5 with 1975's 'Standing Room Only', and No. 1 with 'Sleeping Single In A Double Bed' (1978). She spoke for many country fans with 'I Was Country When Country Wasn't Cool' (1981), featuring guest vocalist George Jones, and hosted her own network television series (1980–82), which also featured her sisters Louise and Irlene. She was voted CMA Entertainer Of The Year in 1980 and 1981, after which she moved on to an acting career.

Brian Golbey
(Vocals, fiddle, b. 1939)

During the 1960s' folk movement in the UK, Brian Golbey and banjo player Pete Stanley became leading international exponents of traditional music. Visiting the USA in 1970, Golbey was invited to appear on Nashville's *Midnight Jamboree* by host Ernest Tubb (who strongly encouraged young, aspiring talents) as well as on WWVA's famed *Wheeling Jamboree* in West Virginia. Back in England, he toured with Americans Patsy Montana and Mac Wiseman, before putting together *Cajun Moon* (1976) with folk singer Allan Taylor.

Ronnie Milsap
(Vocals, piano, b. 1946)

Blind since birth, Ronnie Milsap was a multi-instrumentalist by the age of 12. Working with Elvis Presley's producer Chips Moman, he played piano and sang backing vocals on a Presley recording session, and in 1965 scored a Top 20 US R&B hit with 'Never Had It So Good'. Milsap also worked in J. J. Cale's backing band and played piano at Roger Miller's King Of The Road Motel in Nashville. In 1970 he released the first of his 14 US pop

crossed over to the pop chart. Ten country No. 1s in that period curiously did not include her two million-selling pop chart-toppers – 'Snowbird' (1970) and 'You Needed Me' (1978). Apart from these, Murray delivered 1980's 'Could I Have This Dance' (from the film *Urban Cowboy*) and covers of hits associated with The Everly Brothers, The Beatles and Bruce Channel. Duets with Glen Campbell, Kenny Rogers and others also charted. During her career, her voice has gained greater stylistic qualities, reflected in her 1983 CMA Single Of The Year and country No. 1, 'A Little Good News' – an emotive show of social conscience.

hits, the biggest of which was 1981's '(There's) No Gettin' Over Me' (Top 5). This was also one of 35 country No. 1s he achieved between 1974 and 1989 on RCA Records.

Melba Montgomery

(Vocals, songwriter, fiddle, b. 1938)

Born in Tennessee and raised in Alabama, Melba Montgomery toured with Roy Acuff's band between 1958 and 1962 before going solo. Fourteen of her 30 country hits were duets, initially with George Jones. Her greatest success with Jones – 'We Must Have Been Out Of Our Minds' (1963) – was followed by 'Baby Ain't That Fine' (1966) with Gene Pitney and several with Charlie Louvin. The deep-voiced vocalist's 1974 narration, 'No Charge', her only No. 1, was covered in Britain by J. J. Barrie, but her songwriting is currently gaining many covers, especially with acoustic acts.

Anne Murray

(Vocals, b. 1945)

Arguably one of Canada's finest vocal exports, over 25 of Murray's 50-plus country hits between 1970 and 1991

The Oak Ridge Boys
(Gospel vocal quartet, 1964–present)

With roots stretching back to the Second World War as the gospel Oak Ridge Quartet, The Oak Ridge Boys made the shift to country music in 1973, when the line-up was Duane Allen (lead vocals, b. 1943), Joe Bonsall (tenor, b. 1948), Richard Sterban (b. 1943, bass) and Bill Golden (baritone, b. 1935) – replaced by Steve Sanders between 1987 and 1996. Their first hit was 'Praise The Lord And Pass The Soup' (1973), sharing credit with Johnny Cash and The Carter Family. The quartet impressed hugely during the 1970s and 1980s as one of the most entertaining acts of their era, topping the chart on 17 occasions, with 'Leaving Louisiana In The Broad Daylight' (1979), 'Elvira' (1981) and 'Bobbie Sue (1982) among their most memorable hits. They continue to present a fast-paced stage act accompanied by their own backing group.

Jeanne Pruett
(Vocals, songwriter, b. 1937)

Alabama-born Norma Jean Bowman moved to Nashville with her husband, Jack Pruett (guitarist with Marty Robbins for 14 years), in 1956. In 1963, she became a songwriter for Robbins, gaining her own record deal with Decca in 1971. 'Satin Sheets' (1973) was her biggest hit, a three-week No. 1 that also made the pop Top 30. A 1979 sequel, 'Please Play Satin Sheets For Me', was a minor hit on her short-lived comeback.

Charlie Rich
(Vocals, piano, 1932–95)

Arkansas-born Rich won his greatest success as a country crossover act in the first half of the 1970s, topping both US country and pop charts with 1973's million-selling 'The Most Beautiful Girl'. This was actually his second million-seller that year – 'Behind Closed Doors' had reached the US pop Top 20, and was CMA Single Of The Year. Both singles were also UK Top 20 hits. Rich, who recorded for Sun in the mid-1950s, was well-versed in blues, jazz and rockabilly.

Johnny Rodriguez
(Vocals, songwriter, b. 1951)

Born in Texas, Rodriguez played guitar from the age of seven, starting his career during a jail sentence for stealing a goat. There he wrote songs, occasionally utilizing Spanish lyrics. A prison guard alerted Tom T. Hall to his talent, and Rodriguez moved to Nashville, working as a

Above

Olivia Newton-John has always been on the fringes of acceptance in the country-music world, and many of her hits have been undeniably pop in flavour. However, this did not stop her claiming a CMA Female Vocalist award in 1974.

Olivia Newton-John
(Vocals, b. 1948)

English by birth, but raised in Australia, Olivia Newton-John enjoyed a brief career in country music. Much to the dismay of traditionalist Jean Shepard and her contemporaries among the country music fraternity, Newton-John was voted CMA Female Vocalist Of The Year in 1974, although only a handful of her singles made the US country Top 10 between 1973 and 1976. Her 1973 UK Top 20 hit, 'Take Me Home Country Roads', is arguably her most country release.

guitarist with Hall in 1971–72 and releasing his single debut, 'Pass Me By' (1972). Going solo, he topped the US country chart six times before 1976, once with a cover of 'That's The Way Love Goes' (1973), the final Lefty Frizzell-penned hit song. With 45 country hits by 1989, Rodriguez fell into drug addiction, effectively ending his chart career.

Kenny Rogers

(Vocals, b. 1938)

In the early 1960s Rogers joined The New Christy Minstrels, and formed The First Edition in 1968. The following year, the group became Kenny Rogers And The First Edition. Their worldwide hit, 'Ruby Don't

Take Your Love To Town', was written by Mel Tillis. In 1973, Rogers went solo, and 1977 brought the million-selling 'Lucille', which topped the UK pop chart and was the first of his 20 country chart-toppers. These included seven duets, the first three with Dottie West (the pair were CMA Duo Of The Year in 1978 and 1979). His 1983 duet with Dolly Parton, 'Islands In The Stream' topped the US pop chart, and made Rogers a superstar.

Pete Sayers

(Vocals, banjo, guitar, 1942–2005)

Englishman Pete Sayers visited Nashville in the mid-1960s, and remained there for five years. During this time he hosted his own daily television series. This gave him the confidence to set up his monthly version of the Grand Ole Opry back in Newmarket, where he hosted several television series, featuring guests like George Hamilton IV, John D. Loudermilk and other notable contemporary US acts. An active recording artist over the years, Sayers' last album was titled *Old Mr. Crow* (2002), co-produced by Sayers and BBC radio presenter Nick Barraclough – one-time member of Sayers' Radio Cowboys band.

Above

Multi-instrumentalist Pete Sayers cut his country teeth in Nashville, but later returned to his native England, where he hosted television series that helped bring American country's best-loved artists to the wider world.

Left

A keen photographer, Kenny Rogers published a book of his celebrity pictures in 1987. He has also starred in several movies, including The Gambler *(1980) and* Coward Of The County *(1981) – named after two of his biggest hits.*

Sammi Smith
(Vocals, 1943–2005)

Below
Tanya Tucker started in the music business when she was 13 years old. Her later years have seen equal success, though, and she has released hit duets with Glen Campbell and Delbert McClinton, among others.

Sammi Smith will forever be remembered for her 1971 chart-topping version of Kris Kristofferson's 'Help Me Make It Through The Night', which also made the US pop Top 10. Her one and only No. 1 highlighted her worth as a song interpreter, and choice covers of Steve Goodman's 'City Of New Orleans' (1973) 'Today I Started Loving You Again' (1975) and 'I Can't Stop Loving You' (1977) were among her finest work.

Red Steagall
(Vocals, songwriter, guitar, b. 1937)

Texas-born Steagall learned to play mandolin and guitar as therapy for his left hand and arm during recovery from polio. Moving to California in 1965, he started songwriting, and Ray Charles recorded his 'Here We Go Again', a 1967 US Top 20 hit. Steagall, a rodeo rider and quarter horse breeder as well as playing Texas swing and western music, accumulated 23 country hits between 1972 and 1980 – the biggest was 'Lone Star Beer And Bob Wills Music' (1976). He remains a favourite at rodeo fairs and appears regularly at the annual Cowboy Poetry Gathering in Nevada. His 1990s albums on the Warner Western label are helping to keep the old tradition alive.

Gary Stewart
(Vocals, piano, guitar, 1945–2003)

Kentucky-born Stewart first recorded in 1964, and was a member of rock band The Amps. He co-wrote Stonewall Jackson's 1965 country hit, 'Poor Red Georgia Dirt', and several for Billy Walker and others before signing to RCA in 1973. His first country hit was a cover of The Allman Brothers' 'Ramblin' Man' (1973), and he enjoyed chart success until 1989. His rough-edged vocals perfectly fit his songs of hard drinking and bar-rooms, and can be heard at his best in his 1974 country Top 10 hits, 'Drinkin' Thing' and 'Out Of Hand', and his lone chart topper, 1975's 'She's Actin' Single (I'm Drinkin' Doubles)'. Apart from two duet albums in the early 1980s with Dean Dillon, Stewart recorded briefly for Hightone, and his death is believed to have been drug-related.

Mel Tillis
(Vocals, guitar, songwriter, b. 1932)

CMA's 1976 Entertainer Of The Year caught malaria as an infant, which left him with a speech defect (reflected in the title of his autobiography – *Stutterin' Boy*). Nevertheless, the father of Pam Tillis accumulated 77 country hits between 1958 and 1989, including three duets with Nancy Sinatra.

Equally famous as a songwriter, he wrote
'Detroit City', a hit for both Bobby Bare and Tom
Jones, Kenny Rogers and The First Edition's
'Ruby, Don't Take Your Love To Town' and
'Honey (Open That Door)', a 1984 chart topper
for Ricky Skaggs. 'I Ain't Never' (1972), co-
written with Webb Pierce, was the biggest of his
six No. 1s. 'Coca Cola Cowboy' and 'Send Me
Down To Tucson', were hits from the 1979 Clint
Eastwood film *Every Which Way But Loose*.

Tanya Tucker

(Vocals, b. 1958)

Teenage prodigy Tanya Tucker amazed
everyone when, at the age of only 13, she
charted with 'Delta Dawn', and she reached
No. 1 three times in less than a year throughout
1973–74. The last of these chart-toppers was
David Allan Coe's adult song, 'Would You Lay
With Me (In A Field Of Stone)'. Voted CMA
Female Vocalist Of The Year in 1991, she
attempted a pure pop career in the late 1970s,
but returned to producer Jerry Crutchfield to
score her tenth country chart-topper, 'Strong
Enough To Bend' in 1988.

Conway Twitty

(Vocals, 1933–93)

Born Harold Lloyd Jenkins, Twitty took his stage
name from Conway, Arkansas and Twitty, Texas.
His first success was as a rock'n'roller, topping
the pop chart in 1958 with 'It's Only Make
Believe', and scoring a second gold single with
'Lonely Blue Boy' in 1960. His powerful vocals
and sometimes risqué songs made him one of
country music's greatest hitmakers – with 40
chart-toppers, including five 1970s duets with
Loretta Lynn. 'Hello Darlin'' (1970), his biggest
country single, was his theme song.

Don Williams

(Vocals, guitar, b. 1939)

Texas-born Williams worked in 1964 with folk trio The
Pozo-Seco Singers. Encouraged by producer Cowboy Jack
Clement, his solo career began in 1971, and resulted in
gentle hits like 'Amanda' (1973), 'You're My Best Friend'

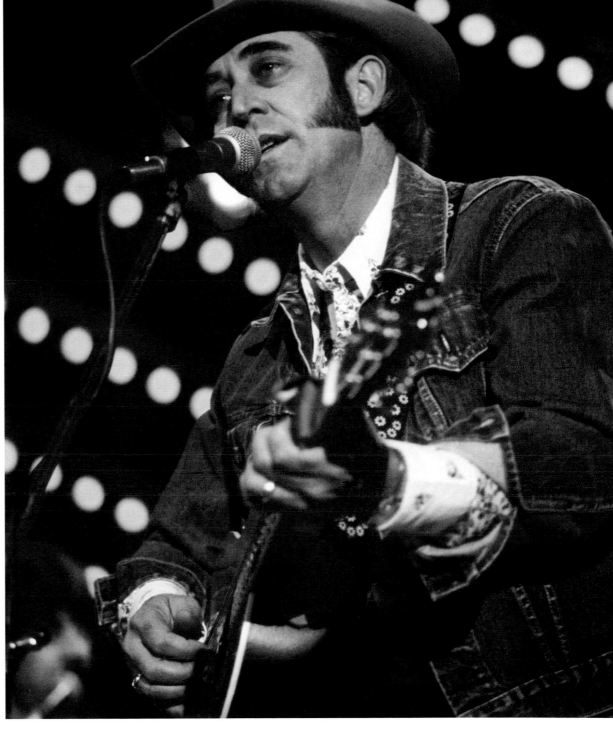

(1976) and 'Tulsa Time' (1978). He enjoyed immense
popularity in the UK, where he had success with 'I Recall
A Gypsy Woman' (1976) and a number of gold albums. In
1983, he topped the charts with Gallagher And Lyle's 'Stay
Young', which emphasized his willingness to find material
outside normal country-music sources.

Above
*The gentle giant of
country music, Don
Williams is greatly loved
for his simple vocal style
and his willingness to
embrace music from
different sources.*

Roses In The Snow:
New Country &
The Neo-Traditionalists

after the 1960s heyday of the cultured Nashville Sound, country music was all but swept aside. It had survived the lasting effect of 1950s rock – rock'n'roll and traditional old-timey music and bluegrass, especially – but it was now the turn of a musical hybrid, country rock, to lead the way for almost a decade.

Country rock was originally played by bands boasting the look of rock acts and determined to make a change. It was like two flints being rubbed together – no one could tell when the spark would become a flame, nor, as was the case with many country-rock bands, when the flame would be extinguished, such was the climate and temperament of the musicians involved. One thing a lot of these young musicians and bands had in common, though, was their appreciation of the history of country music. One such was Ingram 'Gram' Parsons, who introduced Emmylou Harris, and who worked tirelessly to keep the country candle burning. The 1970s also saw the establishment of a new type of musician – the singer-songwriter, and Harris – the queen of country rock – helped bring members of her Hot Band – Rodney Crowell and Ricky Skaggs – to the attention of both country and rock audiences.

West Coast-based Dwight Yoakam and Randy Travis emerged in the mid-1980s, as the neo-traditionalist movement gathered pace. Like Harris and Skaggs, Garth Brooks and Texan George Strait – through his working of bar-room country and western swing – spawned a style of country music that attracted a younger and more mainstream audience, and did much to keep the music on an even keel.

Key Artists

Garth Brooks

Emmylou Harris

Ricky Skaggs

George Strait

Randy Travis

Dwight Yoakam

Influences & Development

New country took many years and miles of travel before its current evolution – not least the new traditionalist movement of the 1980s, which returned country music to its roots. Garth Brooks (b. 1962) did it far more quickly, but that's a different story. Sometimes it seemed like these artists were chipping away at a mountain with nothing more than an ice pick – change and the loosening of old restrictions came painfully slowly. The music is at its best when two idioms collide and the listener doesn't immediately realize it – as in the work of Dwight Yoakam (b. 1956), Ricky Skaggs (b. 1954), Suzy Bogguss (b. 1956), Rodney Crowell (b. 1950), Emmylou Harris (b. 1947) and even Patty Loveless (b. 1957), who, after an exciting run as a top Nashville mainstream act, moved towards the revival, where she took her distinctive sound right back to the bluegrass roots of her rural background.

'I really think that we can make a difference and just let people know that, hey, bluegrass is cool, it's hip and it's awesome, and if it's done in a great way and a great presentation, I don't know who wouldn't like it.' **Ricky Skaggs**

Unbroken Circle

During the 1970s, Waylon Jennings (1937–2002), Hank Williams Jr. (b. 1949) and Willie Nelson (b. 1933), among others, had threatened that it was time for a change.

Waylon's 'Are You Sure Hank Done It This Way?' was virtually a mission statement, and things duly changed – not least when Tompall Glaser's (b. 1933) Nashville headquarters, familiarly known as 'Hillbilly Central', became a focal point for artists and songwriters wanting to do things their way. It was during this period that young acts emerged from bands that had experimented with country rock.

When Vince Gill (b. 1957) appeared, bringing genuine craft to singing, his talents as a song stylist were recognized by the Nashville establishment, which hired him for many years as host of the annual CMA Awards show. Gill has played a vital role in encouraging new talent, as have many others. One of the most influential has been singer-songwriter Guy Clark (b. 1941), who like Gill (but nearly a decade earlier) had been signed to RCA. Gill was signed by Tony Brown, whom he first knew as a fellow member of Rodney Crowell's Cherry Bombs. Others who have made their mark include Texan Lyle Lovett (b. 1957) who, like Clark, has never bowed to commercial demands, and was chosen to accompany Dire Straits on their world tour. Working at their own pace, Lovett and Clark view songwriting as a craft; both of them demonstrate a minimalist, Hank Williams-like approach. The multi-talented Terry Allen (b. 1943) arrived in the mid-1970s with his uninhibited mini road-movie-like songs. The Nitty Gritty Dirt Band's imposing 1971 triple LP, *Will The Circle Be Unbroken*, saw the removal of barriers and was to country music what Woodstock was to rock.

The Roots Of The New Traditionalist Style

Much of the new traditionalist music came – and still comes – through acts who learned their craft playing acoustic music, often bluegrass, as children at festivals, school and church gatherings. Pickers like Skaggs, Keith Whitley (1955–89) and Marty Stuart (b. 1958) all gained experience as teenagers playing with bluegrass greats – Skaggs and Whitley with Ralph Stanley (b. 1927) and Stuart with Lester Flatt (1914–79). And they were not alone. Back in the early 1960s, Peter Rowan (b. 1942), Del McCoury (b. 1939) and others cut their teeth in Bill Monroe's Blue Grass Boys.

In all cases, the greatest forward movements of the new traditionalists have been when musicians have gone backwards to progress – developing, embellishing and placing a definitive spin on the music they inherited, giving old ideas and style an injection of modern spirit. But there's nothing unusual there – after all, bluegrass founder Bill Monroe (1911–96) was doing it himself when he started combining musical styles to create a new genre.

New traditionalists are always going to be emerging – never more so than when country music becomes entangled in repetitive commercialism, as it did with string-laden productions and the watered-down pop/soft-rock efforts of the 1970s. Those of a creative bent are always stripping back the old paint and rebuilding the walls, sometimes stone by stone. At other times – such as the late-1980s, with the so called UK 'new country' marketing campaigns that saw Dwight Yoakam, Randy Travis (b. 1959) and others bringing a breath of fresh air to country music – the combination of an old style with a new approach can make all the difference. Steve Earle (b. 1955), who needed a second chance before he made it, was another pioneer, while The Desert Rose Band, led by ex-Byrd Chris Hillman, combined West Coast country rock with bluegrass and also played their part in the revolution.

Left

Vince Gill was embraced by the traditional Nashville establishment, and became the face of the CMA Awards.

Far Left

Waylon Jennings was one of the artists to sow the seeds of the new country revival that took place in the following decades. His song 'Are You Sure Hank Done It This Way?' was a battle cry for new young bands.

Left

Marty Stuart cut his country teeth with bluegrass great Lester Flatt. The bluegrass influence is still evident in his music.

The Queens Of Country Rock

During the mid-1970s, Emmylou Harris and her friend Linda Ronstadt (b. 1946) brought something to the table of a regenerative leaning, besides their obvious glamour. Both were attractive, stylish women, and Ronstadt, whose career began in a folk trio, at one time used the musicians who later became The Eagles as her studio band. Covering familiar classic songs and supplementing them with material by new writers like Kate and Anna McGarrigle, Neil Young and Andrew Gold, Ronstadt could well have become a greater act than she did. In fact she chose not to, and this has been the case with countless others who did not stay the course, but were more than also-rans.

Breaking away from the restrictions imposed by Nashville's chart-conscious thinking were a bunch of songwriters with their roots in Texas music, who did not always gain recognition earlier in their careers. These include Billy Joe Shaver (b. 1949), the artful and sometimes mystical Mickey Newbury (1940–2002), and Townes Van Zandt (1944–97), who would sometimes stay locked away for 24 hours at a time writing songs when he was a young man.

Right
Emmylou Harris, whose 1980 album Roses In The Snow *set the benchmark for the new traditionalist style for the rest of the decade.*

Below
Along with such key figures as Emmylou Harris and Linda Ronstadt, Gail Davies was one of the most influential female voices in country music in the 1970s and 1980s, and the first to produce her own LP.

Chaos In Country

By the mid-1980s, falling sales were the cause of growing concern for country music's hierarchy, which had been left in tatters by the urban cowboy era. Dolly Parton (b. 1946) had absconded – crossing over to pop, making films and playing Las Vegas – and Columbia Records was clearly at a loss as to what to do. The release of Johnny Cash (1932–2003), who at the time had done more for the label than any other artist, was not particularly well received by his fellow acts. It took Oklahoma's Gail Davies (b. 1948), a singer-songwriter, with her RCA debut album, *Where Is A Woman*, to achieve something that no other female country act had been allowed – producing her own album.

Few acts seemed aware that changes were afoot, and the music needed an injection of artists offering greater depth and less emphasis on the formulaic. John Anderson (b. 1954) and Vern Gosdin (b. 1934) were more discerning in their choice of material than most others, and hung tough as they helped to not only steady, but also propel country during the 1980s. Though their vocal styles differ greatly, Gosdin, like Vince Gill, had risen through the ranks playing bluegrass music, a style noted for producing both fine lead and great harmony vocalists. Pushing back the tide and steadying the waves of discontent as labels shuffled artists around like playing cards may not have stopped altogether, but increasing awareness among the acts was certainly apparent as they gradually began to take control of material and insist on a say in how their music was recorded.

The Rise Of The Neo-Traditionalists

Just prior to the sweeping influx of neo-traditionalism
in 1985–86, came the emergence of new, young session
musicians in Nashville. These included Jerry Douglas,
who worked on Emmylou Harris's 1980 album *Roses In The
Snow*, a project in which his erstwhile partner in Boone
Creek, Ricky Skaggs, was also heavily involved. Douglas
has since become one of the most sought-after players and
is now a pivotal member of top bluegrass act, Alison
Krauss And Union Station.

In the 1980s, Rosanne Cash (b. 1955), produced by her
then-husband Rodney Crowell (b. 1950), blended rock and
country with a little attitude and accumulated 11 US
country No. 1 hits – only slightly less impressive than that
achieved by her late father, Johnny Cash. However,
Rosanne has never made country music the centre of her

universe, unlike the prolific Crowell, whose songs have
been recorded by everyone from Johnny Cash to
Emmylou by way of Guy Clark and The Oak Ridge Boys.
First coming to prominence as duet partner for Emmylou
Harris (replacing Gram Parsons), he has subsequently
become a leading neo-traditionalist and a brilliant
songwriter, capable of either embracing the present or
transporting the listener back in time.

The same is true of Nanci Griffith (b. 1953), a singer-
songwriter who is set to be revered for many years, and
whose early albums were produced by Jim Rooney.
Griffith uses a musical style that she fondly refers to as
'folkabilly'. Rooney also helped revive the career of John
Prine, brought Hal Ketchum to the fore, gave life to the
homespun songs of Iris DeMent, and co-produced Townes
Van Zandt's finest album since the 1970s, *At My Window*.

Above
*Texas-born Guy Clark
has not enjoyed much
commercial success, but
although his output has
not been prolific he
remains one of the most
influential country artists
of the 1970s and 1980s.*

Will The Circle Be Unbroken

The Nitty Gritty Dirt Band started out in 1966 as a student jug band in Los Angeles, and in an early incarnation it included a teenage Jackson Browne. Among the group's founder members was singer and guitarist Jeff Hanna. Both Hanna and multi-instrumentalist Jimmie Fadden are still Dirt Band members 40 years on. The extremely ambitious *Will The Circle Be Unbroken* project was conceived by NGDB manager, William E. 'Bill' McEuen, who was the brother of another band member – banjo man and iconoclast John McEuen. It resulted in the original 38-track, three-LP set in 1972.

An All-Star Album

The band at the time of *Will The Circle Be Unbroken* (also the title of a classic neo-religious country song) was completed by another multi-instrumentalist founder member, Les Thompson, and by Jimmy Ibbotson, who played guitar, keyboards, drums and accordion as well as

contributed vocals. Before Bill McEuen's brainwave, the band was at a crossroads in commercial terms. Their 1970 LP, *Uncle Charlie And His Dog Teddy*, had restored them to the US chart, from which they had been absent for three years. *Uncle Charlie* had contained three US hit singles, including 'Mr. Bojangles', their first Top 10 hit, but the band's next LP, *All The Good Times*, performed far less well commercially, and only included one minor hit single.

Bill McEuen, who was finding that the big wheels at United Artists were taking little notice of his future plans for the band, got the idea for an all-star album after the great Earl Scruggs had complimented John McEuen on his performance of an *Uncle Charlie* song, 'Randy Lynn Rag', which was written by Scruggs. McEuen asked him if he would record with the band. Scruggs agreed. Bolstered by the positive response, the band asked Doc Watson if he would consider playing with them. Watson also agreed, and from there the list of luminary figures grew – Roy Acuff, Mother Maybelle Carter and Merle Travis. They recorded for six days, and the best 38 tracks were released as a magnificently packaged triple LP. It was a huge success, surpassing the heights achieved by *Uncle Charlie*, and becoming the band's first gold album. Gold status depends on the retail value of an album's sales, and since this was a triple LP, its price was at least double that of a single LP.

Volumes Two And Three

In 1989, the Dirt Band – now comprising Hanna, Fadden, Ibbotson and keyboard man Bob Carpenter – decided to repeat the process – with Volume Two not only using Acuff and Earl Scruggs, but also Johnny Cash, The Byrds' Roger McGuinn and Chris Hillman, original Eagle Bernie Leadon, Chet Atkins, Emmylou Harris, Johns Denver, Hiatt and Prine, Ricky Skaggs and several others. This gave the band their first US Top 100 album in nearly a decade.

In 2002 – by which time John McEuen had rejoined – the band decided to attempt the magic one more time. Volume Three featured Cash, Scruggs, McGuinn and Harris as well as Willie Nelson, Alison Krauss, Tom Petty, Dwight

Yoakam and others. Once again, this returned the Dirt Band to the Top 150 of the US album chart, proving that the concept remained a winner. The same year brought a 30th Anniversary reissue of the original *Circle* as a double CD with four bonus tracks. While The Dirt Band (as they called themselves for a few years in the 1980s, before reverting to their full title) were never as influential as The Byrds or The Flying Burrito Brothers, nor as successful as The Eagles, the *Circle* albums were visionary in providing a link between the originators of country music and younger disciples, and for that alone, The Nitty Gritty Dirt Band can be credited with bridging a musical generation gap.

Above
The Will The Circle Be Unbroken *albums have ensured that The Nitty Gritty Dirt Band will have a place in country-music history, bringing original country music to a new, young audience.*

Garth Brooks

Key Artist

'True country music is honesty, sincerity, and real life to the hilt.' **Garth Brooks**

Below

When his debut album, Garth Brooks, received a lukewarm reception in 1989, no one could have predicted the sudden and meteoric rise the artist's career would take in just a few short months.

Country music gained a new face when the Garth Brooks phenomenon swept the stage in the 1990s. Such a huge marketing venture took place that his name virtually became synonymous with country music and the pop crossover style. Yet Brooks' career had started in unspectacular style in 1989, when his *Garth Brooks* album shipped only 20,000 copies. Such was the momentum gathered in the following years that the album went on to sell over nine million copies.

Brooks Fever

The wheels were only being greased in 1989, and Brooks' career was about to blossom in a way that was previously unknown in any musical field. Produced by country veteran Allen Reynolds (whose clients have included Don Williams and Crystal Gayle), his debut album delivered the No. 1 hit single 'If Tomorrow Never Comes'. But a huge transformation was about to take place, through the 16-million selling *No Fences* (1990), *Ropin' The Wind* (1991, 14 million), *The Chase* (1992, eight million) and *In Pieces* (1993, eight million), for the business graduate born on 7 February 1962, in Tulsa, Oklahoma. His mother, Colleen Carroll, had recorded for Capitol Records during the 1950s, but Brooks' albums would debut at No. 1 on both the pop and country charts. Brooks fever swept the USA.

His 2001 album, *Scarecrow*, was his seventh to top the US pop chart, and his ninth to top the country charts. The record books have been rewritten time and again by Brooks, who, through his high-energy shows matched his 113 million album sales in the USA, with record-breaking live shows not only across America, but also in Europe. This massive success contrasts greatly with his first taste of Nashville in 1985 – he had left town after 24 hours. No one would have believed he would soon be selling out venues like the Hollywood Bowl on 22 July 1994, in just over 20 minutes, or selling 896,932 copies of *Sevens* during its first week on release in November 1997. Effortlessly outselling top pop acts – both new and old – this saw Brooks equal Elton John's feat of having three albums simultaneously appear on the *Billboard* Top 200 chart in 1998 – *Sevens*, *The Limited Series* (a six-CD album set) and *Double Live*.

A Record-Breaking Act

On 7 August 1997, Brooks drew the largest-ever crowd for his concert in New York's Central Park, alongside an equally massive television audience, and his star remained in the ascendant throughout the decade. Huge crowds

flocked wherever he went; his eight sell-out dates in Dublin, Ireland, were the subject of a two-hour television special, *Garth Brooks: Ireland And Back* (along with footage shot in Los Angeles featuring songs from *Sevens*). This attracted 15.7 million viewers, topping that night's ratings Stateside.

Brooks has seen great success on the country singles charts as 'The Dance' (1990) and 1991's dramatic, emotion-torn 'The Thunder Rolls' had him act out his part to the full. These songs, alongside 'Friends In Low Places' (1990) and a remake of the newgrass favourite 'Callin' Baton Rouge' (1993), became focal points of his live show, which took on elements of a rock presentation.

Brooks' domination started to falter when he created a character named Chris Gaines for a multi-media attempt at breaking into television and film. *Garth Brooks... In The Life And Times Of Chris*

Gaines (1999) was a failure in comparison with previous projects but, nevertheless, still sold two million copies. In 2005, in the midst of his 'retirement', Brooks displayed his astute marketing skills by announcing an exclusive deal with Wal-Mart stores. Two million sales of *The Lost Sessions*, within a few months, proved that he had lost none of his popularity.

Above

Brooks has attracted a fanatic following, and his live shows rival rock's greatest in terms of presentation and showmanship

Left

Brooks won the award for CMA Entertainer Of The Year in 1991, 1992, 1997 and 1998. Few acts win that title, but it is a measure of his success that Brooks did so four times.

Key Track

'The Dance' (1989)
Brooks, who has a natural talent for acting out a scene, reflects the storyline in his trademark masterly style. His sobering tones are enough to chill even a room boasting a blazing log fire. Unlike with some of his later recordings, the trappings, effective as they might be, do not conflict with the lyrics, as Brooks the artist draws the listener closer to the action and the story.

Emmylou Harris

The undisputed queen of country rock, Emmylou Harris has long been both a student of traditional country music and a peerless innovator. Even now, some 30 years after she debuted with the tormented genius Gram Parsons, she is still the one others turn to for acceptance and support.

Gram Parsons' Influence

Born in Birmingham, Alabama, on 2 April 1947, Harris grew up near Washington, D.C. She cut her teeth as a folk singer, but after an unsuccessful 1969 debut, *Gliding Bird*, Byrd/Flying Burrito Brother Chris Hillman introduced her

EMMYLOU HARRIS·ROSES IN THE SNOW

to Parsons, who was looking for a female vocalist for his *GP* album, and suddenly, the world of country music opened up for her. Though impressed with Harris, months went by before Parsons sent her plane ticket to Los Angeles, and the collaboration began in earnest. The spark and chemistry of their voices was of almost sibling quality, and for a time it seemed that both artists were destined for superstardom. But it wasn't to be. Gram didn't even live to see the result of his second album with Harris, *Grievous Angel* (1974), on which Harris shone.

'I called Linda and told her that Dolly was coming over. This one evening, there was no particular reason for it.' **Emmylou Harris**

After this major setback, and despite her inexperience, Harris continued along the path pioneered by Parsons, taking over the team of stellar musicians he had assembled and forming The Hot Band (ex-Cricket Glen D. Hardin on keyboards, Emory Gordy on bass, Ricky Nelson/Elvis Presley guitarist James Burton, Hank DeVito on pedal steel guitar and John Ware on drums, with the then-

The Queen Of Country Rock

Harris And Her Hot Band, with the occasional personnel change, rolled on for many years until she formed the all-acoustic Nash Ramblers for a 1992 live album, *At The Ryman*. After this she fell under the influence of producer-musician Daniel Lanois and produced the *Wrecking Ball* album, forming her band Spyboy (featuring Buddy Miller) and creating a more contemporary sound.

There have been many twists and turns in Harris's body of work. This is evidenced by the bluegrass/traditional *Blue Kentucky Girl* (1979), the Ricky Skaggs-influenced *Roses In The Snow* (1980), the two Trio records with Dolly Parton and Linda Ronstadt (1987 and 1999), and a duet album with Ronstadt, *Western Walls – The Tucson Sessions* (1999). She has also produced such classic albums as *Quarter Moon In A 10 Cent Town* (1978) and *Cimarron* (1981), and participated in the celebrated movie soundtrack, *Oh Brother, Where Art Thou?* (2001). Other projects have ranged from The Band's *Last Waltz* finale to work with The Chieftains (1992's *Another Country*) and even collaborating with Bob Dylan. The 1980 CMA Female Vocalist of the Year has touched many bases.

Emmylou Harris is not only 'queen of the silver dollar' (somewhat surprisingly not one of her over 50 country hit singles), she is the perfect role-model for any female vocalist who aspires to a career in country music, and seems to be one of the most popular country-music superstars among her peer group. Apart from winning 11 Grammy Awards, a Lifetime Achievement – Performer Award (2002), which was handed to her at The Americana Awards, sums up both past and ongoing efforts on stage and in the recording studio.

unknown Rodney Crowell stepping into Parsons' shoes) to back her both on record and on the road. In 1975 she released not only her breakthrough album, *Pieces Of Sky*, which included her heartfelt tribute to Parsons, 'Boulder To Birmingham', but also *Elite Hotel*, which immediately propelled her to the top of the country-rock pecking order. Her blending of classic country songs from The Louvin and Stanley Brothers and A. P. Carter, with the then-new contemporary writers Rodney Crowell, Jesse Winchester, Townes Van Zandt, Bruce Springsteen and her one-time husband, British songwriter Paul Kennerly, provided a continuation of a vision she once shared with Parsons.

Classic Recordings

Pieces Of The Sky (1975)
'Boulder To Birmingham', 'Queen Of The Silver Dollar', 'Too Far Gone', 'If I Could Only Win Your Love', 'Bottle Let Me Down'

Elite Hotel (1976)
'Together Again', 'Here, There And Everywhere', 'One Of These Days', 'Sweet Dreams', 'Till I Gain Control Again'

Luxury Liner (1977)
'Makin' Believe', '(You Never Can Tell) C'est La Vie', 'Luxury Liner', 'Pancho & Lefty', 'Hello Stranger'

Quarter Moon In A 10 Cent Town (1978)
'Leavin' Louisiana In The Broad Daylight', 'To Daddy', 'Two More Bottles Of Wine', 'Ain't Living Long Like This', 'Easy From Now On'

Blue Kentucky Girl (1979)
'Sister's Coming Home', 'Blue Kentucky Girl', 'Hickory Wind', 'Even Cowgirls Get The Blues', 'Beneath Still Waters'

Roses In The Snow (1980)
'I'll Go Stepping Too', 'Roses In The Snow', 'Gold Watch And Chain', 'Miss The Mississippi And You', 'The Boxer'

Trio (with Dolly Parton and Linda Ronstadt, 1987)
'Making Plans', 'To Know Him Is To Love Him', 'Farther Along', 'Hobo's Meditation', 'Wildflowers'

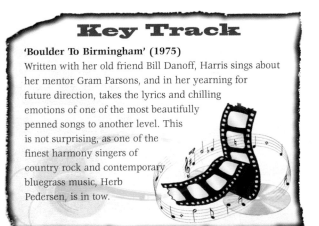

Key Track

'Boulder To Birmingham' (1975)
Written with her old friend Bill Danoff, Harris sings about her mentor Gram Parsons, and in her yearning for future direction, takes the lyrics and chilling emotions of one of the most beautifully penned songs to another level. This is not surprising, as one of the finest harmony singers of country rock and contemporary bluegrass music, Herb Pedersen, is in tow.

Ricky Skaggs

bluegrass band. This was quickly followed by a move to a more contemporary bluegrass combo, J.D. Crowe And The New South. After leaving The New South, Skaggs helped form Boone Creek, with whom he made the albums *Boone Creek* (1977) and *One Way Track* (1978).

In 1978, he replaced Rodney Crowell in Emmylou Harris's Hot Band. He had already worked as a session musician on Harris's albums, playing fiddle and mandolin on *Pieces Of The Sky* (1975) and *Luxury Liner* (1977). On formally joining the band, he appeared on *Blue Kentucky Girl* (1979), *Light Of The Stable* and *Roses In The Snow* (both 1980) and *Evangeline* and *Cimarron* (both 1981). In 1980, Skaggs also released *Skaggs & Rice* with Tony Rice. Sharon White (whom he later married) and her father, Buck White (of the bluegrass/gospel group, The Whites) also appear on several Emmylou Harris albums and Skaggs has both played on and produced their albums.

> *'Country and western is ignored by the intellectuals. They don't look at it as an art form. They think it's just somebody sitting on his couch singing about his life.'*
> **Ricky Skaggs**

Above

Ricky Skaggs has worked in some of country music's greatest bands and with some of its best-loved artists, including Ralph Stanley, Bill Monroe, Flatt And Scruggs and Emmylou Harris.

Above Right

The great Earl Scruggs was one of Skaggs' earliest and most enduring influences. Skaggs appeared on Flatt And Scruggs' television show as a child and much later he collaborated with Scruggs on the album Three Pickers.

Ricky Skaggs was born on 18 July 1954, in Cordell, Kentucky, and from the age of five Skaggs and his trusty mandolin have been almost inseparable. A child prodigy, he was invited on stage to play a tune at a Bill Monroe concert at the age of six, and a year later, he appeared on the Flatt And Scruggs' television show. He then met Keith Whitley, another Kentuckian, who played guitar, and the two teenagers formed a band with Whitley's brother, Dwight. Ralph Stanley was so impressed when he heard them that he invited both Skaggs and Whitley to join his band, The Clinch Mountain Boys, in 1970. The teenagers were confident enough even then to make their own duet album, *Second Generation*, in 1971.

A Country Gentleman

In 1974, Skaggs moved to Washington, D.C., and joined The Country Gentlemen, a long-established traditional

Twenty-First Century Success

From humble beginnings with such early solo albums as *That's It* (1975), *Sweet Temptation* (1980) and *Family And Friends* (1981), his career swiftly blossomed, and he signed to Columbia/Epic, where his albums, *Waitin' For The Sun To Shine* (1981) and *Highways And Heartaches* (1982), set the ball rolling. Over a five-year period, he topped the *Billboard* country chart on no less than 10 occasions. 'Crying My Heart Out Over You' (1982) opened the floodgates for 'I Don't Care', 'Heartbroke', 'Highway 40 Blues' and a wonderful remake of the Bill Monroe classic 'Uncle Pen'– all of which resulted in him becoming one of the great saviours of country music. Skaggs helped steer it back on track, encouraging the new traditionalists, who were waiting patiently in the wings for a bright new dawn to break.

His albums *Don't Cheat In Our Hometown* (1983) and *Country Boy* (1984) may not have included as many chart-topping singles as he had grown used to, but during the late 1980s and early 1990s, the music continued to flow. He found his second wind after signing with Atlantic Records and more recently has launched his own Skaggs Family label.

Despite being more influenced now by gospel music, he has continued to win awards. During his vintage years on Epic he won the CMA's Male Vocalist Of The Year Award (1982), while three years later he was recipient of the prestigious Entertainer Of The Year Award. In 1999 he found favour with his *Soldiers Of The Cross* album

and in 2003, the recording that reputedly gave him the greatest satisfaction, *Three Pickers*, on which he collaborated with Earl Scruggs and Doc Watson. Released on both CD and DVD, it won them all a Grammy Award.

Left
Ricky Skaggs continues to release much-lauded country albums, and to collaborate with country music's huge pantheon of artists.

Key Track

'Uncle Pen' (1983)

Fittingly, one of Skaggs' greatest singles successes was with a song written by his hero, Bill Monroe. 'Uncle Pen', a song about Monroe's uncle Pen Vandiver, a fiddle/mandolin player, boasts some of the most wonderful picking imaginable on fiddle and acoustic, electric and steel guitar, and with Ricky at the peak of his powers, everything falls into place, as if by some divine power.

George Strait

Right

Right

George Strait greets his fans – of which there are many after more than 20 years as a leading light on the country-music scene.

Far Right

Country legend Bob Wills was a major influence on Strait, who endeavoured to emulate his straightforward approach to traditional country music.

The Lone Star State is steeped in tradition, producing both songwriters and swing bands. In the 1980s, the clean-cut George Strait And His Ace In The Hole band took the baton from such earlier legends as Bob Wills, Lefty Frizzell, Ray Price and Hank Thompson. Born on 18 May 1952, in Poteet (south of San Antonio), Strait took to playing country music seriously in 1973, when, stationed in Hawaii in the final year of his three-year stint in the US Army, he got a job as vocalist in a band formed to entertain the troops.

'You don't want to do a song just because it's got Texas in it. Sometimes that can get a little hokey.'

George Strait

Rising Star

Influenced by Bob Wills, whose music he discovered via Merle Haggard's *Tribute To The Best Damn Fiddle Player In The World* (1970), it took until 1981 for Strait to secure a major record deal (MCA), with the help of his manager, Erv Woolsey. It came at a time when the majority of new country faces were leaning towards pop – the glossy urban-cowboy era had helped to accelerate a shift away from country music's older styles, but this all changed as Strait almost single-handedly kept the tradition alive via his blend of honky-tonk, ballad-laden and swing-inflected honest fare. The prime movers of the new-traditionalist movement of the mid-1980s benefited greatly because of his pioneering work.

In 1981, Strait had been working as a ranch foreman in San Marcos, Texas, supplementing his income by playing nights in local bar-rooms and dancehalls. Now he was about to embark on a series of chart-topping hit singles. 'Fool Hearted Memory' was the first of his 51 No. 1s to date, and he drew on songwriters Dean Dillon (who nearly made a career out of writing for Strait), Frank Dycus, Sanger D. (Whitey) Shafer and Hank Cochran (and, more recently, Jim Lauderdale) to continue the trend. A raft of country awards soon followed. Many were from the CMA, including, in 1985, the first of his five Male Vocalist Of The Year awards – the others came in 1986, 1996, 1997 and 1998 – alongside two Entertainer Of The Year Awards (1989 and 1990).

Strait Success

Strait's live shows always attract sell-out crowds, evidenced by his legendary Houston Astrodome gigs, where he outsold even Elvis Presley – the ink on the tickets had barely dried in 1987, when all 49,246 seats had been sold. His songs 'Does Fort Worth Ever Cross Your Mind', 'The Chair' and 'All My Ex's

'Live In Texas' deservedly set side by side with his equally successful versions of country standards like 'Right Or Wrong', 'If You Ain't Lovin' (You Ain't Livin')' and 'Love Bug'. It is little wonder that the likes of Alan Jackson, Garth Brooks and Randy Travis cite him as having inspired them to pursue a life playing country music.

Apart from his recording and stage success, the Stetson-toting Strait also starred in the film *Pure Country* (1992), where he appeared as a country singer who turned his back on the superstar lifestyle. The soundtrack album, which featured the chart-topping, 'Heartland', is one of his biggest sellers, and his album sales to date total in excess of 62 million.

After 25 years, the awards might now have slowed, yet Strait's popularity among country followers remains as strong today as it ever was. Another notable award – his vocal duet with Alan Jackson on Larry Cordle and Larry Shell's controversial 'Murder On Music Row', which was voted CMA Vocal Event in 2000 and Song Of The Year in 2001 – was one of his sweetest achievements.

Left
George Strait continues to wow audiences as well as the country-music establishment. In 2005 he achieved his 51st country No. 1 hit.

Key Track

'Does Fort Worth Ever Cross Your Mind' (1984)
Penned by one of the all-time great honky-tonk songwriters, Sanger D. 'Whitey' Shafer, with a little help from his wife, Darlene, this song has Strait slipping into every emotion and groove of a superb shuffle. Doused in steel guitar, tinkling piano and fiddle from Texas legend Johnny Gimble, a wonderful feeling results.

Randy Travis

Key Artist

'My dad wanted me to play when I was a kid, so I learned to play the guitar. I pursued a career in music because I love it so much and I enjoy what it does to those who hear it.' **Randy Travis**

Born Randy Bruce Traywick on 4 May 1959 in North Carolina, Randy Travis won a talent show at the age of 16, but found his music career progressed painfully slow. Hankering after a more exciting lifestyle, he dropped out of high school in the ninth grade. Music eventually came to his aid, but not without a great deal of hard work. Travis doubled playing music in clubs and bars with cooking and washing dishes at the Nashville Palace. Club manager Lib Hatcher, whom he later married, became his manager and it wasn't until he had suffered rejection by most of Nashville's major labels that a deal was struck with Warner Bros. in 1985.

Storms Of Life

Prior to his breakthrough, Paula Records had released two Randy Traywick singles produced by Joe Stampley in the late 1970s, while an independently released *Randy Ray – Live At The Nashville Palace* album (sold at gigs) had created quite a stir without anything resulting. But tenacity paid off. The new-traditionalist era was bringing previously undiscovered talent to the fore, as though Nashville was opening its doors to a new dawn. Curiously, the first Travis recording for Warner was 'Prairie Rose', on the soundtrack album of the film *Rustler's Rhapsody*. It was perhaps fitting that he started this way, as he was a keen western buff and later appeared in such movies as *The Rainmaker* (starring Jon Voight, Matt Damon and Danny DeVito), *Black Dog* (Patrick Swayze), and *Frank And Jesse* (Bill Paxton and Rob Lowe), as well as a starring role in the film *Texas Rangers*.

However, it won't be as an actor that Randy Travis will be best remembered when the curtain falls on a career that has spanned country, western and country gospel, for this quiet and reserved stage performer. It will be for his head-turning recordings, especially those of the 1980s, when his 1986 debut Warner bros. album *Storms Of Life* was certified triple platinum. It was arguably the finest country album of its time, boasting No. 1 country singles 'On The Other Hand' (his first chart-topper) and 'Diggin' Up Bones'. This started a run that yielded three more No. 1s from his 1987 album, *Always And Forever*, which held the top slot in the country charts for an incredible 38 weeks, and it was no surprise when it was voted CMA Album Of The Year, while its first and biggest single, 'Forever And Ever, Amen', was voted CMA Single Of The Year. With his career very much on a roll, he also scored maximum chart success with a revival of Brook Benton's 1959 million-seller, 'It's Just A Matter Of Time'.

Heroes And Friends

More nostalgia surfaced on 1990's *Heroes And Friends* album, on which not only country acts George Jones, Loretta Lynn, Merle Haggard, Willie Nelson and Dolly Parton duetted with Travis, but also his western idol Roy Rogers. *Wind In The Wire* (1993) was a western album that saw a change in his music, while in 1997 he was one of the first artists to sign for the newly formed Dreamworks label, after 12 albums with Warners. He gave his new label its first No. 1 country single with 1998's 'Out Of My Bones', while his 2003 country gospel album *Rise And Shine* featured 'Three Wooden Crosses', which, apart from topping the country charts, won awards from both Christian and country organizations. *Worship And Faith* (2004) and *Passing Through* (2005) prove that Travis is showing no signs of tiring.

Above
Robert Patrick and Dylan McDermott ride alongside Randy Travis in the 2001 movie Texas Rangers.

Left
Travis's career has so far amassed 21 No. 1 country singles, four Grammy Awards – and a great deal of respect.

Key Track

'On The Other Hand' (1986)
Released in 1985, this song displays Travis' ability with ballads as his cool, unruffled, precise vocal style milks the lyrics and emotions of this song written by Paul Overstreet and Don Schlitz in a superb, heart-stopping, no nonsense manner. Pure country, no gimmicks, just a fine natural singing voice reaching out to the heart of the listener.

Dwight Yoakam

Key Artist

'You'll start out with a master take, the whole band plays it, and then we start doing coverage of each instrument, and it's very similar to filmmaking in terms of the process, time involved and the repetition of performance.'
Dwight Yoakam

Of all the new-traditionalist acts, Dwight Yoakam was arguably the most flamboyant, with his tight-fitting designer jeans and cowboy hat. He was also the most distinctive of those to emerge on the country scene in the mid-1980s. Yoakam was born in Pikesville, Kentucky, on 23 October 1956. He was primarily raised in Columbus, Ohio, before relocating to Los Angeles. There, in the early 1980s, he debuted on the independent Oak label.

Far Right
Buck Owens was one of Yoakam's major influences, and their duet together became Yoakam's first chart-topping single.

Right
Maverick country star Dwight Yoakam turned his back on the Nashville scene, and as a consequence suffered a lack of awards. The situation belies his success – his album sales have topped 24 million.

A Musical Maverick

Hugely influenced by both the music of Bakersfield, as typified by Buck Owens, and by his own Kentucky heritage, Yoakam's songwriting matured during his formative years, and he didn't so much emerge on to the country scene, as explode. The influence and assistance of producer/lead guitarist Pete Anderson – who stuck with Yoakam through both the big years and when Warner/Reprise seemed to turn its back on him – cannot be underestimated. He and Yoakam have done more than most in keeping Bakersfield on the country map.

Ever a maverick, Yaokam played only by his own rules: after pre-fame rejection from the powers that be in Nashville in the mid-1970s, he never returned, deciding to remain on the West Coast to be near Hollywood, where lucrative deals were struck as he also diversified into movie work. Unfortunately this has meant that Yoakam never quite gained the recognition he deserved when it came to awards handed out by Nashville's highest power, the CMA.

Guitars, Cadillacs Etc. Etc. (1986, platinum), *Hillbilly Deluxe* (1987, gold), *Buenas Noches From A Lonely Room* (1988, gold) and the triple platinum *This Time* (1993) helped bring the music to both a wider audience and raise the standard. In all, despite his devoting more attention to films – his starring role in the Oscar-winning *Sling Blade* (1996), *South Of Heaven, West Of Hell* (which he authored) and other movies in which he featured, such as *Rosewell, The Newton Boys* and *The Little Death* – he is still huge in the eyes of the public.

A West Coast Icon

'Streets Of Bakersfield', a duet with Buck Owens, became Yoakam's first No. 1 country single. After eight years in retirement, Owens was persuaded to make a comeback due to the reaction sparked by this revival of a song from a 1972 Owens album. Yoakam's run continued with 'I Sang Dixie', the Grammy Award-winning 'Ain't That Lonely Yet' (US country Top 3), plus the brooding 'A Thousand Miles From Nowhere' (also Top 3) and 'Home For Sale' (the latter three all included on his acclaimed 1993 album *This Time*). Another variation, his film work aside (three movies emerged in 2005 alone), has been where, like his hero Buck Owens, he has recorded covers of classic pop/rock material by The Beatles, Van Morrison/Them, Elvis, The Everly Brothers, The Rolling Stones, The Kinks and even 'Train In Vain' by The Clash, without disturbing his country roots. This resulted in the 1997 album *Under The Covers*. After a long and successful run with Warner/Reprise, which began in 1985 when they licensed his 1984 mini-album from Enigma, ties were finally broken in 2001.

New recordings followed, such as 'Population Me' (Audium, 2003) and 'Blame The Vain' (New West, 2005), which prove that the Yoakam is anything but done with making country music with a distinctive West Coast twang.

Left

Yoakam, who first moved to Los Angeles in 1978 and wowed the thriving club scene, has lost none of his West Coast appeal in the twenty-first century.

Classic Recordings

Guitars, Cadillacs, Etc. Etc. **(1986)**
'Honky Tonk Man', 'Guitars, Cadillacs', 'I'll Be Gone', 'Ring Of Fire', 'Miner's Prayer'

Hillbilly Deluxe **(1987)**
'Smoke Along The Tracks', 'Little Sister', 'Always Late With Your Kisses', 'Johnson's Love', 'Readin', Rightin', Rt. 23'

Buenas Noches From A Lonely Room **(1988)**
'Streets Of Bakersfield', 'I Sang Dixie', 'Home Of The Blues', 'Buenas Noches From A Lonely Room', 'Send Me The Pillow'

This Time **(1993)**
'Pocket Of A Clown', 'A Thousand Miles From Nowhere', 'Home For Sale', 'Ain't That Lonely Yet', 'Try Not To Look So Pretty'

dwightyoakamacoustic.net
'Bury Me', 'Fast As You Can', 'Little Ways', 'If There Was A Way', 'Guitars, Cadillacs'

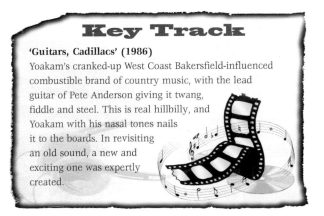

Key Track

'Guitars, Cadillacs' (1986)
Yoakam's cranked-up West Coast Bakersfield-influenced combustible brand of country music, with the lead guitar of Pete Anderson giving it twang, fiddle and steel. This is real hillbilly, and Yoakam with his nasal tones nails it to the boards. In revisiting an old sound, a new and exciting one was expertly created.

A-Z of Artists

Terry Allen
(Vocals, piano, songwriter, b. 1943)

This Texas-raised musician, sculptor and playwright is an American original. His left-of-centre songs about the road and life's characters have created a cult following via such albums as *Juarez* (1975), *Lubbock (On Everything)* (1979) and *Human Remains* (1995). 'New Delhi Freight Train' and 'Amarillo Highway' are his most covered songs.

Below

Terry Allen's songs have been recorded by the likes of Bobby Bare, Little Feat, Robert Earl Keen and Joe Ely.

John Anderson
(Vocals, guitar, songwriter, b. 1954)

Neo-traditionalist Anderson's early Nashville career was unsuccessful, but after 1977, the hits began, including an inspired 1981 version of Billy Joe Shaver's 'I'm Old Chunk Of Coal (But I'm Gonna Be A Diamond Someday)', while early albums *John Anderson* (1980) and *John Anderson 2* (1981) and singles 'Wild And Blue' (1982) and 'Straight Tequila Nights' (1992), are typical of his honest style.

Moe Bandy
(Vocals, b. 1944)

Raised in Texas, Marion Franklin Bandy was a rodeo rider before joining his father's band, The Mission City Playboys. Bandy, a disciple of Hank Williams and George Jones, with his own band, Moe And The Mavericks, specialized in honky-tonk music, cheating songs and steel guitar. His 50-plus US country hits include the novel 'Just Good Ol' Boys' (1979), a duet with Joe Stampley, which earned them 1980's CMA Duo Of The Year award.

Dierks Bentley
(Guitar, vocals, songwriter, b. 1975)

Arizona-born and raised, Bentley moved to Nashville in 1994, playing the clubs as an intimate singer-songwriter. In 2001, he released the self-financed *Don't Leave Me In Love,* backed by friends from the Jamie Hartford Band and bluegrass legend Del McCoury's band. In 2003, a major label deal resulted in his eponymous debut album, which included the country chart-topping crossover hit single, 'What Was I Thinkin''. In 2005, his gold album, *Modern Day Drifter*, and CMA Horizon Award maintained the momentum.

Clint Black
(Vocals, songwriter, b. 1962)

Born in New Jersey and raised in Houston, Black burst on to the scene in the late 1980s. Signed by ZZ Top manager Bill Ham, Black's double platinum debut album, *Killin'*

Time (1989), spawned four chart-topping singles, including 'Better Man' and 'Nobody's Home'. He has duetted with legendary cowboy Roy Rogers, and in 1994, he was *Billboard*'s most-played country act.

Bente Boe

(Vocals, b. 1970)

Bente Boe from Tonsberg, Norway, made her national radio debut aged only nine, and has been singing for her entire adult life. Voted European Female Singer of the Year in 1996, she made her first album in the US, *Cross The River*, in 1998, following three previous albums in Norway.

Suzy Bogguss

(Vocals, b. 1956)

Suzy Bogguss served her apprenticeship travelling across America in a camper van for five years, then appearing daily at Dolly Parton's Dollywood theme park in 1986. Her third album, *Aces* (1992), achieved gold status and gained a firm chart foothold for the folk-influenced troubadour's singles and albums. A highlight of her career was making *Simpatico* (1994) with Chet Atkins.

Jimmy Bowen

(Vocals, record producer, b. 1937)

New Mexico-born Bowen enjoyed three distinctive careers, first as a rock'n'roll artist with Buddy Knox (their 1957 double A-sided single, 'Party Doll'/'I'm Stickin' With You' sold a million copies); then as a West Coast record executive, working with such as Frank Sinatra and Dean Martin; and,

finally, running several of the Nashville record labels with production credits including George Strait, Merle Haggard, Hank Williams Jr., Mel Tillis and Reba McEntire.

Brooks & Dunn

(Vocal duo, 1990–present)

Prior to partnering Ronnie Gene Dunn (b. 1953), Leon 'Kix' Brooks (b. 1955) had made a 1989 solo album, after writing 'I'm Only In It For The Love', a 1983 chart-topper for John Conlee, and 'Modern Day Romance', a 1985 No. 1 for the Nitty Gritty Dirt Band. In 1990, the two songwriters made a demo for Arista, and began a hugely successful career with four No. 1 singles in 1991–92. Subsequently, they have won 13 CMA Duo Of The Year awards and four Entertainer Of The Year awards. 'Only In America' – a single released in the wake of 9/11 – along with their Neon Circus And Wild West Show tour, featuring a mixture of up-and-coming acts, has kept them in contention ever since.

Tracy Byrd

(Vocals, b. 1966)

After sharing a residency with Mark Chesnutt at The Cutters Club in Beaumont, Texas, Byrd followed his route to Nashville two years later. His eponymous 1993 album included 'Holdin' Heaven', his first No. 1 hit. Nine years later, he returned to the top with 'Ten Rounds With Jose Cuervo', one of several novelty singles. His second album, *No Ordinary Man*, went double platinum and included four Top 5 hit singles.

Left
Clint Black's singles have won him CMA awards and a Grammy, and he has successfully combined making movies with music and family life.

Below
Notable hit singles by Suzy Bogguss include John Hiatt's 'Drive South' and 'Outbound Plane' (written by Tom Russell and Nanci Griffith).

Mark Chesnutt
(Vocals, b. 1963)

Steeped in tradition, Mark Chesnutt has followed a path akin to his heroes Merle Haggard and George Jones. Following in his father's footsteps as a honky-honk singer aged only 17, he worked the local Beaumont, Texas, scene for a decade, finally breaking through with 'Too Cold At Home' (1990). Although his first dozen singles all made the Top 10 and included four No. 1s, he is regarded by Nashville as too left-field.

Guy Clark
(Vocals, songwriter, b. 1941)

The archetypal Texas troubadour, Clark cannot be called prolific, having released about 10 original albums since his 1975 debut, *Old No. 1.* Born in Monahans, West Texas, Clark worked in television, as a photographer and building boats and guitars. Influenced by bluesman Mance Lipscomb, he worked the Texas folk circuit, meeting Townes Van Zandt, who remained a close friend until his death.

Admired by his contemporaries, backing singers on his albums have included Emmylou Harris, Rodney Crowell, Hoyt Axton, Waylon Jennings and Steve Earle. Virtually all

Above

Carlene Carter's country-music heritage is evident in her name – descended from the famous Carter Family, she continued the tradition into the twenty-first century.

Carlene Carter
(Vocals, b. 1955)

Born Rebecca Carlene Smith, the daughter of June Carter and Carl Smith, she worked on *The Johnny Cash Show* and with The Carter Family after her mother married Cash. During the first half of the 1990s, she returned to country music, after a period in the rock world and early albums with Dave Edmunds and her then-husband Nick Lowe. Her vibrant vocal style can be heard in her Top 3 country singles 'I Fell In Love' (1990) and 'Every Little Thing' (1993).

Rosanne Cash
(Vocals, songwriter, b. 1955)

Johnny Cash's daughter topped the country charts 11 times in the 1980s, starting with 'Seven Year Ache' (1981). Ten were solo hits and 'It's Such A Small World' (1988) a duet with her then-husband, Rodney Crowell. In 1985, she won a Grammy for Best Country Female Vocal Performance. Covering her father's 'Tennessee Flat Top Box' from her *King's Record Shop* album (1987), saw Cash come closest to Nashville, but she has never followed musical fashion.

Right

Rosanne Cash's 2006 album Black Cadillac *includes songs inspired by the recent deaths of her parents, and is typical of her deeply emotional songwriting.*

his albums have been exemplary, including *Texas Cookin'* (1976), *Better Days* (1982), *Dublin Blues* (1995) and *Cold Dog Soup* (1999). His accomplished acoustic guitar work perfectly complements his weathered vocals.

Mark Collie
(Vocals, songwriter, b. 1956)
Tennessee-born Collie toured the south-west in various bands before his 1982 move to Nashville and a residency at the Douglas Cafe. His debut album *Hardin County Line* (1990), gained critical acclaim, and although success has greeted such songs as 'Even The Man In The Moon Is Crying' (1992), and the albums *Unleashed* (1994) and *Tennessee Plates* (1995), his talent for writing hard-hitting, rocking country songs has yet to make the impact anticipated.

Earl Thomas Conley
(Vocals, songwriter, b. 1941)
Conley's first big break came in 1975, when Mel Street recorded his song 'Smokey Mountain Memories'. Conway Twitty took his song 'This Time I Have Hurt Her More Than She Loves Me' to the top of the US country chart in 1976. On moving to Nashville, his first No. 1 hit, 'Fire And Smoke' (1981), appeared on the independent Sunbird label, which sold his contract to RCA. He made 17 No. 1s for them during the 1980s, including his duet with Emmylou Harris, 'We Believe In Happy Endings' (1988).

Rodney Crowell
(Vocals, songwriter, b. 1950)
A member of The Hot Band from 1975–77 as Emmylou Harris's duet partner, Crowell wrote contemporary classics for her, including "Til I Gain Control Again' and 'I Ain't Living Long Like This'. After a modest start in chart terms with Warner Bros. in the late 1970s, his second Columbia album, *Diamonds And Dirt* (1988), saw his solo career go into orbit. Despite missing the US pop chart, the album included an all-time record of five chart topping-singles, the first a duet with his then-wife, Rosanne Cash.

Gail Davies
(Vocals, songwriter, b. 1948)
Gail Davies initially played jazz, and then formed a duo with her brother, songwriter Ron Davies. After session work in Los Angeles, she moved to Nashville in the mid-1970s. Two breaks came in 1978: Ava Barber's only US Top 20 country hit was Davies' song 'Bucket To The South', and Davies released her eponymous debut album on the Lifesong label. Her plaintive songs brought her single hits on Warner Bros. (1979–84), including the autobiographical 'Grandma's Song' (1982). After five years with RCA in the later 1980s, Davies, now working acoustically, launched her own Little Chickadee label in the 1990s. Her 2005 album, *The Songwriter Sessions*, featuring 'Hometown Gossip' (as covered by The Whites), underlined the talent of one of country's true survivors.

Above
The advent of new country made Earl Thomas Conley's crooning vocal style redundant, but he continued to impress his die-hard fans into the 1990s.

Above
Controversial band The
Dixie Chicks enjoyed
their most successful
year in 2000, when they
won five awards,
including the CMA
Entertainer Of The Year.

Right
Sara Evans has scored
a succession of hit
singles, and is among
the top female vocalists
on the contemporary
country scene.

The Dixie Chicks

(Vocal/instrumental group, 1989–present)

Texas-based band The Dixie Chicks initially included sisters
Martie (vocals, violin, b. 1969) and Emily Erwin (vocals,
dobro, banjo, b. 1972), Laura Lynch (bass) and Robin Lynn
Macy (vocals, guitar). Their debut album, *Thank Heavens For
Dale Evans* (1990), a mixture of folk music and traditional
country, was released on the independent Crystal Clear label.
By 1995, Lynch and Macy had left, and Natalie Maines (b.
1974), joined the soon to be top-selling act. *Wide Open Spaces*
(1997) sold over 12 million copies and 'Ready To Run' was a
hit single. Maines criticized President Bush about the war in
Iraq at a 2003 London show, which resulted in some US radio
stations refusing to play the group's records. *Top Of The World
Tour* (2003), a double album and DVD, regained much lost
ground for the 1999 and 2000 CMA Vocal Group Of The Year.

Steve Earle

(Vocals, songwriter, guitar, b. 1955)

Born in Virginia and raised in Texas, Earle's first tracks in
1983 were ignored. A change of label saw *Guitar Town* (1986)
being hailed as pivotal in the new-traditionalist movement,
spawning Top 10 singles in the title track and 'Goodbye's
All We've Got Left'. His songs 'My Old Friend The Blues',
'Someday' and his third album *Copperhead Road* looked set to
be the sum total of his legacy, until he returned from prison
after recovering from substantial drug abuse. Using seasoned
musicians Norman Blake, Roy Huskey and Peter Rowan, he

recorded *Train A Comin'* (1995), which lacked the self-
indulgence that had blighted his career, and subsequent
albums like *El Corazon* (1997) and *Transcendental Blues* (2000)
indicate that his demons have been banished.

Sara Evans

(Vocals, b. 1971)

Evans moved to Nashville in 1991, where she met her
husband, Craig Schelske. In 1995, her demo of the 1965 Buck
Owens hit 'I've Got A Tiger By The Tail', attracted the
attention of the song's writer, Harlan Howard, and led to her
signing with RCA Records and her much-hailed traditional
country album, *Three Chords And The Truth* (1997). A
consistent chart artist, her number ones have included 'No
Place That Far' (1998) and 'A Real Fine Place To Start' (2005).

Foster & Lloyd

(Vocal/instrumental duo, 1987–90)

Bill Lloyd (b. 1955) and Radney Foster (b. 1959) enjoyed
success writing 1986's 'Since I Found You', the first Top 10
hit for Sweethearts Of The Rodeo, and co-writing 1987's
Top 3 hit, 'Love Someone Like Me' with/for Holly Dunn.
They capitalized on this by acquiring their own record deal
and their eponymous 1987 album included four Top 20
singles. Foster achieved four hit singles in the early 1990s,
and made the album *Del Rio, Tx, 1959* (1992), while Lloyd
has concentrated on songwriting and session work, and
has also made two rock albums.

Vince Gill
(Vocals, guitar, songwriter, b. 1957)

Oklahoman Vince Gill paid his dues, first in high-school band Mountain Smoke, then with Sam Bush in Bluegrass Alliance around 1975, and was a member of Pure Prairie League from 1978–80. Gill joined The Cherry Bombs in 1981, backing Rodney Crowell and Rosanne Cash, and befriended musician/producer/label executive Tony Brown, who first signed him to RCA, resulting in three Top 10 hits, then to MCA. In 1990, 'When I Call Your Name', the title track of his MCA debut album, became his first Top 3 hit. Gill, a smooth tenor, has maintained high standards ever since, achieving an all-time record 18 CMA Awards and hosting the Award Show for 12 years.

Vern Gosdin
(Vocals, b. 1934)

Vern Gosdin was part of *The Gosdin Family Gospel* radio show in the 1950s in Alabama, before moving to California with his brother, Rex Gosdin (1938–83), to form The Golden State Boys, a bluegrass combo who in 1964 became The Hillmen (featuring Chris Hillman, later of The Byrds).

After emerging in 1976 as a solo artist, Gosdin was christened 'The Voice' by his peers and accumulated over 40 US country hit singles. 'Chiseled In Stone' was voted 1989 CMA Song Of The Year.

Nanci Griffith
(Vocals, songwriter, b. 1953)

Texas singer-songwriter Nanci Griffith first emerged via her early 'folkabilly' acoustic fare, and then introduced a broader spectrum to her music, involving country. Exposure to a wider audience than the folk circuit in Texas and neighbouring states came through her Jim Rooney-produced albums, *Once In A Very Blue Moon* (1985) and the Grammy-nominated *Last Of The True Believers* (1986). Her major-label debut *Lone Star State Of Mind* (1987) featured the first cover of Julie Gold's 'From A Distance' and *Little Love Affairs* (1988) saw some of her best work up to that point. However, she topped it with *Other Voices, Other Rooms* (1993), and the follow-up *Other Voices, Too (A Trip Back To Bountiful)* (1998), which featured songs by other artists, is regarded as her greatest achievement.

Above
Nanci Griffith has a reputation for admiring and supporting her peers, as evidenced by the all-star line-ups on several of her albums.

buck owens ⊚128 rosanne cash ⊚260 rodney crowell ⊚261

Above
Faith Hill (who is married to Tim McGraw) won Grammy Awards in 2000 as well as the CMA Female Vocalist Of The Year.

Right
Musicians like Alan Jackson have incorporated rock-based rhythm sections into this music while maintaining a strong country feel through harmony, instrumentation and singing style.

O. J. Hanssen

(Vocals, songwriter, b. 1964)

Norway's O. J. Hanssen is one of Europe's country-music success stories, having made three albums in Nashville. For 11 years, he divided his time between performing and serving as deputy sheriff in his home town of Mosjøen. With numerous nominations from the European CMA to his credit, his first Nashville album *What's It Gonna Take* (2001), was produced by Barry Beckett, while his bluegrass/gospel album, *Blessed* (2004), boasted guest appearances by The Jordanaires.

Ruud Hermanns

(Vocals, songwriter, b. 1950)

One of Holland's premier country artists, Hermanns recorded with the folk group Heating, before joining country act The Tumbleweeds, whose eponymous 1975

album went platinum. Their cover of Merle Haggard's 'Somewhere Between' topped the Dutch pop chart. In 1977, he formed his own country band, Tulsa, touring Europe and making regular visits to the USA.

Faith Hill

(Vocals, b. 1967)

Born Audrey Faith Perry, Hill moved to Nashville in 1986, where she was discovered singing back-up to singer-songwriter Gary Burr at the Bluebird Café. Hill made an instant and huge impact when in 1994 her debut single, 'Wild One', topped the country chart for four weeks. Effortlessly crossing over to pop, her *Take Me As I Am* album (1993) was certified triple platinum. A cover of Janis Joplin's 'Piece Of My Heart' gave her a second No. 1 single, and *Breathe* (1999) not only sold eight million copies, but the title track topped the country singles charts for six weeks and, like *This Kiss* (1998), made the Top 10 in the US pop chart.

Alan Jackson

(Vocals, songwriter, guitar, b. 1958)

Georgia-born Jackson moved to Nashville in 1985. His rise to fame came after a chance meeting between his wife, Denise, and Glen Campbell, and before long, he was a staff songwriter at Campbell's music-publishing company. A traditionalist blue-collar act, he was the first signing to Arista's Nashville branch, and his 1990 debut album *Here In The Real*

World went platinum. His second album, *Don't Rock The Jukebox* (1991), which went double platinum and made the US pop Top 20, included four country chart-toppers.

Gina Jeffreys
(Vocals, songwriter, b. 1968)

Gina Jeffreys has been recognized as Australia's premier female country act since her first hit single, 'Two Stars Fell' (1993). She started playing guitar at the age of 12 and at 15 was playing with the band ONYX. CMA Female Vocalist Of The Year in 1994 – when she toured with Johnny Cash and Kris Kristofferson – she retained her title in 1995 and 1996. Her biggest album to date, *Angel* (2001) was produced in Nashville by Garth Fundis.

The Judds
(Vocal duo, 1983–91)

The Judds were a rags-to-riches story. Divorced mother Diana took her daughters, Ashley (b. 1946) and Christina (b. 1964), to Nashville in 1979. In 1983, renamed Naomi and Wynonna, they clinched a record deal with RCA. Their lilting vocal harmonies warmed by the acoustic guitar of Don Potter resulted in 14 of their first 17 hit singles topping the chart, the first of which was 'Mama He's Crazy' (1984). Naomi and Wynonna won numerous CMA Awards in the latter half of the 1980s, including Vocal Group Of The Year from 1985–87 and Vocal Duo Of The Year from 1988–90. Ill-health forced Naomi to retire in 1991, while Wynonna has enjoyed a successful solo career, selling over nine million albums.

Arly Karlsen
(Vocals, songwriter, b. 1954)

Aged 12, Norwegian Arly Karlsen bought his first guitar, and played with numerous bands in his native country during the 1970s, before forming The Western Swingers with Arne Løland and Liv Jurunn Heia. Their 1983 debut album, *Sin Egen Stil*, sold over 20,000 copies in Norway, and they made four more albums by 1996. In 2001, Karlsen embarked on a solo career. His third album, *Sweet Honky Tonk* (2005), was recorded in Nashville.

Robert Earl Keen
(Vocals, songwriter, b. 1956)

Texan Robert Earl Keen Jr. first came to notice with his self-financed 1984 album *No Kinda Dancer*, which included 'The Front Porch Song', co-written with Lyle Lovett. Keen's

raspy vocals coupled with his conversational styled songs have produced such albums as *West Textures* (1989) and *What I Really Mean* (2005).

Toby Keith
(Guitar, vocals, b. 1961)

Toby Keith's rich, booming voice is best known for his chart-topping 1993 debut single 'Should've Been A Cowboy', which the NFL Dallas Cowboys football team adopted as their anthem, while his eponymous debut album was certified platinum. His 1994 album, *Boomtown*, went gold, and after six years with Mercury he moved to the Dreamworks label in 1999, where he enjoyed even greater success, winning Academy Of Country Music Awards in 2000 for both Album and Male Vocalist Of The year. A 2002 duet with Willie Nelson, 'Beer For My Horses', was another career highlight.

Below

Oklahoma-raised Toby Keith chose a career in music after playing professional American football for the Oklahoma City Drillers, and working in rodeo and the oil industry.

Lee Kernaghan
(Vocals, guitar, songwriter, b. 1964)

With 14 gold albums to his name, Kernaghan is the biggest-selling country artist in Australia. He first visited Nashville in 1986, played at Fan Fair, and met producer Garth Porter, resulting in his 1992 double-platinum debut album, *The Outback Club*. He has recorded with the late Australian legend Slim Dusty.

k.d. lang
(Vocals, songwriter, b. 1961)

Canadian lang's first international album, the Dave Edmunds-produced *Angel With A Lariat* (1987), was critically acclaimed. A duet with Roy Orbison on a remake of his 1961 hit, 'Crying', for the movie *Hiding Out*, was her first country hit. She then teamed up with veteran producer Owen Bradley for *Shadowlands* (1988), which spawned the hit singles 'I'm Down To My Last Cigarette' and 'Lock, Stock And Teardrops', as well as the historic 'Honky Tonk Angels Medley', featuring Brenda Lee, Loretta Lynn and Kitty Wells. Through this, the truly

unique lang endeared herself to country audiences. *Absolute Torch & Twang* (1989) similarly achieved gold status, but she is now regarded as a mainstream performer.

Tracy Lawrence
(Vocals, songwriter, b. 1968)

Born in Texas and raised in Arkansas, Lawrence's early influences included Merle Haggard, Keith Whitley and George Strait. Moving to Nashville in 1990, he signed with Atlantic, who released his platinum debut album, *Sticks And Stones* (1991), which included four Top 10 singles, including the chart-topping title track. 1993's *Alibis* placed his career and personal life at its most stable level, but despite label changes (when Atlantic closed its Nashville office) his brand of honky-tonk music has retained an audience.

Chris LeDoux
(Vocals, guitar, songwriter, 1948–2005)

Chris LeDoux lived out many people's fantasies of being a genuine cowboy and touring rodeo shows as a musician. Garth Brooks paid tribute to him in the song 'Much Too Young (To Feel This Damn Old)', and was backing vocalist on LeDoux's Top 10 single, 'Whatcha Gonna Do With A Cowboy' (1992), LeDoux made well over 30 albums, and would have been an even bigger star had he not been diagnosed with cancer less than 10 years after his major breakthrough.

Albert Lee
(Guitar, vocals, songwriter, b. 1943)

Englishman Albert Lee first attracted attention playing with British R&B singer Chris Farlowe in the mid-1960s, and played in several British bands before working as a 'hired gun' for legendary acts like The Crickets, Jerry Lee Lewis and most notably The Everly Brothers. In 1976, he replaced his hero, James Burton, in Emmylou Harris's Hot Band, playing on at least six of her albums. His 1979 solo album, *Hiding*, which included help from Harris and her band, featured arguably Lee's best-known composition, 'Country Boy', a song with which Ricly Skaggs topped the country singles chart in 1985.

Reg Lindsay
(Vocals, songwriter)

Long regarded as an Australian treasure, Lindsay has written more than 500 songs, and has been the winner of three Golden Guitars at the Australasian Country Music

Below

Born in Herefordshire, England, Albert Lee is a much in-demand session and touring musician, who has recorded occasional solo albums.

Awards, as well as the recipient of the Order of Australian Merit for services to music. He gained his first break on radio in Sydney in 1951, followed by a 12-year stint with the Adelaide-based Reg Lindsay Country Homestead. In 1968, he became the first Australian to appear on Nashville's Friday night Grand Ole Opry show. He continues to record.

Patty Loveless
(Vocals, songwriter, b. 1957)

The daughter of a coal miner, Loveless took her stage name from her first husband, Terry Lovelace, drummer with the Wilburn Brothers, with whom she toured. In 1985, after the marriage crumbled, she moved to Nashville and her first Top 10 single, 'If My Heart Had Windows' (1988), was a revival of a 1967 George Jones hit. She is married to producer/musician/songwriter Emory Gordy Jr. her 2001 album *Mountain Soul*, saw her revisiting her bluegrass roots and gaining considerable acclaim.

Lyle Lovett
(Vocals, songwriter, b. 1956)

Lovett's music spans folk, swing, jazz and country and has remained innovative since his eponymous 1986 album, which included his only Top 10 single, 'Cowboy Man'. Touring with his so-called Large Band, which features the talents of Victor Krauss (brother of Alison), cellist John Hagen and harmony vocalist Francine Reed, he has won four Grammy Awards. Highlights of his catalogue include his 1998 album *Step Inside This House*, a tribute to fellow Texas singer-songwriters.

Wheels And A Dozen Roses'. CMA Female Vocalist Of The Year in 1989 and 1990, Mattea has done much to expand country music's parameters.

The Mavericks
(Vocal/instrumental group, 1992–98)
The Mavericks released their debut album independently, and their major-label debut, *From Hell To Paradise* (1992), gave little hint of the success ahead, as CMA Vocal Group Of The Year in both 1995 and 1996. All have moved on to further ventures, but will be forever linked with the audience-pleasing band whose albums include *What A Crying Shame* (1994), *Music For All Seasons* (1995) and *Trampoline* (1998), which featured 'Dance The Night Away', their signature song.

Reba McEntire
(Vocals, b. 1954)
Multi-award winning Oklahoma-born Reba McEntire's introduction to country music came through singing as a teenager with her siblings, Dale (nicknamed Pake) and Susie, as The Singing McEntires. Red Steagall heard her sing the 'Star Spangled Banner' at the National Rodeo finals in 1974, and she signed to Mercury Records, where mostly minor hits ensued. Moving to MCA, 'Can't Even Get The Blues' (1983) became the first of over 30 No. 1s. CMA Female Vocalist Of The Year for four years and Entertainer Of The Year (1986), McEntire has also developed a career as an actress with starring roles in movies and on Broadway (*Annie Get Your Gun*) as well as her own high-rating sitcom, *Reba*.

Tim McGraw
(Vocals, songwriter, b. 1967)
Louisiana-born Tim McGraw moved to Nashville in 1989. His charisma brought him a record deal in 1993, and after several minor hit singles, he released 'Indian Outlaw', which was certified gold. McGraw has regularly crossed over to the *Billboard* pop chart, both solo and with his wife, Faith Hill. CMA Vocalist Of The Year in 1999–2000, his approach has recently become more creative and roots-based than ever before.

Allison Moorer
(Vocals, songwriter, b. 1972)
Moorer moved to Nashville after college and started songwriting after she met Oklahoma musician Doyle

Kathy Mattea
(Vocals, guitar, b. 1959)
Kathy Mattea joined bluegrass band Pennsboro as a student, before moving to Nashville. After working in Bobby Goldsboro's road show, she signed with Mercury in 1983. Her first two albums were only modest successes, but *Walk The Way The Wind Blows* (1986) included her first Top 3 single – a cover of Nanci Griffith's 'Love At The Five And Dime'. Her folksy style came to the fore on *Untasted Honey* (1987), which included her career song, 'Eighteen

'Butch' Primm, whom she later married. Moorer's debut
album, *Alabama Song* (1998) included 'A Soft Place To Fall',
as featured in the soundtrack to the movie *The Horse
Whisperer*. After four major-label albums, she was released
from her contract, and may have found a more appropriate
home with her album *Duel* (2004) on Sugar Hill.

Lorrie Morgan

(Vocals, b. 1959)

The daughter of country star George Morgan, Loretta Lynn
Morgan first performed at the age of 13 at the Grand Ole
Opry, which she joined in 1984. After two years singing
back-up for George Jones, and singing demos for
publishers Acuff Rose, she made her first Top 10 hit single,
'Dear Me', in 1989. A year after her first husband, Keith
Whitley, died, an electronically engineered duet between
them, 'Til A Tear Becomes A Rose', was 1990's CMA Vocal
Event Of The Year.

Daniel O'Donnell

(Vocals, b. 1961)

Irish-born O'Donnell has gained a large UK audience
through his easy listening-styled covers of sentimental pop
standards, Irish favourites and country ballads, since
signing with Irish label Ritz Records in 1986. In 1991, his
albums held six of the top seven positions in the UK
country chart, and his albums and singles have repeatedly
scored in the pop charts as well. His domestic live concerts
from the 1990s to date have invariably been sell-outs.

The O'Kanes

(Vocal/instrumental duo, 1986–89)

Frustrated by the Nashville system of the mid-1980s,
Kieran Kane (b. 1949) and Jamie O'Hara (b. 1950) worked
together as the O'Kanes from 1986–89, recording three fine
albums. Their six Top 10 singles in less than two years
included 1987's 'Can't Stop My Heart From Loving You',
their only chart-topper. Disillusioned with major labels,
Kevin Welch, Harry Stinson and Kane set up their own
label, Dead Reckoning, in 2000.

Rascall Flatts

(Vocal/instrumental group)

Leaning more towards pop, Jay DeMarcus (b. 1971) and
Joe Don Rooney (b. 1975) already knew each other when
they played a gig with Gary Levox (b. 1970), the second

cousin of DeMarcus, and the trio – 2002 CMA Horizon
Award winners – began. Songs like 'Bless The Broken
Road' and 'Fast Cars and Freedom' have almost become
mission statements and deliver music high on energy and
radio playlist-friendly.

Above
Allison Moorer has enjoyed
some success in Nashville.
Her star seems set to
continue in the ascendance.

the spirit and folklore of western cowboy songs – not least in their stage shows, which include expert yodelling – performing material associated with The Sons Of The Pioneers, Roy Rogers and Gene Autry in both an educational and entertaining fashion.

LeAnn Rimes

(Vocals, b. 1982)

Rimes' career in country music reads more like fiction than reality. Aged 13, she was riding high in the US country and pop charts with her first hit single, 'Blue' (originally recorded by her father at Norman Petty's studio in Clovis, New Mexico). Her 1996 album, also titled Blue, sold eight million copies. Her version of 'How Do I Live' (1997) spent 32 weeks at the top of the US pop chart, and her music has drifted away from country towards pop.

Above

Although The Riders In the Sky are often regarded as a novelty act, their music has kept alive some of the great traditions of country music.

Riders in the Sky

(Vocal/instrumental group, 1977–present)

Formed in 1977 by journalist and music historian Douglas Green (b. 1946), this trio (a quartet since 1988 when Joey Miskulin first played accordion with them) have kept alive

Ricky Van Shelton

(Vocals, b. 1952)

Virginia-born Shelton earned a dozen chart-topping hits from 1987 via his blending of country, rock'n'roll and gospel strains, often covering well-chosen older material,

Right

LeAnn Rimes released her first album, Blue, in 1994, when she was just 13 years old. Although her songs still retain a country flavour, they are now widely regarded as pop.

introduction ◉ **238** *influences & development* ◉ **240** *key artists* ◉ **246**

like his second No. 1, 'Life Turned Her That Way'. He won CMA Male Vocalist Of The Year in 1989. During the early 1990s he combined writing children's books, recording a gospel album and making such hit singles as his 1991 duet with Dolly Parton, 'Rockin' Years'.

Doug Stone
(Vocals, b. 1956)

Stone (born Doug Brooks) found little commercial success until 1990, but made up for lost time with a dozen Top 10 hits, including several No. 1s, with his new-traditionalist approach. 'I'd Be Better Off (In A Pine Box)' (1990) and 1991's 'A Jukebox With A Country Song' are among many tunes through which Stone, a genuine communicator, has touched the hearts of listeners.

Marty Stuart
(Vocals, guitar, mandolin, songwriter, b. 1958)

Aged only 13, Mississippi-born Stuart joined bluegrass legend Lester Flatt and Nashville Grass for six years until Flatt's death. After this he enjoyed a six-year spell in *The Johnny Cash Show*. His first significant solo album was *Busy Bee Café* (1982). The title track of *Hillbilly Rock* (1990) largely sums up his musical stance, especially when in 1992, he began working with rising star Travis Tritt. In 2005, Stuart – who has done much to promote Nashville music, released *Souls' Chapel* – the first album on his own MCA-connected label, Superlatone.

Pam Tillis
(Vocals, songwriter, b. 1957)

The daughter of songwriter Mel Tillis started performing at the age of eight, learning to play various instruments at Nashville's Blair Academy. In the late 1970s, she tried various musical ventures, before singing back-up in her father's road show in the 1980s and releasing five minor chart singles. Emerging country label Arista signed her and the spirited 'Don't Tell Me What To Do' (1991) was her debut Top 5 hit. Her vibrant vocal style was highlighted in 'Maybe It Was Memphis' (1992) and 'Cleopatra, Queen Of Denial' (1993).

Travis Tritt
(Vocals, guitar, b. 1963)

James Travis Tritt burst on to the country-music scene in 1989 with a Top 10 single, 'Country Club'. Utilizing strains of

southern rock and expressing emotions of everyday people, he gained an audience with such singles as 1991's 'Here's A Quarter (Call Someone Who Cares)', his second chart-topper, 'Anymore', and 'The Whiskey Ain't Workin'', a duet with his friend and touring partner, Marty Stuart. His guitar-fired approach to country themes has seen him earn his keep at both Warner Bros. and Sony, which he joined in 2000.

Above
Although he has yet to win the awards his success merits, Travis Tritt has already achieved much in country music.

Shania Twain
(Vocals, songwriter, b. 1965)

Twain's 1993 self-titled debut album little suggested the success that lay ahead. Record producer Robert John 'Mutt' Lange was an early supporter, and the two married six months after their first meeting. Massive sales followed, as her music was embraced by pop and she became more a pop diva than a Nashville country queen. Her albums sold in massive quantities: 1995's *The Woman In Me* sold 19 million copies, and 1997's *Come On Over* 34 million. She became a huge live attraction with all-action shows, which in 1999 alone grossed over $36 million.

his career, Clay Walker – whose 1993 debut single, 'What's It To You' topped the singles charts – has since occupied that position on more than 10 occasions. Without gaining the recognition he might have, the smooth-voiced ballad singer has remained a strong and consistent chart performer and is a good example of just how much talent is found in Nashville.

Gene Watson
(Vocals, b. 1943)

Texan Gene Watson started out in music at only 13 and recorded for local labels in 1965, but it wasn't until 1975 that 'Bad Water' became his first country chart hit, and the same year's 'Love In The Hot Afternoon' started a successful run of hits on Capitol and, later, MCA. He has continued to record on independent labels without letting his standards slip.

Above

Keith Urban was CMA Male Vocalist Of The Year in 2004 and 2005, when he also won the prestigious Entertainer Of The Year award.

Keith Urban
(Vocals, guitar, b. 1967)

New Zealand-born, Australian-raised, Keith Urban represents the slick, rock-slanted visual side of Nashville. In 1988 Urban formed a three-piece band in Australia and gained a good following, signing with EMI Australia in 1990 before making the leap to Nashville in 1992. There he formed The Ranch and signed with Capitol. His self-titled 2001 debut album included the chart-topping single 'But For The Grace Of God', and he has since regularly topped the singles chart.

Right

Clay Walker's early success was marred by his diagnosis with multiple sclerosis. He has continued, however, proving an inspiration to his country-music peers.

Clay Walker
(Vocals, songwriter, b. 1969)

Despite being diagnosed with multiple sclerosis early in

Keith Whitley

(Vocals, guitar, 1955–89)

Initially a bluegrass artist, Whitley began performing at the age of eight on the Buddy Starcher radio show from Charleston, Virginia. In 1970, Whitley and his friend Ricky Skaggs joined Ralph Stanley's Clinch Mountain Boys, and during the 1970s, recorded with J. D. Crowe And The New South. He turned to country music in 1983 and recorded an extended version of Lefty Frizzell's hit 'I Never Walk Around Mirrors'. 'Don't Close Your Eyes'– the title track of his 1988 album – was his first chart-topping single, but just as his career began, his tragic death occurred.

Hank Williams III

(Vocals, songwriter, b. 1979)

The grandson of the late Hank Williams and son of Hank Williams Jr. must have music in his genes, and like his forbears, Shelton 'Hank III' is a rebel. 1996's *Three Hanks* album featured his voice alongside those of his father and grandfather, and he realized that he would forever be judged as country. His debut solo album, 1999's *Risin' Outlaw*, featured songs by his friend, Wayne 'The Train' Hancock, and after personal problems, he returned in style with the alt-hillbilly *Straight To Hell* (2006).

Gretchen Wilson

(Vocals, songwriter, b. 1973)

Raised in rural Pocahontas, Illinois, Gretchen Wilson was one of the biggest acts to emerge on the country scene in some years. She moved to Nashville in 1996, where she eventually met John Rich, of singer-songwriters Big And Rich, and gave him a demo. This led to a deal with Epic, and two hit albums – *Here For The Party* (2004), which was certified quadruple platinum, and *All Jacked Up* (2005). Her good ol' girl image and attitude has seen her break down barriers, and pick up the Female Vocalist Of The Year Award, 2005.

Lee Ann Womack

(Vocals, b. 1966)

From a traditional/bluegrass background, Womack's self-titled debut album, rich in traditional sounds, was released in 1997, and included such hit singles as 'The Fool'. *I Hope You Dance* (2000) sold over three million copies and brought her CMA's 2001 Female Vocalist Of The Year Award, and more awards followed. After a change in her style, *There's More*

Where This Came From, the 2005 CMA Album Of The Year, was a refreshing return to traditional values.

Trisha Yearwood

(Vocals, b. 1964)

Trisha Yearwood initially moved to Nashville in 1985 to study for a degree in music management, but she ended up working as receptionist at MTM. When the label closed down in 1988, she worked singing demos and sessions. In 1991, her first single, 'She's In Love With The Boy', topped the chart, and her user-friendly vocal style has brought further chart success. She was CMA Female Vocalist of the Year in 1997 and 1998. Her 2005 album, *Jasper County*, features assistance from her current husband, Garth Brooks, repaying his debt for her work on his debut album.

Below

Lee Ann Womack has experimented with different styles since her first album was released in 1997. In recent years she has returned to more traditional country sounds.

Winter's Come & Gone:
Alternative Country & The Bluegrass Revival

hank Williams and George Jones would have found the whole notion of alt-country unfathomable. Why would anyone seek an alternative to bestselling country records? For these sons of dire southern poverty, the whole point of making country records was to sell as many as possible and maybe catch hold of the dignity and comfort that a middle-class life might afford. In fact, it was the hunger for such success that gave their early recordings such a compelling edge.

On the other hand, if you were Steve Earle, the son of a San Antonio air-traffic controller, or Lucinda Williams, the daughter of a Lake Charles English professor, middle-class life was already a given. What was most important to them – more important than the *Billboard* country charts – was the ability to express themselves as writers. And because their favourite writers included Bob Dylan, Townes Van Zandt and Johnny Cash, their preferred medium was not poetry or the novel but rather country songs. For them, alternative country was inevitable.

In parallel fashion, most of the bluegrass musicians born before 1950 clung to the format created by Bill Monroe because it represented – much like the church it so often celebrated – a rock of stability in a world of rural hardship. But many of the best young bluegrass pickers born after 1950 craved possibility more than stability, challenges more than tradition. Musicians such as banjoist Bela Fleck, mandolinist Sam Bush and dobroist Jerry Douglas wanted new chord changes, new rhythms. To find them, they created new-grass.

These three streams – the new-grass pickers like Fleck, the country rockers like Earle and the singer-songwriters like Williams – often overlapped, sharing stages and recording sessions. They varied a great deal – especially in volume – but they were united by a determination to pursue an artistic vision rooted in country music's past, even if it meant working at the margins of the current country-music marketplace.

Key Artists

Sam Bush & Bela Fleck

Kasey Chambers

Alison Krauss

Uncle Tupelo

Whiskeytown

Influences & Development

'It's like music theory, which was created to study what already was. Bluegrass exists, and since it's been around long enough there are people who want to talk about it.' **Bela Fleck**

Below

Country rocker Steve Earle emerged from prison to find a brave new world in country music. He became a role model for the aspiring young musicians of a new generation.

When Steve Earle (b. 1955) was released from prison on 16 November 1994, it had been four years since he had released a studio album and three years since he'd done a tour. During that time lost to heroin and crack, much had changed in the world of country music. The charismatic but mainstream-pop-oriented Garth Brooks (b. 1962) was setting new records for country sales and most of the other acts on the country charts were scrambling to imitate Brooks.

Role Models

Pushed aside in the excitement was the progressive-country movement of which the pre-prison Earle had been a part. Earle's heroes, Emmylou Harris (b. 1947) and Guy Clark (b. 1941), had already had their last Top 40 country hits, and so had such peers as Rosanne Cash (b. 1955), Rodney Crowell (b. 1950) and Lyle Lovett (b. 1957). The mainstays of the Outlaws movement – Willie Nelson (b. 1933), Waylon Jennings (b. 1937), Johnny Cash (1932–2003) and Kris Kristofferson (b. 1936) – would never again have a Top 40 single without the crutch of a duet with a younger singer. The movement seemed to have stalled.

Yet, as Earle began to reconnect with the music world, acquiring his first guitar in years and starting to play again, he found glimmers of hope. Several terrific female singer-songwriters had emerged: Lucinda Williams (b. 1953), Iris DeMent (b. 1961) and Mary Chapin Carpenter (b. 1958). Alison Krauss And Union Station, Mark O'Connor and Bela Fleck And The Flecktones were opening new territory for string-band musicians. Down in Australia, The Dead Ringer Band and Paul Kelly were putting their own spin on American country music.

Two Nashville couples – Buddy and Julie Miller and Gillian Welch and Dave Rawlings – were digging deep into traditional country with shovels sharpened by Townes Van Zandt-like songwriting. And several young rock bands that had found the punk format too constricting – most notably Uncle Tupelo, Blue Mountain, The Old 97's, The Jayhawks, The Bottle Rockets, Whiskeytown and The Blood Oranges – had reached out to country music as a vehicle for the same iconoclastic fervor. Many of these younger acts looked to Earle and his generation as role models.

Feeling Alright

Earle's first move after prison was to ease back into the spotlight with an acoustic string-band album. Bluegrass had been a purification rite for progressive-country musicians –

Earle's improbable resurrection from prison and addiction gave the whole alt-country movement reason for optimism. As if making up for lost time, Earle was suddenly everywhere. He and his co-producer, country veteran Ray Kennedy, formed The Twang Trust, which produced Lucinda Williams' 1998 *Car Wheels On A Gravel Road*, Jack Ingram's 1997 *Livin' Or Dyin'*, the V-Roys' 1996 *Just Add Ice*, Cheri Knight's 1998 *Northeast Kingdom* and a new Willie Nelson and Waylon Jennings version of Earle's 'Nowhere Road' for the 1996 reissue of *Wanted! The Outlaws*.

Earle hired the husband-and-wife team of Buddy and Julie Miller as the opening act and as supplemental Dukes for his 1997–98 tour, and sang harmonies on their 1997 albums: Julie's *Blue Pony* and Buddy's *Poison Love*. Earle and his partners Jack Emerson and John Dotson founded a new label, E-Squared Records, to handle many of these projects. Meanwhile, Earle's old colleagues from the 1980s – such as Harris, Crowell, Clark, Lovett and Cash – also found a new home in the alt-country camp.

Left
Mary Chapin Carpenter was once of the new breed of female singer-songwriters to gain much critical success from the 1990s.

Below
Like Mary Chapin Carpenter, Iris DeMent was a talented singer-songwriter. Her collaboration with Steve Earle in 1999 marked a key point in the resurgence of bluegrass.

a way to flush out trendy distractions and to reconnect with essential roots – ever since Emmylou Harris had made *Roses In The Snow* in 1980. Earle hired three of the best bluegrass musicians in Nashville – guitarist Norman Blake, mandolinist Peter Rowan and bassist Roy Huskey Jr. – to record 1995's *Train A Comin'* and finally fulfilled his dream of singing with Harris herself. Earle would return to bluegrass in 1999 by recording *The Mountain* with the Del McCoury Band and Iris DeMent.

But first, having regained his confidence, Earle made a very different album in 1996 – the loud, swaggering country-rock manifesto called *I Feel Alright*. Like the younger bands he admired, such as Uncle Tupelo and Whiskeytown, Earle believed country music's stories about outlaws, death, divorce and family could be strengthened rather that negated by a rock'n'roll rhythm section. Backed by his old producer Richard Bennett, Lucinda Williams and a new version of his rock'n'roll band, The Dukes, Earle confronted the self-destruction and personal betrayals of his lost years and found reason for optimism.

Right
Bands like Hüsker Dü were responsible for changing the style of rock and giving it a more country feel. The edges of many musical styles began to blur and country became cool.

Below
David Grisman plays country music in many forms – bluegrass revival, country-jazz and traditional folk.

Insurgent Country

It was as if they realized that progressive-country was never going to find a place on country radio again, so it needed to set up an alternative infrastructure of labels, production teams, collaborations, media and touring circuits. Whereas Willie Nelson and the Outlaws, and Emmylou Harris and her ex-band members, had invaded the country charts from the outside, this new movement was content to create its own small island between the large continents of country, rock'n'roll and bluegrass. All it needed was its own name.

Many names were proposed. Uncle Tupelo's 1990 debut album, *No Depression*, became the name of an Internet site and then of a magazine that championed this new movement; some people referred to the sound itself as 'No Depression' music. Kevin Welch named his 1992 album *Western Beat* after Europeans had described the music of Nashville's new renegades that way. Chicago's Bloodshot Records, home to many of these acts, labelled the sound 'Insurgent Country'. In 1995, the music-industry trade publication *Gavin* launched a chart for what it called 'Americana' music. When an advocacy group formed in 1999 to promote the music, they called themselves the Americana Music Association.

But the preferred term was alternative-country, a phrase that mimicked the alternative-rock label for the punk bands that languished outside the mainstream (languished, that is, until the 1991 breakthrough of Nirvana's *Nevermind* ushered punk into the mainstream; alt-country is still waiting for a similar event to render its label obsolete). Implicit in the phrase was a willingness to abandon dreams of big success with its attendant compromises in exchange for modest success with artistic freedom. Earle, for one, no longer tried to repeat the Top 10 success that his first three albums had found on the country charts; he satisfied himself with albums that sold 200,000 copies and tours that played small theatres and large nightclubs.

New-Grass

A much older musical label was new-grass, which came from The New Grass Revival, a band that debuted in 1972. The term 'new-grass' was soon applied to anything that might be called alternative-bluegrass, an umbrella big enough to cover two different impulses. One was the tendency by such acts as The Country Gentlemen, the Seldom Scene and J. D. Crowe to reach beyond the standard bluegrass repertoire and embrace contemporary material by such songwriters as Bob Dylan, Paul Simon and Johnny Cash and new songs in the same style. This led to less emphasis on flashy solos and standardized harmonies and more emphasis on song interpretation.

The other, seemingly contradictory impulse was the tendency by pickers such as Tony Rice (b. 1951), Mark O'Connor (b. 1961) and David Grisman (b. 1945) to push the instrumental dexterity of bluegrass beyond the simple chord changes and steady 4/4 rhythms of its past and into the ambitious harmonies and exotic rhythms of jazz, classical and Latin music. But because both impulses challenged the traditions of bluegrass, they both accepted the term new-grass, and because they both regularly collaborated with alt-country artists they accepted that label, too. In the 1990s, Alison Krauss spearheaded the song-interpretation school of new-grass, while Sam Bush and Bela Fleck, both alumni of The New Grass Revival, led the jazz-grass school.

At the other end of the decibel dial, a new kind of country-rock band emerged. Bands such as Uncle Tupelo, the Old 97's and Whiskeytown altered the country-rock recipe by fusing country not with jump blues as Elvis Presley (1935–77) had, not with folk-rock as The Byrds had, not with boogie blues as Lynyrd Skynyrd had and not with British Invasion rock as Earle himself had. Instead these new bands fused their newfound fascination for country music with their original enthusiasm for the punk-rock of the Replacements, R.E.M., Hüsker Dü and X. This recipe gave their country-rock a faster, noisier, more staccato sound than any country-rock that had come before.

But when these new bands claimed in interviews that Johnny Cash and George Jones were punk-rockers in spirit, they weren't kidding. Both Cash and The Replacements' Paul Westerberg would attack any subject with a ruthless honesty, an impatient growl and an unrelenting rhythm. It was that common spirit that these new bands were trying to capture. It was country music, but it was also something more. It was an alternative vision of what country could be.

Above
Paul Westerberg, formerly of The Replacements, forged a solo career that epitomized the alternative-country style of straight-talking, hard-thumping music that carried country into the new millennium.

O Brother, Where Art Thou? & The Resurrection Of Country Music

Right

Fiddle-player John Hartford was one of the many acts to perform on the film soundtrack for O Brother, Where Art Thou? – and take a share of its enormous success.

The most influential country act of 2001 was a band that didn't even exist. The Soggy Bottom Boys were the prime attraction on *O Brother, Where Art Thou?* the soundtrack album that topped the country and pop charts and sold more than four million copies. The group revived the late 1930s and early 1940s sound when old-time string-band music was morphing into bluegrass, but did so with a modern, whoop-it-up energy. One could hail the band's popularity as a triumph for tradition and authenticity – except for the fact that The Soggy Bottom Boys were an entirely artificial construct.

Men Of Constant Sorrow

Below

(L-r): John Turturro, Tim Nelson and George Clooney in the country-music phenomenon of the 1990s, the film O Brother, Where Art Thou?

The group was invented by Joel and Ethan Coen who wrote, produced and directed *O Brother, Where Art Thou?* a movie set in the late 1930s. Ulysses (George Clooney)

and his two sidekicks escape from a prison chain gang and wander around Mississippi, evading the law and trying to reach Ulysses' wife Penelope. The fugitives stumble across a rural radio station where they perform an impromptu version of the old folk song 'I Am A Man Of Constant Sorrow', uncannily anticipating The Stanley Brothers' arrangement of 1949. The song becomes a hit across the South, and the escaped prisoners have to don ridiculous fake beards when they perform in public.

Clooney didn't even sing the song; the vocals were supplied by Dan Tyminski, who was joined on the track by his fellow members in Alison Krauss And Union Station – Jerry Douglas, Ron Block and Barry Bales – as well as three members of The Nashville Bluegrass Band. On 'I'm A Man Of Constant Sorrow' and their version of Jimmie

Rodgers' 1928 song 'In The Jailhouse Now', The Soggy Bottom Boys invested these vintage numbers with a jumpy rhythm that sounded suspiciously like proto-rock'n'roll.

Musical Outlaws

Krauss sang 'Down To The River To Pray' by herself, 'I'll Fly Away' with Gillian Welch and 'Didn't Leave Nobody But The Baby' with Welch and Emmylou Harris. No one personified the artifice of *O Brother, Where Art Thou?* better than Welch. Though she was a middle-class daughter of California television writers, she fell in love with The Stanley Brothers and played old mountain instruments in anachronistic arrangements. But the songs she wrote and sang were starkly original and not at all derivative. She wasn't pretending to be someone she wasn't; she selectively borrowed from the past to make her own art more effective.

Like so much of the alt-country movement, these musicians were not so much interested in what really happened in the 1930s as in what should have happened; they created an imaginary past as a template for the future. By pretending that country music was once devoted to working-class geniuses who borrowed liberally from Celtic ballads, blues and swing tunes and turned the results into highly personal stories about work, death and marriage, the musicians and their fans were really proposing what the music could be now. After all, if three prison escapees and an African-American drifter could team up in the movie to defeat a corrupt governor and the Ku Klux Klan with a jump-blues version of an old mountain lament, why couldn't a new crop of musical outlaws overthrow country radio in real life?

Chart-Topping Success

It worked. Without any support from country radio, the soundtrack topped the country charts for nearly five months and led to a triumphant live tour that featured soundtrack participants such as Krauss, Tyminski, Welch, Harris, The Nashville Bluegrass Band, John Hartford, Chris Thomas King, The Cox Family, Norman Blake and The Whites, as well as natural allies such as Ricky Skaggs, Patty Loveless, Del McCoury, the Flatlanders, Rosanne Cash and Rodney Crowell. There was a live album called *Down From The Mountain*.

Suddenly everyone wanted to make a retro, acoustic album. Once it had been bluegrass acts who wanted to be country stars; now it was country stars who wanted to be bluegrass acts. In the wake of *O Brother, Where Art Thou?* Patty Loveless, Lynn Anderson and Jim Lauderdale all recorded bluegrass projects. They were all seeking the most authentic traditions of country music, even if they were inspired by a totally fictional band.

Below

Rodney Crowell participated in the O Brother tour. Although he did not appear on the film soundtrack, his sympathy with the bluegrass revival and the alt-country movement made him a perfect choice.

Sam Bush & Bela Fleck

Key Artist

'Variety within musical style has always been the thing that keeps me interested.... But the music has to come from bluegrass first.'

Sam Bush

Above

The New Grass Revival – Bela Fleck, Sam Bush and John Cowan – spearheaded the new-grass movement, even giving it its name.

In 1981, Sam Bush (mandolin, vocals, b. 1952) lost half of his band, The New Grass Revival, to road weariness. Courtney Johnson (banjo, 1939–96) and Curtis Burch (guitar, vocals, b. 1945) were exhausted by the tours with Leon Russell and the club and festival dates in between. So Bush and his remaining partner, John Cowan (vocals, bass, b. 1952) had to decide what to do: reinvent the band or fold up the tent.

A New Addition To New-Grass

It would have been a shame to give up. Ever since The Bluegrass Alliance renamed itself The New Grass Revival in 1971, it had been such a leader in progressive bluegrass that the movement eventually took its name from the band. Bush in particular had redefined the mandolin by

adapting fast fiddle solos to the instrument and by inventing rhythm figures that owed as much to Chuck Berry and Keith Richards as to Bill Monroe. To keep going, he'd need to find someone who had redefined another instrument in a similar way.

When Ricky Skaggs married Sharon White in 1981, a skinny, 22-year-old kid from New York City joined in the jam at the reception and played the banjo in a radically different manner. Instead of speeding up his licks as every other banjoist did, he slowed them down so he could explore melodies and harmonies those other players had never attempted. His name was Bela Fleck (banjo, b. 1959) and Bush immediately recruited him for The New Grass Revival.

With fourth member Pat Flynn (vocals, guitar, b. 1952), the revamped New Grass Revival flourished throughout the 1980s. The band struck an apt balance between the instrumental virtuosity of Bush and Fleck and the singing of the folk-flavoured Flynn and the R&B powerhouse Cowan. They became a favourite of folk and bluegrass festivals, signed with Capitol Records, and even placed five singles in the lower reaches of the country charts.

Solo Success

Meanwhile, Bush and Fleck became central figures in a Nashville community that was revolutionizing the possibilities of old string-band instruments even as they were being hired to play on mainstream country sessions. Other key figures included fiddler Mark O'Connor, guitarist Tony Rice, fiddler Vassar Clements, dobroist Jerry Douglas, guitarist Norman Blake, fiddler Stuart Duncan, mandolinist Ricky Skaggs and bassist Edgar Meyer. Out in California, similar experiments were being conducted by mandolinist David Grisman, fiddler Darol Anger, mandolinist Mike Marshall and fiddler Richard Greene.

These pickers dared to ask the questions: why limit these instruments to bluegrass? Why not also play Miles Davis' 'Solar', Sam And Dave's 'Hold On, I'm Coming', Bach's

Partita No. 3 and Bob Marley's 'One Love'? After all, the notes are there on our instruments; all we have to do is find them. Bush and/or Fleck would end up recording all those pieces and would inspire their peers to take similar risks.

These experiments reached a peak when Bush, Fleck, O'Connor, Douglas and Meyer, who had been playing at the Telluride Bluegrass Festival every year, challenged themselves to each compose one tune with each other member. The result was an exquisite chamber-bluegrass album, 1989's *The Telluride Sessions*, credited to Strength In Numbers. The promise of that project was further explored by Bush, Meyer, Marshall and classical violinist Joshua Bell on 1999's *Short Trip Home*; by O'Connor, Meyer and classical cellist Yo-Yo Ma on 2000's *Appalachian Journey*; and by Fleck, Meyer and Bell on 2001's *Perpetual Motion*.

When The New Grass Revival broke up in 1989, Flynn and Cowan both launched solo careers. Bush joined Emmylou Harris And The Nash Ramblers, the singer's string-band outfit, for six years before finally launching a full-time solo career. Fleck recruited Chicago jazz pianist Howard Levy and two Nashville funk musicians, bassist Victor Wooten and his brother Roy 'Futureman' Wooten (who played 'drumitar', a drum machine in the shape of a guitar) to form Bela Fleck And The Flecktones. Fleck was soon popping up in jazz magazine feature stories and polls, even though he played the most unlikely of instruments, the banjo.

Classic Recordings

The New Grass Revival
Friday Night In America (1989)
'Callin' Baton Rouge', 'Let Me Be Your Man', 'Angel Eyes', 'Big Foot'

Strength In Numbers
The Telluride Sessions (1989)
'Future Man', 'Texas Red', 'No Apologies'

Bela Fleck & The Flecktones
UFO Tofu (1992)
'Magic Fingers', 'The West Country', 'After The Storm'

Bela Fleck
Tales From The Acoustic Planet (1994)
'Up And Running', 'The Landing', 'In Your Eyes', 'System Seven'

Sam Bush
Glamour & Grits (1996)
'Same Ol' River', 'Brilliancy', 'All Night Radio'

Above

Banjoist and new-grass pioneer Bela Fleck plays with jazz musician Victor Wooton.

Left

Mandolin-player Sam Bush has enjoyed significant solo success since the demise of The New Grass Revival.

Key Track

'Big Foot' (1989)
This extended instrumental, composed by Fleck, demonstrated his determination and ability to pursue an intriguing theme through variation after variation, altering the melody and harmony with each turn. It was introduced by The New Grass Revival (with Bush playing snaking fiddle lines) on the 1989 album *Friday Night In America* and was revisited on Fleck's 1991 album, *Live Art*.

Kasey Chambers

Key Artist

'I only heard what Dad was listening to at the time.... Lucky he had good taste.'

Kasey Chambers

Below

Kasey Chambers has carried Australia's country-music tradition into the twenty-first century with her rock-crossover style.

It makes sense that Australia would be the one country outside North America to develop an important country-music scene of its own. Like the USA and Canada, Australia had a large, under-populated frontier that was settled by English, Irish and Scotch immigrants who brought their folk songs with them. Roughened and toughened by frontier life, those songs became country music. Australia lacked the African, German and Mexican influences that shaped American country music, but it had a strong oral-poetry tradition that led to the bush ballads, the down-under equivalent of cowboy songs.

Australian Alt-Country

Tex Morton recorded the first Australian country songs in 1936 in the style of his hero Jimmie Rodgers and became a big star in the 1940s. He was soon joined by a similar star, Buddy Williams. The giant of the bush balladeers was David Gordon 'Slim Dusty' Kirkpatrick, who first recorded in 1946 and released more than 100 albums. But it was an alt-country artist, Kasey Chambers (vocals, guitar, b. 1976), who finally enabled Australian country to cross over to the pop charts in the 1990s, a triumph that alt-country never tasted in the United States.

A few months after she was born, her bohemian parents Bill and Diane Chambers took Kasey and her older brother Nash out for a six-month fox-hunting trip on the Nullarbor Plain, an immense red-dirt desert in South Australia that resembles Mars more than anything near Sydney. It was a trip the family would take every year for 10 years, and every day after dinner, the family would sit around the campfire and sing songs by Bill's favourites: Bob Dylan, Johnny Cash, Buck Owens and Emmylou Harris. When the family finally settled down year-round in one place, they began performing the same songs in local clubs as The Dead Ringer Band.

Dead Ringers

Free of the usual influences, the four Dead Ringer Band albums sounded so fresh that they yielded a No. 1 country single and a slew of Best Country Group awards. As a singer and writer of transparently emotional songs, Chambers soon emerged as the family's most formidable asset. When her 1999 debut solo album, *The Captain*, won Album Of The Year from the Country Music Association of Australia, the sight of the spiky-haired, pierced Chambers accepting the award from the wrinkled patriarch Slim Dusty started a media buzz. The album jumped into the pop Top 10, went double platinum, won Chambers the Female Vocalist Of The Year ARIA Award (Australia's equivalent of the Grammies) and was released in the USA the next year.

Classic Recordings

The Captain (1999)
'Cry Like A Baby', 'The Captain', 'Don't Talk Back', 'The Hard Way'

Barricades And Brickwalls (2001)
'Not Pretty Enough', 'The Mountain', 'Still Feeling Blue'

Wayward Angel (2004)
'Pony', 'More Than Ordinary', 'Guilty As Sin'

Left
Vika and Linda Bull were taken under Chambers' wing, and she helped the act raise their profile by crafting some fine songs for the duo.

Chambers' second album, *Barricades And Brickwalls*, featured a duet with Australia's leading roots-rocker, Paul Kelly. Chambers and Kelly sang another duet on his bluegrass album, *Foggy Highway*, and she contributed a song to *The Woman At The Well: The Songs Of Paul Kelly*, an anthology of Kelly's songs interpreted by 16 different Australian women (including Slim Dusty's daughter Anne Kirkpatrick). The tunes deserved such treatment, for they were some of the finest English-language songs of the 1990s.

Also on that album were Vika and Linda – the Bull sisters who made several superb albums with help from Kelly's songwriting and production. Kelly also co-produced the 1990 debut album, *Charcoal Lane*, by Archie Roach, the most gifted singer-songwriter to emerge from the Aborigine community. Eric Bogle, a Scotch native who spent most of his life in

Australia, translated the country and folk impulses of his hero Woody Guthrie into such distinctly Australian songs as the anti-war classic, 'And The Band Played Waltzing Matilda'.

Australians such as Olivia Newton-John, Keith Urban, Diana Trask and Sherrie Austin found success in Nashville by imitating America's pop-country formulas, but the country music with the truest Australian character has been made by Slim Dusty, Paul Kelly, Vika And& Linda, Archie Roach, Eric Bogle and The Chambers Family.

Left
Paul Kelly alternated rock and country-folk projects with the same unpredictability and the same high quality as Steve Earle, Richard Thompson and Neil Young.

Key Track

'Cry Like A Baby' (2001)
When Chambers sings 'I don't hide my pain to save my reputation ... I still cry like a baby' her miraculous voice makes it a statement of both weakness and strength, implying that she is often overwhelmed by emotions but that she's brave enough to let them show in public.

Alison Krauss

Above

Alison Krauss began her musical career as a virtuoso fiddle player, and this is what her first record label thought they were getting when they signed her – until she opened her mouth and sang.

'It sounded like a drag ... so we recorded it.'

Alison Krauss

In 1995, Alison Krauss (vocals, fiddle, b. 1971) achieved a level of success no other bluegrass act had ever matched. Her 1995 retrospective album, *Now That I've Found You: A Collection*, went double platinum, and she won the CMA Awards for Single, Female Vocalist, Vocal Event and Emerging Artist as well as the Grammy Awards for Best Female Country Vocal and Best Country Collaboration With Vocals. If ever there was a time to walk away from small-label bluegrass and take a fling at major-label pop stardom, it was then.

An Inspiration For A Generation

She considered it. She talked to several record companies, but she soon realized that they all wanted her to abandon the very thing that had brought her such success: bluegrass. So she decided to stay on the small folk/bluegrass label where she had begun, Rounder Records. She would stick with the approach that was transforming bluegrass even as it was winning the genre unprecedented visibility.

When Rounder had first signed Krauss in 1986, she was a 15-year-old girl, an Illinois high-school sophomore with red curls and quick fingers who had won nearly every fiddle contest she entered. They thought they were signing a fiddle prodigy like Mark O'Connor, but when they asked her to sing a little on her first solo album, *Too Late To Cry*, she opened her mouth and out came a once-in-a-generation voice – a soprano that never lost its purity or power even as it softened with desire or twisted with heartache. To accommodate this gift, Krauss revamped the usual bluegrass procedure. Rather than emphasizing fast, hard picking and highly stylized harmonies, she stressed good songwriting, patient tempos and personalized singing. With her success, she inspired a whole generation of female bluegrass singers to take a similar approach – most notably Lynn Morris, Laurie Lewis, Claire Lynch, Alison Brown and Alecia Nugent.

Union Station

Krauss soon displayed a knack for unearthing gifted songwriters few people had heard of. She began with her Illinois neighbour and mentor, John Pennell, but soon dug up Todd Rakestraw, Nelson Mandrell, Sidney Cox, Mark Simos and Bob Lucas. These writers fashioned confessional monologues that sounded natural, especially when delivered with Krauss's effortless intimacy.

Her 1989 band Union Station included Pennell on bass, Jeff White on guitar and Mark Harman on banjo. By 1990, her band included banjoist Alison Brown, guitarist Tim Stafford, mandolinist Adam Steffey and bassist Barry Bales. Brown would go on to found the alt-country label Compass Records and to carve out a solid solo career. Stafford would go on to co-found the terrific bluegrass band Blue Highway with fellow singer-songwriter-guitarist Shawn Lane and dobro virtuoso Rob Ickes. Steffey went on to co-found the bluegrass band Mountain Heart.

By 1999, Union Station included Bales, Ron Block, Dan Tyminski (vocals, mandolin, guitar, b. 1967) and Jerry Douglas (dobro, b. 1956). Banjoist Block, a former member of the Weary Hearts and the Lynn Morris Band, evolved into a fine singer-songwriter, whose gospel material was recorded by Randy Travis, The Cox Family, Rhonda Vincent and Michael Smith. Tyminski, the lead singer for the Lonesome River Band and a solo artist, was one of the finest bluegrass singers of his generation. Block and Tyminski always sang several lead vocals in every Krauss concert.

Krauss called Douglas 'the greatest dobro player who has ever lived', and few would argue. The son of an Ohio steelworker, he joined The Country Gentlemen in 1973, joined Ricky Skaggs and Tony Rice in J. D. Crowe And The New South in 1974, co-founded Boone Creek with Skaggs in 1976, released his first solo album 1979, joined the Whites in 1979, became Nashville's dobroist of choice in the 1980s and 1990s, and joined Union Station in 1999. In every setting, he displayed not only speed and dexterity, but also the imagination to pull sounds and effects out of his instrument no one else had dreamed of.

Left
Krauss's voice – amazing as a teenager – has only got better as the years have passed, and she continues to be one of the leading lights of female country artists.

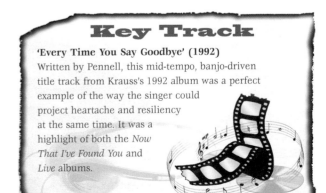

Key Track

'Every Time You Say Goodbye' (1992)
Written by Pennell, this mid-tempo, banjo-driven title track from Krauss's 1992 album was a perfect example of the way the singer could project heartache and resiliency at the same time. It was a highlight of both the *Now That I've Found You* and *Live* albums.

Uncle Tupelo

Above

The original Uncle Tupelo trio joined forces with several other musicians and the band morphed throughout its career, taking different names and with different line-ups.

The Belleville Trio

It was at Belleville West High School in 1984 that Jay Farrar (vocals, guitar, b. 1966) met Jeff Tweedy (vocals, bass, guitar, b. 1967) and drummer Mike Heidorn and formed a trio called Uncle Tupelo. At first they were a punk band, but eventually they incorporated the flavours of the country songs they had previously ignored when their parents and relatives played them on the radio. Farrar had a grainy, nasal baritone that resembled a brooding, hillbilly lament, and Tweedy had an experimental streak that combined acoustic and electric instruments in ways that altered the sound of each.

'I just try to get inside the song and imagine what comes next.'

Jeff Tweedy

Their 1990 debut album *No Depression* introduced Uncle Tupelo's surprisingly natural blend of country and punk-rock, a blend the band refined on 1991's *Still Feel Gone*. The third disc, *March 16-20, 1992*, was an all-acoustic affair produced by R.E.M.'s Peter Buck and named after how long it took to record. On 1993's *Anodyne*, the group (now featuring Farrar, Tweedy, drummer Ken Coomer, bassist John Stirratt and multi-instrumentalist Max Johnston) graduated to a major-label and enjoyed their biggest commercial and critical success yet. After a triumphant tour, they seemed on the brink of a big breakthrough when Farrar suddenly quit the band in 1994.

Farrar reunited with Heidorn and formed Son Volt, a band that isolated his hypnotically ominous, dirge-like contributions to Uncle Tupelo. Tweedy stayed with Coomer, Stirratt and Johnston and recruited guitarist Jay Bennett to form Wilco, a band that drifted steadily from alt-country to alt-rock. Wilco became a media sensation when its album *Yankee Foxtrot Hotel* was turned down by Warner Bros. Records for not being 'commercially viable.' When the band bought back the tapes and turned the album into a critical and commercial triumph in 2002, the story became the subject of a movie, *I Am Trying To Break Your Heart*, and a book, *Wilco: Learning How To Die*.

Belleville is a small town in downstate Illinois, south-east of St. Louis. Like a lot of mid-western towns, it was hit hard in the 1980s by the twin whammy of closing factories and faltering family farms. If punk-rock is the sound of factories and if country music is the sound of farms, it makes sense that a successful blend of the two would come out of a place like Belleville.

Guthrie's Legacy

But Wilco made its most important contribution to Americana when it rescued the lost lyrics of the original alt-country artist, Woody Guthrie. Guthrie had left behind thousands of pages of typed, scribbled and illustrated lines of verse with no music, and his daughter Nora Guthrie invited Wilco and British singer-songwriter Billy Bragg (vocals, guitar, b. 1957) to look through the papers and create new music and arrangements for the most promising items. The musicians found so much terrific material that they recorded not one but two albums: 1998's *Mermaid Avenue* and 2000's *Mermaid Avenue, Vol. 2*. Far from being a musty historical exercise, the results were funny, irreverent, sexy, bouncy and moving, a tribute to the living as well as the dead.

In some ways, however, the most important result of the Uncle Tupelo break-up was not Son Volt or Wilco but rather The Bottle Rockets, the band led by Uncle Tupelo's roadie and frequent sideman Brian Henneman. Unlike Farrar and Tweedy, whose songs tended to be cryptic and evasive, Henneman and his bandmates wrote anthemic choruses, crunchy guitar riffs and lyrics filled with startlingly sharp images, often about their hometown of Festus, Missouri. In other words, the Bottle Rockets had more in common with Neil Young and Lynyrd Skynyrd than with Leonard Cohen or R.E.M. and created two alt-country masterpieces: 1995's *The Brooklyn Side* and 2003's *Blue Sky*.

Classic Recordings

***No Depression* (1990)**
'That Year', 'Before I Break', 'No Depression'

***Still Feel Gone* (1991)**
'Looking For A Way Out', 'Fall Down Easy', 'True To Life'

***March 16–20, 1992* (1992)**
'Grindstone', 'Wait Up', 'Shaky Ground', 'Wipe The Clock'

***Anodyne* (1993)**
'Acuff-Rose', 'The Long Cut', 'Anodyne'

Left

After leaving Uncle Tupelo, founder-member Jeff Tweedy created Wilco with other former Tupelo members.

Left

Woody Guthrie has been adopted by alt-country artists as the father of their genre. Uncle Tupelo members in particular were greatly influenced by him, and created two albums of previously unrecorded material by the great man.

Key Track

'No Depression' (1990)
This obscure 1936 song from The Carter Family had the right mix of bleakness and hope to not only find a place on Uncle Tupelo's first album but to also become the title track. The album attracted so much attention that a website of the same name sprang up. Eventually the website became a magazine that explored all aspects of alternative-country and lent definition to the movement.

Whiskeytown

'It's awesome. They thought we were losing all our starters ... and we come back and we just show them that we all can do it.' **Ryan Adams**

Below

Fuelled by ambition, alcohol and insecurity Ryan Adams' spontaneity mesmerized audiences and collaborators but just as often it alienated them.

The Research Triangle, a cluster of three major universities (Duke, North Carolina and North Carolina State) in the Appalachian foothills, was a natural breeding ground for an alt-country scene, thanks to its rural Southern setting and its density of bohemians. It had been an outpost of the Georgia-centered alt-rock scene that had produced R.E.M., The Swimming Pool Qs, The B-52s, The

Connells, Let's Active and The dBs in the 1980s. But when a younger generation started adding twang to punk, the centre of gravity in south-eastern music shifted to the North Carolina towns of Chapel Hill, Durham and Raleigh.

Major-Label Success

The lively scene eventually produced such acts as Tift Merritt, The Backsliders, The Two Dollar Pistols, Hazeldine, Chatham County Line, Phil Lee, The

Accelerators, 6 String Drag, The Ruins, The Woods and Thad Cockrell. But one band dominated: Whiskeytown – and before long it seemed like half the musicians in the area had served time in the group. Whiskeytown was co-founded in 1994 by punk-rocker Ryan Adams (vocals, guitar, b. 1974) and bar owner/drummer Skillet Gilmore. Before long the line-up included grad-student bluegrass-lover Caitlin Cary (vocals, fiddle, b. 1968), roots-rock guitarist Phil Wandscher and bassist Steve Grothman.

The country leanings of Cary and Wandscher created an Americana frame for Adams' hot-wire tenor and undeniable rock'n'roll songwriting gifts. The results inevitably recalled Uncle Tupelo and its similar blend of influences, but there was a crucial difference. In contrast to the self-effacing demeanor of Tupelo's Jay Farrar and Jeff Tweedy, Adams was a charismatic rock star, an impulsive man-child who would do anything to grab the audience's attention.

Whiskeytown attracted national attention with an EP and the *Faithless Street* album in 1995 and the band signed with the major label Outpost/Geffen in 1996. By the time of the second full-length album, *Strangers Almanac*, there was a new drummer and bassist; soon after Mike Daly replaced Wandscher on lead guitar and a series of guitarists, keyboardists, drummers and bassists trooped through the ranks as Adams' behavior became ever more erratic. But the music remained at a high level, and the band recorded a third album, *Pneumonia*, although its 1999 release was delayed due to turmoil at Geffen and to turmoil within the band itself.

Solo Careers

Pneumonia was finally released in 2001, but by then Whiskeytown was history. Adams was preparing to release his second solo album, *Gold*, and Cary (now married to Gilmore) was preparing to release her debut album, *While You Weren't Looking*, after an earlier solo EP. It was Adams

who got the most attention – he seemed to be in *Rolling Stone* every other issue; he collaborated with everyone from Emmylou Harris to Beth Orton, and he befriended Elton John – but his best music was already behind him.

It was Cary, joining the country heartache of Patsy Cline to the British folk-rock of Sandy Denny, who captured the country-rock magic of Whiskeytown's best moments. Cary's solo and trio projects were produced by Chris Stamey (vocals, guitar, keyboards, b. 1954), former co-leader of the legendary, Beatlesque new-wave band, the dBs. Stamey released eight impressive solo albums and also produced, co-produced and/or engineered Whiskeytown's 1996 *Faithless Street*, the Backsliders' 1996 *From Raleigh, North Carolina*, the Two Dollar Pistols' 1998 *Step Right Up*, Thad Cockrell's 2003 *Warmth & Beauty* and Chatham County Line's 2005 *Route 23*. Stamey had the experience, the skills and the ears to hold the North Carolina alt-country scene together when it so often threatened to blow apart.

Classic Recordings

Strangers Almanac (1997)
'In Town', 'Yesterday's News', 'Houses On The Hill', 'Turn Around'

Pneumonia (2001)
'Reasons To Lie', 'Ballad Of Carol Lynn', 'Crazy About You'

Ryan Adams
Gold (2001)
'New York, New York', 'Wild Flowers', 'Firecracker', 'Goodnight, Holywood Blvd.'

Caitlin Cary
While You Weren't Looking (2002)
'Shallow Heart, Shallow Water', 'Sorry', 'Hold On To Me'

Above

In addition to her solo albums, Caitlin Cary spearheaded an all-female vocal trio, Tres Chicas (which also included Let's Active's Lynn Blakey and Hazeldine's Tonya Lamm), and a hard-country duo with Thad Cockrell.

Key Track

'Don't Wanna Know Why'
This song from Whiskeytown's final studio album was co-written by Adams, Cary and Daly and finds all three harmonizing sweetly on its country-lament melody. The lyrics are sad but the pop pleasures of the vocals and string-band backing suggest everything's going to be okay.

A-Z of Artists

Dave Alvin

(Vocals, guitar, b. 1955)

Dave Alvin did most of the Springsteen-like songwriting and his brother Phil Alvin (vocals, guitar, b. 1953) did all the lead singing for The Blasters, one of the best roots-rock bands of the '80s. Dave left to join X and then left that band for a solo career that increasingly emphasized the country side of his influences. His song about Hank

Williams' last ride, 'Long White Cadillac', became a Top 40 country hit for Dwight Yoakam. Alvin also produced alt-country projects for Sonny Burgess, Big Sandy And His Fly-Rite Boys, Tom Russell, The Derailers, Christy McWilson, Candye Kane and Katy Moffatt. Alvin's best solo albums were 1991's *Blue Blvd.*, 1994's *King of California* and 2004's *Ashgrove*, but the twangiest of Alvin's projects was the part-time band The Knitters, which also featured John Doe and Exene Cervenka of X.

Blood Oranges

(Vocal/instrumental group, 1990s)

Blood Oranges never sold many records, but they made two terrific albums (1990's *Corn River* and 1994's *The Crying Tree*) thanks to some smart songwriting, a savvy mix of bluegrass and British folk-rock and the contrast between fizzy male vocals and melancholy female vocals. The band was founded by Jimmy Ryan (vocals, mandolin, b. 1959), guitarist Mark Spencer and Cheri Knight in Boston in 1987, but drifted apart in 1995. Ryan formed such bands as Wooden Leg, Sunday's Well, The Pale Brothers and Hayride. Knight released two solo albums, including 1998's *The Northeast Kingdom*, co-produced by Steve Earle.

Iris DeMent

(Vocals, guitar, piano, b. 1961)

Iris was the youngest of 14 children in Paragould, Arkansas, and she grew up singing gospel and hillbilly songs in a loud, nasal voice. In 1987 she started writing smart, sharply sketched songs and sang them in her undiluted twang on 1992's *Infamous Angel* and 1994's *My Life*. Merle Haggard declared her the best singer he had heard in years, and she joined his band as a pianist for a few weeks and for his 1996 album. He recorded two of her songs and she recorded one they co-wrote on *The Way I Should*, her 1996 album that was as stirring in its denunciation of the now as her first two had been stirring in their evocations of the past. Then DeMent fell silent, due to a divorce and writer's block. She recorded some Grammy-award-winning duets with John Prine, released an album of old gospel hymns and married noted singer-songwriter Greg Brown.

Alejandro Escovedo

(Vocals, guitar, b. 1951)

Escovedo had played in the country-rock bands Rank And File and The True Believers, but his 1992 solo debut album *Gravity* unveiled an unexpected talent pursuing an unprecedented sound. Using acoustic guitar, steel guitar and cello to create the quiet intimacy of chamber music, his brooding original songs blended alt-country, Mexican folk music and punk-rock with arresting results. He pursued this distinctive blend, both in small combos and in string-laden big bands, on such remarkable albums as 1998's *More Miles Than Money* and 2001's *A Man Under The Influence*. His return in 2006 with *The Boxing Mirror* was universally welcomed.

Robbie Fulks

(Vocals, guitar, b. 1963)

Fulks was so good at writing traditional country song that he had a right to kiss off an uninterested Nashville with a profanity-laced song. But it was that uninhibited irreverence that put the alternative into Fulks' classic honky-tonk tenor and twangy tunes. He spent several years in the Special Consensus bluegrass band before settling in Chicago, where he recorded for the alt-country label Bloodshot. The results were so impressive that Geffen tried to turn him into a mainstream Nashville star in 1998. That led to the angry farewell and a more modest career as one of alt-country's most impressive talents, as displayed on such albums as 1997's *South Mouth* and 2005's *Georgia Hard*.

his bluegrass heroes Frank Wakefield and Red Allen in 1963 and joined their band in 1966. But the same curiosity that led him from Manhattan streets to Carolina hills also led him to improvising jazz and the exotic flavours of klezmer, Latin and swing. It became so difficult to untangle and isolate his many influences that he began to call his sound Dawg Music. The David Grisman Quintet was formed in 1976 and has ever since remained the model for anyone who wants to play acoustic instrumental music with both a love of tradition and the freedom to try new things.

Jayhawks
(Vocal/instrumental group, 1985–present)

The Jayhawks grew out of the same Minneapolis scene that produced Hüsker Dü and The Replacements, but the rock band led by Gary Louris (vocals, guitar, b. 1959) and Mark Olson (vocals, guitar, b. 1961) turned in a folkier, more country direction in reaction to their neighbours. After two small-label albums and two big-label albums gave them a high profile in the alt-country world and a low profile everywhere else, Olson left the band in 1995 to live in California with his wife, the noted alt-country singer-songwriter Victoria Williams. Louris carried on with the Jayhawks, veering into Beatles/Beach Boys pop-rock before returning to alt-country.

Above

The Jayhawks blend elements of country, folk and rock in their music. Despite renown in country-music circles, they have yet to come to the attention of the wider musical world.

Jon Dee Graham
(Vocals, guitar, b. 1959)

Graham was, like Alejandro Escovedo, an alumnus of The True Believers, who found in alt-country an effective catalyst for fusing his Mexican-American childhood and his punk-rock youth. With a rumbling baritone not unlike Tom Waits', Graham wrote haunting songs about real despair and possible redemption on such albums as 2002's *Hooray for the Moon* and 2004's *The Great Battle*. Graham was also a member of the legendary Austin band The Resentments with Stephen Bruton and Scrappy Jud Newcomb.

Jim Lauderdale
(Vocals, guitar, b. 1957)

Lauderdale pays his bills by writing hook-laden hits for mainstream-country performers such as George Strait, The Dixie Chicks, Vince Gill and Mark Chesnutt, but his own recordings reflect a penchant for traditional country and a quirky sense of humour that land him in the alt-country category. He grew up in South Carolina, obsessed with

David Grisman
(Mandolin, b. 1945)

Grisman was a city kid from New York who fell so deeply in love with the bluegrass music of Bill Monroe that he devoted himself to mastering his repertoire and his instrument, the mandolin. Grisman produced a record by

Right

Eclectic singer-songwriter Jim Lauderdale has co-written songs with Grateful Dead lyricist Robert Hunter, honky-tonk songwriter Harlan Howard, alt-country hero Buddy Miller and progressive-country producer Rodney Crowell.

bluegrass, and eventually recorded two albums with his hero, Ralph Stanley. Lauderdale's songs have been recorded by such alt-country acts as Shelby Lynne, Kelly Willis, The Derailers, Donna the Buffalo and Joy Lynn White. He was the first winner of the Americana Music Association Artist Of The Year Award in 2002.

Lonesome River Band
(Vocal/instrumental group, 1983–present)

The Lonesome River Band changed the direction of bluegrass when the quartet's 1991 album, *Carrying The Tradition*, turned away from the jazzy solos and folkie songwriting of new-grass to focus the hard-driving rhythms of Bill Monroe and Jimmy Martin with a rock'n'roll precision and energy. That album's line-up was mandolinist Dan Tyminski, guitarist Tim Austin, bassist Ronnie Bowman and banjoist Sammy Shelor, but the band's sound didn't change all that much when Tyminski was replaced by Don Rigsby and Austin by Kenny Smith. All but Shelor left in 2001, but the banjoist carried on with new pickers. Smith joined his wife Amanda in a new duo; Bowman pursued a pop-bluegrass solo career, and Rigsby emerged as one of the strongest bluegrass vocalists of the new decade.

Buddy Miller
(Vocals, guitar, b. 1952)

Miller is short and stocky, just like Buck Owens, and applies a similar thick hillbilly twang to similar down-to-earth, hard-country songs. Julie Miller (vocals, b. 1956) is as tall and willowy as Joni Mitchell, and writes the same sort of poetic, folk-rock songs for the same sort of reedy soprano. They make an unlikely couple, but even when they release solo albums, they help each other out with

songwriting, harmony singing, arranging and production. They met in Austin in 1976, played music with Jim Lauderdale and Shawn Colvin in New York in 1980, married in Waco in 1981, moved to California where Buddy played sessions and Julie recorded four Christian-pop albums and finally moved to Nashville in 1993 to record their remarkable run of secular alt-country albums.

Above

Buddy and Julie Miller's songs have been recorded by Lee Ann Womack, The Dixie Chicks, Patty Loveless, Brooks And Dunn, Emmylou Harris and Dierks Bentley.

Nickel Creek

(Vocal/instrumental group, 1989–present)

Nickel Creek gave a youthful jolt to the bluegrass scene when the charismatic, virtuosic group released its Alison Krauss-produced, eponymous 2000 debut album before half the quartet had turned 20. The band formed in 1989 when Chris Thile (vocals, mandolin, b. 1981) met the siblings Sara Watkins (vocals, fiddle, b. 1981) and Scott Watkins (vocals, guitar, b. 1977) at a weekly bluegrass show at a San Diego pizza parlour. Chris Thile was the standout soloist early on, and his father Scott Thile was the bassist until 2001, when he was replaced by Tony Rice veteran Mark Schatz. But the Watkins kids soon blossomed, and Nickel Creek's three albums plus its collaboration with Glen Phillips as The Mutual Admiration Society are all democratic collaborations that branch out into Anglo-Celtic folk music and chamber-folk instrumentals. Chris Thile has four solo albums, and Sean Watkins two.

Above

Nickel Creek's innovative sound has been described as 'polystylistic' by critics. Their music reflects their diverse influences, which include Bill Monroe, Bach, Radiohead and Pat Metheny.

Right

O'Brien loved his Irish heritage and recorded several albums of Irish folk songs. In every setting, he displayed understated skill and a contagious enthusiasm for acoustic music.

The Nashville Bluegrass Band

(Vocal/instrumental group, 1984–present)

The Nashville Bluegrass Band put the blues back into bluegrass with their frank borrowings from black gospel quartets and country bluesmen. The band was founded in 1984 by Alan O'Bryant (vocals, banjo, b. 1955), Pat Enright (vocals, guitar, b. 1945), Mike Compton (mandolin, b. 1956) and bassist Mark Hembree, with Stuart Duncan (fiddle, b. 1964) joining in 1986. Bela Fleck produced the group's 1985 debut which featured tight harmonies and Compton's Bill Monroe-like mandolin rhythms. A 1988 tour-bus crash forced Compton and Hembree to leave the group, replaced by Roland White (vocals, mandolin, b. 1938) and Gene Libbea (bass, b. 1953). This line-up won the International Bluegrass Music Association's (IBMA) highest honour, Entertainer Of The Year, in 1992 and 1993. White and Libbea were replaced by Compton and Dennis Crouch in 2000.

Tim O'Brien

(Vocals, guitar, mandolin, fiddle, b. 1954)

Tim O'Brien is a good example of the restless spirit that puts the new in new-grass. He first fell in love with bluegrass during his West Virginia childhood, and he led the 1978–90 Colorado new-grass band Hot Rize that also included Pete Wernick (banjo, b. 1946), Charlie Sawtelle (bass, guitar, 1946–99) and Nick Forster (bass, b. 1955); they were voted IBMA Entertainers of the Year in 1990. But O'Brien also loved mainstream country, so he had the members of Hot Rize adopt funny costumes and funny names and perform as Red Knuckles And The Trailblazers; O'Brien's songs would later be recorded by Garth Brooks, Kathy Mattea and The Dixie Chicks. His sister Mollie O'Brien (vocals, b. 1952) is a powerful folk and jazz singer who has recorded both solo albums and duo projects with her brother.

Mark O'Connor

(Fiddle, guitar, b. 1961)

O'Connor was a child prodigy who won the junior division of the National Old-Time Fiddlers Contest in 1974. Before he graduated from high school in 1979, he had won the all-ages Grand Masters Fiddling Championship and had released three albums for Rounder Records. Right after graduation, he joined The David Grisman Quintet for its tour with Stephane Grappelli. After a stint with the fusion band Dixie Dregs, O'Connor moved to Nashville and became a top session musician who played on 450 albums between 1982 and 1990, the year he won the first of six consecutive CMA Musician Of The Year Awards. Since 1990 he has concentrated on his solo recordings, branching out from new-grass to explore classical music (with Yo-Yo Ma among others) and swing jazz (with Wynton Marsalis among others).

Old '97s

(Vocal/instrumental group, 1993–present)

The Old '97s named themselves, when they formed in Dallas in 1993, after Johnny Cash's version of the 1906 train-wreck ballad, 'The Wreck Of The Old 97'. But the group's chief songwriters, Rhett Miller (vocals, guitar,

b. 1970) and Murry Hammond, seemed influenced as much by the pop-punk of The Replacements as by Cash or Gram Parsons. Miller had a knack for jangly melodic hooks, and those hooks were surrounded by country twang and punk momentum on early records such as 1995's *Wreck Your Life*. As the years wore on, though, the Old 97s became a good but more conventional rock band.

Above
Mark O'Connor brings an elegant bowing technique and a determination to push past clichés to bring something new to every project he takes on.

Above

Jason Ringenberg's strangled tenor initially put off radio, but his unflagging energy and imagination have endeared him to live audiences everywhere.

Jason Ringenberg

(Vocals, guitar, b. 1958)

Ringenberg is perhaps the only alt-country performer who actually grew up on a farm (his daddy raised pigs in Illinois) and that background lent a rural authenticity to his music, whether it was his Dylanesque solo projects or the revved-up rockabilly group, Jason And The Scorchers. That band came together in Nashville in 1981 and recorded three major-label albums.

Peter Rowan

(Vocals, guitar, b. 1942)

Peter Rowan was a member of Bill Monroe And The Blue Grass Boys from 1964 to 1967 and that stint gave him a solid, traditional foundation for everything he did after that, no matter how wild, whether it was the art-rock band Earth Opera (with David Grisman), the folk-rock band Sea Train (with Richard Greene), the new-grass band Muleskinner (with Clarence White), the jam-rock band The Rowan Brothers (with his younger brothers Chris and Lorin), the new-grass band Old And In The Way (with Jerry Garcia), the country-rock band Peter Rowan And The Free Mexican Airforce or the duo Peter Rowan and Tony Rice.

Rhonda Vincent

(Vocals, mandolin, b. 1962)

Vincent won six consecutive Female Vocalist Of The Year Awards (2000–05) from the IBMA for a reason. She has a high, lonesome voice reminiscent of bluegrass pioneers Bill Monroe and Jimmy Martin, and she pushes it ever forward with her hard, driving mandolin riffs. After her mid-1990s fling with mainstream country, Rhonda returned to bluegrass, the music she had played with her family's band growing up in Missouri. She assembled an old school, all-star band, The Rage, that proved the perfect setting for her flinty vocals. Their second album, 2001's *The Storm Still Rages* won her the IBMA's biggest prize, Entertainer Of The Year.

Tony Rice

(Guitar, vocals, b. 1951)

Tony Rice is one of the most inventive, elegant guitarists to emerge from the bluegrass community. As a teenager he was part of the California bluegrass scene with his brothers Larry and Wyatt, his hero Clarence White and his future collaborator Chris Hillman. Rice's virtuosity soon won him jobs with The Bluegrass Alliance, The David Grisman Quintet, J. D. Crowe And The New South and The Bluegrass Album Band. As an artist, Rice was a daring soloist, whether he was interpreting Bill Monroe or Miles Davis, but he was also a fine singer, especially when he interpreted Gordon Lightfoot. Since Rice's voice was disabled by dysphonia in 1993, he has concentrated on guitar picking, often in a duo with Peter Rowan.

Gillian Welch

(Vocals, guitar, b. 1967)

Gillian Welch met David Rawlings at Boston's Berklee School of Music, where most of their classmates were studying jazz and classical music. Welch and Rawlings were drawn instead to lyric-heavy songwriting and concluded that Appalachian string-band music would be the best vehicle for those songs. It was a foreign tradition for them, but they mastered it, settled in Nashville, founded their own record company and released a series of brilliant albums under Welch's name, most notably 1996's *Revival* and 2001's *Time (The Revelator)*.

Lucinda Williams
(Vocals, guitar, b. 1953)
Williams began as a blues revivalist on Woody Guthrie's old label, Folkways, releasing an album of standards in 1979 and an album of originals in 1980. But it wasn't until she formed a partnership with guitarist-producer-arranger Gurf Morlix that her

songwriting and singing became more focused and country in style. Their 1988 album together, *Lucinda Williams*, was her peak achievement. Its country credentials were certified when two of the songs were later turned into Top 10 hits by Patty Loveless ('The Night's Too Long') and Mary Chapin Carpenter ('Passionate Kisses'). Williams made two more superb albums, 1992's *Sweet Old World* and 1998's *Car Wheels On A Gravel Road*, before splitting with Morlix and losing her momentum.

Left
Gillian Welch's songs have been recorded by Emmylou Harris, Alison Krauss, Kathy Mattea, The Nashville Bluegrass Band, The Nitty Gritty Dirt Band, Ryan Adams and Tim O'Brien.

Below
Lucinda Williams garnered something of a cult following in her heyday, but her popularity waned after her split from producer Gurf Morlix.

Instruments & Equipment

from its roots, country music has been associated with simplicity – in melody, in subject-matter and in instrumentation, and it is this that has perhaps ensured its longevity. However, all good musicians make their craft look simple, and the history of country music is packed with virtuosos, from the pioneering banjoist Earl Scruggs, through Bill Monroe's unmistakable bluegrass fiddle, to the masterful guitar-playing of Chet Atkins.

Country music has come a long way since the banjo-on-the-porch days of early hillbilly, but many musicians have remained true to the early sound. Instruments that seem to have an ill-defined place in other types of music have come to characterize the country strain. One of the earliest and most enduring of these is the banjo – that homely mainstay of early vaudeville that is one of the most recognizable sounds in country recording. It has survived and been given a new lease of life in the talented hands of The Dixie Chicks. And where, of course, would country music be without the guitar? Acoustic or electric, from its Spanish origins, and brought into the limelight by The Carter Family, many country musicians since then have made it their own. The recording pioneers such as Eck Robertson and John Carson made their names on the ubiquitous fiddle – an instrument that lends itself equally to the soaring melancholy of a ballad or the toe-tapping lilt of Western swing.

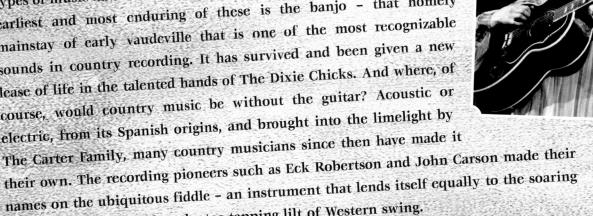

Alongside these staples stands a host of other instruments – from the piano, drums and mandolin to the dulcimer, washboard and harmonica – that have seen periods of popularity and decline during the ebb and flow of changing country styles.

Country Music Instruments

Banjo

The banjo is a refinement of an instrument brought to the Americas by slaves from West Africa. Banjos were often used in early twentieth-century minstrel and vaudeville shows, but more as a comic prop than a serious musical instrument. Pete Seeger and other artists in the forefront of the 1950s folk-music boom were crucial in raising this instrument's profile. Around the same time, banjo master Earl Scruggs, playing first with Bill Monroe's Blue Grass Boys and later with guitarist Lester Flatt, as Flatt And Scruggs, developed an intricate, three-finger picking style. In so doing, Scruggs raised banjo-playing to a new level of virtuosity and established the instrument's importance in bluegrass music. More recently it made a return to mainstream country in The Dixie Chicks' lineup, as played by Emily Robinson.

Mandolin

An off-shoot of the lute, the mandolin assumed its present-day eight-string form in early eighteenth-century Italy. The Gibson Guitar Company's early 1920s introduction of the F-series mandolin, with its enhanced tone and volume, laid the groundwork for the mandolin's rise in traditional country and bluegrass music. It was Kentucky-born Bill Monroe, often lauded as 'the father of bluegrass music', who thrust the mandolin to the forefront as a rhythmic and lead instrument when he began accompanying himself with mandolin on the Grand Ole Opry. Monroe's universally imitated, aggressive, chopping rhythmic style and flurry-like lead picking set the standards followed by more recent bluegrass mandolin virtuosos – Jesse McReynolds, Bobby Osborne, David Grisman, John Duffey and Ricky Skaggs, among them.

Piano

A popular nineteenth-century parlour instrument in the USA, pianos have been present in country music from its inception. Old-time string bands often relied on piano for its bright rhythmic and percussive tonalities. The advent of Western-swing music in the southwestern USA in the early 1930s also gave rise to influential country piano players such Al Stricklin, who played with Bob Wills And His Texas Playboys, and Moon Mullican, a member of Cliff Bruner's band and later a solo artist and Grand Ole Opry member.

Beginning in the early 1950s, piano thumper Del Wood was also a long-time favourite on The Grand Ole Opry. During that same decade, session pianist Harold Bradley enlivened many Nashville recording sessions. And in the 1960s and 1970s, Floyd Cramer played on hundreds of Nashville sessions, had several instrumental solo hits and developed a distinct 'slip-note' style that became almost synonymous with the Nashville Sound. Hargus 'Pig' Robbins was Nashville's most celebrated keyboardist in the 1970s and 1980s. Jerry Lee Lewis, Charlie Rich, Ronnie Milsap, Mickey Gilley and Gary Stewart are among the popular recording artists of the 1960s, 1970s and 1980s who accompanied themselves on piano rather than guitar.

Dobro

The dobro has often served as a bluesy supplement or substitute to the pedal steel guitar in country music. The dobro was invented in 1926 by the Dopyera brothers, who were experimenting with mechanically amplifying the acoustic guitar. The dobro was first established in country music by Cliff Carlisle, who played the instrument on some of Jimmie Rodgers' recording sessions in the late 1920s, and by Roy Acuff, the Grand Ole Opry headliner who featured dobro-players in his band during the 1930s and 1940s. It was Burkett 'Uncle Josh' Graves who largely redefined the dobro as both a lead and rhythmic instrument in bluegrass during the early 1950s when he played dobro with Flatt And Scruggs, a definitive 1950s bluegrass ensemble.

Fiddle

This ancient instrument has been popular in the USA since Colonial times and has always been at the centre of country music. In the early 1920s the very first country records were made by old-time fiddlers John Carson and Eck Robertson. In the 1920s and 1930s

Bob Wills and other pioneers of Western-swing music in the southwestern USA made the fiddle (often two fiddles playing in unison, named 'twin fiddle') an essential ingredient of their sophisticated music. The fiddle was also front and centre in honky-tonk music as it emerged full-blown in the late 1940s and early 1950s. In the late 1940s, Kentuckian Bill Monroe also enlarged the fiddle's influence by making it as crucial to bluegrass music as it had been in bluegrass' antecedent, mountain string-band music.

Guitar

The romantic image of the solo singer with guitar is central to country music mythology. Even so, the guitar lagged far behind the banjo, lute and mandolin in popular usage until as recently as the 1920s. Jimmie Rodgers (who played a Martin guitar) and Mother Maybelle Carter of The Carter Family (who strummed a Gibson) were largely responsible for establishing the guitar at the forefront of country when they played this instrument on their seminal 1920s recordings. In 1950, California guitar maker Leo Fender introduced the solid-body electric guitar which, with its enhanced volume and sustain, could hold its own among the other basic country ensemble instruments. Within a few years electric guitars were being used widely on Nashville recording sessions. Landmark masters such as Chet Atkins, Hank Garland, Harold Bradley and Don Rich would further refine and expand the role of the guitar in country music in the 1950s and 1960s.

Steel guitar

The modern pedal steel guitar first appeared in the late 1930s. It was the invention of Alvino Rey, a musician who invented the pedal steel as a radical enhancement of the non-pedal, lap steel guitars popular during the 1920s. The addition of pedals allowed for smooth modulation of both chords and individual strings. Speedy West, a California steel player, pioneered the pedal steel in country music using his custom-designed, three-neck, four-pedal instrument on many West Coast country recordings. Nashville session player Bud Isaacs raised the pedal steel's profile higher and inspired numerous imitators

when he featured the instrument on the 1954 Webb Pierce hit, 'Slowly'. Pete Drake, Buddy Emmons, Shot Jackson, Ralph Mooney and Lloyd Green were also widely acknowledged masters of the pedal steel.

Bass

The one-string washtub base was a key ingredient in 1930s mountain string-band and jug-band music (and made a brief reappearance in the mid 1950s' skiffle movement, a British country music hybrid). The four-string, acoustic, stand-up bass (often called the 'bull fiddle') was popular in 1940s and early 1950s country and honky-tonk music and is still widely used in bluegrass and acoustic country music. In the early 1950s, California guitar maker Leo Fender introduced the four-string electric bass, which is almost identical in design to a solid body electric guitar. With its enhanced sound and easy portability, the four- and five-string electric bass soon became a staple in country bands and on country recording sessions, as it remains today. During the late 1950s and 1960s, the six-string 'tic tac' bass, with its distinctive, softly percussive clicking sound, was often utilized in Nashville Sound-style arrangements.

Drums

As recently as the 1950s, drums were disdained by many country musicians who considered them too loud or too rock'n'roll. With only a few begrudging exceptions, drums were forbidden on the hallowed stage of the Grand Ole Opry. But by the 1960s, as electrification gradually became the norm for contemporary country music, more and more singers began relying on drums to enhance rhythmic percussion and their live and recorded music. Still, as a rule, drums tend to play a more subdued role in country music's overall mix than in rock'n'roll.

Though less central to the overall sound, the accordion, dulcimer, autoharp, zither and harmonica are among the other instruments often featured in country music for artists in search of a more exotic or old-timey musical feel.

Glossary

A capella Sung without any instrumental accompaniment.

A&R Artists and Repertoire – the department (or representative of the department) of a record company that finds new artists and songs and oversees their production.

African-Americans Also known as Afro-Americans or Black Americans; an ethnic group in the USA whose ancestors, usually in predominant part, were indigenous to Sun-Saharan and West Africa.

.alt-country Alternative country music – music considered to be outside the mainstream of the typical country-music style found on country radio stations and in the country charts.

Arpeggio Playing tones separately in rapid succession, rather than at the same time.

Arrangement The reworking or recomposing of a musical composition or some part of it (such as the melody) for a medium other than that of the original.

Bakersfield Sound The style of country music that developed in Bakersfield, California as part of the West Coast scene in the 1950s.

Ballad Properly, a sentimental love song; also used in reference to any slow piece.

Barn dance A variety radio show that spotlighted country artists. Shows included the *Grand Ole Opry, Louisiana Hayride, Big D Jamboree, National Barn Dance, Renfro Valley Barn Dance* and *WWVA Jamboree.*

Bluegrass A style of country music originating in the South, usually played on fiddle, banjo, guitar or mandolin. Bluegrass often involves improvisation and was named after Bill Monroe's Blue Grass Boys, the band that pioneered the style.

Blues Most commonly, a musical form consisting of a repeated 12-bar pattern with standardized harmony; also a melodic style and a particular mood.

Border radio High-powered radio stations situated in the north of Mexico aimed at US listeners and broadcast in English.

Broadside An advertisement intended for broad distributions. Musical broadsheets are often printed on a single sheet of paper or in leaflet form.

Cajun A native of Louisiana descended from French Canadians. Cajun music usually features fiddle and accordion.

Cantata A composition, often from the Baroque era, comprising solos, duets and choruses, accompanied by orchestra or keyboards. Cantatas can be sacred or secular.

Chord A group of two or more notes sounded simultaneously. There are many descriptors that can be attached to 'chord' to indicate the notes included, for example, 'added sixth chord').

CMA Country Music Association, founded in 1958 as an organization intended to promote and raise awareness of country music. Presidents of the CMA have included famous country-music stars such as Gene Autry, Ken Nelson and Tex Ritter. It presents an annual awards show.

Composition The act of creating a piece of music, and the product of that process.

Conjunto A style of Latin-American music that originated in the Texas border region.

Counterpoint Meaning 'point against point', the art of composing two or more melodic lines.

Country rock A mixture of country and rock music, pioneered in the 1960s by the likes of Gram Parsons and Bob Dylan.

Countrypolitan Another expression for the Nashville Sound – the style of country music that grew out of Nashville, Tennessee in the 1950s.

Cover A version of a song that has previously been recorded by another artist.

Creole Ill-defined term often referring to descendants of French and Spanish settlers in the southern USA and Louisiana in particular. Used by several early country and jazz bands made up of Creole musicians from New Orleans.

Crossover A song that achieves popularity among country-music fans, and fans of other types of music, particularly pop music. Often crossover hits gain a place in both the country and popular-music charts.

Demo A recording intended to showcase the talents of a musician, singer or group to a record producer rather than being released to the general public.

Event song A song, usually a ballad, that took as its subject-matter actual news events of the day such as murders or train wrecks.

Folk music A term that has no clear definition but essentially refers to the traditional music of an indigenous population. Generally lacks an identifiable composer, is passed on aurally (i.e. not notated) and is performed by non-professionals.

Frolic Social gathering where light entertainment and music were performed.

Gospel music Religious songs deriving from evangelical Protestant groups in the USA, both white and African-American, that came to prominence in the early twentieth century. African-American gospel music had a profound influence on country music.

Grace notes Musical notes added as an embellishment rather than part of the main (rhythmic) music.

Grand Ole Opry The best-known and longest-running radio barn dance, broadcast on Saturday nights from Nashville's WSM radio station.

Harmony The combining of a succession of chords to produce a harmonic progression. There are systems governing such progressions, which help to create recognizable harmonic structures.

Hillbilly Style of country music characterized by acoustic instruments such as the guitar, banjo and fiddle from the 1920s – in essence the original country music, which changed its name around the 1940s.

Hoe-down The music played for a square dance (or the dance itself) – a style of country music.

Honky-tonk Style of country music originating in Texas in the 1930s and popular throughout the 1940s, characterized by a louder, heavier beat than traditional country music of the time.

Improvise To invent with little or no preparation.

Jazz A style of music characterized by rhythmic syncopation, repeated harmonic structures and improvisation that has its roots in performing conventions brought to the USA by African-Americans.

Jig A lively dance or the music for such a dance, usually in triple time.

Louisiana Hayride A radio barn dance broadcast from Shreveport, Louisiana. Its heyday was between 1948 and 1960.

Lyrics The words written for a song.

Medley A composition made up of an assortment of songs or musical pieces of various styles and sources.

Melody An organized group of pitches, each sounded subsequently.

Minstrel show An indigenous form of American entertainment consisting of comic sketches and songs performed by actors in blackface.

Music Row A region in Nashville that houses most of the city's music businesses. It is the heart of the country-music industry.

Nashville Sound The style of music that arose in Nashville, Tennessee in the 1950s. Nashville Sound disposed of the honky-tonk nature of traditional country music and moved towards the song structures enjoying success in the pop charts of the time.

Neo-Traditional A style of country music that reverts back to the ethos of original country music.

Newgrass Progressive bluegrass music that incorporates elements of other musical styles.

Notation A means of describing musical sounds visually through symbols representing instructions to the performer.

Note Specifically, the graphic representation of a sound; also used in reference to the sound itself.

Old-timey A term used to describe the 'original' country music of the 1920s and 1930s.

Outlaws A group of country musicians who broke free from the traditional constraints of the genre and added elements of rock and other modern musical style to their form of country.

Picking Playing an acoustic guitar with a pick.

Pitch The quality of a sound that fixes its position in a scale. Sounds that do not belong in a scale (usually percussive sounds) are said to be unpitched.

Pop Applied to a particular group of musical styles that are popular. As a result, the term is subject to constant redefinition.

Progression See *Harmony*

Psalter A prayer book containing the psalms from the Bible.

Ragtime A style of music popular in America between the 1890s and 1920s. Most often played on the piano, it is distinguished by a syncopated (or 'ragged') melody, set against a straight-moving bass.

Recording Used to refer to any method of storing visual images and/or sound. Audio recording was invented in 1877 by Thomas Edison.

Reel An American country dance (also known as the Virginia reel).

Rhythm The variation in the duration of sounds in time. The perception of rhythm in music is related to the use of metre and pulse.

Riff A short, recognizable phrase. Also a pre-prepared melodic phrase used in improvisation.

Rockabilly A style of country music characterized by a strong rhythm and incorporating elements of blues and bluegrass. Rockabilly is largely associated with the early music of Elvis Presley, and paved the way for the rock'n'roll revolution.

Scale A sequence of notes arranged in ascending or descending order of pitch.

Shape-notes A system of music notation designed to help choral singing, in which the shape of the note indicates its pitch.

Standard A tune that has become established in the country-music repertoire.

Swing A style of jazz from the 1930s, characterized by big bands, solo improvisation and strong rhythmic pulse. A rhythmic manner of playing first heard in the swing style.

Syncopation The effect of rhythmic displacement through accents on weak beats or in between beats.

Tex-Mex Music that blends the influences of Mexico and the southern USA, particularly Texas.

Tin Pan Alley Originally an area in New York City in which exponents of the music industry – producers, composers and publishers – ran their businesses.

Vaudeville Originally a satirical French song. In the nineteenth century it came to indicate a musical comedy or music-hall variety show.

Virtuoso An instrumentalist or singer (or indeed any craftsman) of extraordinary technical skill.

Western swing A style of country music with strong jazz and blues influences that saw it achieve great popularity in the dancehalls of the 1930s and early '40s.

1930s–1960s	Acuff, Roy	Old-Timey, traditional	Vocals, fiddle	Tennessee, USA
1990s–	Adams, Ryan	.alt-country, Country-rock	Vocals, songwriter	North Carolina, USA
1970s–1990s	Adcock, Eddie	Bluegrass	Banjo	Virginia, USA
1990s–	Adkins, Trace	New Country	Vocals	Louisiana, USA
1990s–	Akins, Rhett	Neo-traditional	Vocals, Songwriter	Georgia, USA
1970s–	Alabama (Randy Owen, Teddy Gentry, Jeff Cook, Mark Herndon)	Urban Cowboy, Country-rock	Vocals, guitar, songwriter (Owen), vocals (Gentry), vocals, songwriter, various instruments (Cook), drums (Herndon)	Alabama, USA
1960s–1970s	Alan, Buddy	Bakersfield, Honky-Tonk	Vocals, songwriter	California, USA
1980s–1990s	Alger, Pat	New Country	Songwriter, guitar	USA
1990s–	Allan, Gary	New Country, Neo-traditional	Vocals	California, USA
1980s–1990s	Allen, Deborah	Urban Cowboy	Vocals	Tennessee, USA
1990s–	Allen, Harley	New Country	Songwriter	Ohio, USA
1910s–1930s	Allen, Jules Verne	Cowboy Songs	Vocals	American
1950s–1990s	Allen, Red	Bluegrass	Vocals, guitar	Kentucky, USA
1940s–1970s	Allen, Rex	Cowboy Songs	Vocals, guitar	Arizona, USA
1970s–1980s	Allen Jr., Rex	Country-pop, Cowboy	Vocals, guitar	Illinois, USA
1940s–1960s	Allen, Rosalie	Cowboy Songs	Vocals, guitar	Pennsylvania, USA
1970s–1990s	Allen, Terry	.alt-country, Country-rock	Songwriter	Texas, USA
1920s–1940s	Alley, Shelly Lee	Western Swing	Vocals, bandleader, songwriter	Texas, USA
1980s–	Alvin, Dave	.alt-country	Songwriter, producer	California, USA
1970s–	Amazing Rhythm Aces (Jeff Davis, Butch McDade, Russell Smith, Billy Earheart, Barry Burton, James Hooker)	Country-rock	Bass (Davis), drums (McDade), guitar, vocals (Smith), keyboard (Earheart), dobro (Burton), piano (Hooker)	Tennessee, USA
1960s–	Anderson, Bill (born James William Anderson III)	Nashville Sound	Vocals, guitar, songwriter	South Carolina, USA
1970s–	Anderson, John	Outlaw, Honky-Tonk	Vocals	Florida, USA
1960s–	Anderson, Lynn	Nashville Country-pop	Vocals	North Dakota, USA
1980s–1990s	Anderson, Pete	West Coast	Guitar	Michigan, USA
1940s–1990s	Arnold, Eddy	Traditional, Nashville Sound, Cowboy Songs,	Vocals	Tennessee, USA
1970s–2000s	Asleep At The Wheel	Western Swing	Vocals, various instruments	Texas, USA
1940s–1960s	Atcher, Bob	Cowboy Songs, Old-Timey	Vocals, banjo, guitar	Tennessee, USA
1940s–1990s	Atkins, Chet	Nashville Sound	Guitar, vocals, producer	Tennessee, USA
1990s–	Austin, Sherrie	New Country	Vocals, songwriter	Sydney, Australia
1920s–1960s	Autry, Gene	Old-Timey, Cowboy Songs	Vocals	Texas, USA
1970s–1990s	Axton, Hoyt	Country-rock, Contemporary	Vocals, guitar, songwriter, actor	Oklahoma, USA
1990s–	Azar, Steve	New Country	Guitar	Mississippi, USA
1940s	Bailes Brothers	Traditional	Vocals, various instruments	West Virginia, USA
1940s–1950s; 1970s–1980s	Bailey Brothers, The (Charlie & Danny)	Bluegrass, Old-Timey	Mandolin (Charlie), guitar & vocals (both)	Tennessee, USA
1950s–1980s	Baker, Kenny	Bluegrass	Fiddle	Kentucky, USA
1980s–	Ball, David	New Country	Vocals, Guitar	South Carolina, USA
1970s–1990s	Bandy, Moe	Honky-Tonk, Cowboy Songs	Vocals	Mississippi, USA
1940s–1980s	Banes, Tex	Old-Timey	Vocals, guitar	Australia
1950s–1980s	Bare, Bobby	Nashville Sound, Outlaw	Guitar, vocals	Ohio, USA
1980s–	Barnes, Max D.	New Country, Neo-traditional	Songwriter	Iowa, USA
1990s	Barnett, Mandy	New Country, Neo-traditional	Vocals	USA
1930s–1990s	Bashful Brother Oswald	Old-Timey	Dobro, banjo, vocals	USA
1960s–2000s	Begley, Philomena	Traditional country, Irish	Vocals	Ireland
1970s–	Bellamy Brothers, The (Howard & David)	Country-rock, Country-pop	Guitar, banjo, mandolin (Howard), piano, accordion, fiddle, banjo, mandolin (David)	Florida, USA
2000s	Bentley, Dierks	Neo-traditional	Vocals guitar, songwriter	Arizona, USA
1990s	Berg, Matraca	New Country	Songwriter, vocals	USA
1960s–1990s	Berline, Byron	Bluegrass	Fiddle	Oklahoma, USA
1990s–	Berry, John	New Country	Vocals	Georgia, USA
1990s–	Big House (Monty Byrom, David Neuhauser, Chuck Seaton, Ron Mitchell, Sonny California, Tanner Byrom)	New Country	Vocals (Monty Byrom), guitar (Neuhauser, Seaton), bass (Mitchell), harmonica (California), drums (Tanner Byrom)	California, USA
1980s–1990s	Black, Clint	Neo-traditional, New Country	Vocals	New Jersey, USA
1990s–	Blackhawk (Henry Paul, Van Stephenson, Dave Robbins)	New Country	Vocals, mandolin (Paul), vocals, guitar (Stephenson), vocals, keyboard (Robbins)	USA
1970s–	Blake, Norman	Bluegrass	Guitar	Tennessee, USA
1990s	Blood Oranges, The (Jim Ryan, Cheri Knight, Mark Spencer, Ron Ward)	.alt-country, Country-rock	Vocals, songwriter (Ryan), bass, vocals (Knight), guitar (Spencer), drums (Ward)	New York, USA
1930s	Blue Ridge Rangers	Western Swing	Vocals, various instruments	Texas, USA
1930s–1970s	Blue Sky Boys (Bill & Earl Bolick), The	Bluegrass, Old-Timey	Guitar, banjo (Bill), guitar, mandolin (Earl), vocals (both)	North Carolina, USA
1970s–1990s	Bluegrass Cardinals, The	Bluegrass	Vocals, various instruments	California, Virginia USA
1900s–2000s	Boe, Bente	Contemporary	Vocals	Norway
1920s, 1960s	Boggs, Moran 'Dock Lee'	Old-Timey	Banjo	Virginia, USA
1950s–1960s	Boggs, Noel	Western Swing	Steel guitar	Oklahoma, USA
1980s–1990s	Bogguss, Suzy	Neo-traditional	Vocals, guitar	Illinois, USA
1940s–1970s	Bond, Johnny	Cowboy Songs, West Coast	Vocals, guitar, songwriter	Oklahoma, USA
1990s–	Bottle Rockets, The (Brian Henneman & others)	.alt-country	Vocals, guitar (Henneman)	Missouri, USA
1950s–1990s	Bowen, Jimmy	Rockabilly, Contemporary	Vocals, record producer	New Mexico, USA
1930s–1950s	Boyd, Bill	Western Swing	Vocals, guitar	Texas, USA
1990s–	BR549	New Country	Various	Tennessee, USA
1960s	Bradley, Harold	Nashville Sound	Guitar	Tennessee, USA
1950s–1970s	Bradley, Owen	Nashville Sound	Piano, producer	Tennessee, USA
1990s	Brandt, Paul	New Country	Vocals	Alberta, Canada
1940s–1950s	Brasfield, Rod	Traditional, Novelty	Comedian	Mississippi, USA
1940s–1950s	Britt, Elton	Traditional	Vocals	Arkansas, USA
1990s	Brokop, Lisa	New Country	Vocals, guitar	British Columbia, Canada
1990s–	Brooks & Dunn (Leon Eric 'Kix' Brooks III, Ronnie Gene Dunn)	Neo-traditional, New Country	Guitar (Brooks), vocals (Dunn)	Louisiana, USA (Brooks), Texas, USA (Dunn)
1980s–	Brooks, Garth	Neo-traditional	Vocals	Oklahoma, USA
1960s	Brower, Cecil	Western Swing	Fiddle	Texas, USA
1990s–	Brown, Alison	Bluegrass	Banjo	USA
1950s–1990s	Brown, Jim Ed	Nashville Sound, Honky-Tonk	Vocals	USA
1990s–	Brown, Junior	Neo-traditional, .alt-country	Vocals, guitar	Indiana, USA
1990s	Brown, Marty	New Country	Vocals	Kentucky, USA
1930s	Brown, Milton	Western Swing	Vocals	Texas, USA
1980s–	Brown, T. Graham	Urban Cowboy, Country-pop	Vocals	Georgia, USA

1950s–1960s	Browns, The (Jim Ed, Maxine & Bonnie) Arkansas, USA	Nashville Sound, Country-pop	Brother and sisters vocal trio	
1960s–1980s	Bruce, Ed	Outlaw	Songwriter, vocals	Arkansas, USA
1930s–1940s	Bruner, Cliff	Honky-Tonk, Western Swing	fiddle	Texas, USA
1990s	Bryant, Cody (born Jeff Ruff)	Bluegrass, Western Swing	Guitar, songwriter	California, USA
1960s	Bryant, Felice & Boudleaux Wisconsin (Felice), Georgia (Boudleaux), USA	Nashville Sound, Country-pop	Songwriter, fiddle, vocals	
1990s–	Buckner, Richard	.alt-country	Vocals, songwriter	Texas, USA
1970s–	Buffett, Jimmy	Country-rock, 'Island' music	Vocals, guitar, songwriter	Mississippi, USA
1950s; 1980s	Burgess, Sonny	Rockabilly	Vocals, guitar	Arkansas, USA
1920s–1930s	Burnett, Dick	Old-Timey, Traditional	Vocals, banjo, guitar	Kentucky, USA
1950s	Burnette Trio, Johnny	Rockabilly	Vocals, various instruments	Tennessee, USA
1970s–	Burnette, Billy	Country-rock	Guitar, producer	Tennessee, USA
1950s–1960s	Burnette, Smiley	Cowboy Songs	Vocals, songwriter	
1960s–1970s	Burton, James	Country-rock	Guitar	Louisiana, USA
1960s–	Bush, Johnny	Honky-Tonk, Western Swing	Vocals, songwriter, drums, guitar	USA
1970s–2000s	Bush, Sam	Newgrass	Vocals, mandolin	Kentucky, USA
1940s–1960s	Byrd, Jerry	Nashville Sound, hawaiian	Steel guitar	Ohio, USA
1990s–	Byrd, Tracy	New Country	Vocals	Texas, USA
1970s	Byrds, The	Country-rock	Vocals, various instruments	California, USA
1930s–1940s	Callahan Brothers (Homer & Walter)	Old-Timey, Traditional	Vocals, guitar	North Carolina, USA
1960s–	Campbell, Glen	West Coast, Country-pop, Nashville Sound	Guitar	Arkansas, USA
1990s	Campbell, Stacy Dean	New Country	Vocals, songwriter	New Mexico, USA
1950s–2000s	Campi, Ray	Rockabilly	Vocals, double bass	Texas, USA
1930s–1950s	Canova, Judy	Traditional, Novelty	Vocals, comedian, actress	Florida, USA
1990s	Carlin, Bob	Old-Timey	Banjo	New York, USA
1930s–1990s	Carlisle, Bill & Cliff	Old-Timey, Comedy	Guitar, vocals	Kentucky, USA
1980s–	Carpenter, Mary–Chapin	New Country	Vocals	New Jersey, USA
1950s–1960s	Carroll, Johnny	Rockabilly	Vocals, guitar	Texas, USA
1920s–1930s	Carson, Fiddlin' John	Old-Timey	Fiddle	American
1990s–	Carson, Jeff	New Country	Vocals	Oklahoma, USA
1990s–	Carson, Mindy	New Country	Vocals	USA
1920s–1960s	Carter Family, The (Alvin Pleasant Delaney, also A.P., Sara Dougherty, Maybelle Addington)	Old-Timey	Vocals (A.P.), autoharp & guitar (Sara Dougherty), guitar (Maybelle Addington)	Virginia, USA
1960s	Carter, Anita	Traditional, Country-folk	Vocals	Virginia, USA
1970s–1990s	Carter, Carlene	Contemporary, Country-rock	Vocals	USA
1990s	Carter, Deana	New Country, Neo-traditional	Guitar	Tennessee, USA
1950s–1960s	Carter, Mother Maybelle	Old-Timey	Guitar, autoharp, banjo	USA
1930s–1980s	Carter, Wilf	Cowboy Songs	Vocals	Nova Scotia, Canada
1950s–	Cash, Johnny	Rockabilly, Traditional, Gospel, Country-folk	Vocals, guitar, songwriter	Arkansas, USA
1980s–2000s	Cash, Rosanne	Contemporary, Country-rock	Vocals, songwriter	Tennessee, USA
1930s–1940s	Cassell, Pete	Old-Timey	Vocals, guitar	Georgia, USA
1990s–2000s	Chambers, Kasey	.alt-country	Vocals, guitar, songwriter	Australia
1980s–	Chapman, Beth Nielson	New Country	Vocals, songwriter	Texas, USA
1990s–	Chesney, Kenny	Neo-traditional	Vocals, songwriter	Tennessee, USA
1990s–	Chesnutt, Mark	New Country	Vocals, songwriter	Texas, USA
1930s–1950s	Choates, Harry	Western Swing	Fiddle	Louisiana, USA
1960s–1990s	Clark, Gene	Country-rock	Vocals, songwriter	Missouri, USA
1970s–1990s	Clark, Guy	.alt-country, Outlaw	Songwriter	Texas, USA
1950s–	Clark, Roy	Traditional, Nashville Sound	Multi-instrumentalist, vocals, comedian	USA
1990s–	Clark, Terri	New Country, Neo-traditional	Vocals	Montreal, Canada
1990s	Claypool, Philip	New Country	Songwriter, vocals	Tennessee, USA
1970s–1990s	Clayton, Lee	Outlaw	Vocals, songwriter	Tennessee, USA
1970s	Clement, Jack	Outlaw, Contemporary	Songwriter, producer	Tennessee, USA
1970s–	Clements, Vassar	Bluegrass	Fiddle	USA
1930s–1940s	Clements, Zeke	Cowboy Songs	Vocals, songwriter	Alabama, USA
1950s–1970s	Clifton, Bill	Bluegrass	Banjo	Maryland, USA
1950s–1960s	Cline, Patsy	Nashville Sound	Vocals	Virginia, USA
1960s–1990s	Cochran, Hank	Honky-Tonk	Songwriter	Tennessee, USA
1960s–	Coe, David Allan	Outlaw	Songwriter	Ohio, USA
1980s–1990s	Collie, Mark	Neo-traditional	Guitar, piano, vocals, songwriter	Tennessee, USA
1950s–1970s	Collins, Tommy	Bakersfield Sound, Honky-Tonk	Vocals	Oklahoma, USA
1970s–1980s	Colter, Jessi	Outlaw	Piano, vocals, songwriter	Arizona, USA
1970s–1990s	Conlee, John	Neo-traditional	Vocals	Kentucky, USA
1980s–1990s	Conley, Earl Thomas	Urban Cowboy	Vocals, songwriter	Ohio, USA
1940s–1950s	Cooley, Spade	Western Swing	Fiddle	Oklahoma, USA
1930s–1950s	Coon Creek Girls, The (Lily May Ledford, Rosie Ledford, Evelyn Lange, Ester Koehler, later Minnie Ledford)	Old-Timey, Bluegrass	Various	Kentucky, USA
1940s–1970s	Cooper, Wilma Lee & Stoney	Old-Timey, Bluegrass	Fiddle, vocals	West Virginia, USA
1940s–1960s	Copas, Cowboy	Honky-Tonk	Vocals, fiddle	Ohio, USA
1940s–1950s	Cotton, Carolina	Cowboy Songs, Western Swing	Vocals	Arkansas, USA
1960s–1990s	Country Gentlemen, The	Bluegrass	Vocals, various instruments	Virginia, USA
1980s–	Cowboy Junkies, The (Michael Timmins, Alan Anton, Peter Timmins, Margo Timmins)	.alt-country	Guitar, songwriter (Michael), bass (Alan), drums (Peter), vocals (Margo)	Toronto, Canada
1970s–1980s	Craddock, Billy 'Crash'	Country-pop/Rock	Vocals	North Carolina, USA
1950s–1990s	Cramer, Floyd	Nashville Sound	Piano	Louisiana, USA
1950s–2000s	Crowe, J. D.	Bluegrass	Vocals, banjo, guitar	Kentucky, USA
1970s–	Crowell, Rodney	Neo-traditional, Country-rock	Vocals, songwriter, producer	Texas, USA
1930s	Cumberland Ridge Runners, The (Hartford Taylor, Red Foley, Karl Davis, Slim Miller)	Old-Timey, Traditional	Vocals, various instruments	Kentucky, USA
1960s–1970s	Cunningham, Larry	Showband, Country & Irish	Vocals	Ireland
1950s–1990s	Curless, Dick	Truck Driving, Traditional	Vocals	Maine, USA
1960s–1980s	Curtis, Sonny	Rockabilly, Traditional	Vocals, guitar, songwriter	Texas, USA
1990s–	Cyrus, Billy Ray	New Country	Vocals, guitar	Kentucky, USA
1930s–1940s	Daffan, Ted	Western Swing, Country Vocals	Songwriter, bandleader	Louisiana, USA
1920s–1940s	Dalhart, Vernon	Cowboy Songs, Old-Timey	Vocals	American
1970s–	Dalton, Lacy J.	Neo-traditional	Vocals	Pennsylvania, USA
1970s–	Daniels, Charlie	Urban Cowboy, Country-rock	Guitar, fiddle, mandolin	North Carolina, USA
1920s–1930s	(Tom) Darby & (Jimmy) Tarlton	Old-Timey	Vocals (Darby), slide guitar (Tarlton)	Georgia; S. Carolina, USA
1930s–1950s	Darling, Denver	Cowboy Songs	Vocals, guitar	Illinois, USA
1970s–2000s	Davies, Gail	Neo-traditional	Vocals, guitar, songwriter	Oklahoma, USA
1920s–1980s	Davis, Jimmie	Traditional, Gospel	Vocals, songwriter, politician	Louisiana, USA
1990s	Davis, Linda	New Country	Vocals	Texas, USA

1970s 1990s	Davis, Mac	Nashville Sound, Country-pop	Vocals	Texas, USA
1960s–1990s	Davis, Skeeter	Nashville Sound, Country-rock	Vocals	USA
1940s–1980s	Dawson, Smoky	Contemporary	Vocals	Australia
1990s–	Day, Curtis	New Country	Vocals	Kentucky, USA
1960s; 1990s	Day, Jimmy	Honky-Tonk, Western Swing	Steel guitar	Alabama, USA
1990s	Dean, Billy	Neo-traditional	Vocals	Florida, USA
1930s–1970s	Dean, Eddie	Cowboy Songs	Vocals	Texas, USA
1950s–1970s	Dean, Jimmy	Nashville Sound	Vocals, guitar, harmonica, accordion	Texas, USA
1980s–1990s	Dean, Larry	Cowboy Songs	Songwriter	Texas, USA
1930s–1950s	Delmore Brothers, The (Alton, Rabon)	Honky-Tonk, Old-Timey	Vocals (both), guitar (both)	Alabama, USA
1990s	Dement, Iris	Neo-traditional, .alt-country	Vocals, songwriter	Arkansas, USA
1940s–1960s	Denny, Jim	Various	Music publisher, agent	Tennessee, USA
1970s	Denver, John	Country Folk	Vocals, guitar, songwriter	New Mexico, USA
1990s–	Derailers (Tony Villanueva, Brian Hofeldt, Vic Gerard Ziolkowski, Terry Kirkendall)	.alt-country, Honky-Tonk, Country-rock	Vocals, guitar (Villanueva), guitar (Hofeldt), bass (Ziolkowski), drums (Kirkendall)	Texas, USA
1980s–1990s	Desert Rose Band (Chris Hillman, Herb Pedersen, John Jorgenson, Jay Dee Maness, Bill Bryson, Steve Duncan)	Country-rock, Newgrass	Vocals, guitar, mandolin (Hillman), banjo, guitar (Pedersen), guitar (Jorgenson), steel guitar (Maness), bass (Bryson), drums (Duncan)	California, USA
1950s–1960s	Dexter, Al	Nashville Sound, Honky-Tonk, Cowboy Songs	Vocals	Texas, USA
1990s–	Diamond Rio	Contemporary	Vocal/instrumental group	Tennessee, USA
1960s–1990s	Dickens, Hazel	Old-Timey	Vocals	West Virginia, USA
1940s–1960s	Dickens, Little Jimmy	Traditional, Novelty	Vocals	West Virginia, USA
1990s	Diffie, Joe	New Country	Guitar, vocals	Oklahoma, USA
1960s–1990s	Dillards, The (Doug & Rodney)	Country-rock, Bluegrass	Banjo (Doug), guitar (Rodney)	Missouri, USA
1970s–1990s	Dillon, Dean	Neo-traditional	Vocals, Songwriter	Tennessee, USA
1990s–	Dixie Chicks, The (Martie Erwin, Emily Erwin, Natalie Maines)	Neo-traditional, Country-rock	Fiddle (Martie Erwin), banjo, guitar, dobro (Emily Erwin), vocals (all)	Texas, USA
1970s–	Douglas, Jerry	Bluegrass	Mandolin, guitar, dobro	Ohio, USA
1950s; 1980s	Downing, Big Al	Rockabilly, Contemporary	Vocals, piano	Oklahoma, USA
1960s–1970s	Dr Hook	Country-rock	Guitar, vocals	New Jersey, USA
1960s–1980s	Drake, Pete	Nashville Sound, Novelty	Steel guitar, record producer	Georgia, USA
1950s–1960s; 1990s	Driftwood, Jimmie	Old-Timey	Guitar, vocals	Arkansas, USA
1960s–1990s	Drusky, Roy	Nashville Sound	Vocals, songwriter	Georgia, USA
1960s–	Dudley, Dave	Truck Driving, Honky-Tonk	Vocals	Wisconsin, USA
1930s–1970s	Duke of Paducah, The	Narrations, Novelty	Comedian	Missouri, USA
1970s–1980s	Duncan, Johnny	Traditional, Honky-Tonk	Vocals, guitar, songwriter	Texas, USA
1930s–1960s	Duncan, Tommy	Western Swing	Vocals. songwriter	Texas, USA
1980s–1990s	Dunn, Holly	New Country	Vocals	Texas, USA
1950s–2000s	Dusty, Slim	Traditional	Vocals, guitar, songwriter	Australia
1960s–	Dylan, Bob	Country-rock	Vocals, guitar, songwriter	Minnesota, USA
1970s–1990s	Eagles, The (Bernie Leadon, Randy Meisner, Glenn Frey, Don Henley)	Country-rock	Vocals (all), guitar (Leadon, Frey), bass (Meisner), drums (Henley)	California, USA
1980s–	Eaglesmith, Fred	.alt-country	Vocals, songwriter	Ontario, Canada
1980s–	Earle, Steve	.alt-country, Country-rock	Guitar, vocals	Virginia, USA
1980s–	Edwards, Don	Cowboy Songs	Vocals, songwriter	New Jersey, USA
1970s–	Ely, Joe	Outlaw, Country-rock	Vocals	Texas, USA
1970s–2000s	Emery, Ralph	Spoken	Radio & TV personality	Tennessee, USA
1960s–	Emmons, Buddy	Western Swing, Traditional	Steel guitar	Indiana, USA
1990s	England, Ty	New Country	Guitar, vocals	Oklahoma, USA
1990s–	Escovedo, Alejandro	.alt-country	Guitar, vocals	USA
1940s–1960s	Evans, Dale	Cowboy Songs, Country-pop	Vocals	Texas, USA
1990s	Evans, Sara	Neo-traditional	Vocals	Missouri, USA
1970s–1980s	Everette, Leon	Urban Cowboy	Guitar	South Carolina, USA
1950s–1990s	Everly Brothers, The (Don & Phil)	Country-rock	Vocals, songwriter (both)	Kentucky, USA (Don), Illinois, USA (Phil)
1980s–1990s	Ewing, Skip	Neo-traditional	Songwriter	California, USA
1970s	Fairchild, Barbara	Nashville Sound, Gospel	Vocals	Arkansas, USA
1970s–1980s	Fargo, Donna	Nashville Sound	Vocals	USA
1950s	Feathers, Charlie	Rockabilly	Vocals, guitar	Mississippi, USA
1970s–1980s	Felts, Narvel	Rockabilly, Traditional	Vocals	Arkansas, USA
1970s–1980s	Fender, Freddy (Baldemar Huerta)	Tex Mex	Vocals, guitar	Texas, USA
1970s–1980s	Firefall (Rick Roberts, Michael Clarke, Jo Jo Gunne, Mark Andes, Jock Bartley, Larry Burnett, David Muse)	Country-rock	Vocals, guitar, songwriter (Roberts), drums (Clarke), bass (Andes), vocals, guitar (Bartley), vocals, guitar, songwriter (Burnett), keyboard, woodwind (Muse)	USA
1970s; 1990s–	Flatlanders, The (Joe Ely, Jimmie Dale Gilmore, Butch Hancock)	Outlaw, .alt-country	Vocals, songwriter (all)	Texas, USA
1940s–1970s	Flatt, Lester	Bluegrass	Guitar, vocals (Flatt), banjo (Scruggs)	Tennessee, USA (Flatt),
1980s–2000s	Fleck, Bela	Newgrass	Banjo	New York, USA
1940s–1960s	Foley, Red	Honky-Tonk, Nashville Traditional, Country-pop	Vocals	Kentucky, USA
1940s–1980s	Ford, 'Tennessee' Ernie	West Coast, Country-pop, Gospel	Vocals	Tennessee, USA
1980s–1990s	Foster (Radney) & Lloyd (Bill)	Neo-traditional, New Country	Vocals (both), lyricist (Foster), songwriter (Lloyd)	Texas, USA (Foster), Kentucky, USA (Lloyd)
1940s–1950s	Fox, Curley & Ruby, Texas	Traditional	Vocals, fiddle, guitar	Tennessee, Texas, USA
1950s–1970s	Frazier, Dallas	Nashville Sound, Honky-Tonk	Vocals	Oklahoma, USA
1970s–1980s	Fricke, Janie	Nashville Sound, traditional	Vocals	Indiana, USA
1970s–1990s	Friedman, Kinky	Outlaw	Vocals, songwriter	Texas, USA
1950s–1970s	Frizzell, Lefty	Honky-Tonk	Vocals	Texas, USA
1970s–1990s	Froggatt, Raymond	Country-rock, Country-pop	Vocals, guitar, songwriter	England
1990s–	Fulks, Robbie	.alt-country, Neo-traditional	Vocals, guitar	Pennsylvania, USA
1970s–1990s	Gatlin, Larry	Urban Cowboy, Neo-traditional	Vocals	Texas, USA
1950s–1960s	Gay, Connie B.	–	Promoter, manager	North Carolina, USA
1970s–	Gayle, Crystal	Traditional, Country-pop	Vocals	Kentucky, USA
1980s–1990s	Gibbs, Terri	Urban Cowboy	Vocals, keyboard, songwriter	Florida, USA
1940s–1990s	Gibson, Don	Nashville Sound	Guitar, vocals	North Carolina, USA
1980s–	Gill, Vince	Neo-traditional, Bluegrass, New Country	Vocals	Oklahoma, USA
1960s–1990s	Gilley, Mickey	Urban Cowboy, Honky-Tonk	Piano, vocals	Louisiana, USA
1980s–	Gilmore, Jimmie Dale	.alt-country	Vocals	Texas, USA
1970s–1980s	Gimble, Johnny	Western Swing, Bluegrass	Fiddle	Texas, USA
1980s–1990s	Girls Next Door, The (Doris King, Cindy Nixon, Diane Williams, Tammy Stephens)	Nashville Sound, Contemporary	Vocals (all)	USA
1930s–1940s	Girls Of the Golden West	Cowboy Songs, Western Swing	Vocals	Illinois, USA
1950s–1980s	Glaser, Jim	Urban Cowboy	Guitar, vocals	Nebraska, USA
1960s–1990s	Glaser, Tompall	Outlaw	Vocals	Nebraska, USA
1960s–1990s	Golbey, Brian	Old-Timey	Vocals, guitar, fiddle	England
1970s–	Goodacre, Tony	Country-folk, Traditional	Vocals, guitar	England
1970s–1990s	Gosdin, Vern	Traditional	Vocals	Alabama, USA
1990s–	Graham, Jon Dee	.alt-country	Vocals, guitar	USA
1940s–	Graves, Josh	Bluegrass	Dobro	Tennessee, USA
1950s–1960s	Gray, Billy	Western Swing	Guitar	Texas, USA

1920s–1930s	Gray, Otto	Western Swing	Bandleader	Oklahoma, USA
1920s–1930s	Grayson, G.B. (Gilliam Banmon)	Old-Timey	Fiddle, vocals	N. Carolina, USA
1980s–	Greenwood, Lee	Urban Cowboy	Vocal	California, USA
1990s–	Gregory, Clinton	Traditional, Contemporary	Fiddle	Virginia, USA
1930s	Griffin, Rex	Traditional	Vocals, songwriter	Alabama, USA
1970s–	Griffith, Nanci	New Country, Country-folk	Vocals	Texas, USA
1970s–	Grisman, David	Bluegrass	Piano, saxophone, mandolin	New York, USA
1930s–1960s	Guthrie Woody	Topical, Political	Vocals, songwriter, author	Oklahoma, USA
1960s–	Haggard, Merle	Bakersfield Sound, Honky-Tonk, Western Swing	Guitar, vocals, songwriter	Oklahoma, USA
1940s–1960s	Haley, Bill	Western Swing, Cowboy, Rock'n'roll	Vocals, guitar	Michigan, USA
1960s–1990s	Hall, Tom T.	Traditional, Nashville Sound	Songwriter, guitar, vocals	Kentucky, USA
1930s–1960s	Hamblin, Stuart	Cowboy Songs, West Coast, Gospel	Vocals, songwriter	Texas, USA
1980s–	Hamilton, George V	New Country, Country-rock	Vocals, songwriter, guitar	Tennessee, USA
1950s–1980s	Hamilton, George IV	Nashville Sound, Folk-country	Vocals, guitar	North Carolina, USA
1970s–	Hancock, Butch	.alt-country	Vocals, songwriter	Texas, USA
1990s–	Hancock, Wayne	Neo-traditional, .alt-country	Vocals	Texas, USA
1990s–2000s	Hanssen, O.J.	Contemporary	Vocals, songwriter	Norway
1970s–1980s	Hargrove, Linda	Country-rock, Gospel	Vocals, songwriter	Florida, USA
1990s–	Harms, Joni	Cowboy Songs	Vocals	Oregon, USA
1920s–1940s	Harrell, Kelly	Old-Timey, Traditional	Vocals, guitar, songwriter	Virginia, USA
1960s–	Harris, Emmylou	New Country, Country-rock	Vocals, guitar	Alabama, USA
1950s–1970s	Hart, Freddie	West Coast, Country-pop	Vocals, songwriter	Alabama, USA
1960s–	Hartford, John	Old-Timey, Folk-country	Vocals	New York, USA
1950s–1960s	Hawkins, Dale	Rockabilly	Vocals, guitar, record producer	Louisiana, USA
1950s–1960s	Hawkins, Hawkshaw	Honky-Tonk	Vocals, guitar	West Virginia, USA
1960s–2000s	Hawkins, Ronnie	Rockabilly, Country-rock	Vocals	Arkansas, USA
1920s–1940s	Hay, George D	Announcer	Radio showman	Indiana, USA
1950s–1970s; 1990s–Hazlewood, Lee	Country-rock	Vocals	Oklahoma, USA
1950s–1970s	Heap, Jimmy	Honky-Tonk, Western Swing	Guitar	Texas, USA
1970s–2000s	Hermans, Ruud	Contemporary	Vocals, guitar, songwriter	Holland
1990s–	Herndon, Ty	New Country	Vocals	Mississippi, USA
1970s–	Hiatt, John	Country-rock	Songwriter, vocals	Indiana, USA
1980s–	Hickman, Sara	.alt-country	Guitar, vocals	North Carolina, USA
1930s–1940s	Hi-Flyers, The	Western Swing	Vocals, various instruments	Texas, USA
1920s	Hill Billies, The	Old-Timey, Traditional	Vocals, various instruments	Virginia, USA
1990s–	Hill, Faith	New Country, Country-pop	Vocals	Mississippi, USA
1950s	Hofner, Adolph	Western Swing	Vocals, bandleader	Texas, USA
1950s	Holly, Buddy	Rockabilly	Vocals, guitar	Texas, USA
1930s–1960s	Hoosier Hotshots, The (Gabe Ward, Paul Trietsch, Ken Trietsch)	Old-Timey, Novelty	Clarinet (Ward), slide whistle, washboard (Paul Trietsch), guitar, banjo (Ken Trietsch)	Indiana, USA
1950s–1960s	Horton, Johnny	Nashville Sound, Honky-Tonk, Rockabilly	Vocals, songwriter	California, USA
1960s–1970s	Houston, David	Nashville Sound	vocals	Louisiana, USA
1950s–1980s	Howard, Harlan	Honky-Tonk, Country-pop, Nashville Sound	Songwriter, vocals	Kentucky, USA
1970s–2000s	Hubbard, Ray Wylie	Texas Country, Country-rock	Vocals, guitar, songwriter	Texas, USA
1950s–1990s	Husky, Ferlin	Nashville Sound, Honky-Tonk	Vocals	Missouri, USA
1920s	Hutchinson, Frank	Old-Timey	Slide guitar	American
1990s–	Intveld, James	Neo-traditional, Country-rock	Vocals	California, USA
1990s–	Jackson, Alan	Neo-traditional, New Country	Guitar, vocals, songwriter	Georgia, USA
1950s–1980s	Jackson, Stonewall	Nashville Sound, Honky-Tonk	Vocals	Georgia, USA
1950s–1970s	Jackson, Tommy	Western Swing	Fiddle	Alabama, USA
1950s–2000s	Jackson, Wanda	Rockabilly, Traditional, Gospel	Vocals	Oklahoma, USA
1950s–1980s	James, Sonny (Jimmy Loden)	Nashville Sound, Country-pop	Guitar, vocals	Alabama, USA
1990s	Jason (Ringenberg)	.alt-country	Vocals, songwriter	Illinois, USA
1990s	Jefferson, Paul	New Country	Vocals, songwriter	California, USA
1990s–2000s	Jeffreys, Gina	Contemporary	Vocals, songwriter	Australia
1920s	Jenkins, Blind Andy	Old-Timey, Topical, Gospel	Vocals, songwriter	Georgia, USA
1950–	Jennings, Waylon	Country-folk, Outlaw, Country-rock	Guitar, vocals, songwriter	Texas, USA
1930s–1990s	Jim & Jesse (McReynolds)	Bluegrass, country	Guitar (Jim), mandolin (Jesse)	Virginia, USA
1930s–1960s	Johnny (Wright) & Jack (Anglin)	Contemporary	Vocals, guitar	Tennessee, USA
1970s–1990s	Johnson Mountain Boys, The (Dudley Connell, Richie Underwood, David McLaughlin, Eddie Stubbs, Larry Robbins)	Bluegrass	Vocals, banjo, guitar (Connell), banjo (Underwood), mandolin (McLaughlin), fiddle (Stubbs), bass (Robbins)	Washington, USA
1950s–	Jones, George	Nashville Sound, Honky-Tonk	Vocals, guitar	Texas, USA
1930s–1970s	Jones, Grandpa (Louie Marshall Jones)	Old-Timey	Vocals, banjo	Kentucky, USA
1940s–	Jordanaires, The (Bill Matthews, Monty Matthews, Culley Holt, Bob Hubbard), The	Nashville Sound	Vocal group	Missouri, USA
1980s	Judds, The (Naomi & Wynonna)	New Country	Vocals, songwriters	Kentucky, USA
1990s	Kane, Kieran	New Country	Vocals, songwriter	New York, USA
1980s–2000s	Karlsen, Arly	Contemporary	Vocals, songwriter	Norway
1920s–1930s	Kazee, Buell	Old-Timey	Vocals, banjo, songwriter	Kentucky, USA
1980s–	Keen, Robert Earl Jr	.alt-country	Songwriter	Texas, USA
1960s–2000s	Keith, Bill	Bluegrass	Banjo, steel guitar	New England, USA
1990s–	Keith, Toby	New Country	Guitar, vocals	Oklahoma, USA
1960s–1990s	Kentucky Colonels, The	Bluegrass	Vocal/instrumental group	California, USA
1990s–2000s	Kernaghan, Lee	Contemporary	Vocals, guitar, songwriter	Australia
1950s–1990s	Kerr, Anita	Nashville Sound	Vocals, vocal group leader	Tennessee, USA
1980s–	Ketchum, Hal	Neo-traditional	Vocals, drums, songwriter	New York, USA
1960s–1970s	Kilgore, Merle	Traditional, Honky-Tonk	Vocals, songwriter	Oklahoma, USA
1930s–1970s	Kincaid, Bradley	Old-Timey	Vocals	Kentucky, USA
1930s–1970s	King, Pee Wee	Western Swing, Cowboy Songs, Old-Timey	Fiddle, accordion	Wisconsin, USA
1960s–1980s	King, Sid	Western Swing	Vocals, guitar	Texas, USA
1990s–	Kirchen, Bill	.alt-country, Country-rock	Guitar	Michigan, USA
1980s–	Kirwan, Dominic	Country-pop, Irish	Vocals	Ireland
1950s–1960s	Knox, Buddy	Rockabilly, Country-pop	Vocals, guitar	Texas, USA
1980s–	Krauss, Alison	Bluegrass, Neo-traditional	Fiddle	Illinois, USA
1970s–1990s	Kristofferson, Kris	Outlaw, Country-rock	Songwriter, vocals, actor	Texas, USA
1980s–	LaFave, Jimmy	.alt-country	Vocals, guitar, songwriter	Oklahoma, USA
1990s–	Lambchop (Kurt Wagner & others)	.alt-country	Various	Tennessee, USA
1980s–	Landsborough, Charlie	Country-folk, Country-pop	Vocals, guitar, songwriter	Liverpool, England
1980s–	lang, k. d.	Neo-traditional, .alt-country	Vocals, songwriter	Alberta, Canada
1990s–	Lauderdale, Jim	New Country	Vocals	North Carolina, USA
1950s–1970s	Law, Don	Nashville Sound	Record producer	London, England

1990s–	Lawrence, Tracy	New Country	Vocals, songwriter	Texas, USA
1970s–	Lawson, Doyle	Bluegrass	Vocals, mandolin, banjo, guitar	Tennessee, USA
1970s–2000s	LeDoux, Chris	Urban Cowboy, Neo-traditional, Cowboy Songs, New Country	Guitar, harmonica, songwriter	Missouri, USA
1960s–	Lee, Albert	Neo-traditional, Country-rock	Guitar, vocals	Leominster, UK
1950s–1990s	Lee, Brenda	Nashville Sound	Vocals	Georgia, USA
1950s–	Lewis, Jerry Lee	Rockabilly, Honky-Tonk	Piano, vocals	Louisiana, USA
1930s–1940s	Lewis, Texas Jim	Western Swing, Novelty	Vocals, guitar, actor	Georgia, USA
1930s–	Light Crust Doughboys, The	Western Swing	–	USA
1960s–1970s	Lilly Brothers, The (Charles Everett & Michael Burt 'Bea')	Bluegrass	Mandolin, banjo, fiddle (Charles), Guitar (Michael), vocals (both)	West Virginia, USA
1950s–1970s	Lindsay, Reg	Traditional	Vocals, songwriter	Australia
1990s	Little Texas (Tim Rushlow, Dwayne O'Brien, Porter Howell, Duane Propes)	New Country	Vocals (Rushlow), vocals, guitar (O'Brien), guitar (Howell), bass (Propes)	Texas, USA
1940s–1970s	Locklin, Hank	Nashville Sound, Honky-Tonk	Vocals	Florida, USA
1980s–	Lonesome River Band	Newgrass	Vocals, various instruments	USA
1990s–	Lonestar (Dean Sams, Richie McDonald, John Rich, Michael Britt, Keech Rainwater)	Neo-traditional	Various	Texas, USA
1950s–1970s	Long, Hubert	–	Publisher, promoter	Texas, USA
1940s–1980s	Lonzo & Oscar	Traditional, Novelty	Comedians	Kentucky, USA
1950s	Lou, Bonnie	Cowboy Songs	Vocals, fiddle, guitar	Illinois, USA
1940s–1960s	Louvin Brothers, The (Charlie & Ira)	Traditional, Bluegrass	Vocals (both), guitar, mandolin	Alabama, USA
1980s–	Loveless, Patty	Neo-traditional, Bluegrass	Vocals	Kentucky, USA
1980s–	Lovett, Lyle	.alt-country	Vocals, songwriter	Texas, USA
1930s–1950s	Lulu Belle (Myrtle Cooper) & Scotty (Wiseman)	Old-Timey	Vocals, guitar (later politics)	North Carolina, USA
1950s–1970s	Luman, Bob	Rockabilly, Nashville Sound	Vocals, guitar	Texas, USA
1920s–1930s	Lunsford, Bascom Lamar	Old-Timey	Fiddle, banjo, vocals	N. Carolina, USA
1960s–	Lynn, Loretta	Nashville Sound, Honky-Tonk	Vocals	Kentucky, USA
1980s–	Lynne, Shelby	.alt-country	Vocals	Virginia, USA
1970s	Lynyrd Skynard	Country-rock	Vocals, various instruments	Florida, USA
1920s–1950s	Macon, Uncle Dave	Old-Timey	Banjo, vocals	Tennessee, USA
1930s–1960s	Maddox Brothers (Cal, Henry, Fred, Don) & Rose, The	Western Swing, Rockabilly, Bluegrass	Vocal/instrumental group	Alabama, USA
1930s	Mainer, J. E. (& Mountaineers)	Old-Timey, Country Variety	Vocals, various instruments	North Carolina, USA
1980s–1990s	Malchak, Tim	Urban Cowboy	Vocals, songwriter	New York, USA
1960s–1990s	Mandrell, Barbara	Nashville Sound, Countrypolitan	Vocals, multi-instrumentalist	Texas, USA
1940s–1980s	Maphis, Joe	West Coast, Honky-Tonk	Guitar	USA
1950s, 1980s	Martin, Janis	Rockabilly	Vocals, guitar	Virginia, USA
1940s–1990s	Martin, Jimmy	Bluegrass	Vocals, guitar	Tennessee, USA
1930s–1940s	Massey, Louise (& The Westerners)	Cowboy Songs, Western Swing	Vocals, various instruments	New Mexico, USA
1980s–	Mattea, Kathy	New Country, Country-folk	Vocals, guitar	West Virginia, USA
1990s	Mavericks, The (Raul Malo, Robert Reynolds, Paul Deakin)	Neo-traditional	Vocals, songwriter (Malo), bass (Reynolds), drums (Deakin)	Florida, USA
1950s–1970s	McAuliffe, Leon	Western Swing	Steel guitar	Texas, USA
1990s	McBride, Martina	Neo-traditionalist	Vocals	Kansas, USA
1970s–2000s	McCann, Susan	Traditional, Irish	Vocals	Ireland
1970s–1980s	McClain, Charly	Country-pop	Vocals	Tennessee, USA
1960s–	McClinton, Delbert	Country-rock	Vocals, harmonica, songwriter	Texas, USA
1960s–	McCoury, Del	Bluegrass	Banjo, guitar, vocals	North Carolina, USA
1990s–	McCoy, Neal	New Country, Neo-traditional	Vocals	Texas, USA
1990s–	McCready, Mindy	New Country	Vocals	Florida, USA
1970s–1980s	McDaniel, Mel	Traditional	Vocals, songwriter	Oklahoma, USA
1950s–1960s	McDonald, Skeets	West Coast	Vocals, guitar, songwriter	Arkansas, USA
1970s–	McDowell, Ronnie	Traditional, Country-pop	Vocals	Tennessee, USA
1970s–	McEntire, Reba	Traditional, Country-pop	Vocals	Oklahoma, USA
1930s–1970s	McGee, Sam	Old-Timey	Guitar	Tennessee, USA
1980s–200s	McGhee, Wes	Country-rock	Vocals, guitar, songwriter	Leicester, England
1990s–	McGraw, Tim	Neo-traditional, Country-rock	Vocals, songwriter	Louisiana, USA
1990s–	Messina, Jo Dee	Neo-traditional	Vocals	Massachusetts, USA
1980s–2000s	Meyer, Herman Lammer	Traditional, Western Swing	Vocals, guitar, songwriter	Germany
1930s–1940s	Miller, Bob	Various	Pianist, bandleader, music publisher	Tennessee, USA
1990s–	Miller, Buddy	.alt-country, Neo-traditional	Vocals, songwriter, producer	USA
1990s	Miller, Dean	New Country	Vocals, songwriter	Florida, USA
1920s–1950s	Miller, Emmett	Old-Timey, Honky-Tonk	Vocals, songwriter	Georgia, USA
1950s–1980s	Miller, Roger	Nashville Sound, Honky-Tonk, Novelty	Vocals, songwriter	Texas, USA
1960s–	Milsap, Ronnie	Countrypolitan, Country-pop	Vocals, piano	North Carolina, USA
1990s–	Mitchell, Waddie	Cowboy Songs	Vocals	Nevada, USA
1950s–1970s	Mize, Billy	West Coast	Vocals, steel guitar, songwriter	Kansas, USA
1930s–1990s	Monroe, Bill	Bluegrass	Mandolin, vocals	Kentucky, USA
1930s–1990s	Montana, Patsy	Cowboy Songs, Western Swing	Vocals, guitar, fiddle	Arkansas, USA
2000s–	Montgomery Gentry (Eddie Montgomery, Troy Gentry)	Contemporary	Vocal duo	Kentucky, USA
1990s–	Montgomery, John Michael	New Country	Vocals	Kentucky, USA
1960s–1970s	Montgomery, Melba	Traditional, Gospel	Vocals, songwriter	Alabama, USA
1970s	Moore, Tiny	Western Swing, Bluegrass	Mandolin	Texas, USA
1990s–2000s	Moorer, Allison	Neo-traditional, Bluegrass	Vocals, guitar, songwriter	Alabama, USA
1940s–1950s	Morgan, George	Traditional, Country-pop	Vocals	Tennessee, USA
1980s–	Morgan, Lorrie	Neo-traditional	Vocals	Tennessee, USA
1940s–1960s	Mullican, Moon	Honky-Tonk, Western Swing	Piano	Texas, USA
1970s–	Murphey, Michael Martin	Neo-traditional, Country-rock, Cowboy Songs	Songwriter, vocals	Texas, USA
1990s	Murphy, David Lee	Neo-traditional	Vocals, songwriter	Illinois, USA
1960s–	Murray, Anne	Country-pop	Vocals	Nova Scotia, Canada
1980s–1990s	Nashville Bluegrass Band, The (Alan O'Bryant, Pat Enright, Mike Compton, Mark Hembree)	Bluegrass	Banjo (O'Bryant), guitar, vocals (Enright), mandolin (Compton), bass (Hembree)	Tennessee, USA
1950s–1980s	Nelson, Ken	West Coast, Contemporary	Record producer	Minnesota, USA
1950s–1980s	Nelson, Rick	Country-rock	Vocals	USA
1950s–	Nelson, Willie	Outlaw, Nashville Sound, Country-pop	Vocals, guitar, songwriter	Texas, USA
1960s–	Nesmith, Michael	Country-rock	Songwriter, guitar	Texas, USA
1960s–1990s	Newbury, Mickey	Contemporary	Vocals, songwriter	Texas, USA
1950s–1970s	Newman, Jimmy C.	Cajun, Nashville Sound	Vocals, songwriter	Louisiana, USA
1970s–	Newton, Juice	Country-pop	Vocals, guitar	New Jersey, USA
1970s	Newton-John, Olivia	Contemporary, Country-pop	Vocals, actress	Cambridge, England
1990s–	Nichols, Joe	Neo-traditional	Vocals	Arkansas, USA
2000s–	Nickle Creek	Folk, Newgrass	Vocals, various instruments	California, USA
1960s–	Nitty Gritty Dirt Band	Country-rock, Bluegrass	Vocals, guitar, drums, harmonica, bass	California, USA
1990s	Norwood, Daron	New Country	Vocals	Texas, USA
1980s–	O'Connor, Mark	Traditional, Contemporary	Fiddle, guitar	Washington, USA
1950s–1970s	O'Day, Molly	Honky-Tonk	Vocals	Kentucky, USA

Years	Name	Style	Role / Instruments	Origin
1980s–2000s	O'Donnell, Daniel	Country-pop, Irish	Vocals	Donegal, Ireland
1960s	O'Gwynn, James	Contemporary	Vocals, songwriter	Mississippi-born
1990s–	O'Hara, Jamie	Neo-traditional	Vocals, songwriter	Ohio, USA
1980s	O'Kanes, The (Kieran Kane & Jamie O'Hara)	New Country	Vocals	Tennessee, USA
1970s–1980s	Oak Ridge Boys, The (Duane Allen, Joe Bonsall, William Lee Golden, Richard Sterban)	Traditional, Country-pop, Gospel	Vocals	Tennessee, USA
1990s	Old '97s, The	.alt-country	Vocals, various instruments	Texas, USA
1970s	Old & In The Way (Jerry Garcia, David Grisman, Vassar Clements, Peter Rowan, John Kahn)	Bluegrass	Vocals, banjo (Garcia), vocals, mandolin (Grisman), fiddle (Clements), vocals, guitar (Rowan), bass (Kahn)	California, USA
1970s–	Olson, Carla	Country-rock	Vocals	Texas, USA
1950s–1980s	Orbison, Roy	Rockabilly, Country-pop	Vocals, guitar	Texas, USA
1950s–1990s	Osborne Brothers, The (Bobby & Sonny)	Bluegrass	Vocals, various instruments	Kentucky, USA
1980s–	Oslin, K. T.	New Country	Vocals	Arkansas, USA
1980s–	Overstreet, Paul	New Country	Vocals, Songwriter	Mississippi, USA
1970s	Overstreet, Tommy	Traditional, Country-pop	Vocals	Oklahoma, USA
1960s–1970s	Owens, Bonnie	Honky-Tonk	Vocals	Oklahoma, USA
1950s–1980s	Owens, Buck	Bakersfield Sound, Honky-Tonk	Guitar, vocals, songwriter	Texas, USA
1930s–1950s	Owens, Tex	Cowboy Songs	Vocals, guitar	Texas, USA
1990s	Paisley, Brad	Traditional	Vocals, guitar	West Virginia, USA
1990s	Parnell, Lee Roy	Country-rock	Vocals, guitar, songwriter	Texas, USA
1960s–1970s	Parsons, Gram	Country-rock	Piano	Florida, USA
1960s–	Parton, Dolly	Urban Cowboy, Honky-Tonk, New Country	Vocals, songwriter	Tennessee, USA
1960s–	Paycheck, Johnny	Outlaw, Honky-Tonk	Vocals, guitar	Ohio, USA
1940s–1960s	Payne, Leon	Traditional	Vocals, songwriter	Texas, USA
1940s–1960s	Pearl, Minnie	Old-Timey, Topical	Comedienne	Tennessee, USA
1920s–1950s	Peer, Ralph	Old-Timey, Hillbilly	Record producer, talent scout, music publisher	Missouri, USA
1990s	Pennington, J. P.	New Country	Guitar, vocals	Kentucky, USA
1940s–1960s	Penny, Hank	Western Swing	Guitar, vocals	Alabama, USA
1990s–	Perfect Stranger (Shayne Morrison, Richard Raines, Steve Murray, Andy Ginn)	Neo-traditional	Bass (Morrison), guitar (Raines), vocals (Murray), drums (Ginn)	Texas, USA
1950s–1980s	Perkins, Carl	Rockabilly, Country-rock	Vocals, guitar, songwriter	Tennessee, USA
1990s–	Peters, Gretchen	New Country	Songwriter	New York, USA
1950s–1980s	Pierce, Webb	Honky-Tonk	Vocals	Louisiana, USA
1960s–1980s	Poco	Country-rock	Vocals, various instruments	California, USA
1920s–1930s	Poole, Charlie	Old-Timey	Banjo, vocals	American
1960s–1980s	Posey, Sandy	Nashville Sound	Vocals	Alabama, USA
1950s–1970s	Presley, Elvis	Rockabilly, Country-pop	Vocals	Mississippi, USA
1950s	Price, Ray	Nashville Sound, Honky-Tonk	Vocals	Texas, USA
1960s–	Pride, Charley	Nashville Sound	Guitar, vocals	Missouri, USA
1970s–2000s	Prine, John	Country-folk, Contemporary	Vocals, guitar, songwriter	Illinois, USA
1970s	Pruett, Jeanne	Nashville Sound	Vocals, songwriter	Alabama, USA
1920s–1940s	Puckett, Riley	Old-Timey	Guitar, banjo	Georgia, USA
1970s–1990s	Rabbitt, Eddie	Contemporary, Country-pop	Vocals	New York, USA
1950s–1960s	Rainwater, Marvin	Rockabilly, Country-pop	Vocals, guitar	Kansas, USA
1990s	Ranch Romance (Jo Miller, Nancy Katz, Barbara Lamb, Lisa Theo)	.alt-country, Western Swing	Vocals, guitar (Miller), bass (Katz), fiddle (Lamb), mandolin (Theo)	Washington, USA
1960s–1990s	Randolph, Boots	Nashville Sound	Saxophone	Kentucky, USA
2000s	Rascal Flatts (Gary LeVox, Jay DeMarcos, Joe Don Rooney)	Contemporary Country-pop	Vocal trio, various instruments	Ohio, USA
1980s–1990s	Rattlesnake Annie (born Rosan Gallimore)	Outlaw, Country-folk	Vocals	Tennessee, USA
1950s–1980s	Rausch, Leon	Western Swing	Vocals, guitar	Missouri, USA
1960s–	Raven, Eddy	Traditional, Cajun	Vocals, songwriter	Louisiana, USA
1950s–1970s	Ray, Wade	Western Swing	Fiddle, banjo, vocals	Indiana, USA
1990s–	Raye, Collin	New Country, Neo-traditional	Vocals	Arkansas, USA
1970s	Raye, Susan	Bakersfield Sound	Vocals	Oregon, USA
1960s–	Red Clay Ramblers, The	Old-Timey	Banjo, guitar, mandolin, piano, bass, vocals	North Carolina, USA
1930s–1970s	Red River Dave	Traditional, Topical	Vocals, guitar, songwriter	Texas, USA
1960s–1980s	Reed, Jerry	Traditional, Country-pop	Vocals, guitar, songwriter	Georgia, USA
1950s–1960s	Reeves, Jim	Nashville Sound	Vocals	Texas, USA
1990s	Reeves, Ronna	New Country	Vocals, songwriter	Texas, USA
1950s–1990s	Reno, (Don) & Smiley, (Red)	Traditional, Bluegrass	Banjo (Reno), vocals (Smiley)	N. Carolina, USA (both)
1980s–1990s	Restless Heart	Contemporary	Vocals, various instruments	Tennessee, USA
1930s–1950s	Revard, Jimmie (& Oklahoma Playboys)	Western Swing	Vocals, various instruments	Oklahoma, USA
1980s–	Rhodes, Kimmie	.alt-country, Country-rock	Vocals	Texas, USA
1970s–	Rice, Tony	Bluegrass	Guitar	California, USA
1950s–1990s	Rich, Charlie	Rockabilly, Nashville Sound, Country-pop,	Vocals, piano	USA
1990s	Richey, Kim	New Country	Vocals, guitar	Ohio, USA
1990s–	Ricochet (Heath Wright, Jeff Bryant, Junior Bryant, Greg Cook, Teddy Carr, Eddie Kilgallon)	New Country	Various	Texas, USA
1970s–2000s	Riders In The Sky	Cowboy Songs	Vocals, various instruments	Tennessee, USA
1950s	Riley, Billy Lee	Rockabilly	Vocals, guitar, harmonica	Arkansas, USA
1990s–	Rimes, LeAnn	New Country, Country-pop	Vocals	Mississippi, USA
1990s–	Riptones, The (Jeb Bonansinga, Tod Bonansinga, Earl Carter, Andon T. Davis, Tom Harmon)	.alt-country	Guitar, vocals, songwriter (Jeb Bonansinga), vocals, rub board (Tod Bonansinga), bass (Carter), guitar (Davis), drums (Harmon)	Illinois, USA
1930s–1970s	Ritter, Tex	Cowboy Songs, West Coast, Nashville Sound	Guitar, vocals	Texas, USA
1970s–	Rizzetta, Sam	Bluegrass	Hammered dulcimer	West Virginia, USA
1960s–1990s	Robbins, Hargus 'Pig'	Nashville Sound	Piano	Tennessee, USA
1950s–1990s	Robbins, Marty	Nashville Sound, Cowboy Songs, Country-pop	Vocals, guitar, piano, songwriter	Arizona, USA
1940s–1980s	Roberts, Kenny	Cowboy Songs	Vocals	Tennessee, USA
1920s; 1960s	Robertson, Eck	Old-Timey	Fiddle	Arkansas, USA
1990s	Robinson, Bruce	New Country	Vocals, songwriter	Texas, USA
1920s–1950s	Robison, Carson	Cowboy Songs, Old-Timey	Whistler	Kansas, USA
1990s–	Roddy, Ted	.alt-country	Vocals, harmonica, songwriter	Texas, USA
1920s–1930s	Rodgers, Jimmie	Old-Timey	Vocals	American
1970s–1980s	Rodriguez, Johnny	Tex-Mex, Traditional	Vocals, songwriter	Texas, USA
1960s–	Rogers, Kenny	Country-rock, Country-pop	Vocals	Texas, USA
1930s–1960s	Rogers, Roy	Cowboy Songs, Old-Timey	Guitar, mandolin, vocals	Ohio, USA
1960s–	Ronstadt, Linda	Country-rock	Vocals	Arizona, USA
1960s–2000s	Rooney, Jim	Bluegrass, Modern Country	Vocals, guitar	New England, USA
1930s–1950s	Rose, Fred	Traditional, Country-pop	Songwriter, music publisher	Indiana, USA
1950s–1980s	Rose, Wesley	–	Music publisher, producer	Illinois, USA
1970s–1990s	Rowan, Peter	Bluegrass	Guitar, vocals, mandolin	Massachusetts, USA
1970s–1980s	Russell, Johnny	Traditional, Country-pop	Vocals, guitar, songwriter	Mississippi, USA

311

1990s–	Twain, Shania	Contemporary, Country-pop	Vocals	Ontario, Canada
1980s	Twister Alley (Shellee Morris, Kevin King, Amy Hitt, Steve Goins, Randy Loyd, Lance Blythe)	New Country	Vocals (Morris), drums (King), guitar (Hitt, Goins, Blythe), bass (Loyd)	USA
1950s–1990s	Twitty, Conway	Rockabilly, Nashville Sound	Guitar, vocals	Missouri, USA
1990s	Two Dollar Pistols (John Howie & others)	.alt-country	Vocals, guitar, songwriter (Howie)	North Carolina, USA
1940s–1950s	Tyler, T. Texas	Traditional	Vocals	Texas, USA
1970s–1990s	Tyson, Ian	Cowboy Songs, Country-folk	Guitar, vocals	British Columbia, Canada
1990s	Ulisse, Donna	New Country	Vocals	USA
1990s	Uncle Tupelo	.alt-country	Vocals, various instruments	Missouri, USA
1990s–2000s	Urban, Keith	Country-rock	Vocals, guitar	New Zealand
1950s–1960s	Van Dyke, Leroy	Contemporary, Novelty	Vocals, guitar, songwriter	Missouri, USA
1970s–1990s	Van Zandt, Townes	Country-rock, Contemporary	Vocals, guitar, songwriter	Texas, USA
1990s	Vezner, Jon	New Country	Songwriter, vocals, bass	Minnesota, USA
1990s	Vidalias, The (Charles Walston, Henry Bruns, Jim Johnson, Page Waldrop, David Michaelson)	.alt-country	Vocals, guitar, songwriter (Walston), pedal steel guitar (Bruns), bass (Johnson), guitar (Waldrop), drums (Michaelson)	Georgia, USA
1950s–1970s	Vincent, Gene	Rockabilly, Rock'n'roll	Vocals	Virginia, USA
1980s–	Vincent, Rhonda	Bluegrass	Vocals, guitar	Missouri, USA
1990s	Waco Brothers, The (Jon Langford & others)	.alt-country	Various	Illinois, USA
1990s	Wade, Stephen	Old-Timey	Banjo	Illinois, USA
1950s–1980s; 2000s–	Wagoner, Porter	Nashville Sound	Vocals, guitar	Missouri, USA
1940s–1970s	Wakely, Jimmy	Cowboy Songs	Vocals	Arkansas, USA
1940s–1990s	Walker, Billy	Western Swing, Honky-Tonk	Vocals	Texas, USA
1960s	Walker, Cindy	Western Swing, Honky-Tonk	Songwriter, Vocals	Texas, USA
1990s	Walker, Clay	New Country	Vocals, guitar	Texas, USA
1960s–	Walker, Jerry Jeff	Outlaw	Vocals, songwriter	Texas, USA
1990s	Wall, Chris	.alt-country	Vocals, songwriter	California, USA
1960s–1970s	Wallace, Jerry	Country-pop	Vocals, guitar	Arizona, USA
1990s	Walser, Don	.alt-country, Western Swing	Vocals, guitar	Texas, USA
1990s	Ward, Chris	New Country	Vocals	USA
1930s–1940s; 1960s	Ward, Fields	Old-Timey	Vocals, guitar	Virginia, USA
1990s	Warden, Monte	.alt-country	Vocals	Texas, USA
1980s–	Wariner, Steve	Neo-traditional	Songwriter	Indiana, USA
2000s	Warwick, Rachael	Contemporary, Country-rock	Vocals, guitar	Warrington, England
1990s	Watson, Dale	.alt-country	Vocals, songwriter	Alabama, USA
1960s–	Watson, Doc	Old-Timey	Guitar	North Carolina, USA
1970s–1980s	Watson, Gene	Contemporary, Nashville Sound	Vocals	Texas, USA
1990s–	Welch, Gillian	.alt-country	Vocals, songwriter	New York, USA
1990s–	Welch, Kevin	.alt-country	Vocals, songwriter	Kentucky, USA
1940s–1980s	Wells, Kitty	Nashville Sound, Honky-Tonk	Vocals	Tennessee, USA
1950s–1980s	West, Dottie	Nashville Sound, Country-pop	Vocals	Tennessee, USA
1980s	West, Shelly	Urban Cowboy	Vocals	USA
1940s–1960s	West, Speedy	Western Swing, West Coast	Steel guitar	Missouri, USA
1950s–1980s	Western, Johnny	Cowboy Songs	Vocals, guitar	Minnesota, USA
1990s	Whiskeytown (Ryan Adams, Caitlin Cary, Phil Wandscher, Steve Grothmann, Eric Gilmore)	.alt-country	Vocals, songwriter, guitar (Adams), fiddle (Cary), guitar (Wandscher), bass (Grothmann), drums (Gilmore)	North Carolina, USA
1960s–1970s	White, Clarence	Bluegrass	Guitar	Maine, USA
1960s–2000s	Whites, The	Old-Timey, Bluegrass	Vocals, various instruments	Oklahoma, Texas, USA
1980s–1990s	Whitley, Keith	Neo-traditional, Bluegrass	Vocals, guitar	Kentucky, USA
1930s–1950s	Whitley, Ray	Cowboy Songs	Vocals, bandleader	Georgia, USA
1940s–1980s	Whitman, Slim	Traditional, Country-pop	Vocals	Florida, USA
1920s–1930s	Whitter, Henry	Old-Timey, Traditional	Vocals, guitar	Virginia, USA
1950s–1970s	Wilburn Brothers (Teddy & Doyle)	Nashville Sound	Vocals, songwriters, music publishers	Arkansas, USA
1990s–	Wilco (Jeff Tweedy, Ken Coomer, John Stirratt, Max Johnston, Jay Bennett)	.alt-country	Vocals, guitar, songwriter (Tweedy), drums (Coomer), bass (Stirratt), fiddle, banjo, lap steel (Johnston), guitar (Bennett)	USA
1990s	Wild Rose (Wanda Vick & others)	Neo-traditional	Various instruments	USA
1950s–1970s	Wilken, Marijohn	Traditional, Gospel	Vocals, songwriter	Texas, USA
1990s	Williams, Jett	.alt-country, Honky-Tonk, Neo-traditional	Vocals, guitar	Alabama, USA
1940s	Williams, Curly	Western Swing	Bandleader	Georgia, USA
1930s–1970s	Williams, Doc & Chickie	Traditional, Old-Timey	Vocals, guitar, accordion	Ohio, West Virginia
1960s–	Williams, Don	Country-pop	Vocals, guitar	Texas, USA
1940s–1950s	Williams, Hank	Honky-Tonk	Vocals, guitar, songwriter	Alabama, USA
1960s–	Williams, Hank Jr.	Outlaw, Country-rock	Vocals, guitar, songwriter	Tennessee, USA
1990s	Williams, Hank III	.alt-country, Country-rock	Vocals, guitar, songwriter	Alabama, USA
1970s–	Williams, Lucinda	.alt-country	Vocals, songwriter	Louisiana, USA
1940s–1980s	Williams, Tex	Western Swing	Vocals, guitar	USA
1940s–1960s	Willing, Foy	Cowboy Songs	Vocals	Texas, USA
1960s–1970s	Willis Brothers, The (James 'Guy', Charles 'Skeeter', John 'Vic')	Traditional, Western Swing, Novelty	Vocals, guitar (James), fiddle, vocals (Charles), guitar (Joe)	Oklahoma, USA
1990s–	Willis, Kelly	New Country	Vocals, songwriter	Oklahoma, USA
1950s	Wills, Billy Jack	Western Swing	Vocals	Texas, USA
1930s–1970s	Wills, Bob	Western Swing	Mandolin, guitar, fiddle	Texas, USA
1940s–1970s	Wills, Johnnie Lee	Western Swing	Fiddle	Texas, USA
1990s–	Wills, Mark	New Country	Vocals	USA
2000s	Wilson, Gretchen	Neo-traditional	Vocals, guitar	Illinois, USA
1940s–1990s	Wise, Chubby	Traditional, Bluegrass	Fiddle	Florida, USA
1950s–	Wiseman, Mac	Bluegrass, Traditional	Vocals	Virginia, USA
1990s–	Womack, LeeAnn	New Country	Vocals	USA
1940s–1960s	Woods, Bill	Bakersfield Sound	Musician, bandleader	Texas, USA
1940s–1970s	Wooley, Sheb	Cowboy Songs, Country-pop, Rockabilly	Vocals, guitar, actor	Oklahoma, USA
2000s	Worley, Darryl	Contemporary	Vocals, guitar, songwriter	Tennessee, USA
1980s–1990s	Wright, Michelle	New Country	Vocals	Ontario, Canada
1990s–	Wylie & The Wild West Show (Wylie Gustafson & others)	.alt-country, Western Swing	Vocals, guitar (Gustafson)	California, USA
1960s–1990s	Wynette, Tammy	Nashville Sound, Honky-Tonk, Country-pop	Vocals, guitar	Missouri, USA
1990s	Wynonna (Judd)	New Country	Vocals, guitar	Kentucky, USA
1990s–	Yearwood, Trisha	New Country	Vocals	Georgia, USA
1980s–	Yoakam, Dwight	Neo-traditional, .alt-country, Bakersfield Sound	Vocals	Kentucky, USA
1950s–1990s	Young, Faron	Nashville Sound, Honky-Tonk	Vocals	Louisiana, USA
1960s–	Young, Neil	Country-rock	Songwriter, vocals	Toronto, Canada
1970s	Young, Steve	Country-rock, Contemporary	Vocals, guitar, songwriter	Georgia, USA

Further Reading

General

Alden, Grant and Peter Blackstock (Eds), *The Best of No Depression: Writing About American Music*, University of Texas Press, 2005

Bogdanov, Vladimir, Chris Woodstra, Stephen Thomas Erlewine, *All Music Guide to Country*, Backbeat UK, 2003

CMT 100 Greatest Songs of Country Music, Hal Leonard Publishing, 2004

Daley, Dan, *Nashville's Unwritten Rules: Inside the Business of Country Music*, Overlook Press, 1999

Einarson, John, *Desperados: The Roots of Country Rock*, Cooper Square Press, 2001

Escott, Colin, *Lost Highway: The True Story of Country Music*, Smithsonian Books, 2003

Green, Douglas B., *Singing in the Saddle, The History of the Singing Cowboy*, Vanderbilt University Press, 2002

Hemphill, Paul, *The Nashville Sound*, Everthemore Books, 2005

Hinton, Brian, *South By Southwest: A Roadmap to Alternative Country*, Sanctuary Publishing, 2003

Kienzle, Rich, *Southwest Shuffle: Pioneers of Honky-Tonk, Western Swing and Country Jazz*, Routledge, 2003

Kingsbury, Paul (Ed.), *The Encyclopedia of Country Music: The Ultimate Guide to the Music*, Oxford University Press, 2004

Kingsbury, Paul, *Vinyl Hayride: Country Music Album Covers 1947-1989*, Chronicle Books, 2003

Larkin, Colin (Ed.), *The Virgin Encyclopedia of Country Music*, Virgin Publishing, 1998

Lomax, John A., *Cowboy Songs and Other Frontier Ballads*, Schirmer Books, 1986

Malone, Bill C., *Country Music, U.S.A.*, University of Texas Press, 2003

Malone, Bill C., *Don't Get Above Your Raisin': Country Music and the Southern Working Class*, University of Illinois Press, 2006

Nickerson, Ross, *The Banjo Encyclopedia: Bluegrass Banjo from A to Z*, Mel Bay Publishing, 2004

Oermann, Robert K. and Mary Bufwack, *Finding Her Voice: Women in Country Music, 1800-2000*, Vanderbilt University Press, 2003

Poore, Billy, *Rockabilly: A Forty-Year Journey*, Omnibus Press, 2002

Rouda, Bill, Lucinda Williams and David Eason, *Nashville's Lower Broad: The Street that Made Music*, Smithsonian Books, 2004

Rubin, Dave, *Best of Rockabilly*, Hal Leonard Publishing, 2004

Streissguth, Michael, *Voices of Country*, Routledge, 2004

Tosches, Nick, *Country: The Twisted Roots of Rock 'n' Roll*, Da Capo Press, 1996

Whitburn, Joel, *Billboard Presents Joel Whitburn's Top Country Songs 1944-2005*, Record Research Inc., 2006

Willman, Chris, *Rednecks and Bluenecks: The Politics of Country Music*, The New Press, 2005

Wolfe, Charles K. and Ted Olsen (Eds), *The Bristol Sessions: Writings About the Big Bang of Country Music*, McFarland and Co., 2004

Wolfe, Charles K., *Classic Country: Legends of Country Music*, Routledge, 2001

Biographies

Allen, Bob, George Jones: the Life and Times of a Honky-Tonk Hero, Birch Lane Press

Brown, Jim, *Emmylou Harris*, Fox Music Books, 2004

Cash, Johnny, *Cash: The Autobiography*, HarperCollins Publishers, 2000

Cash, Johnny, *The Original Carter Family*, Hal Leonard Publishing, 1999

Cochran, Michael and Chet Atkins, *Chet Atkins: Me and My Guitar*, Omnibus Press, 2003

Cooper, Daniel, *Lefty Frizzell*, Little, Brown, 1996

Cray, Ed, *Ramblin' Man: The Life and Times of Woody Guthrie*, WW Norton & Co., 2006

Eggar, Robin, *Shania Twain: The Biography*, Pocket Books, 2005

Escott, Colin, *Hank Williams Revealed: Snapshots from the Lost Highway*, Da Capo Press, 2001

Ewing, Tom, *The Bill Monroe Reader*, University of Illinois Press, 2006

Haggard, Merle, *The Best of Merle Haggard*, Hal Leonard Publishing, 2000

Hemphill, Paul, *Lovesick Blues: The Life of Hank Williams*, Secker and Warburg, 2005

Jennings, Waylon, *Waylon: An Autobiography*, Time Warner International, 1996

Jones, Margaret, *Patsy: The Life and Times of Patsy Cline*, Da Capo Press, 1999

Judd, Wynonna, *Coming Home to Myself*, New American Library, 2005

Lynn, Loretta, *Still Woman Enough*, Hyperion Books, 2003

McWhorter, *Cowboy Fiddler: Bob Wills' Band*, University of North Texas Press, 2006

Miller, Stephen, *Smart Blonde: The Life of Dolly Parton*, Omnibus Press, 2006

Nash, Alanna, *Dolly: The Biography*, Cooper Square Press, 2002

Nelson, Willie, *The Tao of Willie*, Gotham Books, 2006

O'Neal, Bill, *Tex Ritter: America's Most Beloved Cowboy*, Eakin Press, 1998

Piazza, Jim, *The King*, Black Dog & Leventhal, 2005

Pugh, Ronnie, *Ernest Tubb: The Texas Troubadour*, Duke University Press, 1998

Schlappi, Elizabeth, Roy Acuff: The Smoky Mountain Boy, Pelican Publishing Company, 1993

Sgammato, Jo, *American Thunder: The Garth Brooks Story*, Ballantine Books, 2000

Sgammato, Jo, *Keepin' It Country: The George Strait Story*, Ballantine Books, 1998

Shaver, Billy Joe, *Honky-Tonk Hero*, University of Texas Press, 2005

Streissguth, *Johnny Cash at Folsom Prison: The Making of a Masterpiece*, Da Capo Press, 2004

Streissguth, Michael, *Johnny Cash: The Biography*, Da Capo Press, 2006

Streissguth, Michael, *Like a Moth to a Flame: the Jim Reeves Story*, Rudledge Hill Press, 1998

Streissguth, Michael, *Like a Moth to a Flame: The Jim Reeves Story*, Rutledge Hill Press, 1998

Thomson, Graeme, *Willie Nelson: The Outlaw*, Virgin Books, 2006

Travis, Randy, *Randy Travis: Worship and Faith*, Word Music, 2003

Urbanski, Dave, *Man Comes Around: The Spiritual Journey of Johnny Cash*, James Bennett Pty Ltd, 2004

Walker, Jason and Sean Body, *Gram Parsons: God's Own Singer*, Helter Skelter Publishing, 2006

White, Raymond E., *King of the Cowboys, Queen of the West: Roy Rogers and Dale Evans*, Bowling Green University Popular Press, 2005

Wills, Bob, *Bob Wills and His Texas Playboys*, Creative Concepts, 2000

Wynette, Tammy, *Stand by Your Man*, Pocket Books, 1999

Zwonitzer, Mark and Charles Hirshberg, *Will You Miss Me When I'm Gone: The Carter Family and their Legacy in American Music*, Simon & Schuster, 2004

Practical Guides

Capplinger, Dennis, *Bluegrass Banjo Basics*, International Music Publications, 2004

Duncan, Brett, *Country Guitar*, LTP Publications, 2004

Harrison, Mark, *Country Piano: The Complete Guide*, Hal Leonard Publishing, 2004

Hodgson, Lee, *Hot Country: The Comprehensive Guide to Lead and Rhythm Country Guitar Playing*, Sanctuary Publishing, 1997

Sokolow, Fred, *Complete Bluegrass Banjo Method*, Hal Leonard Corporation, 2003

Soto-Morettini, Donna, *Popular Singing: A Practical Guide to jazz, Blues, Rock, Country and Gospel*, A&C Black, 2006

Thomson, Eric, *Bluegrass Guitar: Know the Players, Play the Music*, Backbeat UK, 2006

Trovato, Steve, *Country Solos for Guitar*, Hal Leonard Publishing, 2000

Author Biographies & Picture Credits

Tony Byworth
(General Editor; There's A New Moon Over My Shoulder)

Tony Byworth is one of the few Brits to be wholly involved in country music for over 30 years, building connections through frequent visits to Nashville. A founding member of the consumer BCMA and twice elected Chairman of the trade CMA (GB), he edited the monthly magazine *Country Music People* for six years, was a contributing editor for *Billboard*, *Music Week* and *The Stage*, and provided columns for pop music publications. In 1984 he co-founded Byworth-Wootton International, the UK's first county-music services company, which led to working with many top US artists. Latterly he provided pr on behalf of Garth Brooks and George Strait as well as developing various country projects, including an internet site and the London based radio station Ritz 1035. The author of several books, numerous sleeve notes and album compilations, Tony Byworth is the recipient of many awards, including the CMA's prestigious Wesley Rose (Foreign Media Achievement) Award especially pleasing as he had worked for Acuff-Rose Music two decades earlier.

Bob Allen
(Consultant Editor; Tonight We're Settin' The Woods On Fire; When Two Worlds Collide; Instruments and Equipment)

Bob Allen has spent the last quarter century as a country-music journalist, historian and critic. He is former Nashville editor for – and has been a regular contributor to – the popular Nashville-based fan magazine *Country Music Magazine* since 1977. His writing on country music has appeared in *Esquire*, *Rolling Stone*, the *Washington Post*, the *Atlanta Journal* and the *Baltimore Sun*. Allen is the author of *The Life And Times Of A Honky-Tonk Legend*, the (unauthorized) biography of George Jones, and he has contributed to various historical and reference books on country music in recent years. He resides in Eldersburgh, Maryland.

Kevin Coffey
(I've Sold My Saddle For An Old Guitar)

Kevin Coffey was born and reared in Texas. He has written extensively about American roots music, with a particular emphasis on western swing. In addition to publishing numerous articles and CD sleeve notes, he compiled *A Discography of Western Swing & Hot Swing Bands, 1928-1942* with Cary Ginell.

Geoffrey Himes
(Foggy Mountain Breakdown; Are You Sure Hank Done It This Way?; Winter's Come And Gone)

Geoffrey has written about music on a weekly basis in the *Washington Post* since 1977 and has been a contributing editor to *No Depression* magazine since 1998, and has contributed to countless other publications. He has been honoured for Music Feature Writing by the Deems Taylor/ASCAP Awards, by the Abell Foundation Awards and by the Music Journalism Awards. His book on Bruce Springsteen, *Born In The USA*, was published in 2005. He has contributed entries to *The Blackwell Guide to Recorded Country Music*, *Will The Circle Be Unbroken*, *The Music Hound Folk Album Guide* and *The Rolling Stone Jazz & Blues Album Guide*. He is currently working on a book about Emmylou Harris, Roseanne Cash, Rodney Crowell and Ricky Skaggs for the Country Music Hall Of Fame.

Maurice Hope
(Working Nine To Five; Roses In The Snow)

Maurice Hope has written about country and folk music since the 1980s, contributing to *Country Music Round-Up*, *Get Rhythm*, *Rock'n'Reel*, *Songbook* etc. He has also written sleeve notes on Merle Haggard and Slim Whitman.

Howard Mandel
(For The Wonder State We'll Sing A Song)

Howard Mandel is a writer and editor specializing in jazz, blues, roots, new and unusual music. Born in Chicago, now living in New York City, he is a senior contributor for *Down Beat*, produces arts features for National Public Radio, teaches at New York University, is President of the Jazz Journalists Association and edits website *www.jazzhouse.org*. He has written *Future Jazz* (OUP, 1989) and written for *Musical America*, *The Wire*, *Swing Journal* and many other periodicals. He has recently taught an intensive class on 'The Roots of American Music'.

Tony Russell
(There Is Sunshine In The Shadows)

Tony Russell is a music historian with a special interest in country music of the 1920s–40s. He wrote *Blacks, Whites and Blues* (1970), founded the magazine *Old Time Music* and edited it from 1971 to 1989, and spent two decades researching *Country Music Records: A Discography, 1921-1942* (Oxford, 2004). He has written voluminously on country music, blues and jazz for a wide variety of periodicals, from *Mojo* to the *New Humanist*, and has been a consultant, scriptwriter or presenter on many TV and radio programmes. His most recent book is *The Penguin Guide To Blues Recordings* (Penguin, 2006).

John Tobler
(Working Nine To Five; Roses In The Snow)

John Tobler has been writing about popular music since the late 1960s, during which time he has written books on Abba, The Beach Boys, The Beatles, Elton John, Elvis Presley, Cliff Richard and several generic titles. He has written for numerous magazines including *ZigZag*, *Billboard*, *Music Week*, *Melody Maker*, *NME*, *Sounds*, *Country Music People*, *Folk Roots*, etc. He has written literally thousands of sleeve notes.

Ian Wallis
(All My Friends Are Boppin' The Blues)

Born in Upminster, Essex, Ian Wallis is a life-long rockabilly enthusiast. For more than 25 years he has contributed magazine articles on the subject and has had two books published. He jointly promotes the Rockers Reunion Party held in Reading every January and helps organize European tours for American rockabilly artists. He has travelled many thousands of miles in pursuit of the greatest music in the world.

Index